BEING AND MEANING

BEING AND MEANING

Paul Tillich's Theory of Meaning, Truth and Logic

by IAN E. THOMPSON *for*

the Edinburgh
University
Press

EDINBURGH UNIVERSITY PRESS
22 George Square, Edinburgh
ISBN 0 85224 388 X
Set in Monotype Times New Roman
by Speedspools, Edinburgh
and printed in Great Britain by
Redwood Burn Limited
Trowbridge

Foreword

When I was invited to write this foreword I readily agreed not only because I have followed Dr Thompson's career with interest, but more particularly because this is a highly individual contribution to Tillich studies. Ever since our first meeting in 1968 I have held Dr Thompson in high esteem as a philosopher of religion, and his noble, distinguished work with the Council of Churches and other such bodies in South Africa has given a dimension of wider significance to his philosophising. Kierkegaard's hesitations about the use of the phrase 'witness to the truth' in connection with Bishop Mynster might well have been overcome in such a context. Certainly one of the most interesting features of Dr Thompson's study of Tillich is the way in which he teases out of Tillich's often opaque writing a metaphysic of truth which can properly be said to have some Kierkegaardian features. I say this for a variety of reasons. The connection between Tillich and Kierkegaard is not lost on Dr Thompson. His sensitivity enables him to appreciate that, despite appearances to the contrary, both thinkers had a very definite metaphysic which neither succeeded in articulating completely. Moreover, the lives of both authors exemplify the practical purposes from which metaphysics springs and which it serves. Bradley's celebrated description of metaphysics as the finding of bad reasons for what we believe naturally has a new relevance in our post-Freudian age. One might therefore expect that the connection between metaphysics and praxis is appreciated all the better. Yet few indeed are the philosophers who discuss metaphysics in this way. Tillich's philosophy, both as an intellectual creation and as an activity of teaching, was this kind of thing – and this is what Dr Thompson discusses.

What I like so much about Dr Thompson's approach is that it is at once so very human a philosophical stance and also so scholarly. Familiar as he is with Tillich and with Tillich scholarship he is also positively steeped in mediaeval and modern philosophy. So he presses Scotus and Charles Peirce into service as he marshals his philosophical criticism of Tillich. This makes the critical analysis exciting to read. I have no doubt that even when readers will find themselves thus faced with unfamiliar themes and technical, difficult discussion the excitement will carry them along. Nobody will abandon the hunt just because the terrain is difficult and the going rough; and everyone will agree that it was a great ride. The author is doing more than saying what he thinks of Tillich: he is trying to think what Tillich thought, and say what Tillich intended to say. In that way it resembles the musicologist's completion of an unfinished masterpiece – a precarious but very satisfying and illuminating task. When I saw Tillich shortly before he died he complained that too few of his critics had succeeded in understanding him and that of those few who did there were too few who agreed with him! Dr Thompson has understood him very well and this makes his criticism all the more useful. In his preface to the first volume of *Systematic Theology* Tillich defined the purpose of his theological system as a 'help in answering questions'. It is as a useful and faithful guide both to the evaluation of that help and to the primary activity of asking and answering these questions that it gives me great pleasure to commend Dr Thompson's study of Tillich.

J. Heywood Thomas

Contents

Preface

I would not have begun this study of the thought of Paul Tillich had I not been gripped first by his sermons. These I read as an undergraduate student while wrestling with the problem of how to achieve an integrated vision of the relations between science, religion, art and philosophy. His faith in the ultimate significance and possible synthesis of all forms of the human quest for meaning in personal and cultural life excited me and encouraged me to explore his work further.

Against the background of Sharpeville and subsequent political events in South Africa, I became aware of his pre-war writings on Religious Socialism. In *Die sozialistische Entscheidung* he had set out with devastating clarity the choices facing pre-war Germany. As he saw it his contemporaries had to choose between National Socialism, Communism and Religious Socialism. These were precisely the choices facing South Africans in the 50s and 60s. The overriding need was for an ideology in terms of which individuals, both black and white, could define their identity, make sense of their experience and rationalise their will-to-power. The choices were clearly between different kinds of belief systems – a nationalism built of the myth of racial superiority, a revolutionary atheistic communism, and various forms of democratic socialism which sought to preserve faith in transcendent values. It became apparent that Tillich's thought had continuing relevance for our times, and in spite of its difficulty warranted careful re-examination.

Struggling with Tillich's theology and philosophy I became convinced of two things. Firstly, that some of the theoretical difficulties I felt with his system were not the result, as so many critics had suggested, of his being over-systematic, but rather of his being over-hasty in the attempt to systematise his insights. Secondly, that the key to his thought was not to be found in the analysis of his philosophical presuppositions alone since it was inspired by painful existential and political experience, but that the latter provided the inspiration for which the former were the *ex post facto* rationalisation. This study is an attempt to defend a new interpretation of Tillich as a Christian ideologist in which his pre-war and wartime experience is regarded as definitive in providing the impulse towards the systematic formulation of his ideas. His true greatness and his limitations cannot be appreciated except against that background.

This study of the dimensions of Tillich's understanding of Meaning,

Truth and Logic in their relation to Being, would not have been under-
taken, continued or completed without the encouragement, advice and
practical assistance of many people. I am particularly indebted to my
former teachers: to Professors Robert Craig and Wolfgang Yourgrau,
formerly of the University of Natal, who introduced me to the work of
Paul Tillich; to Professor Martin Versfeld of the University of Cape
Town who inspired in me an interest in mediaeval philosophy and suggested how illuminating it might be to compare Tillich with St Thomas
Aquinas; to Professor John Heywood Thomas and Dr Paddy Fitzpatrick
who provided me with practical assistance and encouragement as well as
constructive criticism of my work during the two years I spent doing
research in the University of Durham. Their moral support inspired me
to continue doing research in South Africa during a most trying period of
political difficulties, and it has been indispensable in helping me complete
this work now that I and my family have settled in Britain.

I am very grateful to the University of Witwatersrand for two generous
travel-grants and for favourable terms of sabbatical and study-leave that
made it possible for me to visit Durham, to Fr Fergus Barrett, OFM, whose
financial assistance from the post-graduate research fund of the National
Catholic Seminary in Pretoria helped with academic fees and the cost of
books, and in particular to my parents for their unfailing faith in the value
of this enterprise and their unstinting financial aid in times of crisis.

Were it not for the encouragement of Professor Donald Mackinnon,
who suggested that this work, which was originally presented as a PhD
thesis in the University of Durham, should be published, I would not have
had the courage to approach the Edinburgh University Press with it. I
owe to the Secretary, Mr Archie Turnbull, and the technical staff much
gratitude for their help in preparing this book for publication, to Mrs Nan
Hamilton for her patient and precise work in typing various drafts, to
Arlette Nathanael and Andrea Heëseman for checking my German trans-
lations, and particularly to George Morice who painstakingly laundered
and ironed out some of the more obvious infelicities in my prose. What
remains with its many imperfections must be my responsibility.

Finally, I give thanks for my wife's faith and understanding, courage
and good humour, and for our children's love and patience that has
helped to keep us both human.

                                              Autumn 1980, Edinburgh

Abbreviations

DBU	*Der Begriff des Übernatürlichen*
DSW	*Das System der Wissenschaften*
GW	*Gesammelte Werke*
HCT	*A History of Christian Thought*
IH	*The Interpretation of History*
MSA	*My Search for Absolutes*
OB	*On the Boundary*
P	*Perspectives on Nineteenth and Twentieth Century Protestant Theology*
PE	*The Protestant Era*
ST1	*Systematic Theology*, volume 1
ST2	*Systematic Theology*, volume 2
ST3	*Systematic Theology*, volume 3
TC	*Theology of Culture*
TPT	*The Theology of Paul Tillich*
..'R	*What is Religion?*

To my parents

Chapter 1
Introduction: Paul Tillich's Rhetoric

1. *Style as the key to an author's work*

Paul Tillich, writing in 1942 of 'Kierkegaard as Existential Thinker', in a style still heavy with Germanisms, makes the following revealing remark: 'But it must be said, with respect to Kierkegaard as to every great writer: You do not know him if you have not read him and are caught by the power of his own style'.[1] It is equally true of Tillich that, unless we have been caught by the power of his style, we cannot say that we know him or understand the significance of his work. Even the clumsy sentence about Kierkegaard tells us a great deal about Tillich. It tells us about his interest in existential philosophy and theology. It expresses something of the difficulty he had in translating the Germanic form of his thinking into the inhospitable prose of English sentences. The date of the article reminds us that it was written in the middle of the Second World War. The time should remind us of the painful circumstances that forced him to emigrate from his native Germany and of the difficulties he faced in re-establishing himself in academic life, in America. It may even cause us to reflect on the change in his socio-political role from being a participant in the European cultural and political scene to being an interpreter of that scene for the English-speaking world.

Style was important to Tillich but it is also important to the interpretation of his own work. Speaking of the 'theology of culture' he says: 'Concerning the method of such a theological analysis of culture the following might be said. The key to the theological understanding of a cultural creation is its style' (*ST1*, 45). From such early papers as 'Über die Idee einer Theologie der Kultur' (1919) to the concluding volume of his *Systematic Theology* (1963), he uses style as a principle for the theological hermeneutic of culture. This is the practical expression of his belief that 'Religion is the substance of Culture, and Culture the form of Religion' (*PE* 63). However, it is a corollary of this principle that the significance of Tillich's own philosophico-theological system, *qua* cultural and theological creation, is connected with its style.

There are superficial aspects of his style, such as those adverted to above, that reveal much about Tillich, and his life concerns; but there are deeper questions, connected with the dialectical form in which his thought is cast, that relate to the deepest motivations of his life and reveal the specific nature of his religious faith and the philosophical eros that drove him in his quest for truth. 'There is a style of thought, of politics, of social life, etc. The style of a period expresses itself in its cultural forms, in its choice of objects, in the attitudes of its creative personalities, in its institutions and customs' (*ST1*, 45). Whether we admire or criticise Tillich, he is undoubtedly one of the creative personalities of our period, and his work challenges us to interpret its style. This demands that we recognise that 'It is an art as much as a science to "read styles", and it requires religious intuition, on the basis of ultimate concern, to look into the depth of a style, to penetrate to the level where an ultimate concern exercises its driving power' (*ST1*, 45).

2. *Some peculiarities of Tillich's style*

Reactions to Tillich's style vary from uncritical fascination to irritation and impatience. The liturgical solemnity of his prose at its best can exercise a literal enchantment. On the other hand, one may sympathise with G. E. Moore, the Cambridge philosopher, who remarked after hearing Tillich lecture, 'Now really, Mr Tillich, I don't think I have been able to understand a single sentence of your paper. Won't you please try one sentence, or even one word, that I can understand?' (*TPT* 133). More typical of the reaction of English and American commentators are such ambiguous remarks as that Tillich was a 'difficult' thinker but 'undoubtedly profound'; inclined to use too much philosophical jargon, but still a 'successful communicator'.[2]

Tillich's style requires some apology for English-speakers; for, both the superficial form of what O'Connor calls its 'workmanlike German seriousness' and the laborious dialectic of the philosophical style he inherits from Kant, Fichte, Schelling and Hegel are alien to British and American traditions. What are taken to be signs of earnestness and profundity in German thought may appear suspect and even comic to English taste.

Donald Davie, in a review of George Steiner's, *After Babel*, argues that '[w]hat are signs of earnestness in one language are signs of flippancy in another. The difference between British and American English is striking in this respect.' He suggests that if this is true here, it is *a fortiori* true of the difference between English and German, and explains why someone raised in the one language may be rhetorically ill at ease in the other, no matter how skilfully they master the second language. He makes some further observations that are profoundly relevant to the understanding of Tillich's style:

> In a one-language community at some one time a terse pithiness, a dry or casual tone, and a conversational or colloquial vocabulary, are taken for signs that a writer is in earnest; in a neighbouring language-community, or in the first language at another period, earnestness is signalled on the contrary by copiousness, by 'hammering home' (i.e., saying one thing in different ways, many times over), by an excited or urgent tone, and by a vocabulary that darts or

ranges all the way from the racy to the ornate and the proudly erudite.[3]

Tillich was painfully aware of the need to modify his literary style to make his words more acceptable to English and American readers (*PE* xxiv). However, in spite of his efforts, the overwhelming characteristics of his rhetoric remain. He could hardly be better described than in some further words of Donald Davie: 'an eloquent, ornate and driving writer, above all a copious one'. Tillich's written prose has the character, the cadences, and the eloquence of his sermons. His theology is written with the insistent driving emphasis of a preacher. It is copious because its burden is to persuade and cajole rather than to convince by sustained argument. Like St Augustine's, it is discursive in the sense that it is a 'method of digression', because it follows the order of charity rather than the order of intellectual knowledge.[4] Above all it is serious. In fact, he canonises seriousness as a theological virtue, equating faith with 'ultimate seriousness';[5] a fact to which we shall return. Alan Watts comments on Tillich's notion of faith as ultimate seriousness:

> On the one hand, Tillich is associating the deep with the weighty and the grave in thinking of God as 'what you take seriously without any reservation'. The domain of God is the domain of 'ultimate concern', since the dimension of depth is where we address ourselves to what *really matters*, to what is 'no laughing matter', and also confront (though that doesn't seem to be the right way of approach to the deep) the *mysterium tremendum* – the interior strangeness of Being that makes us shudder and wonder.
>
> I am afraid Tillich's God is, for all the transposition into depth, still morally speaking – the old God 'out there', the Protestant– Biblical Jehovah who lacks real depth to the extent that he lacks humour. Does anyone want the End, the Final Ground of all things, to be completely serious? No twinkle? No gaiety? Something rigid and overwhelming and ponderously real? Such a profound seriousness might be the anteroom, but not the presence chamber.[6]

In spite of differences between what counts as humour in different linguistic and cultural traditions, it is doubtful that anyone would deny that seriousness is overwhelmingly characteristic of Tillich as man, as preacher and as theologican. This seriousness relates both to the moral earnestness of his tone and to the spirit of ultimate concern in which he approaches the fundamental questions of human existence. However, it also relates to the absence of humour: to the fact that Tillich's recipe for theology lacks the pinch of salt.

It is amazing how often the word 'serious' and its cognates crop up in his writing, and in the writings of commentators.[7] He also deals predominantly with grave themes: death, guilt, anxiety, estrangement, doubt, meaninglessness and unconditional commitment. He seldom deals with the positive themes of hope, joy, peace and the other theological virtues, although he does have much to say about faith and love. In a rare treatment of the theme of joy, he admits the justice of Nietzsche's

criticism that 'His disciples should look more redeemed'.[8] Religion and
Christian joy are undoubtedly solemn matters (in the strictly literal sense,
from *sollus & annus*, that is, concerned with the celebration of the annual
festivals and high moments of human life), but are they necessarily
serious? Tillich tends to suggest that they are, and this is related to the
way he views religious and theological language. Seriousness is not a
matter affecting only the tone and style of his theology, and the choice of
subjects that he regards as weighty enough to warrant attention; it also
marks an inclination of Tillich's to regard theology itself as being, like
preaching, a solemn proclamation of the Word.

By contrast, Newman suggests that the rhetoric of theology and of
religious devotion differ. It is in the context of their solemn enunciation
in the liturgy that the Creeds are to be understood; not as a series of theological propositions requiring philosophical analysis and criticism, since
'they are devotional acts, and of the nature of prayers, addressed to God;
and, in such addresses, to speak of intellectual difficulties would be out of
place'.[9] Conversely:

> Our devotion is tried and confused by the long list of propositions
> which theology is obliged to draw up, by the limitations, explana-
> tions, definitions, adjustments, balancings, cautions, arbitrary pro-
> hibitions, which are imperatively required by the weakness of human
> thought and the imperfections of human languages. Such exercises
> of reasoning indeed do not increase and harmonise our notional
> apprehension of the dogma, but they add little to the luminousness
> and vital force with which its separate propositions come home to
> our imagination, and if they are necessary, as certainly they are, they
> are necessary not so much for faith, as against unbelief.[10]

What makes Tillich's theology and his sermons so serious is their
earnest moral purpose and didactic character. They aim to teach and
edify, but unlike Kierkegaard, who drew a clear distinction between the
two, Tillich tends to conflate sermons and discourses.

> Kierkegaard developed very precise notions of why his religious
> essays were discourses and not sermons. Primarily it is that sermons
> are properly a work 'absolutely and entirely through authority, that
> of Holy Writ and of Christ's apostles'. They presuppose a priest who
> in virtue of ordination speaks categorically and definitively on God's
> behalf. But discourses, or addresses as they may also be called, use
> as their point of departure, not the authoritatively given content,
> but the human situation. They deal with doubt, and, hence, they are
> not categorical and declaratory as much as accommodating to, and
> eliciting of, the religious potentiality in the listener or reader.[11]

Because Kierkegaard was keenly aware of the difference between the
apologetic function of 'maieutic communication' and preaching the
Word, or 'direct communication', he was able to use the former with
devastating effect to satirise Hegel, whom he accused of treating philosophical dialectic as a source of revelation. Tillich, however, lacked his
understanding of irony, of the incongruities of existence, and thus lacked

the commanding advantage of humour in resisting the bewitchment of Hegelian dialectic. The following remarks of Kierkegaard are not without some relevance to the ambitions of Tillich's *Systematic Theology*: 'There were philosophers even before Hegel who took it upon themselves to explain existence, history. And it is true of all such attempts that providence can only smile at them. Though perhaps it has not always exactly roared with laughter at them; for there was always something honest, human and serious in them'.[12] The detachment required for humour is not unconnected with the detachment that makes possible a proper discrimination between different modes of communication: in this case, between the rhetoric appropriate to the communication of the Christian Faith in preaching and worship and the dialectical activity of the philosophical appraisal of the Christian Faith, including the second-order examination of religious language in its first-order usage.

3. *Tillich's style of thinking*

So far, we have dealt mainly with the superficial characteristics of Tillich's literary style, but we must consider more closely its relation to his style of thought. There are three features of this that have provoked comment: first, although Tillich's style was obscure and difficult he yet proved to be a popular thinker; secondly, while he appeared enormously erudite, his methods of scholarship were almost casual and were certainly suspect among specialists in the many fields that his thought encompassed; thirdly, his work is informed by a spirit of criticism and seriousness that affects both its style and content. Each requires interpretation.

The paradox that while Tillich's thought was almost bafflingly difficult he yet was very much in demand as teacher, popular lecturer and contributor to scholarly and popular journals has been remarked upon by many commentators.[13] However, Tillich's prestige was not accidental to his work. He was essentially a popular theologian, despite all appearances to the contrary, because it is the express apologetic intention of the work to address itself to the common existential concerns of modern man. He had an ear for the dialect in which his contemporaries spoke, especially that of the *avant garde* in Europe and America. He did not speak the language of any particular academic specialty – his use of even philosophical and theological language is odd – but he did catch the tone of concerned people of his time.

Even as hostile a critic of Tillich's obscurity as Leonard Wheat thinks him sufficiently successful to warrant the writing of a book to prove that his popularity was due to the fact that, while masquerading as a theologian, he was really a dialectical humanist in disguise.[14] What Wheat regards as a vice in Tillich, namely, that he sought to become secular man to secular men, dialectical humanist to dialectical humanists, many others regard as a chief virtue. For example, Kegley and Bretall remark:

> What could be more abstract than 'Being'? But in this 'theology of the New Being' the abstract metaphysical term becomes filled with emotional and volitional content – a content which stems partly

from our Christian inheritance, but mostly from that very 'existential situation' of our time, in which we feel ourselves separated from all that religion has meant by 'salvation', 'regeneration', and 'eternal life'. This probably is what makes Tillich pre-eminently an apostle to the sceptics, the 'intellectuals', and the disillusioned of our era; but it is also what makes his philosophy in a sense classical, because the 'intellectuals' are only those who feel more deeply and coherently what the masses obscurely feel.[15]

The fact that Tillich chose to speak and write in what is clearly a self-consciously sophisticated and academic language is surely connected with the fact that he lived in and largely ministered to an academic community. He sought to address himself primarily to the 'cultured despisers' of religion. It is also a fact that his *Systematic Theology* grew out of his lecture notes prepared for students (*ST1*, Preface). It is not implausible to suggest that we cannot understand why his apologetic takes the form it does unless we realise that it was written for and in response to students.

That Tillich was a popular theologian is both a merit and a limitation of his work. Insofar as he successfully addressed himself to the interests of his colleagues, students and contemporaries, his relevance for the period between and following the two World Wars cannot be denied. He is now considered somewhat *démodé* and this is not surprising, given the fickleness of academic fashions and the concern of students with what is contemporary. Whether Tillich will continue to be of contemporary relevance remains to be seen. Perhaps it is the proper fate of a theologian to be overtaken by history, for it certainly is his responsibility to be 'of his times'. His task is to mediate the truth of the Christian message to his generation: 'Theology moves back and forth between two poles, the eternal truth of its foundation and the temporal situation in which the eternal truth must be received' (*ST1*, 3). Thus does Socrates suggest that his situation may become the locus of an understanding of the universal situation of men; his understanding of dislocation become illuminating for all who suffer dislocation.[16] Whether Tillich was a philosopher and theologian in this full sense will be for posterity to decide; it is undoubtedly true that he was sufficiently in tune with his times to be in the genuine sense a popular theologian. His limitations may well turn on the question whether he was fully contemporary with his times; whether his ultimate concern really was with the ultimate in being and meaning or with the particular expression of it in a specific philosophical or theological tradition. Certainly, he had an ability to adapt what he had to say to changing times and circumstances. This accounts for his continuing popularity for two decades after Bonhoeffer's death, a popularity that tends to contradict the latter's somewhat ungenerous assessment of his significance: 'Tillich set out to interpret the evolution of the world itself – against its will – in a religious sense, to give it its whole shape through religion. That was very courageous of him, but the world unseated him and went on by itself: he too sought to understand the world better than it understood itself, but it felt entirely *mis*understood, and rejected the imputation'.[17]

What he did communicate was an attitude of concern with and yet criticism of all cultural creations to the extent that they claim ultimate meaning. He may not have been as critical of his own system as we should like, but he did attempt to build into it the principle of its own criticism: the Protestant Principle (*PE* xxiii–xxiv). This, perhaps, justifies us in applying to him Kierkegaard's remark: that '[i]t is possible that there was more truth in the Socratic ignorance as it was in him, than in the entire objective truth of the System, which flirts with what the times demand and accommodates itself to *Privatdocents*'.[18]

Tillich *did* tend to 'flirt with what the times demand'. For example, his early studies of Schelling and his attack on supranaturalist theology are very much in keeping with the liberal, idealist mood of German theology before the First World War. Again, the emphasis on existentialism and depth psychology, which characterises much of his American writing after the Second World War, fits well with fashionable interests of the time. However, Tillich was not afraid to challenge reigning attitudes; for example, on the basis of a radical belief-ful realism, he challenged popular idealism in philosophy and theology, and he developed his Religious Socialist critique of the reigning bourgeois idealism in politics and showed this, combined with a demonic nationalism, was leading to totalitarian Nazism, war and catastrophe. Similarly, his determined insistence on the importance of ontology was directly contrary to the anti-metaphysical bias of Anglo-Saxon empiricism and positivism and the anti-essentialist view of popular existentialism. His emphasis on the religious and ontological dimensions in depth psychology ran counter to the secular and individualistic emphasis in popular depth psychology.

Tillich's popularity had a different source and character from that of the merely fashionable theologian, partly because of the seriousness with which he took the concerns of modern man. He was able to find formulations of fundamental ideas, in a wide range of contemporary disciplines, that made these disciplines excitingly relevant and meaningful to his contemporaries. The catholicity of his own interest in contemporary culture, his ability as a Christian to affirm its positive meaning and value and his ability to make the ultimate concerns of modern culture real to people, was partly due to his capacity to interpret contemporary culture in its own terms and to relate it to its traditional Christian apologist's task as that of finding common ground with his contemporaries: 'In my search for this common criterion I discovered that the modern trends of thought which are rooted in the Enlightenment, are substantially Christian, in spite of their critical attitude towards ecclesiastical Christianity. They are not, as they are often called, pagan' (*OB* 16). It is his confidence that this is the case that makes it possible for him to recommend a new understanding of the relevance of the Christian Faith and a deeper understanding of their own culture to his contemporaries. The extent to which he succeeded is a measure of his stature as an apologist, and of his greatness as a popularist. The style and character of his philosophical theology is essentially connected with the fact that it is as both that he expounds it.

The second anomalous feature of Tillich's work is the quality of his scholarship. On the one hand there is his undeniable erudition; manifest in the catholic scope of his knowledge and interests and the massiveness of his literary output. On the other hand, specialists were invariably critical of his lack of systematic rigour and his disregard for the appropriate conventions of scholarship, whether in the theological disciplines or in philosophy, psychology, art history, the history of ideas, sociology or politics. It is remarkable that he could command respect and attention by what he had to say on any of these subjects; yet he was not in any unambiguous sense recognised to be great in any field but theology, and even theologians found him difficult to accommodate within their familiar categories.

Part of the explanation is given by Tillich himself, speaking with disarming frankness of the effect of romanticism on his philosophical imagination:

> It has been good in that it has given me the ability to combine categories, to perceive abstractions in concrete terms (I would almost say 'in colour') and to experiment with a wide range of conceptual possibilities. It has been of doubtful value insofar as such imaginative ability runs a risk of mistaking the creations of the imagination for realities, that is, of neglecting experience and rational critique, of thinking in monologues rather than dialogues, and isolating itself from co-operative scientific effort. Whether good or bad, this imaginative tendency (plus certain other circumstances) prevented me from becoming a scholar in the accepted sense of the word. Amongst intellectuals of the twenties there was a kind of aversion against the scholar in the restricted sense of 'expert'. (*OB* 25)

However, this is only part of the story because in one sense Tillich was an ordinary professor with a strong instinct for reality and normality. His academic career was a fairly normal and successful one and not untypical for those who lived through the two World Wars. He enjoyed the rewards of academic success and was sensitive to criticism of his work. On the other hand, he does not conform to the accepted image of a professor in professing some specialty, for he neither stuck to a single specialty nor was he rigorous and meticulous in the pursuit of a single method. In fact, he experimented with a variety of approaches to the subjects he taught and there are, as a result, conflicting trends at work in his system.

Perhaps the most revealing thing in the passage just quoted is the parenthesis 'plus certain other circumstances', for contained in that parenthesis is a world of personal suffering and experience, outside the university, that Tillich never discusses openly. The parenthesis brackets out his personal experience of the First World War, the socio-economic chaos that followed in Germany, and the impact of the Russian Revolution and the political upheavals that followed in Europe. It also conceals the breakdown of his first marriage, and the tensions following his remarriage, to artist and bohemian Hannah Werner. It brackets out the crisis of the clash between Church and State, and his banishment from homeland, friends, family and all that German culture meant to him. These events undoubtedly influenced the character of his scholarship as they informed his compassion for other people.

One respect in which the circumstances of his life affected the character of his scholarship concerns his different roles in German and American society. Even a cursory examination of Tillich's writings reveals that his scholarship had different orientations before and after his emigration to America.

Apart from his early academic studies of Schelling and post-Kantian supra-naturalist theologians, the bulk of his work from 1919 to 1936 is concerned with non-academic subjects. In 1919, there is already evidence of his practical concern with the predicament of the masses, disorientated youth and the confrontation of Christianity and Socialism. Between 1919 and 1925 Tillich published several important papers elaborating the theoretical foundations of his new 'theology of culture', and an important book *Das System der Wissenschaften nach Gegenstanden und Methoden* (1923). However, the orientation of his thinking is practical and related to his concern to understand the cultural, political and religious movements of his time. In the course of his work, he began to develop an interpretation of the world-historical significance of Protestantism. This analysis provided the ideological foundation for Religious Socialism and the framework within which his *Systematic Theology* began to take shape, although the more traditional academic environment in which he found himself in America made him fall back on idealist forms to provide it with a respectable academic appearance.

By contrast with this very practical orientation, his writing took on a much more academic flavour after his forced emigration to America; a form that was more appropriate to his situation as an honoured refugee professor at Union Theological Seminary. Instead of being part of the German Church Struggle and involved in the war and the European situation, he was now removed from both and obliged to adopt the detached role of critical observer and interpreter of these events to others.[19] The same difficulty beset him elsewhere. Instead of being involved in practical politics, he was set up as the expert on Religious Socialism. It is notable, too, that, apart from comment on the existential character of Schelling's philosophy, Tillich wrote nothing directly on Existentialism until he emigrated to America.

Between 1936 and 1948, Tillich was mainly concerned with adjusting to his new life and career in America. Many articles published during this period continue to reflect his preoccupation with the War and the question of post-War reconstruction. However, it is striking that, from 1948 until his death in 1965, his books and articles tend to cluster around the publication and themes of the three volumes of his *Systematic Theology*, and that the character of his work becomes more scholastic in flavour as he becomes preoccupied with the elaboration of his world-view and the completion of his *magnum opus*. This is, undoubtedly, partly a function of advancing age, but it is also a sign of the constraints within which he had to operate, even as one of the most lionised academics of his day.

As a scholar Tillich was a kind of cultural polyglot; an Erasmian figure who combined some of the promethean qualities of a man of the Enlightenment or Counter-Reformation with a comprehensive vision of the relation of religion and culture in our time. He inspired his disciples to devote themselves to the interpretation of contemporary culture in its meaning and depth. This is true of his students, colleagues and friends such as Herbert Marcuse, Karl Mannheim, Theodor Adorno, Erich Fromm, and Mircea Eliade. Rollo May, whose notable study of anxiety was conducted under Tillich's supervision, has this to say: 'But the wonderful thing about Paul Tillich was that he never made disciples of us, nor did he attract mere followers. His whole life was an embodiment of Nietzsche's clarion call "Follow not me but yourself". He made us colleagues, co-workers and co-creators'.[20]

Part of the secret of his popularity was that he adopted the rhetorical style of a scholarly popularist, but this is also the reason for the feeling of uneasiness with which he left more careful scholars. The rhetoric is more impressive than the dialectical analysis offered in its support. This may be a serious defect of Tillich's work, insofar as one judges it by the canons of conventional scholarship. However, it may be more just and more illuminating to seek to understand it in its own terms as a work of theological rhetoric that provides us with both a definition-in-use of theological rhetoric and an insight into the workings of belief-systems. To examine Tillich's employment of concepts like meaning, truth and logic is to clarify both the rhetoric with which he communicates his theological insights and his understanding of the practical significance of philosophy and theology for human life.

Connected with the popular character of his style of thought is something more profound about his thinking; namely, its canonisation of the spirit of criticism. Tillich identifies faith or ultimate concern with seriousness, doubt and the spirit of criticism. In a typical passage, he says concerning those in a state of critical doubt: 'The criticism according to which they should judge themselves is the seriousness and ultimacy of their concern about the content of both their faith and their doubt' (*ST1*, 17). This embodies an insight from an early and crucially important paper[21] of Tillich's, in which he explores the relation between faith and existential doubt, and distinguishes the latter from the methodological doubt of science and philosophy. From this point on, ultimate concern is built into his theology as both a constitutive and a regulative principle. First let us consider it as a constitutive principle.

Perhaps the pivotal assertion of his systematic theology is his definition of man. Man is that being who 'is ultimately concerned about his being and meaning'.[22] This ultimate concern serves as the foundation for both of the formal criteria by means of which Tillich defines theology:

> This then is the first formal criterion of theology: *The object of theology is what concerns us ultimately. Only those propositions are theological which deal with their object so far as it can become a matter of ultimate concern for us.* (*ST1*, 15)

> Our ultimate concern is that which determines our being or non-being. Only those statements are theological which deal with their object in so far as it can become a matter of being or non-being for us. This is the second formal criterion of theology. (*ST1*, 17)

Faith has two sides: it is an affective, volitional and intellectual involvement with its object, for which Tillich chooses the word 'concern'; and that with which it is involved must be ultimate in being and meaning. The former is the translation of faith in terms of *agape*, in accordance with the spirit of the two great commandments; the latter expresses the emphasis on the unconditional transcendence of God in the first of these commandments.[23] The first formal criterion defines God as that which is the object of ultimate concern and is ultimate in meaning. The second formal criterion defines God as that which is the object of ultimate concern and is ultimate in being. Faith, and God as the ultimate ground of being and meaning, are correlated in the existential relationship of ultimate concern. Tillich's existential concern with ontology and the metaphysics of meaning, truth and logic meet in this fundamental relation of ultimate concern.

It is important that Tillich does not only write about ultimate concern. The definition that 'Man is ultimately concerned with his being and meaning' could be a biographical description of Tillich himself. His own life and work expresses this quality of ultimate concern, and constitutes a profound challenge to theologians and philosophers to become similarly involved. His work challenges philosophers to accept their vocation seriously, to wrestle with the questions of being and meaning and not merely to talk about ontology and the philosophy of meaning. Similarly his challenge to theologians is to become participants in the *ministerium verbi divini*, instead of indulging in meta-theological talk or commenting in rabbinical fashion on the theologies of others. Tillich seeks to point us beyond his system to the Ultimate Ground of all Being and Meaning and shares with Kierkegaard an uneasiness about those who would come after him grubbing in his work for material for doctoral and licentiate theses.

The doctrine of faith as ultimate concern is developed as the regulative principle of his theology in the form of the Protestant principle. We learn from *The Protestant Era* that the Protestant Principle is derived from the classic Pauline and Lutheran doctrine of justification through faith. It is variously defined, but is presented first as an instrument for the critique of human culture. For example: 'The Protestant principle as derived from the doctrine of justification through faith rejects heteronomy (represented by the doctrine of papal infallibility) as well as a self-complacent autonomy (represented by secular humanism). It demands a self-transcending autonomy, or theonomy' (*PE* xxi). However, it is also specifically developed as a principle of theological criticism: 'The Protestant Principle is the restatement of the prophetic principle as an attack against a self-absolutising and, consequently, demonically distorted church. Both prophets and reformers announced the radical implications of exclusive monotheism' (*ST1*, 252). In the second chapter of *Systematic Theology* Volume 1, but also throughout the rest of the system, the Protestant principle is applied as a protest 'against the identification of our ultimate concern with any creation of the church', for example, the biblical writings, the liturgical and theological traditions of the church, and church history. Tillich's application of the principle is less consistent and uncompromising than the equivalent doctrine of justification by faith alone in the work of Karl Barth, but to the extent that it tends towards an extreme affirmation of a divine mono-energism and a denial of the efficacy of secondary causes as means of grace, it leads to difficulties in Tillich's Christology and doctrine of the Church and Sacraments, and in his philosophy, in particular, in his account of symbols.[24]

The identification of faith with a dominative critical seriousness is responsible not only for the relative neglect in Tillich's work of the other theological virtues and the more joyful fruits of the spirit, but also for a curious lack of detachment about his own work. Ultimate seriousness is acceptable so long as it doesn't take itself seriously; the self-absolutising tendency is at work in Tillich's system in that what he produces for our consumption is not prepared and presented *cum grano salis*. Lacking Kierkegaard's sense of irony and caustic wit, he tends to identify the Protestant principle with the Kantian critical principle, and drives philosophy and theology into similar antinomies in spite of his attempt to offer us a comprehensive alternative world-view. It is precisely because Tillich is so anxious to get his view across that he adopts the hectoring tone and the pedantic, even pompous, language of the self-styled popularist, and lacks the scholarly detachment expected of so erudite a man. It is the measure of its greatness, and the source of its chief weaknesses, that his system is primarily a work of theological rhetoric.

4. *Rhetoric and dialectic in theology*

It is perhaps necessary to emphasise that the term 'rhetoric' is not here used disparagingly, but in order to make an important distinction between two kinds of theological system: those that are primarily systems of theoretical knowledge, and those that are primarily concerned with the communication of a vision or world-view; between those that aim to achieve rational assent and those that are more concerned with volitional commitment (although the two are clearly not entirely separable). Knowledge-systems have been traditionally connected with demonstrative and dialectical methods of reasoning, and belief-systems with the methods of rhetorical communication and the art of persuasion.[25] This does not mean that the content of a belief-system cannot be subjected to critical analysis; but the application of dialectical and demonstrative methods to its subject-matter tends to transform it into a system of theoretical knowledge.

It is our contention that Tillich's *Systematic Theology* has the character of a belief-system rather than a system of theoretical knowledge. This is shown by his insistence that his theological system is apologetic in character. His description of the method of correlation suggests that he was concerned with the provision of specific theological answers to existential questions; but it is rather the case that the system as a whole, *qua* belief system, is conceived as an answer to man's existential predicament.[26] His system is an outstanding example of a coherent, well articulated belief-system, inspired by a single, over-riding conviction: that if we are to speak of God at all it is as the Ultimate Ground of Being and Meaning. The working out of that insight is doubly instructive: it is illustrative of the nature of belief-systems in general and, because Tillich seeks to rationalise his method, it is a particularly instructive study of the inner logic of such systems.

Although Tillich calls this way of rationalising his method of communication 'dialectical' (whether as 'method of correlation', 'apologetic theology' or 'theonomous systematics'), it corresponds more closely to the subject matter and method of Aristotle's classic *Rhetoric*, in which he says that the function of Rhetoric as a science is 'not to persuade but to discover the available means of persuasion in any subject'.[27]

Tillich's usage of the term 'dialectic' derives principally from Kant, Fichte, Schelling and Hegel, but it is also connected with the Platonic tradition. In this tradition 'rhetoric' has a primarily negative connotation, connected with sophistry and illusion, whereas 'dialectic' is used for knowledge of true being and, at the same time, to describe the existential process of discovery of this knowledge. The chief difficulty in this tradition, whether in its ancient or its modern form, is that in its eagerness to condemn the misuse of rhetoric it fails to realise the importance of the rhetorical element in all communication. But, as Aristotle says,

> For it is not the faculty but the moral purpose which constitutes the sophistical character. But *there is the difference between Rhetoric and Dialectic, that*, while in the former the name 'rhetorician' is descriptive either of the science or of the moral purpose, there is in the atter the name 'sophist' to describe the moral purpose, and 'dialectician' to describe not the purpose but the faculty.[28]

In consequence, the tradition stemming from Plato fails to make clear the real distinction between rhetoric and dialectic. This ambiguity remains in the tradition as a whole, and in later German philosophy there is no clear way of distinguishing between philosophical communication and philosophical knowledge. In Hegel the ambiguity is deliberately exploited to develop a 'dynamic' theory of the relation between the rational and the real, or between truth and being.

In Aristotle's *Organon* and other logical works, he analysed the diverse uses of language and reasoning as instruments of human thought and communication. In general, the scope of his logic is the whole of human discourse, reasoning and communication. Although the term 'logic' was only introduced much later[29] it is obvious that Aristotle does not equate logic with proof-logic or what we call formal logic. He divides the subject-matter of his logical works into the art of persuasion and the art of demonstration. Within the latter art, dialectical reasoning or the logic of disputation is distinguished from demonstrative reasoning in that it is the science of argument from non-evident premisses.[30] Kant's use of the term 'dialectic' is still fairly traditional. In general, he means by it the logic of disputation, and applies it to the critique of antinomies and illusions resulting from transcendental judgements that profess to pass beyond the limits of experience. The identification of dialectic with the transcendental method would accord roughly with the classical view of dialectic as concerned with philosophical knowledge, but with Fichte's generalisation of the process of the movement of thought from thesis to antithesis to synthesis and Hegel's forcible introduction of the Real into logic, the value of the traditional distinction is lost. The term becomes so extensive that it can apply to anything from rational communication to rigorous logical proof, and confuses, in particular, the relations between rhetoric and dialectic and their different but complementary functions in knowledge. To the extent that Tillich is heir to this tradition he is heir to some of this vagueness and these confusions.

However, it is also important to stress that Tillich stands in a philosophical tradition that seeks to emphasise that truth is not merely a theoretical and extensional relation, but is an existential and intentional one. He also stands in a theological tradition that emphasises that preaching and communication of the Word are of primary importance. In fact, Tillich's dialectic bears a striking resemblance to what may be called Plato's 'existential dialectic', which represents, on the one hand, a kind of connatural knowledge of being-itself, apprehended under the forms of the good, the true and the beautiful, and on the other, the painful existential process by which one overcomes one's moral and spiritual self-alienation and becomes capable of reaching that knowledge.[31]

Tillich's *Systematic Theology* sets out, in a panoramic vision, a picture of God as the ground and source of all being and meaning, of man's alienation from God, and of the dialectical process whereby the divine *logos*, in the person of Jesus as the Christ, mediates in human existence the judgement and correction necessary to restore man and the Creation from their alienated state to essential spiritual reunion with the ground and source of all being and meaning. Tillich calls this process 'dialectical', but he also refers to theological method as dialectical. We wish to emphasise that it is more helpful to understand the nature of Tillich's system in terms of its over-riding practical and rhetorical purpose.

The celebrated debate between Barth and Tillich on the nature of theology, which centres on the question of whether it is kerygmatic or apologetic is, at its broadest, about the nature of the communication of the Christian Faith in the contemporary world; but, at its narrowest it is also about the relative merits of two different kinds of theological rhetoric. To Barth's *either-or*, Tillich offers an Hegelian *both-and*. Tillich wants to have it both ways and, in a sense, gets it both ways – this is the genius of his system.

The concern of Tillich with correlation and a theology of culture reflects a common Protestant preoccupation with preaching, apologetics and communication. It has its counterparts in Barth's concern with exegesis, Bonhoeffer's with religionless Christianity, Bultmann's with demythologising the kerygma, Kraemer's with communication and Cox's with secularisation. It is not surprising that this concern with communication should express itself in the English-speaking world in linguistic philosophy and the efforts of linguistic theologians to clarify the 'logic' of religious language. The work of philosophers like Ian Ramsey, Anthony Flew and H. A. Hodges involves a study of theological rhetoric and a critique of knowledge systems as well. Flew, for example, explicitly presents a critique of the knowledge claims that are made for statements such as 'God exists' and 'Man is free'. What is surprising, is that it is not more commonly acknowledged that such studies are studies of rhetoric, and that Protestant theology is more concerned with the rhetorical logic of belief-systems than with the dialectical and demonstrative logic of a theology conceived as a science.

The distinction between kerygmatic and apologetic theology is partly artificial, at least from a methodological point of view, for they could be equally well described as two styles of preaching or as two styles of apologetic. Comparing kerygmatic theology unfavourably with his own apologetic theology, Tillich says; 'Apologetic theology is "answering theology". It answers the questions implied in the "situation" in the power of the eternal message and with the means provided by the situation whose questions it answers' (*ST1*, 6). This can be taken as a paraphrase of what he later calls the 'method of correlation', on which the structure of his theology is built. However, it could equally well be taken as a description of his sermons and kerygmatic assertions. It is not inappropriate to describe Tillich's theological system as evangelical. The point is emphasised by Kegley and Bretall, in discussing the role of his method of correlation in both his preaching and his *Systematic Theology*: 'Here is modern evangelicalism whose significance and applicability in preaching – especially to the "unsaved", the religiously illiterate, and the alienated – are almost unlimited . . . The evangelical note, moreover, rings out free from any hint of fundamentalism or fideism'.[32] David Kelsey makes a similar point: 'a balanced interpretation of Tillich's theology is possible only if justice is done to his explicit intent to be "in accord with Scripture"'.[33] Louis Racine uses Tillich's sermons to illustrate the central concerns of his theology: in particular his concern to forge a new language for the communication of the Christian Faith in the modern world.[34]

What all this indicates is that if we are to understand the precise nature of Tillich's system, we must appreciate that it is a profoundly skilful and articulate system of theological rhetoric. To describe him as a great rhetorician is not to derogate from his significance as a theologian: after all he shares this distinction with that other theologian and professor of rhetoric, to whose thought his is so akin, St Augustine. We may complain that Tillich's theoretical understanding of logic was deficient, but as a practical rhetorician he deserved his success. For he had a fine sense of what Aristotle described as 'the faculty of discovering all the possible means of persuasion in any subject'.[35] Thus he was fully aware that different subject-matters demand different methods and that therefore standards of precision are different in theology and in science and mathematics.[36] However, religion and ethics may be of greater significance for us in spite of the fact that their conclusions are not so easily demonstrated.[37] In addition Tillich possessed the qualities that Aristotle enumerates as requirements of the good rhetorician: 'unless he is competent to reason logically, to study human characters and virtues, and thirdly to study the nature and quality of the several emotions, the sources from which they spring and the methods of exciting them'.[38]

Tillich's theological and philosophical writings have more in common with the occasional addresses and discursive theological writings of St Augustine, which address themselves to specific situations, problems and needs, than they have with the 'disputatious science' of St Thomas Aquinas or of his mediaeval contemporaries, with their emphasis on dialectical and demonstrative argument and contemplative knowledge. There are philosophical and theological pre-suppositions underlying these differences: for example, the priority of will over intellect in the definition of being, and the stress on the preaching of the Word rather than the contemplation of the sacramental mysteries. These differences are not accidental but essential to the form of Tillich's theological system and determine its rhetoric. His approach to questions of meaning and truth is practical and existential. 'Philosophy and theology ask the question of being. But they do so from different perspectives. Philosophy deals with the structure of being in itself; theology deals with the meaning of being for us' (*ST1*, 25). Tillich would profoundly agree with Kierkegaard when he says, at the conclusion of *Either/Or*, 'Only the truth that edifies is the truth for thee'. We may say of Tillich's sermons, lectures and systematic theology what Kierkegaard said of his *Edifying Discourses*: 'They were written for instruction'.

5. *Rhetoric and dialectic in philosophy*

Philosophers of different kinds have reacted to Tillich's style of philosophising with embarrassment. Its urgent driving character, its didactic form, its challenging and provocative tone and its loose, discursive pattern of argumentation have puzzled his philosophical critics. Also, his thought is eclectic and syncretistic in a manner that makes it difficult to identify him with any particular school. Thomists such as Weigel, Foster, Keefe, Osborne and Mondin find his ontology a curious mixture of existentialist themes and idealist jargon, and reject his claim that his doctrine is the same as St Thomas's doctrine of *analogia entis*. Philosophers of an idealist bent, for example, Hook, Hartshorne and Randall, find him disturbingly unorthodox. Existentialist critics find his thought too essentialist; examples are Hamilton, Hammond, Kaufmann and McLean. Such Marxists as Marcuse and Lukacs would presumably find his thought too Christian, as did many of the early critics of Religious Socialism. Hepburn, Mitchell, Smart, Hick, Heywood Thomas and other British philosophers are puzzled by the ontological speculation and lack of analytical rigour in the exposition and defence of his views.

The fact is that Tillich belonged to the 'age of ideology', and his thought has the rhetorical style and ideological form of the types of *Lebensphilosophie* that were popular earlier this century. It does not have the rigorous coherence of a philosophical system, nor is it merely an irrational affirmation of belief. Rather, it is the expression of a conviction that a Christian and realist philosophy of being could be developed out of a synthesis of idealism, Marxism and Existentialism. Tillich's *Systematic Theology* does not pretend to be a theological system in the conventional sense. His work has the aesthetic coherence of a vision, but lacks the back-up of a worked-out theory to support and justify that vision. In examining the critical perspective from which Tillich criticises supranaturalism in religion and nominalism in philosophy, and in scrutinising his metaphysics of meaning, truth and logic, we shall be attempting to clarify the theoretical basis of his Christian world-view.

Tillich is ultimately concerned to recommend to others the need for ultimate concern. However, he is also concerned to recommend the object of his ultimate concern: God as Being-itself, as the New Being, and as Spirit overcoming the split between essence and existence. Insofar as he devotes his attention to these two concerns he is, by his own criteria, doing theology; the question of being and meaning remains the implicit rather than the explicit focus of his thinking. However, when the attention shifts from ultimate concern to being and meaning, then, by his own criteria, he is doing philosophy. This distinction bears some relation to traditional definitions but it is also subtly different. The difficulty is expressed by theologians who complain that he ontologises theology and by philosophers who find it impossible to disentangle his metaphysics of meaning, truth and logic from his theology. If what Tillich offers us is a Christian ideology for our times, then it may be possible to explain both the rhetorical style of his thought and the fact that it is not dialectical in a sense that would make it a system of theological or philosophical knowledge in the traditional manner. If the primary purpose of Tillich's writing was to get across the form and substance of his ultimate concern, then it may be possible to admit both that his thought lacks the dialectical analysis and justification that we expect of a philosophical theology and that it contains challenging insights that ought to provoke us to test their validity. Faced with the problem of defining Tillich's philosophy, we must recognise that part of the difficulty arises out of our different conceptions of the scope and nature of philosophy. The range and significance of the terms 'philosophy' and 'theology' is much more specific and restricted in

Britain than it was in Tillich's Germany or Tillich's America. It is not so much a matter of differences in the formal definitions of terms as it is one of the roles of philosophers in different societies.

British culture, with its almost unbroken tradition of empiricism and a high degree of conformism in religion and morals, has typically produced a conservative and scholastic type of philosophy. In this respect it compares with neo-Kantian scholasticism in Germany in the nineteenth century and with the scholasticism of an unbroken mediaeval tradition. By contrast, the speculative, idealistic and ideological character of German and American philosophy in the first half of this century is associated with a constructive, revolutionary impulse in philosophy.

The less ambitious and narrower concern of British philosophers with logic, semantics, epistemology and meta-ethics, and with the attempt to develop a neutral and objective analytical method, reflects the role of philosophy in a highly conformist society. Empiricism has served an ideological purpose in determining social attitudes and in shaping cultural and political institutions. The fact that a kind of empiricism has characterised theory and practice in Britain for centuries makes logical empiricism almost synonymous with common sense for Britons generally as it was for Moore and Russell in particular. Because there has been a remarkable degree of agreement about common values there has been little questioning of those values, and it was possible for Moore to assert that values can be immediately intuited like colours and for Ayer and the emotivists to assume that majority opinion is right. Instead of being involved in the fundamental criticism of his culture the British philosopher tends to perform an essentially conservative function in society. His role as a scholastic clerk is to examine the niceties of the grammar of morals and to analyse, defend and justify the established ideology.

In contrast, Tillich lived in a period of social and cultural upheaval and of radical questioning of traditional values. He belonged to a generation that set out to change the world not to contemplate it; and he formulated his critique of European culture and his ideological alternative with these revolutionary ambitions in mind. He shared his reforming zeal with the Marxists and Existentialists of the 1920s; but it was also something he inherited from such nineteenth-century idealists as Fichte, Schelling and Hegel. As Franz Nauen has pointed out,[39] Schelling, Hölderlin and Hegel, as members of the *Tübinger Stift*, shared a determination to be to German society and its coming revolution what Rousseau and Voltaire had been to French society and the French Revolution. Tillich stood in this idealist tradition and was inspired by its romantic utopianism, its apotheosis of freedom and its enthusiasm for a revolutionary transformation of Europe spearheaded by Germany. Like his idealist predecessors, he was concerned to reinterpret the cultural history and destiny of Europe and on this basis to develop a credible and persuasive system of belief, that would express the spirit of the times. To the extent that this spirit expressed itself in the revival of German nationalism, Tillich was not unaffected by its mood and optimism, especially in his earlier writings.

Tillich was profoundly indebted to this idealist tradition, and it is possible to appreciate the importance of his later critiques of German nationalism, utopianism and the idealist doctrine of freedom only if we appreciate how deeply he was immersed in the spirit of revolutionary idealism and German nationalism.[40] That he became one of the chief theorists of the Religious Socialist movement is not an accidental feature of his thought; it is intrinsically connected with the nature of his social and religious concerns and the ideological style of his thinking. He assimilated and re-interpreted those elements of Marxism and Existentialism that are compatible with Christianity, and expressed them in a revolutionary doctrine of the world-historical significance of Protestantism and a new vision of the mission of the church in the modern world: to communicate with modern man through the religious forms of his own cultural creations, and to subject these to the challenge and judgement of the New Being in Jesus as the Christ.

This enthusiastic and revolutionary style of Tillich's thought is what recommended him to his contemporaries in Germany in the 1920s and to Americans in the 1930s. As Kegley and Bretall have remarked, the time of Tillich's arrival in America was particularly propitious. On the one hand, the social situation was not dissimilar to that in Germany: 'Tillich appeared on the American scene during the great economic depression of 1929–1935, a time as decisive and creative for American Protestant thought as the years immediately after World War 1 had been for Continental Protestantism. Idealistic liberalism, which broke down in Europe after 1914, remained vigorous in America through the First World War, and through the decade of prosperity that followed the war' (*TPT* 34). On the other hand, the idealistic world views of Royce, Hocking, Whitehead and others provided a background similar to that with which Tillich was familiar in Germany. The ideological bent of American idealist philosophy and the emergent new socialist realism provided a natural environment in which Tillich's thought could take root. Although politicians in the British Labour party were sympathetic to Tillich's Religious Socialism,[41] the mood of British philosophy was increasingly inimical to metaphysics of the kind that preoccupied Tillich. It is not surprising, therefore, that he resisted attempts to persuade him to accept an academic appointment in Britain and accepted instead Reinhold Niebuhr's invitation to Union Theological Seminary. Again, as Kegley and Bretall have pointed out, the belief-ful realism of Tillich's book *The Religious Situation* and *The Interpretation of History* found a responsive audience in America, where '[r]ealism of every sort was gaining ascendancy in those difficult days: Steinbeck's literary realism, Niebuhr's political-economic realism, Whitehead's "provisional realism" in philosophy, and the "religious realism" of a whole group of writers who published a symposium in 1931. Tillich's term "belief-ful realism", derived from the realm of art, fell into combination with all these other realisms' (*TPT* 35).

The upshot of the preceding argument is that if we are to understand

Tillich's thought we must take account of its urgent practical and existential character. To describe it as ideological in character requires some qualification, for Tillich himself uses the term in a predominantly pejorative sense. However, in its colloquial and contemporary usage, as roughly synonymous with an articulated practical philosophy of life, 'ideological' is a usefully neutral term that enables us to distinguish the style of his thought from more conventional philosophy and theology.

Tillich's own usage owes much to Marx, as he readily admitted: 'I owe to Marx an insight into the ideological character not only of idealism, but also of all systems of thought, religious and secular, which serve power structures and thus prevent, even if unconsciously, a more just organisation of reality. Luther's warning against the self-made God is the religious equivalent of what ideology means for philosophy' (*OB* 85). Like Karl Mannheim and other members of the Frankfurt School, Tillich uses the term 'ideology' to cover the religious, political and philosophical rationalisations by which the ruling classes rationalise their interest in preserving the social and economic *status quo*. These compare with the utopian dreams of the oppressed and of those idealistic liberals who identify with them and strive for reform. With these, Tillich contrasts the 'fighting truth' of the radical proletariat or the Christian who recognises that to be grasped the truth must be 'done'.

> Expressed in more concrete terms, the church or the fighting proletariat is the place where truth has the greatest chance to be accepted. In all other spheres the general distortion of our historical existence makes it difficult, if not impossible, to find a true insight into the human situation and through it into being itself. (*PE* 297)

With Marx and Kierkegaard he argues that the fate of self-deception and the tendency to develop ideologies are common to all men except those groups who have faced ultimate anxiety, despair and meaninglessness. Then, on the boundary, when the ultimate meaning of human life is called in question, new possibilities can arise.

> If all ideological veils are torn down and self-deception is no longer possible, truth can appear and can be acted upon. And it is revealed only in the measure it is acted upon. The protest of the reformers against the 'self-made' gods or idols and the protest of Marx against the self-made ideas or ideologies challenge the same spiritual danger of man in his present existence: to make the truth a means of religious pride or political will-to-power. (*PE* 280)

This attitude characterises belief-ful realism, Religious Socialism, and Tillich's thought in general. To the suggestion that his mind had changed and that he had progressed beyond religious socialism he retorted, in 1952: 'If the prophetic message is true, there is nothing "beyond religious socialism"' (*TPT* 13). This concern with ultimate concern, this emphasis on being-in-the-truth, itself needs to be characterised. Tillich recognises that to the extent that beliefs are necessarily subject to formulation in words and symbols they are also liable to demonic distortion. He admits the ideological character of Marxism and Christianity in practice, hence the use of the term 'ideological' to describe the kind of belief- and value-system that he propagates is perhaps not unjust. He might well have agreed with Michael Polanyi that 'Ideologies are fighting creeds'.[42] If we interpret Tillich's thought as in this sense ideological we can explain a number of features that are puzzling to philosophers: his impatience with theoretical analysis, his eclecticism and the urgent, even propagandist, tone of his writing.

As a thinker he was more concerned with the existential problems of individuals and the dynamics of alienation in society, than with the theoretical analysis of being. Although he sketches what his philosophical ontology might be like, he is much more concerned with the personal and historical quest for meaningful be-ing.[43] As an ideologist concerned with winning converts and changing the world he is less concerned with comprehensiveness and logical detail than with practical insight and memorable phrases. He offers us a system of well-informed eclecticism, a synoptic vision of modern culture based on a hermeneutic principle that, as ultimate concern, is religious in character and, as Protestant principle, is critical of the relativity of all cultural forms.

Tillich's thought can be instructive to us if we examine it as a well-articulated example of such an ideology or belief-system. It shares with nineteenth century idealism, a concern to transform history and reality by a revolutionary ideal. However, it is, in intention, realistic, and that in a double sense: he identifies himself with the mediaeval tradition of ontological realism; and he advocates an anti-idealist doctrine of man, a philosophy of history and a theory of alienation that derive from Christian, existentialist and Marxist sources. In examining his Metaphysics of meaning, truth and logic we shall be concerned not only with his semantic and epistemological theories in the conventional sense but also and precisely with its character as a philosophy of life.

In exploring Tillich's logic (in the more conventional sense) it is illuminating to place him in the tradition of realist philosophy and intentional logic, from Duns Scotus and John of St Thomas to Brentano and Husserl.[44] The parallels between his critique of empiricism and idealism as off-shoots of nominalism, and similar critiques in Peirce, Maritain and Veatch are illuminating because of their common indebtedness to mediaeval ontological realism and their common efforts to develop an intentional logic appropriate to the hermeneutic of language and culture.

6. *Ultimate concern in theology and philosophy*

Tillich's concern to restore the existential dimension to theology and philosophy leads him to define both in terms of man's 'ultimate concern with being and meaning', where the accent in theology falls on ultimate concern and in philosophy on being and meaning. In what follows, we examine some of the anomalies created by his attempt to express the relation between philosophy and theology in terms of the method of correlation.

Tillich characterises philosophy in the following terms: as the detached and objective investigation of being and its structures; as the attempt to examine reality as a whole and to describe its universal features; and as the abstract statement of the cosmological significance of ontological categories. Theology, by contrast, is defined in terms of the theologian's existential involvement with the object of his ultimate concern; his concern not with the universal *logos* but with the *Logos* 'who became flesh'; and his concern with the soteriological significance of ontological categories and the quest for the new being.[45]

In spite of his attempt to contrast philosophy and theology in terms of the detached objectivity of the philosopher and the involvement of the theologian, he cannot sustain this distinction. He virtually assimilates them, by using the term 'ultimate concern' equally for the philosopher's interest in being and the theologian's involvement with it:

> Every creative philosopher is a hidden theologian (sometimes even a declared theologian.) *He is a theologian* in *the degree to which his existential situation* and *his ultimate concern shape his philosophical vision.* He is a theologian in the degree to which his intuition of the universal *logos* of the structure of reality as a whole is formed by a particular *logos* which appears to him on his particular place and reveals to him the meaning of the whole. And he is a theologian in the degree to which the particular *logos* is a matter of active commitment within a special community. There is hardly a historically significant philosopher who does not show these marks of a theologian. (*ST1*, 28–9).

To the extent that his method of correlation depends on this kind of tendentious argument and persuasive definition, it simply presupposes what it wants to prove: namely, an ultimate identity between philosophy and theology understood as correlative aspects of man's quest for being and meaning.

This may appear to be a damning criticism of Tillich. However, it may be argued that his method of correlation is a poor rationalisation of his actual practice, and that his work retains its value if the method of correlation is abandoned. This case may be argued on several grounds: i) that the method is too simple an account of theological procedure, including his own; ii) that it caricatures the relation between philosophy and theology; and iii) that it fails to account for the distinctive character of his own philosophy of religion.

i) That Tillich's account of theological method in terms of the method of correlation is simplistic is shown by the fact that it does not account adequately for his own work. What it does account for is the particular method of exposition that he adopts in setting out the various divisions of the *Systematic Theology*. 'Systematic theology uses the method of correlation. . . . The method of correlation explains the contents of the Christian faith through existential questions and theological answers in mutual interdependence' (*ST1*, 67–8). But questions are never entirely theory-neutral, and there is a pre-existent correlation of form between question and answer. If this is pressed far enough, Tillich's method of correlation must contradict the possibility of revelation. Secondly, it is simplistic in failing to recognise that apologetic involves dialogue: theology addresses questions to secular culture as well as suggesting answers to its existential questions. Revelation, as Chesterton suggested can often be potently expressed in the form of a challenging question that calls our ordinary beliefs and self-assurance in question. 'The riddles of God are more comforting than the solutions of men.'[46] Similarly, Tillich's own practice involves a theological critique of secular culture as well as an attempt to interpret the Christian Faith in such a way that its relevance to the predicament of contemporary man can be seen.

In his 'theology of culture', or philosophy of religion, Tillich attempted, and to a great extent achieved, two things: firstly, to provide a credible theological interpretation and critique of modern culture, using 'man's ultimate concern with Being and Meaning' as his hermeneutic principle; and secondly, on the basis of this analysis, to set out a new Christian world-view for modern man. It is important to grasp the fact that Tillich sought to formulate a comprehensive alternative ideology for modern man in place of the secular and scientific-technical one. He was in business as both theologian and philosopher, and concerned with the practical and existential significance of such belief systems. He was engaged in doing for contemporary philosophy and culture what Augustine did for Neoplatonic philosophy and Roman culture, and what Bonaventura and Thomas Aquinas did for Aristotelian philosophy and mediaeval culture: namely, attempting to christen it. Tillich seeks to make explicit the implicit religious concerns and substance of modern culture, and in his interpretation of idealism, Marxism and Existentialism, he produces a new synthesis informed by his deeply Christian point of view. In spite of what he says in the *Systematic Theology*, his own apologetic does not involve correlating theological answers with existential questions so much as addressing searching theological questions to the answers offered by secular culture to man's predicament. Alternatively, it involves holding up to the present world a vision of the eternal truth that demonstrates the relativity and finitude of our human, all too human, science and philosophy.

ii) The method of correlation tends to caricature the relations of philosophy and theology in a number of ways. Firstly, because it distinguishes them according to subject matter and method instead of functionally. Secondly, the assumption that philosophy asks the questions and theology answers them conceals the differences between the kinds of questions asked by philosophers and theologians, and between their methods of answering them. Thirdly, it conceals the facts that both philosophy and theology can be existential in propounding philosophies of life, and both can be theoretical and detached in seeking philosophical means for the justification of such beliefs.

On the first point, Tillich inherits the traditional view, based on the division of disciplines or faculties, that justifies these different subject-matters. In *Das System der Wissenschaften nach Gegenständen und*

Methoden, he seeks to define a subject matter for philosophy in terms of its concern with the principles of being and meaning, that is, with 'the meaning-giving functions and categories,' and defines its method as 'metalogical, that is logical with respect to its critical investigation of thought forms and dialectical in going beyond these to consider their import for man's being' (*DSW* 224–6, 230–8). However, in the general introduction to the same work he identifies the meta-logical method with the normative cultural sciences in general (*Geisteswissenschaften*), and these include both philosophy and theology. In 'Religionsphilosophie', he speaks of the metalogical method as the method proper to the philosophy of religion (*WR* 50–6). These examples from Tillich's own work illustrate the general fact that the nature of the subject-matter of philosophy is problematical. Philosophers have rarely agreed about the subject-matter of philosophy, and some have even maintained that it has no special subject-matter and is simply a method of logical or conceptual or semantic analysis. He partly recognises this difficulty when he attempts to explain how the subject-matter of philosophy is related to, but different from, that of the other sciences 'Just as all sciences have their origin in philosophy, so they contribute in turn to philosophy by giving to the philosopher new and exactly defined material far beyond anything he could get from a pre-scientific approach to reality. Of course, the philosopher, as a philosopher, neither criticises nor augments the knowledge provided by the sciences' (*STI*, 26). However, it is not clear whether philosophy is distinguished from theology and the other sciences by its content or by its method. Likewise, theology does not have a single defining method. Its method can vary from the rhetorical and practical concerns of kerygmatic and apologetic theology to the philosophical concerns of a dialectical and demonstrative system of theoretical knowledge.

Tillich's difficulties in defining philosophy and theology by subject-matter and method (*'nach Gegenständen und Methoden,'*) illustrate the dangers of hypostatising the two disciplines instead of considering them functionally and in their dynamic interdependence. Implicit in *Das System der Wissenschaften*, and 'Religionsphilosophie' is a broad and very interesting theory of intentionality in terms of which Tillich might have arrived at a more helpful account of the differences between philosophy and theology. It is the purpose of our interpretation and critique of Tillich's metaphysics of meaning, truth and logic to clarify this theory.

The analogy between different kinds of belief-systems does not make them theological, except in an extended and metaphorical sense of 'theological', and the difficulty with his very general definition of faith as ultimate concern is that it makes it virtually impossible to distinguish one belief-system from another. In general, however, the same argument holds good for Tillich's philosophy as we have used in discussing his theology: namely, that what he propounds is a belief-system, a Christian world-view or philosophy of life, that is presented in the rhetorical mode, that is, kerygmatically or apologetically. It is the task of this work to demonstrate in what sense Tillich's system is an example of a coherent Christian philosophy of life, and to show how it illustrates some of the typical features of the logic of belief systems.

iii) Referring to Tillich's style of thought, Edward D. O'Connor says: 'The single flaw of which one gradually became aware . . . was an occasional disconcerting shift of perspective, joined to a failure sometimes to reach the fundamental issue of a question'.[47] Developing this criticism, he remarks on the fact that the distinctive thing about Tillich's thought was its metaphysical tone; the fact that he treated all problems in metaphysical language. Yet, he concludes, 'Tillich [was] more at home on the phenomenological level of the history of philosophy than in the depths of ontological mystery . . . his writing abounds with instances of obvious disregard for fundamental distinctions between the orders of being – as between the substantial and accidental, between the real and ideal orders.'[48]

This shift of perspective is the tendency for Tillich to move, without announcing the fact, from the rhetorical mode of communication about man's practical and existential needs to transcendental analysis of the constitutive and regulative principles of philosophy and theology. When Kant's *Groundwork for the Metaphysics of Morals* purports to give us a meta-ethical analysis of the constitutive and regulative principles of ethics, it attempts to provide a basis from which we can evaluate second-order moral theories and relates only indirectly to first-order ethical living. In contrast, Tillich's philosophy of religion provides us with a kind of groundwork for the metaphysics of philosophy and theology, in combination with a kind of kerygmatic statement of his practical, Christian philosophy of life. What is omitted in each case is the intermediate level of philosophical and theological theory. We move from first-order religious experience to the tertiary level of transcendental analysis without the intermediate dialectical stage of comparative study and criticism of philosophical and theological theories. We are concerned in the formal part not so much with philosophical and theological argument, but with something like what O'Connor calls 'phenomenological' analysis, at the level of the history of philosophy and theology. A further consequence of this shift from the practical level to the transcendental and back again is that the transcendental analysis that purports to be a neutral phenomenological description of philosophical and theological method becomes coloured with the rhetoric of the first-order apologetic communication. The transcendental analysis becomes prescriptive.

The point may be brought out by citing two different reactions to Tillich's work: one is that he reduces faith to philosophy, and the other is that his philosophy is propagandistic.

Tavard's criticism is that in Tillich's philosophy of religion faith, defined as ultimate concern, becomes mere faith in faith rather than faith in Christ. On this basis it is impossible to distinguish between one creed and another, since faith is a disposition without a specific object.[49]

Independently of the dogmatic grounds on which Tavard argues his case, his criticism is justified because, at least from the transcendental point of view, Tillich is concerned with 'a preconceived phenomenological notion of faith at large' rather than with the faith of Christianity. However, this is not inconsistent with claims that Tillich is an evangelical preacher. As Tavard admits: 'Tillich's theology drives this principle to an ultimate logical implication: whether they are aware of it or not, Christ is the unconditional concern of all men . . . This explains the messianic eloquence which now and again comes to the surface in the writings of Paul Tillich'.[50]

The fact is that both emphases are there. Tillich speaks at two levels. He speaks from within the theological circle with a conviction that is consistent with the tradition of orthodox Christianity; he also speaks from the transcendental standpoint of the philosophy of religion, and it is not always clear which he regards as proper theology. In a sense neither is. The first is a pre-theological affirmation of faith; the second is a metatheological statement about the logical function of faith in theological discourse.

The truth in the criticism that Tillich is not a philosopher but an apologist for Christianity is that his philosophy of life is uncompromisingly Christian. In spite of his attempt to develop a neutral philosophy of religion, the core of his thought is Christian. However, the philosophical part of his system, as we have argued, is also ideological in that it is presented in a rhetorical style as a kind of propaganda for a world-view that is rooted in what he calls 'belief-ful realism'.

Tillich's interest in symbols is not only historically connected with his vocation as an apologist, evangelist and reformer in Germany in the 1920s, but has to do with the ideological character of his thought. He understood intuitively that, if you wish to influence mass attitudes and behaviour, symbols are more important than rational discourse: and that the clash between ideologies is the clash between different symbols and their adequacy to express man's deepest longings and desires.

Both as chief ideologue of the Religious Socialist movement and as theologian Tillich was concerned with propaganda. The difficulty that academic philosophers and theologians have had in understanding Tillich's work is partly that he was a propagandist, both in the sense of creating and circulating new symbols, for example, *kairos, the demonic* and *the New Being*, and in the sense of being an important opinion-maker and moulder of people's ideas.

The task of the propagandist is to redefine the responses towards certain objects by the management of the available supply of symbols – A consideration of the diversity of meanings attached to specific symbols by particular persons shows why ambiguity is an aid to concerted action. A high degree of generality is essential to popular appeal; symbols must be sufficiently vague to enable the individual to transfer his private loves and hates and hopes and fears to the slogans and catchwords of the movement.[51]

Clearly, Tillich had limited access to the mass media and was not concerned with the deliberate manipulation of people's attitudes, but there is no doubt that he was seriously concerned to persuade people to change their attitudes and behaviour. The vagueness, generality and element of deliberate mystification that characterise Tillich's doctrine of symbolism is not accidental, but is due to the fact that his primary concern was the evangelical one of promoting a new Christian world-view or philosophy of life.

Part One

THE CRITICAL NEW PERSPECTIVE

Chapter 2

The Critique of Naturalism and Supranaturalism: The World-view of Theology

1. *Tillich's critique of the world-view of modern philosophy and theology*

The development of Paul Tillich's Christian philosophy of life is associated with the evolution of his metaphysics of meaning, truth and logic, or what, in more general terms, we may call his 'metaphysics of knowledge'.[1] By 'metaphysics of knowledge', Tillich means an approach that transcends ordinary epistemology, semantics and logic, and the antinomies to which, he believes, they give rise in philosophy and theology. Fundamental to his case is his belief that the philosophical tradition we have inherited is nominalistic, and that the logic, theory of knowledge and theory of meaning associated with that tradition drives theology to choose between two equally unsatisfactory alternatives: naturalism and supranaturalism. Equally, he believes this nominalist tradition compels philosophy to choose between an objective but atomistic materialism and subjective idealism.

From his earliest tentative efforts in *Der Begriff des Übernatürlichen, sein dialektischer Character und das Princip der Identität, dargestellt an der supranaturalistischen Theologie vor Schleiermacher* to his posthumous historical works, Tillich was constantly involved in the critique of naturalism and supranaturalism. He sees them as two sides of the same coin, and generated by an inadequate nominalist ontology. Naturalism exists by way of protest against the supranaturalist view of revelation and miracle as violations of the laws of nature, while supranaturalism exists as a protest against the self-sufficient finitude of the naturalist world-view. 'In this sense, the life of naturalism is based on the existence of supranaturalism, and therefore, in the sense of our subject, we are beyond naturalism if we are beyond supranaturalism. They are interdependent, and in removing the one we remove the other. This is exactly the primary implication of the concept of existence, it liberates us from naturalism by liberating us from supranaturalism.'[2] His conviction is that this dichotomy of naturalism and supranaturalism is a false one that springs from the antinomies inherent in the nominalist tradition.

The manner in which, he believed, these antinomies could be transcended by his metaphysics of knowledge was by recognition of the existential character of the act of knowing, that is, of man's existential involvement in the question of being and meaning. In 'Participation and

Knowledge: Problems of an Ontology of Cognition', we have a fairly elaborate statement of his general position that without a recognition of the active contribution of the existing subject to the act of knowing we are forced by the logic of nominalism to treat subjects and objects in abstraction from the ontological situation in which knowledge arises. The doubts about the reality of the external world and other minds that have dominated discussion in the empiricist and rationalist traditions are rooted in the tendency to confuse the abstract epistemological subject with the existing historical subject, and the logical object with the ontological object. An artificial dichotomy is thereby established between the abstract subject and the abstract object, whereas in actual experience they exist in correlation with one another. This argument underlies the rather cumbersome discussion in *Systematic Theology* Volume 1,[3] and is more fully elaborated in his lecture series 'Christianity and the Problem of Existence':

> Now let us take the fourth step, in which the full meaning of 'existence' as used in the philosophy of existence becomes visible – namely, the implications of this concept in its criticism of the Cartesian philosophy. Descartes starts with the famous statement, 'I think, therefore I am'. The existentialists attack him on the ground that he never asks what the Latin word *sum* ('I am') means; he never answers the question of what 'I am' means. 'I am' – this points neither to a thing in the realm of 'extension', to a mere object, nor to a merely thinking being, a mere epistemological subject. 'Existence' is the concept which undercuts the division of subject and object. This is its decisive function in philosophy, art, and all other expressions of existentialism.
>
> Both Naturalism and Idealism are based on the reduction of man into an object on the one side and a subject on the other, whereby the one tries to swallow the other . . . You can never arrive at the object from the subject (although many Idealist philosophers have tried to do so), nor can you ever arrive at the subject from the object (although contemporary Naturalists try to find a way to do that). Subject and Object have no independent, ultimate reality. They are abstracted from existence. Existence precedes them ontologically.[4]

Tillich's metaphysics of knowledge is consciously developed therefore as an alternative to the nominalist world-view. It is not simply an historical fact that Tillich set out to criticise the nominalist foundations of modern philosophy and theology; because he feels this to be the most pervasive character of the modern world-view he recognises that he must have something to put in its place. His thought is driven by the urge to transcend nominalism and to offer a new Christian philosophy of life to modern man that will give adequate expression to man's ultimate concern with being and meaning. How is the ontological question to be raised, and how can it be answered? he asks.

> Ontology is the elaboration of the 'logos' of the 'on', in English of the 'rational word' which grasps 'being as such'. It is hard for the

modern mind to understand the Latin *esse-ipsum*, being itself, or the Greek ON HEI ON, being-in-so-far-as-it-is-being. *We are all nominalists by birth*. And as nominalists we are inclined to dissolve our world into things. But this inclination is an historical accident and not an essential necessity. The concern of the so-called realists of the Middle Ages was to maintain the validity of the universals as genuine expressions of being. It is however not realism to which I want you to turn from the naive nominalism in which the modern world lives, but I want you to turn to something older than both nominalism and realism: to the philosophy which asks the question of being before the split into universal essences and particular contents . . . It is the philosophy which asks the question: What does it mean that something *is*? What are the characteristics of everything that participates in being? And this is the question of ontology.[5]

This ultimate concern with being and meaning is the basis for Tillich's critique of naturalism and supranaturalism. The former fails to examine the relation between finite beings and being-itself, and the latter creates an unbridgable gulf between infinite being-itself and finite beings. The critique of naturalism and supranaturalism plays a formative part in the elaboration of his metaphysics of meaning, truth and logic and is a constant theme in his writings. For example, when he sums up his theological position in the introduction to *Systematic Theology* Volume 2, he describes it in these terms: 'Beyond Naturalism and Supranaturalism' (*ST2*, 5). However, it is a central concern in the other volumes, from the discussion of supranaturalism, naturalism and dualism as 'three inadequate methods of relating the contents of the Christian faith to man's spiritual existence', in Volume 1, to the discussion of the unsatisfactory implications of supranaturalism and naturalism for the development of the doctrine of the End of history and eschatology, in Volume 3. In what follows, we examine the origin and development of his critique of naturalism and supranaturalism, before we turn to consider the constructive alternative that he offers us in his metaphysics of meaning, truth and logic.

2. The influence of Schelling, and Tillich's distinctive ideas

There is a consensus among scholars that the early influence of Schelling was decisive in determining the form and content of Tillich's thought. In an early comment, R. Allan Killen asserts that '[Tillich's] epistemology is an adaptation of Schelling's philosophy of identity'. Kenneth Hamilton remarks that Tillich's method of correlation is inspired not by existentialist but by idealist sources and Schelling's 'identity ontology'. In a more recent work, Kenan B. Osborn attempts to establish that Tillich's doctrine of the New Being, and in particular the key notion of essentialisation, are derived from Schelling.[6]

On the face of it, this is a natural conclusion. Tillich's first two dissertations were concerned with the interpretation of the work of Schelling; namely, *Die religionsgeschichtliche Konstruktion in Schellings positiver*

Philosophie, ihre Voraussetzungen und Prinzipien and, *Mystik und Schuldbewusstsein in Schellings philosophischer Entwicklung.* Also, throughout his work, Tillich makes reference to Schelling and, in particular, attributes the beginnings of existentialism to his doctrine of existence.[7]

The Schelling studies are such obvious examples of academic research that it is dangerous to conclude from them more than that they reflect the predictable interest of a young theologian in the reigning philosophy of his day, the attitudes of his teachers Martin Kähler and Fritz Medicus in particular, and an understandable preoccupation with the current problems of apologetics. To conclude that both the form and the content of Tillich's thought are determined by the early influence of Schelling is simplistic. He derived many of his fundamental categories and conceptual distinctions from Schelling, but the substance of Schelling's philosophy of religion undergoes a profound change in Tillich's system under the impact of Kant, existentialism and Marxism, not to mention biblical criticism and Christian theology, as Tillich himself insists (*OB* 46–58).

In his first Schelling study, *Die religionsgeschichtliche Konstruktion in Schellings positiver Philosophie*, for example, he contrasts supranaturalism and naturalism unfavourably with Schelling's positive philosophy of religion.[8] Superficially, *Der Begriff des Übernatürlichen* appears to be a natural continuation of this line of argument, using the principle of identity to overcome the antinomies in the theory of knowledge on which supranaturalism and naturalism are based. However, the striking thing about this work, completed in 1915, is that in it we already witness Tillich becoming critical of the philosophies of identity, although he still relies heavily on them for his arguments against nominalism. Paraphrasing his attitude to Schelling at that time, Tillich says:

> Schelling's philosophical interpretation of Christian doctrine opened the way, I thought, to a unification of theology and philosophy. His development of a Christian philosophy of existence, as opposed to Hegel's humanistic philosophy of essence, and his interpretation of history as *Heilsgeschichte*, moved in the same direction. I confess that even today I find more 'theonomous philosophy' in Schelling than in any of the other German idealists. (*OB* 51–2)

This was written in 1936 with the wisdom of hindsight, and emphasises as central the themes of existence and history, whereas in his Schelling studies these themes are secondary to other concerns. The origins of Tillich's distinctive ideas are to be found not so much in these early Schelling-studies as in *Der Begriff des Übernatürlichen*, where, in taking issue with the views of supranaturalists of the day, Tillich was forced to clarify and defend some of his presuppositions. In this critical encounter, the nature of Tillich's central concerns and convictions begins to emerge. In this work, he is preoccupied with Kant rather than with Schelling, and this accords with his own admission: 'My own philosophical position developed in critical dialogue with neo-Kantianism, the philosophy of value, and phenomenology' (*OB* 53). In what follows, we discuss in some detail how Kant's thought determined Tillich's central questions and the nature of his solutions both negatively and positively. However, two further observations need to be made.

First, it is undoubtedly true that Tillich was influenced by the sweeping new world-view of Schelling and by his own metaphysical ambition to create a new theology that would transcend and synthesise theology and philosophy. In opposing supranaturalism in theology and nominalism in philosophy, Tillich was concerned not simply with an academic critique of these attitudes, but with the enthusiastic propagation of an alternative world-view. He appreciated that the world-views of supranaturalist theology and naturalistic science and philosophy have many ramifications in social and political life and culture. In the intellectual crisis of supranaturalism and naturalism, Tillich anticipated some of the features of the coming cultural crisis in Europe, for example, the confrontation between a dynamic political fideism and established rationalist and essentialist bourgeois interests. It is to Tillich's credit that he recognised very early in his career the social and political dimensions of philosophical and theological standpoints. He not only shares the reforming zeal of the idealists in his critique of traditional philosophical and religious positions, but seeks to transform church and society by his new 'theonomous philosophy'. However, he was also aware, and we must give full weight to this, of 'the experience of the abyss', and how in particular the personal suffering and chaos of the period from 1914 to 1920 called in question, easy syntheses worked out on the basis of the philosophies of identity.[9]

Secondly, we must note that the emphasis Tillich gives to the Christian philosophy of existence and *Heilsgeschichte*, in Schelling's thought postdates the First World War, when the experiences of personal suffering, social chaos and revolution transformed his appreciation of existentialism from a notional one in to something much more real; he became more aware of the reality of human alienation and man's anxious quest for the redemptive reality of the New Being in Christ. Although there is an unresolved tension in Schelling between the philosophy of identity and the philosophy of existence, the fact that Tillich later found it necessary to stress the indebtedness of existentialist philosophers to Schelling shows that, in the light of his suffering and experience between the two World Wars, Tillich chose to re-interpret Schelling as prototypical existentialist and to play down idealist elements in his thought. Likewise, the emphasis he gives to the decisive experience of guilt in the realisation of personal and concrete historical existence goes beyond Schelling's abstract alienation of essence and existence, and the mystical intuition of being-itself as the means of transcending the atomism of a world of discrete individuals is translated into a much more specifically Christian form.

3. *The unresolved difficulties in the Kantian legacy*

Like most of his contemporaries in philosophy and theology, Tillich was preoccupied with Kant and the problems Kant had set. Descartes' scepticism, expressed in his 'methodical doubt', never achieved its full expression until the publication of Kant's three *Critiques* and his *Religion Within the Limits of Pure Reason Alone*. Kant gave a methodological justification and a systematic form to methodical doubt and thus set a new programme for philosophy and theology. In *Mystik und Schuldbewusstsein*, Tillich sees the value of Schelling's thought in terms of the solutions it suggests to Kant's problems.[10] Likewise, in 'Kairos und Logos: Eine Untersuchung zur Metaphysik der Erkenntnis', he discusses methods in terms of the contrast between the critical 'methodicism' of the philosophical tradition from Descartes to Kant, and the 'mystic metaphysical' line from Nicolaus of Cusa to Schelling (see *IH* 123–9).

He emphasises the predominant importance of the critical methodical tradition, but argues for recognition of the alternative tradition 'whose symbol is the name of Jakob Böhme. It goes back to the mysticism and nature-philosophy of the late Middle Ages and the Renaissance, and has received no small impulses from Duns Scotus and Luther' (*IH* 124). He argues that the two traditions are not mutually exclusive but complementary; a type of method should be developed that combines the critical rigour of the methodical tradition and the intuitive insight of the mystical tradition. Later, he identifies these two traditions as the 'critical' and the 'dialectical', and argues for a critical method qualified by a recognition of the dialectic of existence, and for a dialectic of existence that respects the need for a critical and methodical account of theoretical knowledge.[11] This 'critico-dialectical' method he identifies with what he calls 'meta-logic' which we shall discuss in detail later.

Tillich was one of a number of philosophers brought up on Kant and the German classical schools who found, through Schelling, a way back to appreciation of the mystical realism of the late middle ages and of Duns Scotus in particular. Peirce, Heidegger, Brentano and Husserl were all influenced by Schelling and the Scotist tradition to a greater or lesser degree. In the case of Peirce, we know that this was due to the specific schooling he had in mediaeval and nineteenth-century German philosophy.[12] However, they all were subject to this influence to the extent that they were introduced to philosophy *via* the great German histories of philosophy of Ueberweg, Windelband and Schwegler. These emphasised the continuity of the Platonic-Augustinian line through Böhme, Cusanus, Duns Scotus and Luther to Schelling and Hegel. In Tillich's work, we find only occasional references to these authors, but the frequent use he makes of themes from their work, and the fact that philosophers generally do not admit how much philosophy they learn at second-hand from histories, makes it likely that part of Tillich's interest in mystical realism derives from these sources.[13]

The effect of Kant's work was to raise again with a new urgency the traditional issues that had featured so prominently in mediaeval philosophy: the nature of universals, the relation of finite and infinite, the relations of truth and being, the nature of the categories, and the relations of being, existence and essence. It is not surprising, therefore, that Tillich and his contemporaries were inclined to re-examine the mediaeval tradition.

In a crucial article, 'Two types of Philosophy of Religion', Tillich develops his ontology in terms that make explicit his dependence on the Platonic-Augustinian-Franciscan tradition from Bonaventura and Alexander of Hales to Anselm and Duns Scotus (*TC*, ch. 2). Likewise, in his posthumously published historical works, *Perspectives on Nineteenth and Twentieth Century Protestant Theology* and *A History of Christian Thought*, he discusses the importance to his own thought of the tradition of mystical realism, and of Duns Scotus in particular (*HCT* 180–91, 206–7), and the impact of this tradition on nineteenth-and-twentieth-century Protestant thought, and on thinkers as diverse as Bergson, Nietzsche, Schopenhauer, Heidegger, and Husserl (*P* 192–5).

Perhaps most revealing of his general attitudes is the footnote from the *Systematic Theology*: 'The word "realism" means today almost what "nominalism" meant in the Middle Ages, while the "realism" of the Middle Ages expresses almost exactly what we call idealism today. It might be suggested that, whenever one speaks of classical realism one should call it "mystical realism" (*ST1*, 197n). In view of the fact that Tillich called the ontology that he developed to resolve the Kantian dilemmas 'belief-ful realism', it is important both to emphasise the connection between idealism and mediaeval realism in Tillich's mind and to pay attention to the way in which the idealism of Schelling and Hegel is qualified by the Christian and realist elements derived from that tradition.

The influence of Kant turns on the unique way in which he asked the question about the meaning of metaphysics, in a form that signified the need for a new metaphysics of meaning, truth and logic. Kant's procedure raises in a fundamental way the question of the possibility of metaphysics, and tends to identify metaphysics with the transcendental method. In particular, the question of the meaning of metaphysics hinges on what Peirce called 'the Kantian principle that metaphysical conceptions mirror those of formal logic'[14]: that they are, in effect deducible from an analysis of logical forms. The classical instance of this is the deduction of the table of categories from the table of types of judgement.[15] In addition, in his three *Critiques*, Kant fundamentally reinterpreted the philosophical approach to the Platonic ultimates, the true, the good and the beautiful, by introducing once again his transcendental method. By this method we no longer ask what the true, the good and the beautiful are, but ask instead what they mean; that is, we ask what are the *a priori* principles presupposed in and necessary to science, ethics and aesthetic experience, considered as forms of knowledge or understanding. Alternatively, the question is one about the constitutive and regulative principles of these different domains considered as universes of discourse.

The first point to emphasise is that, long before the so-called 'revolution in philosophy',[16] which is supposed to have drawn our attention for the first time to the centrality of questions of meaning, Kant, by questioning the meaning of metaphysics and reversing the traditional conception of the dependence of logic on metaphysical principles, had raised with a new urgency the issue of the metaphysics of meaning, and this issue has come to dominate philosophy since his day, as it did philosophical discussion in the late Middle Ages. Such issues as the metaphysics of meaning, the status of universals, the respective claims of realism, nominalism and conceptualism, the ontological foundations of knowledge, and the relation of logic and ontology, all of which were central to the philosophical debates of the thirteenth and fourteenth centuries, arose again, and the solutions of Scotus and Ockham acquired a new relevance.

Kant's treatment of the relations of thought and language and of language and reality, presupposes a triadic intentional relation between reason, judgement and reality. The controversial doctrine of the transcendental ego, with its ambiguous formulation in Kant, dominates discussion of the relations between the forms of judgement and the *a priori* categorical forms of reason. Since it is never quite clear if the transcendental ego is simply the finite empirical ego reflecting upon itself, or the transcendent and infinite ego that unites all finite egos in a pre-established harmony that guarantees the coherence of all knowledge of finite knowers and the universal applicability of the categorical imperative, the way was open for the idealist apotheosis of the transcendental ego, and the construction of the speculative metaphysical systems of Fichte, Schelling and Hegel.

The similarly ambiguous doctrine of the thing-in-itself dominates discussion of the intentional relations between judgements and reality. Since the doctrine is based on the paradox that the thing-in-itself is required as a ground for the possibility of knowledge yet is unknowable in itself, the way was open for Fichte to drop it altogether, and with it any finite limitation on the range and possible fulfilment of thought. The expansion of Kantian epistemology into an idealist system of metaphysics, embracing the cosmos, became possible. It was the intention of the philosophies of identity to overcome the oppositions between finite and infinite, subject and object, existence and essence and thought and being.

Difficulties in Kant's treatment of the relation between language and reality not only call in question his general position that metaphysics can be derived from reflection on the forms of logic (a position that lends itself to idealist exaggeration) but also raise the question of the adequacy of the logic that is presupposed and used for this purpose. By almost universal consensus, the extravagant metaphysics of idealism is as much a result of over-ambitious development of Kantian principles as it is the result of taking for granted the watered-down Aristotelian logic that Kant inherited. The vague intentionalist theory of the relations between logic, language and reality, encouraged the deduction, from the crude subject-predicate logic, of a range of metaphysical distinctions that generate their own philosophical problems: finite and infinite, subject and object, existence and essence, universal and particular and abstract and concrete. These dichotomies result in part from a preoccupation with the logic of classes, a failure to understand the importance of relations, the tendency to take substantives and adjectives as paradigms for understanding universals, and the tendency to confuse first- and second-order discourse and to attribute to second intentions (the fictions of logic) the same mode of being as belongs to first intentions (or concepts of things, events and persons).

The development of philosophy in the past century may be seen as an attempt to grapple with the fundamental problems concerning the relations of metaphysics and logic, and here I refer not only to Hegel's *System of Logic*, Husserl's *Logical Investigations* and Marxist discussions of dialectic, but also to the existentialist rejection of formal logic as a paradigm for knowledge – summed up by Kierkegaard in the ironic paradox: 'A logical system is possible . . . an existential system is impossible' – and the existentialist concern with the problem of meaning and truth as an ontological problem. However, the revolution in logic associated with the names of Boole, Peano, Frege, Russell, Ramsey and others was also related to this debate about the metaphysics of logic. It was perhaps more obvious to people like Peirce, Whitehead and Wittgenstein than it is to us, that the debate *was*, about the metaphysics of logic. They insisted that the new logic was an attempt to give expression to a purely extensional and truth-functional logic that would satisfy the strictest demands of a revamped empiricist and nominalist metaphysics.

Again, the issues are those that engaged the attention of the late mediaeval philosophers, particularly Ockham and Duns Scotus. It is hardly surprising that thinkers facing those problems should have sought, in these mediaeval philosophers, solutions to the problems of the metaphysics of logic, or that they rediscovered, in mediaeval logic means for the criticism of the inadequate notions of nineteenth-century logic, and in this way were able to lay the foundations of modern logic. This is obvious in Peirce, Brentano and Husserl, and it is arguable that Frege was much more influenced by his contemporaries and the German tradition than is implied by Dummett.[17]

The third area in which Kant's influence created a new sensitivity to the solutions offered by Ockham and Scotus was the philosophy of religion. The constraints placed on faith by reason, and the limitations placed on reason by finitude, in Kant, leading to a dichotomy between the truths of faith and the truths of reason, have often been compared to the solutions of Ockham and Cusanus. However, it is precisely these constraints that are abandoned by Hegel in his enormously influential new system of Christian philosophical gnosticism, in which faith and religion are seen as inferior stages to be transcended in the progress towards a mystical and idealistic religion of reason in which reason is identical with being-itself. The Hegelian attempt to develop and overcome the Kantian philosophy of religion, and the analogous system of Schelling, bear striking resemblances to the mystical realism of Scotus, Cusanus and the tradition of German mysticism from Meister Eckhardt and Jakob Böhme to Luther and after.

However, in our preoccupation with Kant as an epistemologist, we tend to ignore his enormous influence on German theology. In fact, he is as important to Protestantism as is Aquinas to Catholicism; the Ritsch-lians referred to him explicitly as the philosopher of Protestantism. The development of German theology in the nineteenth century is unintelligible unless we see how it is provoked by the challenges of Kant's *Religion Within the Limits of Pure Reason Alone*, and his critique of the traditional proofs of the existence of God. Not only does he revive the mediaeval debate about the relations of philosophy and theology, faith and reason and revealed and natural religion in a new form, but he has a deeper significance and a deeper connection with late mediaeval philosophy than Anglo-Saxon thought tends to be aware of.

Crucial to the understanding of the significance of Kant in later German philosophy, and in the thought of Paul Tillich in particular, is the following passage from the latter's *Systematic Theology*:

> The nature of finite reason is described in classical form by Nicolaus Cusanus and Immanuel Kant. The former speaks of the *docta ignorantia*, the 'learned ignorance', which acknowledges the finitude of man's cognitive reason and its inability to grasp its own infinite ground. But, in recognising this situation, man is at the same time aware of the infinite which is present in everything finite, though infinitely transcending it . . . In spite of its finitude, reason is aware of its infinite depth . . . Finitude is essential for reason, as it is for everything that participates in being. The structure of this finitude is described in the most profound and comprehensive way in Kant's 'critiques'. *The categories of experience are categories of finitude.* They do not enable human reason to grasp reality-in-itself; but they do enable man to grasp his world, the totality of the phenomena which appear to him and which constitute his actual experience. The main category of finitude is time. Being finite means being temporal. Reason cannot break through the limits of temporality and reach the eternal . . . The only point at which the prison of finitude is open is the realm of moral experience, because in it something unconditional breaks into the whole of temporal and causal conditions. But this point which Kant reaches is nothing more than a point, an unconditional command, a mere awareness of the depth of reason. (*ST1*, 90–1)

Before we continue with the elaboration of Tillich's metaphysics of knowledge, we must examine in more detail the evolution of his critique of supranaturalism and naturalism in theology, and nominalism in philosophy. We return to his early tentative efforts to formulate his own critique of the world-view of contemporary theology in *Der Begriff des Übernatürlichen, sein dialektischer Charakter und das Princip der Identität, dargestellt an der supernaturalistichen Theologie vor Schleiermacher.*

4. *Tillich's attack on naturalism, supranaturalism, and the philosophies of identity*

In this last named work, Tillich may appear to be concerned with a parochial dispute between two opposing schools in German theology. This is true, but in this work we can discern that he was already conscious of the wider cultural and political ramifications of the issues being discussed. His critique of the narrow school of supranaturalist and somewhat fundamentalist theologians is the beginning of what was to develop into a philosophico-theological critique of modern society and Protestant culture.

The central argument of *Der Begriff des Übernatürlichen* is that supranaturalist theology runs into difficulties because it is based on an inadequate metaphysics of knowledge. The three areas isolated for discussion are: a) the subject-object relation; b) intuition; and c) reason. The argument concentrates on the Kantian and nominalist presuppositions on which supranaturalism is based. The implications of these presuppositions for our knowledge of God are discussed under three headings: i) proofs of the existence of God; ii) the doctrine of faith; and iii) *Gotteserkenntnis*.

a) Tillich believes that the subject-object dichotomy is a fundamental part of our Kantian and nominalist inheritance with the most damaging consequences for theology. Supranaturalists fail to examine the presuppositions on which the distinction is based.

> The primary opposition of concepts upon which supranaturalism is based, is, without question, that of subject and object – that is, in the sense of an exclusive opposition. Thus it is seen as the task of knowledge to ensure that subjective ideas come to harmonise with objective reality. To know the truth is only possible when this harmony (reminiscent of Leibniz's pre-established harmony) has been reached. The main opportunity to discuss this issue for supranaturalist theologians was the polemic against Schelling who negated this entire kind of knowledge in principle, through the introduction of the principle of identity. (*DBU* 76)

Supranaturalists take for granted the Ockamist dissolution of universals or essences into things and therefore cannot distinguish significantly between real beings and beings of reason. This, Tillich concludes, drives them in the direction of a subjectivist epistemology. He quotes Flatt as saying, rather dogmatically, 'All our judgements referring to reality, in as far as they rest upon the application of our subjective laws of thought to the object, can only be considered true if we presuppose harmony and analogy of the former and the latter' (*DBU* 76). This insistence on correspondence between finite subject and object creates an irresoluble tension between ordinary rational knowledge and revelation. Revelation must accommodate itself to the subjective laws of thought in a way that bypasses the subject-object relationship. Instead of seeing that a theory based on the dichotomy excludes revelation *a priori*, the supranaturalist postulates a miraculous intervention in the rational process: 'Flatt's above quoted remarks about inspiration as a divine production of ideas in the human mind which – because divinely made – are necessarily adequate to their object (i.e. true), are characteristic of the subjectivism of supranaturalist epistemology. Recognition without any contact of subject and object' (*DBU* 78).

b) In turning to *the role of intuition* in our knowledge of God, Tillich points out critically that supranaturalists accept the Kantian doctrine that 'concepts without intuitions are empty and intuitions without concepts are blind', but do not admit that we have sensible intuitions of God, or that God is a mere concept. 'In many statements [it is admitted that] knowledge without experience is impossible, usually in connection with the question of recognising [knowing] the supersensible. Steudel, for example, says: "One can never know whether a revelation took place as the supersensible cannot be the object of experience' (*DBU* 79). Supranaturalists, in fact, are driven into sophistry in an attempt to maintain that knowledge of God is possible on strict Kantian principles.

Tillich argues that part of the dilemma faced by these theologians is that they endorse Kant's scepticism on theological grounds. On the basis of the doctrine of Total Depravity, they question the competence of reason to attain knowledge of the essential structures of being. On the basis of the *Extra Calvinisticum* ('finitum non capax infiniti') they deny that secondary causes can have efficacy as instruments for the revelation of knowledge of God. They are thus faced with two equally unsatisfactory alternatives: either they must adopt a kind of irrational fideism and affirm that revelation consists in an interruption of the laws of nature and reason; or they must accept the sceptical implication of the Kantian position, that God cannot be regarded as the constitutive principle of all being, but is merely a regulative idea that is necessary to guarantee the coherence of moral discourse.

The first alternative is adopted by Süskind, who bases his fideist supranaturalism on a sharp distinction between intuition and experience: 'I do not see why a [miraculous] apparition or occurrence in the sensible world should not as such be an object of intuition, even if it is no object of experience. [It follows that] a miracle means that this apparition belongs to the innumerable mass of objects which we cannot know by experience, and which is thus excluded from the domain of reason' (*DBU* 80). The second alternative is followed by Bretschneider, whom Tillich quotes as saying: 'Knowledge is belief based on inner or outer experience, and accordingly our idea of God is not intuitive, is no intuition, and is consequently not knowledge in the strictest sense, but discursive' (*DBU* 80). That is the idea of God is arrived at mediately through deduction, as a necessary regulative idea. Tillich rejects both alternatives, for neither yields a coherent doctrine of theological knowledge and, further, they ultimately lead to irrationalism. His constant theme is that a fundamental re-examination must be made of the epistemological and metaphysical presuppositions on which the argument depends.

These alternatives are strongly reminiscent of the position that Scotists elaborated when, developing the doctrine of the priority of will over intellect in God, they arrived at a doctrine of divine freedom as absolute and ultimately irrational, and maintained that the being of God embodies the principle of indeterminacy. Knowledge of God was possible only on the basis of supernatural revelation and/or the infallible authority of

Scripture or Church. Alternatively, the idea of God, as a mere logical concept, could be deduced from the independently existing exemplars of the ideal natures of things. Both the mediaeval and modern forms of supranaturalism, as Tillich has pointed out, are attempts to deal with the nominalist denial of knowledge of the essential being of things.[18]

Yet another approach shown by Tillich to lead to the idealist solution of the philosophies of identity, was based on the attempt to maintain a distinction between kinds of intuitions, in addition to that between concepts and intuitions. There are intuitions of sense experience and there are intellectual intuitions. Knowledge of God, it is argued, *is* intuitive, that is, it is based on intellectual intuition and is not mere conceptual knowledge. The supranaturalists move in this direction but baulk at the full-blown idealist principle of identity.

> Supranaturalistic views of perception, intuition and experience constitute a strong concession to immediacy. They show that the subject-object opposition cannot be maintained inflexibly and tends to be enlarged under the influence of Kant's principle of identity to include the immediate unity of subject/object as given in sensible intuition. This is, however, a unity which does not really go beyond the subject: it is the momentary influence of object upon subject, but not the object itself. Subject and object are connected in a causal relationship but remain independently existing side by side. Intuition is but the interior process of the subject which – though somehow conditioned by the object – does not nullify the opposition between the two. (*DBU* 80–1)

Tillich shows his own preference for a solution similar to Schelling's:

> Intuition corresponds to the individual natural object in its immediate being; experience corresponds to the system of nature – i.e. experience as knowledge which transcends the individual and connects it with the system as a whole. Not every intuition is experience, but each experience contains intuition . . . At the same time that Schelling equated material and formal nature intuition of a natural object became intuition of nature in itself. In each intuition the whole of nature is given; there is no longer any necessity to go beyond the natural object to nature itself by means of causality, experience and intuition are one i.e. intuition is intellectual . . . Surely there can be no knowledge through the operations of reason. (*DBU* 81–2)

At this early stage the reservations expressed by Tillich about Schelling are tentative. Only much later does he become convinced that Schelling's solution falls short of the demands of both faith and realism, and that his belief-ful realism, especially in combination with Religious Socialism, involves a more fundamental critique of idealism.

c) The third subject in supranaturalist epistemology that Tillich examines is the doctrine of reason inherited from the rationalist tradition from Descartes to Kant. This, in turn, is connected with the nominalist tradition going back to Ockham. The limitations that Ockham places on reason, namely, that for finite reason only individual beings exist and essences are fictions of the mind or mere names, reduce reason to an instrument for the logical analysis of abstract concepts or words. God becomes *a* being, whose existence is problematic, instead of the ground and source of all existing things. If reason cannot grasp being-itself as the internal principle of all that is real, and grasp this through participation in being and reflection upon the act of being, then the traditional functions of *intellectus*, for example, the contemplation of being, are emptied of meaning, and it is only the instrumental *ratio*, that is, analytic and discursive reason, that remains as the faculty of knowledge. This 'technical reason', in contrast to 'ontological reason',[19] is confined to an external knowledge of individual things and a 'controlling knowledge' acquired by the manipulation of things in accordance with the practical dictates of human appetite and need.

Tillich commences by quoting two definitions from Reinhard's *Dogmatik*: firstly, of subjective reason: '*vis rerum distincte et per principia cognoscendi*', and secondly, of objective reason: '*cognitio ea, quam mens humana efficit e contemplatione hujus universi*, and that is one with philosophy'.[20] These definitions conflate knowledge and the faculty of knowledge. This is hardly surprising, since the *vis rerum* that are known by reason are not the instantiated essences of things-in-themselves, but the essences of things in general, which become indistinguishable ultimately from the *a priori* categorical forms of reason as such. Knowledge of things and reasoning about things are conflated. Scepticism about our knowledge of the nature of things-in-themselves, combined with the insistence that nothing but the world of nature may be a ground for knowledge (*Erkenntnisgrund*), leads to almost insurmountable difficulties for these theologians: '[A]s soon as reason as faculty of knowledge directs itself towards something other than the world or what follows from it, it leaves the sphere of reason in the material sense' (*DBU* 82). On the other hand, 'Tittmann postulates as a principle of supranaturalism that a revelation can contain nothing which contradicts the general and necessary truths of reason' (*DBU* 83). But, on the other hand, it is hardly satisfactory to maintain that the content of revelation is confined to knowledge of 'the laws governing the nature of reason: the law of contradiction, of causality, of purpose, according to which a manifold, (harmoniously ordered, a causality according to concepts) presupposes an intelligent first cause' (*DBU* 83–4). The result is a compromise, whereby, 'According to supranaturalist pre-suppositions the process of knowing consists of intuition and also in the action of justification, the referring of objects back to each other in their connection through categories, and just this is rational knowledge' (*DBU* 83).

What this means is that in addition to our ordinary intuition of objects there is also 'a divine production of ideas in the human mind which – divinely made – are necessarily adequate to their object (i.e. true)'.[21] Theology becomes simply the retrospective rational justification of revealed ideas by the demonstration that they 'contain nothing which contradicts the general and necessary truths of reason'. This is directly analogous to the function of ethics in providing, *ex post facto*, a logical justification for the directly intuited unconditional imperative.

A theological epistemology based on these principles Tillich finds completely unsatisfactory; firstly, because it concedes so much to scepticism that theology in general is virtually evacuated of significance, and secondly, because it is obviously inadequate to the needs of a specifically Christian theology. His concluding criticisms are worth quoting in detail as they highlight the issues in epistemology that are central for him:

> The already quoted doubts as to the certainty of knowledge through experience, as well as the whole section about the mere probability of revealed knowledge and the thoughts about the imperfection of human reason, show the prevalence of a sceptical mood. The duality of sources of knowledge (intuition and experience), which does not lead to the unity of intellectual intuition, is the root of this uncertainty. Sensible intuition and, based upon it, experience in the uncritical sense are neither necessary nor general, but to be able rationally to fit objects into the causal context of material nature, a knowledge of the entire context is necessary if there is to be certainty. What neither of the two sources of knowledge is able to achieve by itself, their union is equally unable to attain – through the addition of the two sources individual problems are in no way altered.
>
> Indeed, intuition as such has certainty if it wants to be nothing but intuition: it is then only self-consciousness affected in some way. The object remains beyond. The forms of rational knowledge have certainty as well, they are but reason's consciousness of its own nature. No doubt is therefore directed against these principles, they are above scepticism due to the presupposed self-certainty of reason. But just as intuition remains limited to the material-objective of pure, formless impressions; so are the laws of reason limited to the formal-objective of pure actuality, empty of content. Neither of the two factors reaches knowledge or trans-subjective certainty: self-criticism on the subject of the fundamental subject-object opposition, is required. (*DBU* 84–5)

The subject-object opposition is, for Tillich, the most basic of philosophical problems requiring re-examination. He criticises supranaturalists for failing to understand how the doctrines of Schleiermacher, Fichte and Schelling point to a solution to their dilemmas and to the possibility of a theory of knowledge that would be more adequate to the needs of theology.

He argues that, because of their prejudiced subjectivist standpoint, they radically misunderstand the conception of feeling implied in Schleiermacher's 'feeling of absolute dependence'; they consequently 'cannot understand how the opposition of subjectivity and objectivity can be annihilated in feeling' (*DBU* 78). Similarly, they fail to appreciate how, in the discovery of the moral *a priori*, there is achieved not merely formal but substantive knowledge of the unconditioned. He, continues: 'In moral consciousness there was unity of subject and object in an age where this was lost everywhere else; at this point it transcended itself from the beginning; and through this point it consciously transcended itself in Fichte – there is only one natural existence where reason is both a formal and a material principle, where it recognises itself and experiences intellectual intuition' (*DBU* 86). However, Tillich reserves his fire chiefly for the supranaturalist rejection of Schelling's principle of identity. Schelling arrived at this idea by two kinds of arguments. First, he pointed to the fact that in intellectual intuition there is an immediate experience of the identity of the intuiting and the intuited self; while in Criticism (Fichte) this is interpreted as the intuition of the identity of the self with the Absolute Subject, and in Dogmatism (Spinoza) as the intuition of the identity of the self with the Absolute Object,[22] for Schelling 'the implication is that the Absolute must transcend the distinction between subjectivity and objectivity and be subject and object in identity'.[23] Secondly, he proffers a different interpretation of the logical principle of identity. 'The profound logic of the ancients distinguished subject and predicate as antecedent and consequent (*antecedens et consequens*) and thereby expressed the real meaning of the principle of identity.'[24] On the basis of this definition, Schelling argues that the relationship of God and nature is that of antecedent and consequent, and thus there is a creative unity between them. God is the ground of nature, and nature is the expression of his self-revelation; distinguishable in principle though antecedent and consequent are, nature as immanent in God is ultimately identical with God.

Now, Tillich would interpret this principle differently, but he agrees that the only alternative to scepticism of the nominalist and Kantian kind is a restatement of the mystical realism that he, like Schelling, derives from the mediaevals *via* Bruno and Nicholas of Cusa: the doctrine that the absolute or unconditioned as pure identity, *qua coincidentia oppositorum*, transcends the split between subject and object.

Tillich insists that 'the greatest problem of philosophic thought since the beginning of the modern age – the question whether subject and object coincide, are analogous, adequate or harmonise – is not properly experienced in its full impact (by the supranaturalists); the most profound solution which Leibniz could offer is caricatured by popular philosophy; the result being that the simple opposition subject/object dominates thought in the most rigid way' (*DBU* 78).

The principle on which his argument is based is that, rejecting the possibility of ontology, as the supranaturalists do (on the basis of Kant's refutation of the ontological argument and his scepticism with regard to knowledge of the *an sich*), they are not able to sustain either their physicocosmological or their moral arguments for the existence of God, their doctrine of faith remains irredeemably subjective, and their doctrine of knowledge collapses into empty formalism or scepticism.

i) Tillich shows that the most that theoretical or moral proofs for the existence of God can establish, without ontological presuppositions supplied by the principle of identity is the abstract concept of a necessary first cause, or the abstract principle of the unconditioned as demanded in the moral proof. We cannot make any assertions about the being of such a first cause or the unconditioned, let alone equate either with a really existing God. The upshot is that the supranaturalist cannot give a coherent account of the theoretical and moral proofs, as proofs of God's existence.

Similarly, he argues, unless one recognises the ontological relations of subjectivity, that is, the basis of affective experience *interest* in the subject's contingent existential relations with other beings *inter-est*, it is impossible to develop a doctrine of faith that will escape the consequence that faith is no more than capricious private emotion or an inferior form of rational assent. Faith as an act that includes experience, feeling and reason is possible only on the basis of a proper ontological understanding of the foundations of subjectivity, and the groundedness of the subject-object relation in the structures and dynamics of being.

ii) With regard to the certainty claimed for faith by these theologians, Tillich points out that by rejecting the possibility that the agreement between subject and object could have any ontological foundation independent of inference, they effectively set up an antithesis between the natural and the supranatural, and reduce knowledge of the supernatural to the subjective:

> Knowledge of the supernatural is subjective because it remains without intuition; 'subjective' means reached by inference and not through experience – postulated but not empirically realised.
> (*DBU* 104)

> There is no point of identity in the sense of an intuition between natural subject and supranatural object; with what justification, then, does the subject transcend itself and the natural object? This is the answer given by supranaturalism: through theoretical and practical rational conclusions, the former based on the natural object, the latter on the natural/supranatural subject itself.
> (*DBU* 105)

However, the subjective certainty claimed for faith either proves to be the empty certainty of tautologies or yields certainty only in knowledge of the natural, and fails to reach the supranatural. Whether the argument is interpreted as 'All being has a cause, the world is a being, therefore it has a cause', or as 'Everything conditioned demands an unconditioned, the world is conditioned therefore there must be an unconditioned', the result is the same:

> The major premiss is taken out of our knowledge of the natural and therefore always factually subsumes the supranatural under the natural, or negates the natural and with it the significance of the entire antithesis. Thus it becomes clear that the terms employed in the inference from the natural to the supernatural are correlative terms which can never be brought into the relation of opposition: natural/supranatural. The argument is basically a tautology masquerading as a genuine conclusion, because there is always the un-

conditioned in the concept of the conditioned, the cause in the concept of the effect. Through such rational inference not knowledge of the supranatural is won, but knowledge of the foundation of natural knowledge. (*DBU* 106)

There is a further difficulty, and this is that the certainty of the syllogism proves to be an uncertainty, a not-knowing, when applied to the supranatural, unless there is an intellectual intuition that will negate this not-knowing. But it is precisely this course that is denied to the supranaturalist because of his epistemological presuppositions. Supranaturalist epistemology has blocked this exit by giving up the identity of subject and universe, and thus any form of pre-established harmony. The harmony of these theologians of reflection is no pre-established one but merely that of an ideal correspondence at which they aim; but, due to the fixed opposition between subject and object, this is infinitely unattainable. Faith, then, is both tautological certainty and infinite ignorance: this is the dialectical meaning of the formula: 'belief is subjective certainty'. (*DBU* 107)

iii) Finally, Tillich objects to the supranaturalist's doctrine of Gotteserkenntnis or God-knowledge, for a doctrine of knowledge in which knowledge of being is denied, and things-in-themselves can be inferred only indirectly from mediate phenomenal knowledge, leads to intolerable consequences for theology: 'Supranaturalist epistemology effects the declaration that knowledge of God is impossible on the one hand, while on the other hand, it gives rise to a number of concepts which are transferred from a natural to a supranatural level. If the catchword in the former case was: subjective, not objective, certainty; it is now: symbolic not real, knowledge – obviously an analogous move' (*DBU* 108).

Tillich attacks the presuppositions of this negative theology with great vehemence. He quotes Süskind and Planck who maintain that everything positive which is about the nature and character of the divine must be thought of as a picture or a symbol; whether it be natural or supernatural revelation, the divine can be grasped only negatively by human knowledge. He concludes: 'The foundation of the entire argument is the distinction between the supernatural-in-itself; and the supernatural-in-relation-to-the-natural. About the former one can only know that it is not the natural, about the latter one can only talk by means of ideas taken from the natural – in terms of analogies which do not grasp the thing itself, but are only symbols of it' (*DBU* 109–10). He proceeds to show that this argument proves at once too much and too little. On the one hand, 'to determine God in every respect as non-nature means to determine him entirely through nature, thus total ignorance is turned into total knowledge; on the other hand, this knowledge gained by inference from the divine-in-relation-to-nature immediately disappears into the obscurity of the divine-in-itself. Tillich summarises his argument in these terms: 'The symbolic nature of knowledge of God is not turned into ignorance because the symbol is not the thing itself, but because the thing itself (the effects of God) are themselves only a symbol of his in-itself. Thus, knowledge of God becomes the symbol of a symbol, i.e. utter ignorance' (*DBU* 111). And thus he concludes that 'the dialectic of the *supra* leads to utter contradiction'.

We have expounded the argument of *Der Begriff des Übernatürlichen* in considerable detail because it reveals, in an interesting way, what it was that Tillich was fighting, and because it has been given such scant treatment in the literature.[25] This work illustrates many of the themes that preoccupied Tillich throughout his entire life, especially his life-long battle against supranaturalism and nominalism. Already in this work, Tillich was concerned to point out how supranaturalist theology creates an impossible opposition between philosophy and theology by denying the possibility of ontology. But he was also concerned with the wider implications of such a theology: for example, how it leads to theological heteronomy, encourages authoritarian tendencies in the church and cuts off religion from culture and the church from involvement in the world (*PE* xxxii–xxxv). Tillich lived to see his fears for such a subjectivist, irrational, other-worldly and politically quietist church confirmed by the acquiescence of the 'German Christians' in the policies of Hitler.

Tillich's work abounds in strictures against supranaturalism.[26] It is perhaps not surprising, considering what happened in the German church, that this is a particularly prominent theme in what he wrote after his eviction from Germany. But this passionate opposition to supranaturalism, on political as well as theological and philosophical grounds, is characteristic of his writing from the beginning. It is what brought him into early controversy with Barth, soon after the publication of the latter's *Romerbrief*, and it is what provoked Barth to accuse him of 'still fighting against the Great Inquisitor' (*TPT* 8). Barth did not appreciate how dangerous supranaturalist theology could be.

He attacked it again and again in his early papers, 'On the idea of a Theology of Culture' (*WR* 158, 177), 'The Conquest of the Concept of Religion in the Philosophy of Religion' (*WR* 131), 'Church and Culture' (*IH* 219–41) and 'The Philosophy of Religion' (*WR* 37, 83f.). These papers are concerned mainly with the hiatus between religion and culture that develops in supranaturalism. However, running parallel to these papers are his writings on socialism, on the masses and on contemporary art, in which we see him beginning to explore the wider implications of supranaturalism.

In a decisively important paper, 'Rechtfertigung und Zweifel' Tillich returns to a fundamental re-examination of theological aspects of his earlier critique, and lays the foundations for his ontological interpretation of the doctrine of faith in the *Systematic Theology* and *The Dynamics of Faith*. In the same year, however, we see the convergence of his socio-political interests and his theological critique of supranaturalism in 'Church and Culture', where he is definitely concerned with the social dangers of this type of theology. This critique becomes sharper and more urgent in *Die religiöse Lage der Gegenwart*[27] and increasingly from that time in the development of his belief-ful realism and his Religious Socialist critique of church and society. For example, he says very unequivocally:

> Self-transcending realism requires the criticism of all forms of supranaturalism – supranaturalism in the sense of a theology that imagines a supranatural world beside or above the natural one, a world in which the unconditional finds a local habitation, thus making God a transcendent object, the creation an act at the beginning of time, the consummation a future state of things. To criticise such a conditioning of the unconditional, even if it leads to atheistic consequence, is more religious, because it is more aware of the unconditional character of the divine, than a theism that bans God into the supranatural realm – A Christian who unites his supranaturalistic belief with the continuous denial of his historical situation (and the historical situation of many others for whom he is responsible) is rejected by the principles of a self-transcending realism that is always also historical realism. (*PE* 92)

Finally, by the time he wrote *Die Sozialistische Entscheidung* in 1933, the crisis of the German church had begun. The question at this stage was: can Christians give a lead, and find a way out of the impasse; or is a cataclysmic war inevitable? Supranaturalist and neo-supranaturalist theology was facing the trial of its life. What began as a critique of a relatively small group of fairly insignificant theologians and the views they expounded in their theological magazine, 'Magazin für christliche Dogmatik und Moral,' published between 1796 and 1812, had broadened into critiques of the philosophical presuppositions of modern thought and of traditional Protestant theology and its relation to Protestant culture, and had finally crystallised into a new Protestant, socialist and existential *Weltanschauung* in which Tillich became a prophet of the doom that was to fall on German society and the German church. Beyond that, it formed the basis of what was to become perhaps the most radical and impressive theological construction of this century.[28]

For evidence of the fact that Tillich was constantly preoccupied with the question of supranaturalism we need only consult the indexes of his major works; but the evidence is clearer than that, for in 1957, nearly half a century after the publication of *Der Begriff des Übernatürlichen*, in the introduction to *Systematic Theology*, Volume 2, Tillich restates the fundamental character of his theology in the terms, 'Beyond Naturalism and Supranaturalism' (*ST2*, 5–11).

For Tillich, as we have seen, naturalism and supranaturalism are but two sides of the same coin. Supranaturalist theology is determined and limited in advance by the fact that it accepts the metaphysical, epistemological and logical principles of naturalism. Tillich's point is that it is not enough to criticise the inconsistencies and sophistries of supranaturalist theology; it is also necessary to question both the ideological pretensions and the philosophical presuppositions of naturalism.

On the first point, it is necessary to recognise the ideological character of naturalism and its limitations as a philosophy of life. The emergence in this century of positivism, in combination with a militant secularism, as a self-conscious philosophy of life claiming to be the true expression of the scientific-technical world-view, is a new development that reveals for the first time the true character of naturalism. Theology is confronted no longer merely by naturalistic criticisms of individual religious beliefs, but by a complete alternative belief and value system that challenges religion's traditional hold on men's hearts and minds. This fact, Tillich appreciated, is of the greatest theological significance for the interpretation of the contemporary religious situation.

In *Die religiöse Lage der Gegenwart*, he significantly commences his analysis of the contemporary religious situation not with the churches but with a discussion of the scientific-technical world-view. He begins with a critique of the alliance between 'mathematical natural science, technique and capitalist economy'.[29] Naturalism is not the neutral and objective philosophy it purports to be, but exists in combination with materialistic values, and serves the will-to-power of the ruling elites in both conventional capitalist societies and the state capitalism of authoritarian communist states. He also demonstrates how the anti-metaphysical stance of positivism obscures its own metaphysical presuppositions, and how the brave rhetoric of a self-styled 'scientific philosophy' conceals the doubts and anxieties about the foundations of being and meaning inherent in naturalism.

However, this kind of ideological critique of naturalism, which is a recurrent theme in his writings on religious socialism, is matched by a corresponding concern to examine the philosophical presuppositions of contemporary naturalism. He traces its origins to the sceptical dissolution of the traditional doctrine of being in the late Middle Ages and the emergence of a victorious nominalism with its atomistic metaphysics, empiricist epistemology and attempt to de-intentionalise logic. Before discussing Tillich's critique of Nominalism, we propose to conclude this chapter with some remarks on the significance of scepticism and relativism to Tillich's thought, in general, and to the discussion of naturalism, supranaturalism and the philosophies of identity, in particular.

5. *Scepticism: naturalism, supranaturalism and the philosophies of identity*

Tillich's interest in scepticism is not narrowly methodological, but embraces the change of orientation that came about in Western culture with the Renaissance and the Reformation. The emergence of autonomous man as a new ideological stereotype – the critical, self-determining promethean man of Kant's essay 'What is Enlightenment? – marks the emergence not only of a new questioning mood and a new psychological model, but also of a new doctrine of man and a new ontology.

Discussing the significance of Luther as an individual whose life had a paradigmatic significance for the emergence of autonomous man, the social historian and psychiatrist Erik Erikson observed:

In some periods of his history, and in some phases of his life cycle, man needs ... a new ideological orientation as surely and as sorely as he must have air and food.

> [In this context] ideology will mean an unconscious tendency underlying religious and scientific as well as political thought: the tendency at a given time to make facts amenable to ideas, and ideas to facts, in order to create a world image convincing enough to support the collective and the individual sense of identity. Far from being arbitrary or consciously manageable ... the total perspective created by ideological simplification reveals its strength by the dominance it exerts on the seeming logic of historical events and by its influence on the identity formation of individuals.[30]

In his seminal paper 'Über die Idee einer Theologie der Kultur', Tillich discusses the significance of Luther's championing of spiritual autonomy against the 'heteronomy' of Rome. Here, for the first time, he introduces the distinctions that are crucial to his theology of culture: autonomy, heteronomy and theonomy. Discussing the dissolution of mediaeval theonomy under the impact of scepticism, he stresses the ideological and cultural form that this critical protest takes in the emergence of the type of autonomous man and the ideal of autonomous culture. Supranaturalist theology is one expression of the defensive reaction against autonomy. Heteronomy in religion and culture is an attempt to reaffirm the unconditioned under the impact of the relativising naturalism to which modern man appeals in the defence of his spiritual autonomy.

Tillich's categories, autonomy, heteronomy and theonomy, recur again and again throughout the entire corpus of his writings from his earliest papers on the theology of culture to the discussion in 'Life and the Spirit' in *Systematic Theology*, Volume 3. What is important for our purposes is that Tillich uses these categories to refer not only to particular cultural forms but also to three different kinds of ideology or belief and value system:

> Autonomy asserts that man as the bearer of universal reason is the source and measure of culture and religion – that he is his own law. Heteronomy asserts that man, being unable to act according to universal reason, must be subjected to a law strange and superior to him. Theonomy asserts that the superior law is at the same time, the innermost law of man himself, rooted in the divine ground which is man's own ground: the law of life transcends man, although it is, at the same time, his own. (*PE* 163)

By identifying naturalism and supranaturalism with autonomy and heteronomy respectively, Tillich broadens considerably the basis of his critique of supranaturalism and naturalism, and commits himself to the development of a theology of culture in which an attempt is made to provide an alternative world-view. In so doing, he commits himself to a view of cultural history, that like the theories of Schelling and Hegel, attempts to encompass the world-historical development of culture as a spiritual process with a recognisable inner dialectical movement. While his interpretation of this dialectic is very different from theirs it has a remarkable similarity of form.

In Tillich's case, the dialectical process involves the recurrent interaction of theonomy, autonomy and heteronomy as different spiritual attitudes suggesting different world-views. The process begins with the emergence, in either primitive or developed form, of a theonomous culture, this is, a culture in which the religious substance, or the unconditioned ground of being and meaning, is transparent in the particular cultural forms of the society at a given time. Scepticism, or the spirit of critical autonomy, arises in the first instance as the individual protest, the expression of 'the critical judgement of the Unconditioned against the unity of meaning' that theonomous culture purports to express on behalf of all. 'Autonomy therefore is always at the same time obedience to and revolt against the Unconditional. It is obedience insofar as it subjects itself to the unconditioned demand for meaning; it is revolt insofar as it denies the unconditioned meaning itself. Autonomous culture is as the myth puts it, always at the same time *Hybris* and a gift of the god' (*WR* 75). The antithetical reaction to the spirit of critical autonomy takes the form of a religious or political ideology that 'takes refuge in particular symbols which it exempts from autonomous criticism and to which it ascribes unconditionedness and inviolability' (*WR* 77). Although heteronomy submits itself to the unconditioned meaning, it can become guilty of a religious *hybris* in its attempts to force acceptance of the particular symbols to which it attributes unconditional validity. In defending the religious substance of culture, it fails to recognise the unconditional value implicit in secular cultural forms. According to the logic of the continuing interaction between autonomy and heteronomy, this process ought to give rise to a new theonomy.

Tillich believed that against the naturalistic and autonomous character of modern secular culture, supranaturalistic and heteronomous political and religious ideologies had arisen in protest. Supranaturalism in theology, and totalitarian political ideologies of the extreme right and the extreme left, had arisen in the attempt to remedy the spiritual bankruptcy of bourgeois culture. He considered these reactions equally dangerous. The impetus towards the development of a constructive alternative came from his critique of naturalism and supranaturalism; he hoped that his own belief-ful realism and Religious Socialism might be significant contributions towards the creation of a new theonomy. In this dialectical process, which Tillich sees repeating itself throughout history and which he believes has reached a moment of crisis in the twentieth century, scepticism plays a key part as the catalyst of change. He sees scepticism as a spiritual attitude identified with the emergence of autonomous culture and, in particular, identifies its role in the dissolution of the traditional doctrine of being at the end of the Middle Ages, and in the disintegration of the synthesis of religion, art, science and philosophy in Enlightenment culture at the end of the nineteenth century. He was interested in scepticism as a generalised spiritual attitude before he was concerned with scepticism in scientific or philosophical method.

Robert Scharlemann has rightly argued that reflection and doubt stand in a polar relationship in Tillich's thought, and that together they account for its inner dialectic.[31] However, Scharlemann's interest is primarily epistemological, in the sense that he wishes to do justice to Tillich's view of the nature of historical thinking, and he fails to stress sufficiently that scepticism is an essential category in Tillich's hermeneutic of the history of culture. In his somewhat laboured attempt to press Tillich's thought into a particular dialectical mould, he fails to grasp the metaphysical significance of scepticism for Tillich's ontology.

Tillich was to some extent concerned with the epistemological significance of scepticism, but he was much more interested in its ontological and existential implications. In what follows we shall examine briefly what Tillich has to say about scepticism and method and their relation to historical thinking, but we shall be much more concerned with what he has to say concerning their relation to the doctrine of being, and to doubt, anxiety and guilt as existential attitudes.

In discussing Descartes, Tillich is concerned to emphasise the primary importance of the revolution in ontology brought about by Cartesian scepticism. The traditional realism makes being the primary datum, and consciousness is contingent upon it. Descartes' scepticism consisted not simply in the introduction of a critical method of doubt, but more fundamentally in questioning the foundations of this realism, by directing attention upon the subjective experience of doubting or thinking and, through the *Cogito ergo sum*, making being contingent upon thought. Tillich sees several important consequences as following from this profound change in orientation; first, that epistemology and logic tend to take precedence over ontology; secondly, that recourse has to be made to the mystery of faith to secure the system against absurdity; thirdly, that 'being' comes to refer to individual finite beings *qua* objects of thought, rather than to being itself as the ground of all possible thought; and fourthly, that, because mathematical certitude is pursued as an ideal, the certainty of the traditional symbols of man's faith and knowledge are undermined, leading to anxiety and despair of all meaning.

On the first point, Tillich has a great deal to say. He conceived the whole of his theological epistemology as an attempt to answer this Cartesian and Kantian reversal of the order of priority of ontology, logic and epistemology. 'Epistemology, the "knowledge" of knowing, is a part of ontology, the knowledge of being, for knowing is an event within the totality of events. Every epistemological assertion is implicitly ontological' (*ST1*, 79). He is quite clear about the primary ontological significance of Cartesian scepticism: namely, that it 'presupposes the autonomy of the spiritual over against every immediately given existing thing'.[32] To avoid the dilemma of having to choose between epistemological idealism, which assumes that spirit gives laws to nature, and epistemological realism, which assumes that nature gives laws to the spirit, Tillich advocates a critical-dialectical method that aims to achieve a belief-ful realism:

'It must assume that the principles of meaning to which consciousness submits itself in the spiritual act are at the same time the principles of meaning to which being is subjected. It must assume that the meaning of being comes to expression in the consciousness informed by meaning' (*WR* 42).

There is a fascinating relationship between scepticism and mysticism in the history of Western philosophy, from Plotinus and pseudo-Dionysus to Wittgenstein. It is not our purpose to examine this tradition here, but it is important to understand that Tillich identifies himself with it and, in his doctrine of the co-incidence of opposites, scepticism and mysticism belong together.

In 'The Finitude and the Ambiguities of Actual Reason', Tillich specifically mentions Nicolaus of Cusa as the source of the doctrine of the essential finitude of reason, the doctrine 'which acknowledges the finitude of man's cognitive reason and its inability to grasp its own infinite ground. But, in recognising this situation, man is at the same time aware of the infinite which is present in everything finite, though infinitely transcending it' (*ST1*, 90).

Tillich's aim is to combine the critical and dialectical, and the methodical and the mystical, in a philosophical theology that unites both. This is a source of many difficulties in his metaphysics of meaning, truth and logic, for the kind of realist ontology that he seeks to resurrect from mediaeval philosophy requires more secure rational foundations than the tradition that he traces back to Cusanus will allow. The roots of the Naturalist/Supranaturalist dilemma are to be found, as Gilson has suggested, in Cusanus.[33] The dilemma cannot be transcended within the system of presuppositions that create the dichotomy. There is, in the Mediaeval tradition, a form of realism that avoids these dichotomies, but it is one that questions the basis of scepticism and requires confidence in the power of reason to grasp being immediately. In exploring Tillich's thought, we will be exploring the relations between two kinds of realism, which have their roots in mediaeval philosophy: the extreme realism that derives from the Platonic tradition and finds its most subtle expression in Duns Scotus, and the moderate realism associated with the Aristotelian tradition and Thomas Aquinas.

On the significance of scepticism for theology, Tillich is clear, and again he attributes the change chiefly to Descartes:

> Beginning with Galileo the mathematically-oriented natural sciences banished the supernatural. Nature becomes purely objective, rational, and technical; it becomes divested of the divine. It is now possible to have a concept of the world without having a concept of God. In this manner the way was made free for the dominance of the concept of religion. This becomes immediately evident at the beginning of the whole development, namely in Descartes. The basis for certainty is the self, and God is inferred from the self. (*WR* 128–9)

However, there is a fundamental difference between the intentions of Augustine's *Si fallor sum* and Descartes' '*Cogito ergo sum*':

But the real change in the total situation is to be seen in the contrast of the post-Cartesian outlook with, for example, that of Augustine. For no longer is the Unconditional element extracted out of self-certainty in order through it to apprehend God, but rather is the rational principle extracted, in order from it to deduce God . . . The certainty of God is made to rest upon the certainty of the world and the power of logical inference. (*WR* 129)

Scepticism thus not only produces questioning of traditional religious beliefs, but is identified with a change in spiritual attitude towards nature and the supernatural. Both are seen in a new light in which we begin with subjective mental contents and infer the existence of the external world and of God from clear and distinct ideas. When Kant described his Transcendental Method as comparable to a Copernican revolution in philosophy, he was simply drawing out the consequences of a revolution in spiritual attitudes that began with Descartes. The dichotomy, naturalism or supranaturalism, is an antithesis generated by thought, which regards these spheres as mutually exclusive and collectively exhaustive. In attempting to transcend the dichotomy, Tillich's chief concern is to re-establish the ontological foundations of thought in general. To scepticism, which rests on the assumption of the self-sufficiency of finite human reason, Tillich opposes the paradox of the unconditioned infinite that reveals itself in the contingency of finitude: the Absolute that reveals itself in man's ultimate concern with his being and meaning. The philosophies of identity are judged inadequate in that they suggest that the realisation of the good, the true, and the beautiful is possible by means of a purely rational dialectic. For Tillich the experience of the Holy involves a 'shaking of the foundations': the Unconditioned breaks into human experience and history from without, in a form that is paradoxical, and judges our self-saving attempts, demonstrating the relativity and finitude of our empirico-rational structures of thought (*STI*, 64).

Tillich saw supranaturalism and idealism as attempts to short-circuit the tension between the contingent and the absolute by avoiding the existential challenge of scepticism. What he appreciated was that Descartes, by dignifying scepticism as the supreme expression of man's quest for spiritual autonomy, had drawn attention to the human and historical character of truth. Christianity has claimed to be an historical religion but it has not been prepared to face the radical implications of this position; namely, that truth, like man's being, is historical. Rejecting the idea of an infallible church or scriptures, Tillich is committed to developing a doctrine of being in which the historical dimensions of revelation, the be-ing of God, the doctrine of the Christ, the life of the Spirit, and the doctrines of the Kingdom and Eschatology can be brought out.

What was required was a consistent interpretation of truth as existential. Scepticism makes the truth for me contingent on my experience; Tillich seeks to avoid the destructive consequences of an egocentric scepticism by identifying being-itself with the historical process and the realization of truth *en kairos*. In 'Kairos' and 'Kairos und Logos: Eine Untersuchung zur Metaphysik der Erkenntnis' applying the categories of autonomy, heteronomy and theonomy to the philosophy of history, he argues that the meaning of history can be revealed in these different spiritual attitudes, in particular in theonomy: 'Theonomy is the answer to the question implied in autonomy, the question concerning a religious substance and an ultimate meaning of life and culture . . .' 'Theonomy unites the absolute and the relative element in the interpretation of history, the demand that everything relative become the vehicle of the absolute and the insight that nothing relative can ever become absolute itself' (*PE* 53). Elsewhere, Tillich speaks of the 'Kairos and the Absolute Position', and advocates a belief-ful relativism: 'that relativism which overcomes relativism'. This is the paradoxical position that affirms and transcends of the subjectivity of the knower and the ambiguity of the known at the point where the unconditioned and the conditioned meet, and yet maintains that this experience can never become the subject of a judgement that claims unconditional validity (*IH* 170–1).

R. Allan Killen expresses anxiety about these formulations and suggests that they do not meet the challenge of scepticism and relativism. We may be inclined to agree with him. However, the inadequacy of these early formulations does not vitiate Tillich's ontological theology in the way Killen hastily concludes.[34] Tillich's attempt to come to terms with the historicity of truth is a courageous one, and he answers the challenge by elaborating a philosophy of history and a doctrine of being in which the concept of *kairos* is central. For all its ambiguity, this has been a seminal notion in contemporary theology:

> Kairos in its *unique* and universal sense is, for Christian faith, the appearing of Jesus as the Christ, Kairos in its *general* and special sense for the philosopher of history is every turning point in history in which the eternal judges and transforms the temporal. Kairos in its *special* sense, as decisive for our present situation, is the coming of a new theonomy on the soil of a secularised and emptied autonomous culture. (*PE* 53)

Robert Scharlemann is confident that Tillich has succeeded in providing a rationale for historical thinking that does meet the challenge of sceptical relativism:

> Tillich's solution is that historical thinking reaches a certainty of some reality or some presence not by constructing an 'absolute' whole, not by subordinating reflection to response [doubt], or conversely; but by a correlation of reflection and response that is made possible when thinking grasps or responds to a paradox.[35]

This formulation suggests that Tillich devised a neat dialectic to meet this challenge. However, the challenge of scepticism cannot be met in this way but requires a life-time commitment to truth, that is, a living demonstration of ultimate concern with being and meaning. It is significant that, in his last lectures to the Chicago University Law School in 1965, Tillich returned to this early theme of scepticism and relativism, and the quest for the true, the good and the holy. The lectures were published under the title, *My Quest for Absolutes*. Here, he explores once again the way in which scepticism and relativism, if taken seriously, bring man face to face with the question of the unconditioned and of the ultimate foundation of being and meaning. The words of T. S. Eliot are reminiscent of Tillich's life: 'In my beginning is my end . . . In my end is my beginning'.[36]

Paradoxically, the answer Tillich gives to the scepticism that dissolves being-itself into discrete and finite beings is also existential: being is understood as a dynamic relation, as the state of being rather than as a material substance. The Cartesian divorce between *res cogitans* and *res extensa* tends to reinforce a crude materialistic paradigm of substantial being, and since the connections between individual extended things are insubstantial and cognitive, being-itself becomes a construct of thought. The only appropriate ontological answer to such consequences of scepticism was to emphasise that the knowing subject is not an abstract epistemological subject but an existing historical person. This, as we have seen is fundamental to Tillich's critique of naturalism and supranaturalism.

Finally, we return to the narrower epistemological sense of Descartes' methodological doubt, and discover that Tillich consistently tries to emphasise its importance for philosophical and theological method: 'The doubt which is implicit in faith is not a doubt about facts or conclusions. It is not the same doubt which is the life-blood of scientific research. Even the most orthodox theologian does not deny the right of methodological doubt in matters of empirical inquiry or logical deduction'.[37] This emphasis can be traced back to an early but seminal paper, 'Rechtfertigung und Zweifel', in which he first developed the distinction, so crucial to his thought, between methodological doubt and existential doubt. In it, he argued that so far from being opposed to faith, existential doubt can be an expression of ultimate concern with truth and with the quest for the Holy. Such doubt Tillich argues is a doubt that justifies just as faith justifies the believer. Because such doubt 'does not reject every concrete truth, but is aware of the element of insecurity in every existential truth', it expresses both humility and courage: the humility that eschews claims to proprietorship of the truth and the courage that can include doubt about itself.

In fact, existential doubt is to be contrasted with the scepticism that demands mathematical certitude and yields either to cynicism or to dogmatism. 'The skeptical doubt is an attitude toward all the beliefs of man, from sense experiences to religious creeds. It is more an attitude than an assertion. For as an assertion it would conflict with itself.'[38] Tillich understood very well that the Cartesian demand for indubitable certainty was based on the cult of the calculus: the demand for a language of univocal terms and unambiguous and mathematically precise truth. He understood that such an attitude is removed from reality, where we have to live with ambiguity and uncertainty, and leads to dogmatism and despair. Both religious fundamentalism and positivism in philosophy demonstrate these characteristics. The existential doubt that recognises the limitations of knowledge, of goodness and of man's cultural creations can live with anxiety, guilt and meaninglessness, because it understands that faith begins with the acceptance of creaturely finitude.

The critique of naturalism and supranaturalism begins and ends with the analysis of faith in both its cognitive and its existential dimensions. Scepticism and relativism as expressions of a defiant assertion of man's spiritual self-sufficiency may be challenged at the level of their existential authenticity, but they also challenge most fundamentally the ontological assumptions of philosophy and theology. Tillich's thought is an attempt to meet this challenge, not so much by elaborating particular answers to particular sceptical questions, but by elaborating an alternative world-view and Christian way of life.

Chapter 3
The Critique of Nominalism:
The World-view of Science and Philosophy

1. *Tillich's life-long fight against nominalism*

Tillich sees nominalism as at the root of most difficulties in contemporary philosophy and theology. In a revealing passage, he states in an informal way how the struggle against nominalism is of decisive importance for him:

> There is hardly a day that I do not fight against nominalism on the basis of my comparatively mediaeval realistic kind of thinking, which conceives of being as power of being. That is a sin against the 'holy spirit' of nominalism, and thus also very much against the 'unholy spirit' of logical positivism and many other such spirits. And I fight this because I believe that although extreme realism is wrong, namely, that realism against which Aristotle was fighting in Plato which regards universals as special things somewhere in heaven, there are nevertheless structures which actualise themselves again and again. So I can say the power of being always resists non-being. For this reason I believe we cannot be nominalists alone, although the nominalist attitude, the attitude of humility towards reality, of not desiring to deduce reality, is something we must maintain. (*HCT* 143)

This frank but somewhat emotive passage reveals that Tillich saw the type of ontological realism that he espoused as having direct parallels with mediaeval realism. He develops his own ontology in critical dialogue with nominalism. In 'The Two Types of Philosophy of Religion', he distinguishes between the ontological and the cosmological types of philosophy of religion. He identifies the cosmological type with nominalism and describes it as expressing the way of encountering God as a stranger; as an alien being whose existence has to be proved like a material object. The ontological type he identifies with mediaeval realism; it is a way of overcoming estrangement by the re-affirmation of God as Being-itself or the ground of all being and meaning. He summarises the argument:

> It is the purpose of this essay to show: (i) that the ontological method is basic for every philosophy of religion; (ii) that the cosmological method without the ontological as its basis leads to a destructive cleavage between philosophy and religion, and (iii) that

on the basis of the ontological approach and with a dependent use of the cosmological way, philosophy of religion contributes to the reconciliation between religion and secular culture. (*TC* 10–11)

While this paper re-states some of the arguments against supranaturalism, which he links with nominalism and the cosmological approach, it is also an important source for his philosophical ontology. He aligns himself with the mystical realists of the Franciscan school of thirteenth-century scholasticism, such as Alexander of Hales, Bonaventura, and Matthew of Aquasparta, who developed the ontological line of the philosophy of religion. Of this tradition he says, 'The Augustinian tradition can rightly be called mystical, if mysticism is defined as the experience of the identity of subject and object in relation to Being itself' (*TC* 14). On the basis of this identity, he argues that the ontological argument is rightly attacked by the nominalists insofar as it claims to demonstrate the existence of God *qua ens realissimum*. The prime function of the argument is to demonstrate the principle that, in relation to human thought in general, God is the *primum esse*. He concludes:

> On this basis the ontological argument for the existence of God must be understood. It is neither an argument, nor does it deal with the existence of God, although it often has been expressed in this form. It is the rational description of the relation of our mind to Being as such . . . This Absolute as the principle of Being has absolute certainty. It is a necessary thought because it is the presupposition of all thought. (*TC* 15)

However, Tillich's formulations sound suspiciously like those we find in the philosophies of identity of Schelling and Hegel. He admits the similarity:

> The word 'realism' means today almost what 'nominalism' meant in the Middle Ages, while the 'realism' of the Middle Ages expresses almost exactly what we call 'idealism' today. It might be suggested that whenever one speaks of classical realism, one should call it 'mystical realism'. (*ST1*, 197)

Tillich does tend to identify idealism and mystical realism, but this tells us more about Tillich and his assumptions than about either of these traditions. Mediaeval realism, whether extreme, moderate or mystical, has as its fundamental assumption the conviction that being is the primary datum and thought is contingent upon being, and not, as Tillich asserts, that 'the principle of Being has absolute certainty . . . is a necessary thought, because it is the presupposition of all thought'. The latter makes being a necessary regulative principle for thought. Being is inferred from thought as its necessary foundation. This position corresponds to what Gilson calls 'ontologism', not 'ontology'.[1] The fact is that both idealism and mystical realism undergo a transformation when taken up into Tillich's theological ontology. The form of much of what Tillich says remains idealist, but the substance of his thought is realist in intention and it will be part of our task to demonstrate this.

Tillich was not alone among his generation in opposing nominalism.

The idealist tradition was necessarily hostile to nominalism. Hegel's philosophy was inimical to nominalism, for example, his doctrines of the concrete universal and of the identity of the rational and the real, however, he opposes chiefly the atomistic epistemology and psychology of nominalism. The English philosopher Bradley specifically attacks the nominalist theory of relations as fictions of the mind, and opposes to it his own doctrine of internal relations. The standard German histories of philosophy, written from a broadly idealist standpoint, reinforce the anti-nominalist bias.

Among philosophers espousing a realist ontology, Tillich was not alone in his opposition to nominalism. T. E. Abbot, in *Scientific Theism*, argues against nominalism and defends the view that Christian theology necessarily demands a realist philosophical base. Peirce and Maritain, both of whom embrace mediaeval realism, insist that modern philosophy is excessively nominalistic.[2]

Among philosophers who opposed the increasingly dominant scientific-technical world-view it was fashionable to attack the nominalistic presuppositions of modern science. However, they did not always agree as to who should be included in the category of nominalists. Tillich includes Hegel and Schelling among the realists, while Peirce and Maritain maintain that the idealists were tainted with nominalism. The question whether this opposition to nominalism by self-styled realists was simply a matter of rhetoric or provided a more serious philosophical basis for their criticism of nominalism is particularly pertinent to our discussion of Tillich.

One philosopher who considers that Tillich's opposition to nominalism is unfortunate is Alisdair M. Macleod. In his highly critical study of the role of ontology in Tillich's philosophical theology, he remarks, in a somewhat patronising manner: 'The view discussed in the last two chapters [according to which the task of the philosopher is the clarification of concepts] is both, at one level, fundamentally correct and, at another level, monumentally wrong-headed. It is correct in that Tillich is quite right to insist on the importance of conceptual clarification and also right to regard this as a characteristically philosophical task. But it is also monumentally wrong-headed because Tillich allows his fixed hostility to what he calls 'nominalism' and his flirtation with the delusive charms of etymology to induce him to propose ontological solutions to merely conceptual problems'.[3]

While there is some justice in what Macleod says about Tillich's fixed hostility to nominalism' and his 'flirtation with the delusive charms of etymology', it is difficult to avoid the impression that the argument is deliberately disingenuous. Firstly, there is plenty of evidence that Tillich was able to appreciate the positive features of nominalism, for example, its rejection of *a priorism* in philosophy, its contribution to the development of rational autonomy, its emphasis on the dynamic contribution of the will in the act of knowledge and resistance to the static ontology that reduces God to *actus purus* (see *HCT* 143; *PE* 78 and *ST1*, 63 and 186).

Thus Tillich's opposition to nominalism was based on rational, and not merely emotive, grounds. Secondly, while it is true that Tillich uses arguments from etymology frequently and sometimes in a dubious manner, it does not follow that he is led 'to propose ontological solutions to merely conceptual problems'. The argument proceeds the other way round: because Tillich maintains that knowledge depends upon the given structures and dynamics of being, he believes that a phenomenological investigation of essences is possible. Further, he believes that the etymology of words can provide us with a key to the understanding of essences that some words were originally intended to express. The possibility of a formal ontology rests, in Tillich's view, upon the possibility of a phenomenological investigation of the structures and dynamics of being. Whether or not we believe, with Tillich, that etymology has a part in such a phenomenological investigation, we cannot caricature Tillich's argument, in the way Macleod does, as making his ontology rest on etymology.

Macleod shows a surprisingly naive confidence in his definition of philosophy as clarification of concepts. He assumes that it is self-evident what we mean by concepts, and that neutral and presuppositionless analysis of concepts is possible. He nowhere develops his theory of concepts. He begs the very question at issue; namely, the epistemic and ontological status of concepts. His disingenuousness is shown in the fact that he doesn't clarify his own ontological and epistemological presuppositions, and does not admit his own fixed hostility to ontology. For example, his concluding remarks are either insincere or facile and misleading. On the one hand, he proposes that radical de-ontologisation of Tillich's thought is necessary if anything of value is to be preserved: 'For the ontological language in which he consciously formulates his basic doctrines is not only inessential but also presents a formidable obstacle to the very comprehension of what he has to say'. On the other hand, he admits that 'As Tillich himself believed, the ontological cast of his system is not incidental to the system: to object to its ontological cast is to object to the system'.[4] Ironically, Macleod fails to come to terms with the fact that his own epistemology and the ontology presupposed in his method are nominalistic.

Tillich's opposition to nominalism is essentially connected with the theological and philosophical system he sought to develop. However, insofar as Tillich sought to formulate a Christian *Weltanschauung*, an alternative philosophy of life, he was not beyond using rhetorical devices in his polemic against nominalism and in defence of belief-ful realism. The rational and the rhetorical merge, for Tillich was much more concerned to discredit the nominalistic world-view than he was concerned with the careful and detailed criticism of individual doctrines. Unlike Peirce and Maritain, who developed their philosophical criticisms in considerable detail, Tillich scatters his criticisms throughout his writings; in order to systematise his insights on the metaphysics of meaning, truth and logic we have to separate these aspects somewhat artificially from the fabric of his system. In general, it is true to say that if the rationale for the construction of his system is ideological and apologetic, by the same token his critique of other philosophies is not philosophical so much as rhetorical and polemical. The logic of his opposition to nominalism is to be understood in terms of his ultimate concern with being and meaning. In fact, Tillich would maintain that the critique of different philosophies of life can never be a matter of mere clarification of concepts, any more than his own systematic theology can be reduced to that. The choice of one's fundamental world-view or philosophy of life is a matter of pre-philosophical faith; a matter of ultimate concern.

References to nominalism abound in almost all of Tillich's works, but the most important sources for the philosophical aspects of his discussion are: *Systematic Theology* Volumes 1 and 2, *The Protestant Era*, chapters IV and V, and *The Theology of Culture*, chapter II. The references in the earlier works are scattered, and it is significant that it is only as Tillich became more practically involved in the crisis of Western culture represented by the Second World War, and as he began to give more systematic expression to his ontology, that he developed a more explicit critique of nominalism.

It would be difficult to know where to begin the examination of Tillich's critique were it not that he himself has given us a convenient summary of his reasons for doing battle with nominalism. Discussing William of Ockham, he mentions the following kinds of criticisms: ontological, socio-political and cultural, logical and epistemological, theological, and arguments relating to language and symbolism, to the possibility of rational psychology, and to law and authority (*HCT* 198–201). The order in which these arguments are mentioned is not deliberate, but it is revealing. Ontological questions are of predominant importance, but Tillich's concern with ontology is not abstract. It could be said to arise out of his engagement with the crisis of Western culture and man's renewed concern with his being and meaning.

2. *Tillich's criticisms of nominalism*

a) *Arguments relating to society and culture, ethics and politics.* Tillich objects first to the nominalistic dissolution of universals, with its consequence that the world is atomised into discrete individuals, so that the term 'being' has no reference except to particulars. This seemingly abstract philosophical doctrine has profound consequences for human society and culture.

> Mediaeval realism maintains the powers of being which transcend the individual; mediaeval nominalism preserves or emphasises the value of the individual. The fact that the radical realism of the early Middle Ages was rejected saved Europe from Asiatisation, that is, from collectivisation. The fact that at the end of the Middle Ages all universals were lost resulted in the imposition of the power of the church on individuals, making God himself into an individual who, as a tyrant, gives laws to other individuals. This was the distortion

which nominalism brought along with itself, whereas the affirmation
of the personal was its creative contribution. (*HCT* 144)

The nominalist/realist dispute was not simply a logical game that the
nominalists, for the time being, won. 'Rather it represented a change of
attitude toward reality in the whole of society. You will find nominalism
and realism discussed in books on the history of logic, and rightly so, but
that does not give the full impact of what this controversy meant. This
was a debate between two attitudes towards life. Today these attitudes
are expressed in terms of collectivism and individualism' (*HCT* 199).
The clear implication is that the issue is basically an ideological one.

In criticising nominalism at this level, Tillich identifies a number of
central issues bearing on the fundamental decisions facing modern
Western society. First, he discusses nominalism and the rise of individualism in the West:

> The immediate importance of nominalism was that it disrupted the
> universals, which were understood not only in terms of abstract
> concepts but also of embracing groups, such as family, state, friends,
> craftsmen, all groups which precede the individual. At the same time,
> the danger of mediaeval realism was that the individual was pre-
> vented from developing his potentialities. Therefore, nominalism
> was an important reaction, so important that I would say that with-
> out it the estimation of the personality in the modern world – the real
> basis of democracy – could not have developed. (*HCT* 143–4)[5]

This development has ambiguous consequences for social life, for it
undermines the significance of participation in community and, in
making the relations of individuals subject only to abstract contracts and
conventional laws, it opens the way to totalitarian democracy.[6] Nominalism confronts modern man with the seeming need to choose between
individualism and totalitarianism; in *Die sozialistische Entscheidung*
Tillich argues that the only radical alternative is a socialism that is aware
of the religious foundations of personal and communal life, and is based
on belief-ful realism, which can rediscover being-itself as the unconditioned ground of all being and meaning.

Secondly, Tillich discusses how nominalism leads to romanticism and a
divorce between the psychological and ontological aspects of love, that is,
between love as feeling and love as 'the power of being'. The consequence
is that love comes to be identified with private sentiment, and justice with
formal, positive law enforced by external authority.[7] Anselm's doctrine of
atonement suggests a solution: 'It implies the ontological insight . . . that
ultimately love must satisfy justice in order to be real love, and that justice must be elevated into unity with love in order to avoid the injustice of
eternal destruction'.[8] Tillich identifies justice with the form in which
being actualises itself under the motive force of love in the encounter of
power with power. This highly abstract statement is an attempt to re-
interpret the doctrine of natural law in ontological rather than legal
terms. On the basis of his ontological analysis, which owes a great deal to
mediaeval realism, he asks how the essential unity of love, power and

justice may be re-established. 'The answer is obvious: Through the manifestation of the ground in which they are united. Love, power and justice are one in the divine ground, they shall become one in human existence. The holy in which they are united shall become holy reality in time and space.'[9]

The danger of nominalism is that because it denies the presence of universal powers of being in things, that is, denies the tendency of an existing being to strive towards its *telos*, it denies an intrinsic connection between being and value. The relationship between 'is and 'ought' becomes logically unintelligible, and this leads to theories of value that canonise the arbitrary or the conventional, and to what Tillich calls 'moralism' (*TC* 133–45). The subjective emotivism of the empiricist tradition and the authoritarian formalism of the ethic of duty for duty's sake in the rationalist tradition are equally moralistic and equally products of nominalism. Utilitarianism, although it seeks to ground decisions of value in reality by considering the real effects of actions, collapses into subjectivism because happiness is treated as a subjective emotion and not as an ontological state of well being. The answer to nominalism in ethics is a theonomous ethics that can rediscover the element of the unconditional in being-itself as the ground of meaning and value. This is the main burden of Tillich's writings on ethics from 'Religion and Ethics' in *The Protestant Era* to *Morality and Beyond*.

A third and constant theme is his attack on nominalism for the way it leads to heteronomy in religion and politics. This is the result of 'the escape into authority, which is the consequence of the dissolution of universals and the inability of the isolated individual to develop the courage to be oneself. Therefore the nominalists built the bridge to an ecclesiastical authoritarianism which surpassed everything in the early and late Middle Ages and produced modern Catholic collectivism'.[10] Another factor that Tillich links with the tendency towards ecclesiastical and political authoritarianism is the voluntarism deriving from the Ockhamist exaggeration of will over intellect. Accordingly, because the divine will is omnipotent, 'God cannot be approached at all through autonomous knowledge, he is out of reach. Everything could be the opposite of what it is. Therefore, God can be reached only by subjecting ourselves to the biblical and ecclesiastical authorities. And we can subject ourselves to them only if we have the *habitus*, the habit of grace' (*HCT* 188). However, as he says elsewhere: ' "[n]ominalism" was in danger of completely losing the concept of grace. Without an understanding of "being" and "the power of being", it is impossible to speak meaningfully of grace' (*ST2*, 144). When translated into the secular terms of the General Will and a sovereignty not based on divine right or natural law, this leads directly to the dictatorship of majority opinion: *Vox populi, vox dei*! Political voluntarism is on the way to becoming totalitarian because it recognises no restraints in reality on the unlimited expression of the political will-to-power. Tillich believes that only a religious foundation and socialist political structures can secure democracy against the tyranny of those who manipulate public opinion to create the appearance of a general will.

Fourthly, Tillich was concerned with the effect of nominalism on our view of cultural forms. In his view nominalism, like supranaturalism, tends to empty cultural creations of their ultimate significance by denying any connection between finite forms and the infinite source of meaning. Nominalism emphasises the purely utilitarian functions of reason, since its power to grasp the essential structures and dynamics of being is denied. Art, literature, music and drama increasingly are seen as the expressions of private feelings and attitudes or as purely conventional symbols, rather than as disclosures of reality in a form that is complementary to science and philosophy. Tillich attacks the spirit of nominalism for the way it evacuates man's cultural creations of any ultimate meaning and develops a realist doctrine of symbols that will express man's essential concern with being and meaning.[11]

In his exposition of 'Masse und Geist' in which Tillich uses examples from the history of art to illustrate changing attitudes towards the masses, James Luther Adams points out:

> A late Gothic or an early Renaissance picture, for example in Holland or Germany, conveys a different idea of the meaning of life and the meaning of the masses in the period . . . The mystical mass of the earlier period has become a conglomeration of separately depicted, and interesting, individuals . . . The leader has become the agitator. In other words, the picture shows that mediaeval society is decomposing. Supranaturalism is receding before the newly discovered naturalism. The realism of the idea is destroyed by nominalism. The particular is coming to the throne. It is the time of social revolution, the harbinger of the Peasants' Revolt.[12]

The nominalism that expresses itself in the emergence of the abstract masses also reflects itself in the rest of culture in its manifold expressions. Nominalism has to be opposed in all its forms, if it is to yield to a theonomous view of culture, science and religion.

The general significance of Tillich's critique of nominalism, as distinct from those of Peirce or Maritain, for example, is that Tillich is much more concerned with the global character of nominalism. He is preoccupied with such factors as make possible a significant choice between one world-view and another, for example, the ability to form a comprehensive picture of the attitudes, beliefs and values involved. While he recognises that the total world-view implicitly determines the way we look at issues in logic, epistemology, ethics, politics, psychology, art and ontology, he is primarily concerned with its adequacy as a philosophy-of-life, that is, as a means to disclose the ultimate meaning of being.

Tillich examines the different ways in which various *Weltanschauungen* point to the unconditioned ground of being and meaning. In this way, the discussion of ideologies becomes appropriate subject-matter for theology in terms of his two formal criteria for theology (*ST1*, 255). On the one hand, they have to be judged according to the question whether that for which they claim unconditional validity really is ultimate. The norm involved is sometimes referred to as 'The Protestant Principle', which expresses the prophetic protest against the idolatrous identification of the object of ultimate concern with some finite being or institution. On the other hand, *Weltanschauungen* have to be judged according to the kind of meaning and fulfilment they offer to human existence. The material norm by which ideologies are judged is 'The New Being in Jesus as the Christ'; this is the measure of the validity of unconditional claims made on man's spiritual allegiance.[13]

It is not surprising, therefore, that in setting out his objections to nominalism, he considers first its ethico-political and existential aspects. Questions of epistemology, logic, language and psychology, which we might consider more important, are seen by Tillich as becoming significant only when a man has made a decision for or against nominalism as a way of life. This holds good even for the discussion of specific theological objections, for it is only when nominalism is considered as a comprehensive belief- and value-system that it raises challenging problems for theology. However, before discussing these, we proceed to examine his ontological criticisms of nominalism.

b) *Arguments relating to being, essences and existence.* In a variety of contexts, Tillich points out that the nominalist reduction of universals to mere names undermines not only the doctrine of essences but also the traditional doctrine of being. In a typical passage, he says:

> On the basis of its dissolution of the universals, nominalism objects to the concept of a universal power of being or to the concept of being-itself. But nominalism cannot escape the implicit assertion that the nature of being and knowing is best recognised by a nominalistic epistemology. If being is radically individualised, if it lacks embracing structures and essences, this is a character of being, valid for everything that is. The question then is not whether one can speak of being-itself but what its nature is and how it can be approached cognitively. (*ST1*, 255)

In other words, the nominalist cannot avoid making ontological claims, namely those of an atomistic metaphysics. However, it does not follow that it raises the ontological question in the way Tillich suggests that it does: '[T]he experience of ultimacy implies an ultimate of being and meaning which concerns man unconditionally because it determines his very being and meaning. For the philosophical approach this ultimate is being-itself, *esse ipsum*, that beyond which thought cannot go, the power of being in which everything participates' (*ST1*, 255). While we may admit the general drift of this argument, the relation between what it means to have being and being-itself is not explained. This kind of vagueness, unfortunately, is all too common in Tillich's arguments, and is a sign that he is more concerned with the rhetoric of persuasion than with the logic of proof.

We shall deal briefly with his ontological criticisms of nominalism in relation to what he says about being-itself, the nature of essences, and the relation of essence to existence.

First, with regard to being-itself, it is obvious that he is most concerned with the theological consequences of the nominalist rejection of being-itself as the basic transcendental.

> In classical theology God is, first of all, Being as such. *Deus est esse.* Being in this sense is not the most abstract category, as a mistaken nominalism asserts; it is the power of Being in everything that is, in everything that participates in Being... When Being lost its symbolic power under the influence of nominalism and when, more definitely in the second half of the Renaissance, Being became the object for a subject, to be calculated and controlled, God ceased to be Being-itself and Being ceased to be divine. (*PE* 70; cf. *TC* 12–16, *STI*, 227–231)

As this passage illustrates, Tillich believes that the doctrine of abstraction is partly to blame for the tendency to see being-itself as the highest abstraction. This is a doctrine that he tries to qualify by the principle that, in the act of knowing, subject and object participate in a common reality. This principle is one of the foundations of Tillich's realism.

He is also disturbed by the consequences of the nominalist denial of reality to being-itself, except as the highest abstraction, for our interpretation of the other transcendentalia *verum ipsum* and *bonum ipsum*. If these are mere abstractions, too, then epistemology and ethics collapse into arbitrary conventionalism or subjectivism. In opposing these conclusions, he appeals to the Augustinian tradition in which it is argued that 'Our mind implies *principia per se nota* which have immediate evidence whenever they are noticed: the transcendentalia, *esse, verum, bonum*' (*TC* 15; cf. *STI*, 229). This argument from the intuitive self-evidence of the transcendentalia proves persuasive only within the acceptance of mystical realism. The formal demonstration of the ontological foundations of ethics is a more laborious task; one that Tillich attempted in *Love, Power and Justice*, and in the elaboration of his metaphysics of meaning, truth and logic, the foundations of which were first sketched out in *Das System der Wissenschaften*.

Tillich's concern with categories, which he inherits from Kant and Hegel, is reflected in the last-named work. Here, he argues the general case against Kant's attempt to deduce the categories from the logical forms of judgement: 'The philosophy of knowing, that is to say the study of Essences and Categories in Science, demonstrates that the subject-matter and methods of Science alike are grounded in common categories. Categories are the constitutive functional principles of the world of appearances' (*DSW* 147; cf. *STI*, 182–6, *MSA* 75–80). Tillich's answer to the nominalist doctrine, which would make the categories subjective fictions of the mind, is to be found in the elaboration of his theory of intentionality. This we shall discuss in the course of our examination of his metaphysics of logic, although it is implicit in his discussion of meaning and truth.

The second area to which Tillich turns in his critique of nominalist ontology concerns the nature of essences and their relations to universals and individuals. This issue is 'one of the most difficult problems connected with the ontology essences' (*ST1*, 283). He argues that the more individualised the conception of essences becomes, the more they tend to constitute a duplicate of reality.

It is understandable that nominalism abolished this duplication of the world and attributed being only to individual things, but nominalism cannot deny the power of the universals which reappear in every individual exemplar and which determine its nature and its growth. And even in the individual, notably in the individual man, there is an inner TELOS which transcends the various moments of the process of life. (*ST1*, 283)

Tillich offers two kinds of solution to the question of the relations between form and matter, and between act and potency, in determining the nature of individuated being. He cites the Augustinian claim that it is self-evident that in the divine life there is no difference between potentiality and actuality. He concludes: 'The essential powers of being belong to the divine life in which they are rooted, created by him who is everything "through himself"' (*ST1*, 283). On the other hand, by analogy, as individuals approximate to the fulfilment of their essential nature, the distinction between potentiality and actuality is transcended in the process of essentialisation. Tillich envisages the New Being, the condition of life in the Spirit, as a process in which the hiatus between essence and existence, caused by sin and alienation, is overcome in the ontological process of essentialisation.[14] This move is typical of Tillich's approach: he translates his concern with being into essentialist terms, that is, into a consideration of the significance of ontological doctrines for the meaning of human existence. In other words, Tillich stresses how nominalism, in attacking a Platonic two-world theory of universals as well as Augustinian exemplarism, anticipated the existentialist attack on abstract essentialism.[15]

The third question, the relation of existence to essence, is continuous with the preceding discussion. However, Tillich was also more directly concerned with the theoretical problems of individuation, that is, with the intelligibility of singulars and the doctrine of relations. In his solutions to the problems raised by Ockham, he shows his preference for theories like those of Bonaventura and Duns Scotus.

In rejecting what he regards as the static essentialism of Aristotelian metaphysics, Tillich is reacting against two things that tend to be conflated: an ontological doctrine that makes matter alone the *principium individuationis*, so that the universal, timeless and unchanging form requires to be 'filled' with matter before it becomes actual as an instantiated individual species; and a related epistemological doctrine that, while it is a *conditio sine qua non* that universals must be instantiated in existing individuals in order to be known, individuals *per se* cannot be possible objects of knowledge. The radical alternative of Ockham, that universals have no *fundamentum in re* and are either merely verbal signs for conventional linguistic symbols, or mental signs for intellectual fictions, is unacceptable to Tillich. He argues that this leads to an atomistic meta-physics that denies ontological status to anything but individuals, and to a subjectivist epistemology in which universals, *qua* the intentional objects of the act of knowing, become the creations of the knowing subject (*HCT* 198–201; cf. *ST1*, 255–6).

Tillich opts for a realist doctrine of universals in which the universal element is identified with a dynamic formative and teleological principle in the evolving nature of individual and species. This is expressed in the passage quoted above where he speaks of 'the power of the universals which reappear in every individual exemplar and which determine its nature and its growth ... [the] inner TELOS which transcends the various moments in the process of life' (*ST1*, 283). In an early paper on belief-ful realism he describes knowing as an act of union between knower and known, and the cognitive will as the will of a separated life to unite itself with other life. He compares this doctrine to the Greek view that sought the power of the thing that can be grasped by the logos: 'THEORIA is union with the really real, with that level of a thing in which the "power of being" (OUSIA, *Seinsmächtigkeit*) is situated. Every real has different levels with more or less power of being' (*PE* 76–7). Such an understanding of being as power is the way to give an ontological foundation to the theory of value and to restore to *Theoria* its existential significance: 'Of course, if being is defined as "object of thought" no matter what content it has, the idea of "degrees of being" is senseless. But if being is "power" the assertion of such degrees is natural, and it is a vital necessity for the mind to penetrate into the strata in which the real power of a thing reveals itself' (*PE* 77).

Tillich traces the origins of this doctrine to Bonaventura and Duns Scotus and the tradition of mystical realism (*HCT* 30, 78–9). However, in the same context he mentions Bergson, and it is likely that he derives the voluntarist element in his doctrine of essences as powers of being from the French philosopher rather than from mediaeval source. Never-theless, it is significant that he endorses the doctrine of Scotus that 'the species plus the individual difference accounts for the existence of the singular'.[16] This doctrine has ontological, epistemological and historical consequences for Tillich.

The ontological consequence is that matter alone cannot be the prin-ciple of individuation in things, but requires to be complemented by the dynamic principle of form. It is only in the specific union of form and matter that the particular individual comes into existence as a recognis-able, unique individual.

Because the formal and the material are combined in the definition of the individual, Scotus maintains that the singular is *per se* intelligible to the human mind. This doctrine is very attractive to Tillich, with his desire to emphasise that knowledge consists in an existential relation, and it gets round the essentialist principle that only universals can be immediately known. However, the doctrine is not without its difficulties, as Tillich fails to distinguish between immediate knowledge of being-itself and knowledge of individual existents. His belief-ful realism inclines him to accept the possibility of the former while his Kantian scepticism inclines him to doubt the possibility of the latter.

This doctrine of universals as dynamic elements or powers of being is very important to Tillich's philosophy of history, because it suggests that the essences of things are not timeless and unchanging; on the contrary, like the *rationes seminales* so favoured in the Augustinian tradition, they create in the philosophy of nature a view of nature as a dynamic evolutionary development of new forms and species. This spiritual Darwinism, which expresses itself in Tillich's account of Life and Spirit and of History and the Kingdom of God in *Systematic Theology* Volume 3, is inspired, like Teilhard de Chardin's *Milieu Divin*, by a dynamic view of the relation between matter, form and existence that is reminiscent of Bonaventura and Scotus, but probably derives from Bergson.

Finally, Tillich attacks the view that relations are subjective fictions of the mind or *a priori* forms of intuition. Central to his argument that relations are real is a stress on being as a state rather than as an entity: as the dynamic condition connected with participation, rather than as the static notion of being that identifies it with first substance. As he says in a key passage: 'In polarity with individualisation, participation underlies the category of relation as a basic ontological element. Without individualisation nothing would exist to be related. Without participation the category of relation would have no basis in reality' (*ST1*, 196).[17] This emphasis on the reality of relations is a constant theme in Tillich's writings on epistemology. For example, it is central to the argument of 'Participation and Knowledge: Problems of an Ontology of Cognition'. It is present also as a theme in his metaphysics of logic, however and, in this case, perhaps owes more to the idealist doctrine of internal relations.

Tillich's doctrine of space and time is consciously anti-nominalistic. He emphasises that the categories, including Space and Time, are 'categories of finitude'. They have both a structural character, in determining the form of finite experience, and an existential significance, in that man's existence is spatio-temporally contingent; they thus relate to man's experience of mortality and existential isolation. His formulations are intended to avoid the subjective overtones of the Kantian theory of space and time as subjective forms of intuition. In *My Search for Absolutes*, he describes them as 'forms of perception' and 'universal structures of being' (*MSA* 76). This emphasises the dual significance of the categories as forms of being and forms of knowing. The following formulation attempts to combine the best of both worlds: the idealist perception of the categories as formative principles in knowledge, and the realist emphasis on them as determining modes of being.

> The categories are to be distinguished from logical forms which determine discourse but which are only indirectly related to reality itself. The logical forms are formal in that they abstract from the content to which the discourse refers. The categories, on the other hand, are forms which determine content. They are ontological, and

therefore present in everything. The mind is not able to experience reality except through the categorial forms. (*ST1*, 213–14)

c) *Arguments relating to epistemology and logic, language and symbolism.* Tillich's discussion of epistemological aspects of nominalism is neither as detailed nor as searching as his criticism of the epistemological presuppositions of supranaturalism, partly because he considers that the two are related, and that he has already dealt with the main problems. Nevertheless, the few explicit criticisms of nominalist epistemology and logic, together with his criticisms of supranaturalist epistemology, serve to define the main outlines of his metaphysics of knowledge or ontology of cognition.[18]

First, there are criticisms of the theory of abstraction and our knowledge of universals. This is a subject to which he frequently returned. He paraphrases the views of Ockham in the following terms:

Now, if only individual things exist, what are the universals according to Ockham? The universals are identical with the act of knowing. They rise in our minds, and we must *use* them, otherwise we could not speak. They are natural. He called them the *universalia naturalia*. Beyond them are the words which are the symbols for these natural universals which arise in our minds. They are the conventional universals. Words can be changed; they exist by convention. The word is universal because it can be said of different things. (*HCT* 199)

To put the matter in traditional terms, Tillich believes that the doctrine of abstraction leads naturally to nominalism and ultimately to subjective idealism. If the process is taken to begin with perception, to continue with the comparison of different individuals of the same species in order to identify and abstract their common properties, and to conclude with the formulation of words or concepts to express this common nature, this seems to make the concept of a universal irredeemably subjective. Whether this expresses itself, as in the case of Berkeley, in the denial of the objective reality of the external world or in the early Kantian view that the Understanding makes Nature, it is self-defeating.

Tillich recognised that a naive realist interpretation of the doctrine was not satisfactory either, for the universal in nature and the universal in the mind are logically and ontologically distinct. Nor is the Hegelian apotheosis of the Transcendental Ego an adequate answer. The objectivity of knowledge cannot be guaranteed by making it contingent upon the subjectivity of the Absolute Subject. In his belief-ful realism, Tillich seeks to do justice to the creative contribution of the knowing subject while emphasising the objectivity of the structures and dynamics of being that make knowledge possible. While he does not use the mediaeval terms, his doctrine implies a distinction between the universal as it exists in the mind (the *verbum mentis*) and the universal as it exists in things (*quidditas qua fundamentum in re*). This commits him to a correspondence theory of truth and to a double theory of intentionality. On the one hand, he takes over from Husserl the analysis, derived from mediaeval sources through

Brentano, of a cognitive act, as always a consciousness *of* something, and the correlative doctrine that the immediate object of consciousness is an essence. On the other hand, he maintains that there is a structural and intentional relationship between self and world that provides the context within which the correspondence between the *logos*-structures of mind and reality is expressed in the creative process of the discovery and formulation of knowledge (*ST1*, 29, 83–7, 183).

Secondly, we must mention the epistemological aspects of the nominalist doctrine that only individuals are real. Throughout his discussion of the ontological implications, Tillich constantly implies that an atomistic metaphysics cannot lead to a coherent theory of knowledge, for it must deny objectivity to relations (*ST1*, 184–6; *MSA* 64–83). If all relations are subjective then the relation of similarity, which must be presupposed as a basis for any doctrine of universals, is subjective. Nominalist epistemology must lead to scepticism, as it did in Hume's case, through the denial of ontological status to the principles of identity and causality.

Tillich emphasises, in discussing the significance of the Ontological Argument, that its chief value lies in its stress on the necessary structural identity between thought and being-itself as the presupposition of all knowledge. He would not argue, as Hegel does, that we can deduce substantive conclusions from this fundamental identity. The function of the principle of identity is to ground the possibility of knowledge, not to prove a source of knowledge in its own right. The principle has a primarily protective function, in defending the possibility of knowledge and guaranteeing the coherence of all thoughts in a meaningful totality.

The theory of intentionality has relevance here, too. Again and again, Tillich stresses that knowledge arises in an existential encounter between self and world. The knowing relation is thus a three-term relation: the knower, the known and the knowledge-act that unites them. We cannot ignore the existing subject, and treat the knowing relation abstractly as a relation between knowledge and the known (cf. *ST1*, 83f., 90f.).

The preoccupation of idealist philosophy with dialectical triads suggests that it inclines towards realism and it may be thought that Tillich derives his theory from idealist sources. This is misleading, because in idealist thought the relation between the rational and the real is a notional identity not an ontological correspondence, and because the dialectical triad of thesis, antithesis and synthesis is generated by thought and not given with the structure of being and experience. For Tillich, the fundamental datum, given in pre-reflexive intuition, is the reality of being-itself; and the polarities of self and world, essence and existence, and individuation and participation are differentiated within this fundamental reality.

Thirdly, he attacks the nominalist tendency to equate contingency with chance, and the indeterminacy and irrationalism that this introduces into the theory of knowledge. The ontological meaning of contingency, that is, the given relations of dependence and inter-dependence in which finite things stand is confused with the cognitive meaning of 'accidence', that is, the notion of chance is substituted for the notion of the non-essential: 'The emphasis on the contingency of everything that exists makes both the will of God and the being of man equally contingent. [The nominalist doctrine] gives to man the feeling of a definite lack of ultimate necessity, with respect not only to himself but also to his world. And it gives him a corresponding anxiety'.[19]

Fourthly, there is voluntarism and its similar effect in introducing an irrational element into the nominalist doctrine of knowledge, whether applied to our knowledge of God or applied to our knowledge of things.

> Scotus defined God as will and nothing other than will. In another Franciscan, William of Ockham, this became an irrational will ... If God is sheer will, he can do what he wants. He has within himself no intellectual limits. There is no logos structure which would prevent him from doing what he wants. The world is in every moment dependent on something absolutely unknown. Ultimately nothing in the world can be calculated. Only insofar as it is ordered by God can it be calculated, but God can withdraw both the natural and the moral orders. (*P* 194; cf. *HCT* 142, 188, 191 and *ST1*, 274)

As with indeterminacy, the only corrective to this destructive voluntarism, is an understanding of the proper ontological foundations of the concepts of will and contingency. In particular, he tries to preserve the dynamic conception of reason implied in the nominalist stress on will, but the extravagances of that doctrine are avoided by emphasising that reason is dependent upon the *logos*-structure of reality for its intelligibility, and is limited by the categorical forms, which are forms of finitude.

Fifthly, Tillich connects the scientific-technical world-view with nominalism: 'Controlling knowledge is the epistemological expression of a nominalistic ontology; empiricism and positivism are its logical consequences' (*ST1*, 196). In developing his own doctrine of belief-ful realism, Tillich emphasises that there is a moderate nominalism that is almost synonymous with contemporary scientific realism. He sums up this attitude:

> One concedes to things only so much power as they should have in order to be useful. Reason becomes the means of controlling the world. The really real (OUSIA) of things is their calculable element, that which is determined by natural laws. Anything beyond this level is without interest and not an object of knowledge. This relation to reality is called 'realistic' today. Through technical science and its economic utilisation this realism is so predominant in our social and intellectual situation that the fight against it seems romantic and almost hopeless. (*PE* 78; cf. 70–1)

Tillich, however, attacks this so-called 'realism', because he is hostile not to science and technology but to an uncritical nominalism that distorts their nature and encourages an a-moral and a-cosmic view of science that can easily be made to serve political, military and commercially profitable ends. A nominalistic science is a science divorced from values because its ontological roots and significance are ignored. Science as an expression of man's participation in being along with other beings yields to the naked expression of man's will-to-power over nature and a will-to-dominate other men. True realism involves the humility to recognise the ontological grounds of scientific knowledge: 'Even the empiricist must acknowledge that everything approachable by knowledge must have the structure of "being knowable". And this structure includes by definition a mutual participation of the knower and the known. Radical nominalism is unable to make the process of knowledge understandable' (*ST1*, 197).

The sixth and final criticism of nominalism that we consider here, relates to the nominalist theory of symbolism. In numerous contexts, Tillich identifies nominalism with an attitude to symbolism that is inconpatible with an adequate ontology or theology. For example: 'According to nominalism, only the individual has ontological reality; universals are verbal signs which point to similarities between individual things. Knowledge, therefore, is not participation. It is an external act of grasping and controlling things' (*ST1*, 196; cf. *ST2*, 21). His objection is not so much that nominalism reduces the meanings of words to human convention – rather that it implies that such conventions are arbitrary. He is concerned not so much with semiotic theory as with the metaphysics of meaning. Interpreted as a formal semiotic theory, his theory of symbolism is naive, but against the background of his ontology it has some similarity to the view of structural linguistics that the 'deep grammar' of language reflects structural features of reality as we experience it. At this level, nominalism is indeed inadequate, for it not only reduces semiotics to syntax and semantics (ignoring the importance of pragmatics), but is not able to explain the foundations of logical syntax or the theory of meaning.[20] Tillich's insistence on the fundamental importance of the assertion that being-itself is the unconditioned ground of meaning relates to the same point. We examine these issues in more detail in the next chapter.

William Rowe has suggested that Tillich's critique of nominalism is connected with the attempt to argue that being-itself is a universal.[21] Admittedly, Tillich's doctrine is ambiguous, in spite of his argument that 'God is being-itself' is non-symbolic and univocal (*ST1*, 264–5). However, he does try to consistently maintain that *esse ipsum* is a basic transcendental, and that it logically and ontologically precedes the distinction between particular and universal. To argue that *esse ipsum* is a universal is to misunderstand Tillich's critique of nominalism and the dynamic and personal sense of being that he applies to God when he refers to God as Being-itself.

Perhaps more revealing of Tillich's doctrine of symbolism is the following observation on the change brought about by nominalism: 'In the early centuries of the Christian Church the visual function was predominant in religious art and in the sacraments. Since Duns Scotus, and even more since Ockham, the hearing of the Word becomes most important, and not the seeing of the sacramental embodiment of the reality' (*HCT* 206). The point Tillich emphasises is that for the realist, the paradigmatic instances of symbols are things, that is the objects of nature and art, and even words are treated as things insofar as their iconic functions are emphasised. In nominalism, it is words as conventional signs that serve as paradigms for our understanding of symbols generally. This comment is not of merely historical interest; it is an indicator of Tillich's own attitudes and of the importance he gives to art and visual forms in the interpretation of symbolism. In several places, he remarks on the excessively verbal character of Western culture and, in the *Systematic Theology*, returns to the theme in discussing the importance of vision, touch and taste (*ST1*, 46, 136, 176, 278; cf. *PE* 109f., 119, 209).

Several important consequences follow from this emphasis: first, art and visual symbolism are of central importance in shaping Tillich's understanding of symbolism; secondly, he suggests that modern philosophy prejudges the question of being and meaning by adopting linguistic semantics as the norm for the interpretation of meaning in general; thirdly, he tends to focus attention on iconic verbal signs, that is, on those words that have a particular symbolic value as objects of religious reverence, and to neglect other types of verbal signs and the diversity of linguistic functions.

d) *Arguments relating to philosophy of religion and theology.* Since Tillich's is a self-confessed 'ontological theology', one cannot overemphasise the importance of his critique of nominalism (*ST2*).

I now identify the central problems. First, there is the nominalist denial of God as *Esse-ipsum*; He thereby becomes a being among beings, not Being-itself. There are two sides to this, one of which is the denial of reality to anything but particulars, by which argument God is at best a *res singularissima* (Ockham). The other is the denial of reality to the transcendentalia, being, truth and goodness, by which argument they become mere, albeit the highest, abstractions. The clearest statement is in 'Religion and Secular Culture': 'If God is called *ipsum esse* Being-itself, he can also, and must, be called *ipsum verum* the true itself. But if God is a being beside others which may or may not exist, or a person beside others whom we may or may not discover, a statement like "*Deus est veritas*", "God is truth", has no meaning' (*PE* 70, 71). This is an argument of central importance to his systematic theology.

Secondly, there are difficulties, for those who are nominalists, that arise immediately in the understanding of traditional Christian dogmas. Tillich cites two crucial examples: the doctrine of the *Logos* and the doctrine of the *Trinity*.

> If one is not used to thinking in terms of universals as powers of being, such a concept as Logos remains impossible to understand. (*HCT* 30)

> Those who are nominalists by education have great difficulty in understanding the trinitarian dogma. For nominalism everything which is must be a definite thing, limited and separated from all other things. For mystical realism, as we have it in Plato, Origen, and the Middle Ages, the power of being in a *universal* can be some-

thing quite superior to and different from the power of being in the individuals. (*HCT* 78–9)

Thus, for ontological reasons as well as for reasons deriving from its semantic theories, nominalism makes nonsense of much of the traditional language in which theologians and councils have spoken about God.

Thirdly, Tillich emphasises that the nominalist doctrine that elevates the will to pre-eminence in God's nature has the most serious consequences for theology. The element of indeterminacy in nominalist voluntarism introduces a dynamic element that serves as a corrective to '"realistic" attempts to fix God to a static structure of being' (*ST1*, 186). Similarly, the Aristotelian doctrine of God as *actus purus* (which Tillich takes to mean pure form) is criticised (*ST1*, 199; cf. *ST2*, 25). Again, the concept of intentionality finds its counterpart in the divine being in the polarity of will and intellect; a dynamic interpretation that would not be possible without the Augustinian and Scotist emphasis on the divine will (*ST1*, 274).

However, these positive emphases, which are primarily to be found in Duns Scotus, become dangerous distortions when subject to the exaggerations of Ockham. The mystical tradition of the Franciscans, in which the will as love is decisive in the interpretation of the nature of God, becomes the *potentia absoluta* in Duns Scotus, and irrational will in Ockham: 'The irrational, commanding, absolute God of nominalism and the Reformation ... is partly an expression of the anxiety produced by the basic social conflict of the disintegrating Middle Ages'.[22] The effect on theology was to produce an extreme heteronomy; a divorce of reason and authority that afflicted the Reformers as much as the Roman Catholic church. 'The moment that God became defined as will – determined by his will and not by his intellect – the world became incalculable, uncertain, unsafe. So we are compelled to subject ourselves to what is positively given. All the dangers of positivism are rooted in this concept of Duns Scotus. So I consider him the turning point in the history of Western thought' (*HCT* 191).

A related area in which this doctrine had a profound effect was the revival of the controversies about freewill and predestination; nominalism contributed to the extreme form in which the doctrine of Predestination was expressed by Calvin. This is discussed by Tillich against the background of his critique of the nominalist denial of ontological participation (see *ST1*, 283, 290, 300, 316; cf. *HCT* 195–6).

Fourthly, there is the related question of the fideism to which nominalism gives rise, and its consequences, less for knowledge than for the doctrine of faith: 'It separates the intellectual component of belief (*fides*) from the volitional component of trust (*fiducia*), and divorces these from the ontological state of being grasped by the power of being-itself'.[23] This point is central to the argument of both *The Courage to Be* and *The Dynamics of Faith*. However, the historical connection of fideism with nominalism is a recurring theme of *A History of Christian Thought*, where there is this classic statement:

In his [Ockham's] view God cannot be approached at all through autonomous knowledge; he is out of reach. Everything could be the opposite of what it is. Therefore, God can only be reached by subjecting ourselves to the biblical and ecclesiastical authorities ... Only if grace is working in us can we receive the authority of the church. Cultural knowledge, the knowledge of science, is completely free and autonomous, and religious knowledge is completely heteronomous. (*HCT* 188; cf. 139, 187, 200–1. See also *TC* 16–19)

This led to the dangerous theory of 'double truth', with the incoherent conclusion that 'in reality a statement on the matter can be both theologically true and philosophically false, and vice versa' (*HCT* 189).

Fifthly, there is the nominalist denial of the sacramental idea of participation, and of the related tendency to deny efficacy to sacramentals and ultimate meaning to religious symbols. These are attitudes that Tillich sees as inimical to the very spirit of religion, and he attacks them again and again throughout the development of his theology. They are the explicit subjects of discussions of the collective manifestations of the courage to be through participation,[24] of the sacraments[25] and of symbols of faith.[26] However, the crucial attempt to answer this aspect of nominalism is his doctrine of religious symbols in *Systematic Theology*, Volume 1.[27]

Sixthly, Tillich objects that, on the basis of nominalism, 'it is impossible to construct a rational psychology which proves the immortality of the soul, its pre- or post-existence, its omnipresence in the whole body, etc. If such things are affirmed, they are matters of faith, not of philosophical analysis' (*HCT* 201). In two seminal works, *The Courage to Be* and *The Dynamics of Faith*, Tillich was driven both to extend this criticism of nominalism and to develop his own theory of the ontological foundations of psychology. In the ontology of anxiety that he elaborates,[28] the anxiety of fate and death, emptiness and meaninglessness, and of guilt and condemnation are not individual psychological experiences but are embedded in the permanent structure of human experience. This highly controversial doctrine of the ontological basis of anxiety has had extensive influence on contemporary psychology, as the work of R. D. Laing, Rollo May and Erich Fromm attests.[29] This exemplifies how, in attempting to develop a comprehensive answer to nominalism, Tillich was able to make highly original contributions in some of the many fields that were included within the scope of his alternative world-view.

Seventhly, Tillich objects to the way nominalism tends to deprive religious and cultural symbols of their ultimate meaning by its radical restriction of the meaning of being to finite individual things. The ruthless application of 'Ockham's razor' (*pluritas non est ponenda sine necessitate*) leads to the denial of reality to universals and being-itself, except as words or abstractions. This effectively undermines the possibility of a bridge between the finite and the infinite, and leads to supranaturalism and the denial of natural theology.

However, Tillich's own Protestant principle comes close to a translation of Ockham's razor into a theological principle. As Tillich admits, there is a tension in his own theology between the Extra Calvinisticum (*finitum non capax infiniti*) and the Infra Lutheranum (which asserts that the finite *is* capable of the infinite), or between the critical prophetic protest represented by the Protestant Principle and the theology of mediation that discovers the religious substance in the forms of human culture (*TPT* 5; cf. *PE* xxvii–xxxi).

Paradoxically the emphasis on the Protestant Principle leads to an exaggeration of the distinction between the conditioned and the unconditioned, to depreciation of the empirical and finite in knowledge and elevation of the ideal and absolute. The more Tillich emphasises the Protestant principle, the more he moves away from the existential towards a formal and abstract ontology. The more he emphasises the participation of the finite in the infinite the more he moves towards a mystical realism, characteristically expressed in what he calls 'theology of culture'. There is a striking resemblance between Tillich's classic paper 'Ueber die Idee einer Theologie der Kultur' and Bonaventura's work *On Reducing the Arts to Theology*. Of the latter, Gilson says, in words that virtually summarise Tillich's theology of culture:

[T]he ultimate meaning of our arts and techniques, of our various sciences and of philosophy itself, is *to symbolise on a lower plane* the perfection of the divine art and of the divine knowledge. That is what they are, but, left to themselves they do not know it. It is the proper function of theology to bring them to a complete awareness of their proper function, which is not to know things but to know God through things. Hence the title of St Bonaventura's treatise; the human arts should be reduced to theology, and thereby to God.[30]

Thus Tillich's critique of nominalism commits him to the elaboration of a total alternative. His theology of culture is in effect the elaboration of a Christian *Weltanschauung* or philosophy of life. It has to be judged by his own criteria: is the object of its ultimate concern really the unconditional in being and meaning; and does it offer man ultimate fulfilment? However, it has to be judged by the philosophical criteria of adequacy, also: is it comprehensive, coherent and consistent? The main task of this work will be to consider if the Christian belief and value system that Tillich offers us satisfies these criteria.

3. *The significance of the critique of nominalism for Tillich's thought*

In discussing Tillich's critique of nominalism, we have tried to illustrate, firstly, the particular features of his theology of culture that are brought out in this confrontation, and secondly, the way in which his thought attempts to be systematic by being inclusive of all aspects of life. These serve, like his critique of supranaturalism, to illustrate that Tillich understood his task as philosopher and theologian to be to revolutionise the world-view of his contemporaries. Whether his Christian philosophy of life is called 'belief-ful realism', 'Religious Socialism', 'systematic theology', 'philosophy of religion' or 'theology of culture', it has the same purpose: the conversion of contemporary man, and the reorientation of his beliefs, attitudes and values. Both the critique and the elaboration of alternatives are more suggestive than convincing; they aim to persuade rather than to prove.

However, certain things emerge from these critiques that have profound consequences for his philosophical and theological method: a commitment to a realist ontology and a phenomenological investigation of the structures and dynamics of being; a commitment to a realist epistemology that emphasises the existential character of the act of knowing as a participation of the knower in the known; and a commitment to a realist logic, that is, a logic founded on the concept of intentionality. Each of these will be discussed in detail in the following chapters.

If we are to isolate a single issue that dominates Tillich's thought it must be the nominalist destruction of the ontological argument, and his conviction that the argument must be reinterpreted if an adequate philosophical theology is to be developed in the twentieth century.

Although implicit in his earliest works on Schelling, and mentioned in *Der Begriff des Übernatürlichen*, the first explicit discussion of the importance of the ontological argument occurs in 'Die Überwindung des Religionsbegriffs in der Religionsphilosophie' (*WR* 128–37), where he mentions the importance of Augustine's *Si fallor, sum* argument, and Descartes' reversal of the dependence of thought on being. Tillich sees Kant's criticism of the ontological argument as the last in a line that begins with the mediaeval nominalists and ends in the divorce of thought and being. This divorce must be overcome, if philosophy and theology are to be set on the right course, and in a key paper, he sets out his philosophical creed:

> The ontological approach to philosophy of religion as envisaged by Augustine and his followers, as reappearing in many forms in the history of thought, if critically re-interpreted by us, is able to do for our time what it did in the past, both for religion and culture: to overcome as far as it is possible by mere thought the fateful gap between religion and culture, thus reconciling concerns which are not strange to each other but have been estranged from each other. (*TC* 29)

The first step in the ontological approach involves the re-statement of the *Si fallor, sum* argument, which he paraphrases as follows: 'Man is immediately aware of something unconditional which is the *prius* of the separation and interaction of subject and object, theoretically as well as practically' (*TC* 22).

The second step involves the re-interpretation of the ontological argument as an argument from human experience that points to the necessity for an unconditioned ground of being and meaning if the relationship between thought and being is to be made intelligible:

> [T]he argument is not an argument for *a* highest being, but an analysis of human thought. As such the argument says: There must be a point at which the unconditional necessity of thinking and being are identical, otherwise there could be no certainty at all, not even the degree of certainty which every skeptic always presupposes. This

is the Augustinian argument that God is truth, and truth is the pre-supposition which even the skeptic acknowledges. (*HCT* 164–5)

The third step is to expand the concept of the ultimate or uncon-ditioned, which is the *prius* of the relationship of thought and being, to include, besides the true, the good and the beautiful. The analysis is thus interpreted not only to apply to the relationship of philosophy and reli-gion, but to embrace the whole of culture. The unconditioned of which we are immediately aware in the pre-reflexive intuition of being is the ground of all being and meaning: 'God is identical, then, with the experi-ence of the unconditional as true and beautiful and good. What the onto-logical argument really does is to analyse in human thought something unconditional which transcends subjectivity and objectivity' (*HCT* 164; cf. *ST1*, 228–9). The immediate intuition of the unconditioned as the ground of all being and meaning is the *conditio sine qua non* for the realisa-tion of truth, goodness and beauty. The philosophical and religious absolutes meet in the fundamental formula: *Deus est esse:* 'The *Deus est esse* is the basis of all philosophy of religion. It is the condition of a unity between thought and religion which overcomes their, so to speak, schizo-phrenic cleavages in personal and cultural life' (*TC* 22).

This argument, in its three stages, represents in outline what Tillich understands by ontological realism, that is, an ontology based on the principles of mystical realism.

Before we proceed to a critical discussion of Tillich's ontology, there are some general points of his argument that should be remarked: these are, his treatment of the Platonic ultimates of the good, the true and the beautiful; and his concern with the being of being-itself rather than with the being of finite beings.

We said earlier that Kant's transcendental method had revolutionised the approach to the Platonic ultimates, by asking the question concerning the metaphysical foundations of truth, goodness and beauty. In speaking of the nineteenth-century 'back to Kant' movement, that is, 'the Kant-Ritschl-Harnack line of thought that led to Troeltsch in Germany', Tillich remarks: 'You recall what we said about Kant's prison of finitude. Kant's critical epistemology determined that we cannot apply the categories of finitude to the divine. But, there was one point of break-through in the sphere of practical reason, namely, the experience of the moral imperative and its unconditional character. Here alone can we transcend the limits of finitude' (*P* 215).

Tillich was impressed by the way Schelling transcended the 'prison of finitude' in the direction of the ultimate in art, by building on Kant's *Critique of Judgement*. He saw, in Hegel's *Phenomenology of Spirit and Logic*, how the *Critique of Pure Reason* could be used to transcend the prison of finitude in the direction of an unconditioned truth in which rational and real are one. Tillich commends Troeltsch for being the first to develop the philosophical implications of this analysis:

I will speak first of Troeltsch as a philosopher of religion. His main problem dealt with the meaning of religion in the context of the human spirit or man's mental structure. Here Troeltsch followed Kant by accepting his three Critiques, but he said that there is not only the theoretical *a priori*, man's categorical [sic] structure, as Kant developed it in the *Critique of Pure Reason*, not only the moral, as Kant developed it in the *Critique of Practical Reason*, not only the aesthetic as he developed it in the *Critique of Judgement*, but there is also a religious *a priori*. (*P* 231)

Essentially, Tillich's concern with ontological realism stems from the problems set by Kant and the example of the idealist philosophers in showing how Kant's prison of finitude might be transcended. However, he rejects the idealist implication that Kant's prison of finitude can be transcended in reality as in thought. He seeks to do justice to the realistic element in Kant's doctrine of finitude, and, in his phenomenological method, follows closely the model suggested by Troeltsch: namely, a structural analysis of cognitive, moral and aesthetic experience that manifests the unconditional principles that underlie each, and that points to the unconditioned in being and meaning as their import. Tillich realises that such a phenomenological method must lead to pure formalism unless it is based on faith that the ultimate form in which the good, the true and the beautiful are realised is being-itself, or God.[31] This faith in God as Being-itself is what prevents the good, the true and the beautiful from becoming mere abstractions; it guarantees their import and gives them an ultimate reference. It is for this reason that Tillich disagrees with Troeltsch about the possibility of a religious *a priori*, for he argues that the religious foundation of all cultural forms is not another cultural function alongside the epistemological, the aesthetic and the moral, but is rather the ground of their possible meaning and truth.

The immediate effect of Tillich's subordination of the cosmological approach to the ontological approach is the denial of validity to natural theology insofar as this suggests that it is possible for unaided human reason to prove the existence of God. The burden of Tillich's argument is that the cosmological type of argument as *demonstrationes ex finito*, remains within the finite and cannot reach the infinite. However, he argues that it also has the effect of disrupting the relation between knower and known, because the immediacy of the knowing relation is replaced by mediate causal inferences. The conclusion is that cosmological arguments, in both theology and philosophy, lead to destructive scepticism with respect to knowledge of being-itself or of things-in-themselves. The only alternative, in Tillich's view, is to reinterpret the cosmological approach within the ontological principles that are actually implied in it but not normally recognised. 'If this basis is given, the cosmological principle can be stated in the following way: The Unconditioned of which we have an immediate awareness without inference, can be recognised in the cultural and natural universe' (*TC* 26).

Since the cosmological approach underlies the attitude to reality that derives ultimately from the Greeks and is expressed in the modern scientific-technical world-view, what Tillich proposes is a revolutionary change in our view of things: an entirely different paradigm of being. In the Greek tradition, being is identified with substance. Tillich is concerned with the Biblical 'I am' of personal being rather than with the 'is' of substantial being. According to the cosmological approach, the ultimate in being is the first cause, prime substance or cosmic purpose: a nature or object to which we are externally related by causal and teleological principles. The ontological approach, following both the Biblical view of God as the 'I am that am' and the absolute subject of idealism, emphasises that *Deus est esse* as self-affirming, self-communicating, personal being is experienced immediately as the presupposition and ultimate import of our own being.

The consequence of this approach for Tillich's thought is that the ontological questions concerning the nature and existence of God, which are a matter of doubt and uncertainty in theologies based on the cosmological approach, are objects of immediate certainty to him, as they were to the mediaeval Franciscans. (These are the doctrines which belong to the eternal truth, such as the immediate awareness of God as *esse ipsum*, *ipsum verum* and *bonum ipsum*.) By contrast, the more obviously theological issues, such as the traditional doctrines of the Trinity, Salvation, and the Kingdom, which are, for the supranaturalist, the subjects of an incorrigibly certain revelation, are issues that are secondary and contingent for Tillich, as they were for Franciscans such as Alexander of Hales (*TC* 17). The freedom with which Tillich questions traditional dogmas, for example, the Christological dogmas and the doctrine of the Church, is based on his profound and unshakeable faith in God as the power of being in which every being participates, and the conviction that particular institutions, symbols and dogmas are simply the particular historical and concrete expressions of man's relation to being-itself as the unconditioned ground of all being and meaning.

Tillich's realist epistemology is based on the assertion of the fundamental reality of being-itself as the ground of all possible knowledge. However, a fundamental problem of Tillich's thought concerns the relation of the reality and intelligibility of finite beings to the immediate reality and intelligibility of being-itself.

Another effect of Tillich's subordination of the cosmological approach to the ontological approach is an ontology that approaches being from the standpoint of being-itself rather than from an analysis of the structures and dynamics of finite being. In spite of his professed attempt to do justice to the structures of finitude, Tillich tends to be concerned with the structures and dynamics of being in general and does not do justice, at the level of explicit epistemological theory, to the relationship between our knowledge of unconditioned and of conditioned being.

In addressing himself to the divorce between the finite and the infinite and to the hiatus between subject and object that we find in nominalism and supranaturalism. Tillich insists that we cannot proceed from an analysis of the being of beings to the being of being-itself. According to his view, we have to begin with being-itself as the power of being:

The power of being is the *prius* of everything that has being. It precedes every separation and makes every interaction possible, because
it is the point of identity without which neither separation nor interaction can be thought. This refers basically to the separation and
interaction of subject and object, in knowing as well as acting. The
prius of subject and object cannot become an object to which man
as subject is theoretically and practically related. God is no object
for us as subjects. He is always that which precedes this division.
(*TC* 25)

This may help to demonstrate that the nature of being-itself is logically
peculiar. However, it does not explain in what sense finite subjects and
objects are real, or how the immediate certainty of being-itself bears on
our knowledge of finite real things.

Tillich hesitates to say that we can know the natures of finite things
immediately, as epistemological realism and the intentional logic of
Scotus and John of St Thomas maintain. He is influenced by Kant's
scepticism about knowledge of things-in-themselves, and seeks to ground
his realist epistemology and logic on an argument that supposedly demonstrates the possibility of belief-ful realism in epistemology and logic in
general. Both in his metaphysics of truth and in his metaphysics of logic
there is an area of considerable vagueness about the relationship between
particular truths and truth in general: between the structural intentionality of the self-world relationship and the intentionality of particular propositions. In general, Tillich felt that the main task he faced was to attack
the metaphysical foundations of nominalism and to demonstrate the
possibility of a realist metaphysic of meaning, truth and logic. In the
details of his semiotic theory, epistemology and logic, his thought is unclear and often confused, but many valuable insights occur along the way,
including the outlines of theories that deserve critical examination.

Tillich's approach to nominalism was based on criticism of the most
general kind. This is in keeping with his overall apologetic purpose: to
undermine its credibility and to recommend an alternative world-view.
He intuitively recognised that, as Bertrand Russell once remarked, philosophies are superseded rather than refuted. They die of neglect and abuse
rather than yield to criticism. His strategy for conducting philosophical
criticism is to build up a picture of the position to be attacked that may
well involve over-simplification, exaggeration and even caricature. He
does not discuss theories in detail, and seldom quotes the authors he
attacks directly. He paraphrases his opponent's argument, and sets it in
the context of a discussion relating to his own general line of thought,
rather than criticising the opposing argument on its own terms. As we
said in the Introduction, Tillich is to be judged as a pedagogue and
preacher rather than as a philosopher, and as a philosophically minded
rhetorician rather than as a theoretical dialectician. His own exposition
is all-important. The rest is grist to his mill.

In general, Tillich's arguments are lacking in the tentativeness and
analytic caution that we associate with philosophers when they get down

to the discussion of specific theories and problems within the defined boundaries of an established and accepted *Weltanschauung*. There is a striking similarity between his style and that of a political journalist or a philosopher campaigning for a new point-of-view, when either is involved with an opponent of a different philosophical persuasion. The style appropriate at the campaigning stage is different from that required when a theory has become settled and orthodox. Arguments for and against a new theory are never as dispassionate or objective as arguments conducted on the basis of accepted theory. For Tillich, the issue of man's commitment, of his choice of ultimate concern, is never a matter of indifference. We may well ask whether adequate attention has been paid in philosophy and theology to the difference between the situation where a man's faith is at stake, where his ultimate presuppositions are called in question, and the situation where it is possible to dispute dispassionately about the content or form of particular beliefs.

Part Two

METAPHYSICS OF MEANING, TRUTH AND LOGIC

Chapter 4

The Metaphysics of Meaning: A Theonomous Science of the Norms of Meaning

1. Reasons for beginning with Tillich's metaphysics of meaning

We begin our exposition of Tillich's thought with his metaphysics of meaning for an obvious reason; he himself insists on its central importance. His early book *Das System der Wissenschaften*: expresses his fundamental ideas on the possibility of theology as a science, and attempts to clarify the logical relations between theology and other sciences 'by classifying all of the methodological disciplines as sciences of thinking, being, and culture; by maintaining that *the foundation of the whole system of the sciences is the philosophy of meaning* (*Sinnphilosophie*); by defining metaphysics as the attempt to express the Unconditioned in terms of rational symbols, and by defining theology as theonomous metaphysics' (*OB* 55; italics added).

Secondly, Tillich belonged to a generation of philosophers and theologians in Germany who saw questions of meaning as central to both disciplines. Michael Dummett has credited Frege with effecting a shift in philosophical perspectives comparable to that initiated by Descartes: for Descartes, epistemology is central to philosophy, whereas for Frege the theory of meaning takes this place.[1] It might be possible to claim a similar distinction for Tillich in theology were it not that both he and Frege were part of a general revolution in thought that took place in the early decades of this century. They made major contributions to the revolutions in theology and philosophy, but both were undoubtedly influenced by the prevailing tendency to turn from epistemology to the philosophy of meaning for the solution of fundamental questions. This tendency could be said to begin with the attempt of the idealists to classify the constitutive and regulative principles of every universe of discourse, following the example of Kant's three great *Critiques* dealing with the theoretical, moral and aesthetic spheres. Roughly speaking, Hegel concentrates on the first sphere. Fichte on the second and Schelling on the third; however, each was concerned to explore the other spheres of culture also. This concern with *Sinnphilosophie* was characteristic not only of Frege, Carnap and Wittgenstein, but also of an earlier generation of philosophers such as Dilthey, Brentano, Husserl, Windelband and Hartmann. It was also a fundamental theme in the theological writings of Ritschl, Troeltsch and, more recently, Barth and Brunner.[2]

Tillich notes that the philosophy of Kant provokes philosophers to consideration of the 'correspondence between reality and the human spirit which is probably expressed most adequately in the concept of "meaning"'. Hegel's thought also can be interpreted as concerned in a fundamental way with meaning: '*When idealism elaborates the categories that give meaning* to the various realms of existence, it seeks to *fulfill that task which alone is the justification for philosophy*' (*OB* 82–3). Tillich is obviously in sympathy with this view.

There is a third reason for beginning with Tillich's metaphysics of meaning rather than his metaphysics of truth or logic, and this relates to our general thesis that Tillich is an ideological thinker: he is concerned most fundamentally with what he has graphically called man's 'anxiety of meaninglessness';[3] with his need for a meaningful *Weltanschauung* by which to live. Referring to the critical period between 1919 and 1924, when he taught in Berlin, Tillich speaks of his theology of culture as a response to the oppressive sense of meaninglessness that dominated the period:

> The situation during these years in Berlin was very favourable for such an enterprise. The political problems determined our whole existence; even after revolution and inflation they were matters of life and death. The social structure was in a state of dissolution, the human relations with respect to authority, education, family, sex, friendship and pleasure were in a creative chaos. Revolutionary art came into the foreground, supported by the Republic, attacked by the majority of people. Psychoanalytic ideas spread and produced a consciousness of realities which had been carefully repressed in previous generations. The participation in these movements created manifold problems, conflicts, fears, expectations, ecstacies and despairs, practically as well as theoretically. All this was at the same time material for an apologetic theology. (*TPT* 13–14)

Tillich, in other words, sought to develop a practical belief and value system – what he alternately calls a 'philosophy of meaning' and a 'theology of culture' – that might serve as an answer to the anxiety of meaninglessness expressed by his contemporaries.

In general, the influence of socialism on Tillich's thinking antedates the influence of existentialism. This may well be because in 1919 he and his contemporaries were preoccupied more than anything else with politics, and that as a matter of life and death. During the period from 1919 to 1925, he was constantly engaged with the question of socialism, not merely as a political movement but also as an ideology.[4] With the rise of National Socialism it became more urgent to clarify the philosophical and theological foundations of Religious Socialism. In 1933, *Die sozialistische Entscheidung* marked the parting of the ways for the two movements, and resulted in the dismissal of Tillich from his professorial chair at Frankfurt and his forced emigration from Germany. This work is not a political tract but a serious attempt at an intellectual critique of the Nazi and Communist versions of socialism. Tillich's metaphysics of meaning is thus not a merely abstract philosophical theory, but an integral part of a coherent philosophy of life.

In the early stages of the development of his theory, the influence of existentialism was limited, but he mentions the early influence of Kierkegaard's critique of Hegel, and the importance of the analysis of anxiety and despair in making him adopt a more critical attitude towards idealism. He also mentions Nietzsche's affirmation of life and his critique of the life-denying character of the moralistic and religious attitudes of bourgeois culture. However, it was not until his brief stay as professor of theology at Marburg in 1924 and 1925 that he was confronted by the challenge of modern existentialism in the person of Heidegger. He was slow to assimilate the specific doctrines of existentialism (see *TPT* 14).

He speaks of the influence of Kierkegaard and Marx in making him aware that idealism is an ideology. To Marx he attributes the insight that idealism, or the philosophy of essence, obscures the contradictions between social classes and veils the ambiguities within social reality. To Kierkegaard he attributes the insight that the philosophy of essence conceals the ambiguities within individual existence and ignores the tragic dimensions of alienation. He attributes to both a new definition of truth: 'A new definition of truth follows from the repudiation of the closed system of essentialism. Truth is bound to the situation of the knower: to the situation of the individual for Kierkegaard, and to that of society for Marx. Knowledge of pure essence is possible only to the degree in which the contradictions within existence have been recognised and overcome' (*OB* 85). The paradoxical insight, which is fundamental to Tillich's philosophy of meaning, is that which is achieved when we are liberated from ideological illusion by being placed in the boundary situation of anxiety and despair: 'the highest possibility for achieving non-ideological truth is given at the point of profoundest meaninglessness' (*OB* 86). Existentially relevant truth about being and meaning is revealed when man in such a situation is grasped by ultimate concern.

By commencing our exposition of Tillich's thought with his metaphysics of meaning we not only wish to emphasise its centrality and importance in his philosophy and theology, but also wish to stress its particular character and thus to illustrate our general thesis. As James Luther Adams has observed: 'Tillich was confronted with the necessity of coming to terms with the intellectual struggle of his generation for a new *Weltanschauung*'.[5] This struggle was partially related to what Nietzsche called 'the crisis of science' and, because of the crisis of confidence in philosophic and scientific rationality, what was required was something with a more intuitive appeal, that is, a new world-view. 'A philosophical treatment of history and culture was therefore required as a supplement to or perhaps even as a substitute for the earlier philosophical treatment of natural science.'[6] Tillich's theology of culture purports both to give an account of the metaphysical foundations of meaning in general and to offer a new *Weltanschauung*.

2. *The general features of Tillich's metaphysics of meaning*

Tillich made his debut at the Kant Society in Berlin in 1919 with his paper 'Über die Idee einer Theologie der Kultur'. Using the concept of 'standpoint' (*Stellung*), he contrasts the methodological approaches of the empirical sciences and the systematic cultural sciences. 'In the empirical sciences one's standpoint is something that must be overcome. Reality is the criterion by which what is right is measured, and reality is one and the same. As between two contradictory standpoints, only one can be right, or both can be wrong. The progress of scientific experience must decide between them' (*WR* 155). However,

> The situation is different in the systematic cultural sciences; *here the standpoint of the systematic thinker belongs to the heart of the matter itself*. It is a moment in the history of the development of culture; it is a concrete historical realisation of an idea of culture; it not only perceives but also creates culture. Here the alternative 'right or wrong' loses its validity, for there is no limit to the number of attitudes which the spirit can adopt toward reality. (*WR* 155–6)

He understates his case, for he assumes that universal agreement is possible in science. The possibility of irresoluble theoretical disagreements, for example, between particle and wave theories of the nature of matter, does not occur to him. At this point, he is more concerned to question the universal applicability of objective scientific methods based on measurement. By the time he wrote *Das System der Wissenschaften nach Gegenständen und Methoden* he had come to realise that even the empirical sciences are creative forms of human self-expression, embodying different methodological standpoints and different human perspectives on the world; that they too are cultural forms that require interpretation within a comprehensive metaphysics of meaning.

However, in this early paper he is at pains to point out that, in the systematic cultural sciences (*Geisteswissenschaften*), an existential standpoint is a *conditio sine qua non* of the existence of these value-based sciences. Values are the expression of human decisions and commitment, thus however we abstract and generalise they are related to the existential standpoints of individuals: 'Every universal concept in cultural science is either useless or a normative concept in disguise' (*WR* 156). Insofar as the cultural sciences attempt universal descriptions, they fail to do justice to the concrete situation of commitment from which values acquire what public relevance and significance they have. The commitment of the individual, if it is not a matter of arbitrariness, is always related to his commitment to a group.

> A standpoint is expressed by an individual; but if it is more than individual arbitrariness, if it is a creative act, it is also, to a greater or lesser degree, a creative act of the circle in which the individual moves. This circle, with its peculiar spiritual quality, has no existence apart from the cultural groups that surround it and the creative acts of the past on which it rests. Thus, in the same way even the most individual

standpoint is firmly embedded in the ground of the objective spirit, the mother soil from which every cultural creation springs. From this soil the concrete standpoint derives the universal forms of spirit. (*WR* 156)

In order to grasp this existential dimension in the normative cultural sciences, what is necessary is an approach that Tillich describes as 'meta-logical'. This approach transcends the formal-logical method of analysis of universal thought forms, and the empirical method of investigating particular beings, and demands a recognition of the reality of spirit as essentially creative of meaning.

It is not possible to grasp the essence of spirit without grasping meta-logically the two basic elements of knowledge (thought and being) . . . In the logical analysis of thought the being-element is usually neglected while psychological analysis neglects the thought-element. Both neglect the tension of these elements. However, spirit is not a thought-form just as it is not a type of being. In spite of its dependence upon both, spirit is a separate and particular form. Spirit is the form of thought in the existential mode. (*Geist ist des seiendes Denkens*) (*DSW* 210)

James Luther Adams has given an admirable paraphrase of Tillich's discussion of spirit in this context:

Spirit is, in short, *creative in the realm of meaning.* Although spirit is not divorced from the realm of causality, it is characteristically oriented to the realm of meaning; where individuality *expresses itself by living in and beyond reality*, by accommodating itself to the realm of being but by also *giving to being a novel expression* . . . Every spiritual act is, therefore, an individual meaningful act fusing thought and being. It is an individual meaning-fulfilling act.[7]

It is not surprising that Tillich, seeking to give concrete cultural examples of what he means by spirit, begins with art, and Expressionism in particular. Art, as we shall see when we consider the specific application of his theory of meaning to signs and symbols, is a paradigm for the self-expression of spirit in Tillich's thought. Having developed his general analysis of the way meaning is created, expressed and fulfilled in art, he then applies this *mutatis mutandis* to philosophy, ethics and politics. He notes that the fundamental categories of his philosophy of religion and culture were developed out of reflection on art, and remarks how Expressionism made him aware that 'the substance of a work of art could destroy form' and give expression to a 'creative ecstacy' in which new dimensions of being are revealed to consciousness. 'The concept of "breakthrough", which dominates my theory of revelation, is an example of the use of this insight' (*OB* 28). Because of the importance of art as a paradigm of Spirit as meaning-creating and directed towards the fulfilment of meaning in the disclosure of the transcendent and unconditional, it is worth quoting at length his earliest, and in some ways definitive, discussion of Expressionism:

To start with, it is clear that in Expressionism content has to a very great extent lost its significance, namely content in the sense of the external factuality of objects and events. Nature has been robbed of her external appearance; her uttermost depth is visible. But, according to Schelling, *horror dwells in the depths of every living creature*; and this horror seizes us from the work of the Expressionist painters, who *aim at more than the mere destruction of form in favour of the fullest, most vital and flourishing life within*, as Simmel thinks. In their work a *form-shattering religious import is struggling to find form*, a paradox that most people find incomprehensible and annoying; and *this horror seems to me to be defined by a feeling of guilt*, not in the properly ethical sense, but rather in *the cosmic sense of the guilt of sheer existence. Redemption*, however, is the transition of one individual existence into the other, the wiping out of individual distinction *the mysticism of love achieving union with all living things.* (*WR* 169; italics added)

The reference to Schelling is significant, for Tillich was undoubtedly influenced by Schelling's elevated view of art as a medium for the revelation of ultimate truth. In his *System of Transcendental Idealism*, Schelling expresses a new conception of philosophy modelled on art and aesthetic intuition: 'The objective world is only the original, still unconscious poetry of the Spirit: *the universal organon of philosophy* – and the keystone of the whole arch – is the *philosophy of art*'.[8] Schelling asks what it is in a work of art that gives a feeling of infinite satisfaction; why it is that, with the completion of the product, the creative impulse is satisfied and there is an assurance that all contradictions are reconciled and all riddles solved. It is because 'beauty exists where the particular [the real] is so in accord with its idea that this idea itself, as infinite, enters into the finite and is intuited *in concreto*'.[9]

The difference between Schelling and Tillich, however, is that Schelling tends to subordinate theology to the philosophy of art, whereas in Tillich's case art is put to use in the service of theology; the philosophies of art, history, ethics and politics are subject to the overall categories of his theology of culture. For example, the concept of a standpoint is translated into faith as ultimate concern, the circle of commitment becomes the theological circle from within which the theologian must develop his theonomous systematic of culture, and the concept of breakthrough illuminates the concepts of revelation, miracle and ecstacy (*ST1*, 14f., 12, 124–31).

In developing his theonomous systematic of culture, Tillich clarified his ideas in constant dialogue with Ernst Troeltsch. During his early years as a *privatdozent* of theology in the University of Berlin, he was impressed by the example of Troeltsch in seeking a general systematic of culture. As we have seen, Tillich accepts Kant's analysis of the categories as categories of finitude as of decisive importance for our understanding both of the limitations of man's theoretical knowledge and of the finite and contingent nature of human being. As we have also seen, Tillich credits Troeltsch with having grasped the systematic implications of

Kant's suggestion that the way out of this prison of finitude is revealed in moral experience, because in it something unconditional breaks into the realm of temporal and causal existence. Troeltsch develops this insight by suggesting that there is a theoretical *a priori*, a moral *a priori*, an aesthetic *a priori* and a religious *a priori*, that in each of these spheres reveals itself as the unconditioned and unconditional ground of meaning.[10]

Tillich was also impressed by Troeltsch's analysis of the world-historical significance of Protestantism, and this suggested to him the possibility of a distinctively Protestant *Weltanschauung* (see *P* 230-4). However, he did not hesitate to disagree with the general presupposition of his 'ethics of cultural values'. Troeltsch had used Kant's *Groundwork to the Metaphysics of Morals* as a model for his systematic of culture. Tillich objected that this made religion and the religious *a priori* merely another cultural function alongside the theoretical, aesthetic and moral. This relativises religion by contradicting its claim to reveal the unconditioned in a way that is definitive for other points of view.[11] He also argued that if theology is subordinated to a general ethics of cultural values then theology must in turn be subordinated to theological ethics. He concludes that what is required is not an ethics of cultural values, but a theology of culture or a 'theonomous metaphysics of meaning': 'What was essentially intended in the theological system of ethics can only be realised by means of a theology of culture applying not only to ethics but all the functions of culture. Not a theological system of ethics but a theology of culture' (*WR* 160). He agrees with Troeltsch that an adequate systematic of culture must involve three related aspects: a philosophy of culture that is concerned with the *a priori* and universal forms of all culture; a history of cultural values that examines the abundant variety of concretisations of cultural values; and a normative science of culture, based on a concrete individual standpoint that has been given systematic form.[12]

Tillich believes that only theology, as the concrete and normative science of religion, can provide the basis for an adequate metaphysics of meaning: firstly, because 'religion is directedness towards the Unconditional' and as such is concerned with the ultimate substance or import of all meaning; secondly, because the specific commitment involved in a concrete religious standpoint demands a systematic expression that only theology can give.

In 'Religionsphilosophie', he describes philosophy as 'the science of the functions of meaning and their categories', embracing metaphysics, science and aesthetics, which together comprise the theoretical and 'world-embracing' functions of meaning. Metaphysics involves a scientific and aesthetic element, but stands over against them in that it is directed not to conditioned forms but toward the unconditional itself. It is an attempt to express the unconditioned in rational and symbolic terms. 'Metaphysics functions not as a science, but as a spiritual attitude influencing science' (*WR* 35-6).

However, the scientific function also is meaning-creating, and implicitly directed towards the fulfilment of meaning insofar as it is governed by the aim to achieve universal and unconditional validity. 'In relation to the functions of meaning, the knowing process is always receptive as well as productive. It is determined by the independent, creative process of every sphere of meaning. It is, however, at the same time determinative for that process. The act of knowing in the cultural sciences stands over against its object not merely objectively, but in the process of knowing the object itself is affected' (*WR* 30). The theory of intentionality implicit in the account is of decisive importance not only for Tillich's metaphysics of meaning, but also for his metaphysics of truth and logic. Since all these theoretical functions are concerned with the meaning-creating functions of spirit and the relation of these to the unconditional import of meaning that is their ultimate fulfilment, their interpretation demands a theonomous metaphysics of meaning. This will be the task of a systematic that includes: a philosophy of religion that explicates the religious function of meaning and its categories; a cultural history of religion that gives a general account of the symbols and myths in which the unconditioned has been historically expressed; and a normative theology of culture, based on a specific religious commitment.

The philosophy of religion faces a double demand: 'It must abstract the formative principles from the reality that is informed by meaning. And it must bring the principles of meaning into a unified and necessary relationship' (*WR* 41). For this task it requires a method that is both critical and dialectical. This method 'presupposes the autonomy of the spiritual over against every immediately given existing thing'. However, he insists that the method does not commit him to either epistemological idealism or naive realism. It need not assume that spirit gives laws to nature or *vice versa*. 'It must assume that the principles of meaning to which consciousness submits itself in the spiritual act are at the same time the principles of meaning to which being is subjected. It must assume that the meaning of being comes to expression in the consciousness informed by meaning' (*WR* 42). What is required is that this critico-dialectical method should be modified by an approach that is intuitive and dynamic, by which he means one that does justice to the concrete standpoint. Such an approach would, in his terms, be meta-logical: 'It is *logical* in the sense that the orientation to pure rational forms, involved in the critical method, is retained. It is *meta* logical because it goes beyond pure formalism in a double sense, on the one hand in that it apprehends the import inhering in the forms, on the other in that it sets up norms in an individual-creative way' (*WR* 50).

What meta-logic investigates is the dynamic interrelation of thought and being, or the actual existential engagement of subject and object in a given spiritual act. Tillich thus tries to meet Kierkegaard's objection to Hegel's systematic that 'The systematic Idea is the identity of subject and object, the unity of thought and being. Existence, on the other hand, is their separation'.[13]

Tillich's first move is to insist that the unconditioned is not only the

ground but also the abyss of all meaning. Under the conditions of existence man grasps the truth *and* its contradiction. Not only is knowledge
imperfect but man is estranged from his essential being and he experiences
the systematic Idea ambiguously. Tillich attributes to Hegel the recognition that contradiction and ambiguity are intrinsic to existence in its
attempt to grasp the unity of thought and being (*IH* 167–8). While 'The
employment of ambiguity as a principle of historical dialectics is an
achievement of decisive importance', he admits that Hegel failed to apply
this principle to his own synthesis of syntheses: he attempted to eliminate
all contradiction and ambiguity. Tillich's systematic theology, on the
other hand, is an attempt to express the structure of the essential in such
a way that 'the ambiguity of every solution becomes visible in the solution
itself'.

Secondly, by speaking of the identity of subject and object, or the unity
of thought and being as achieved in the individual spiritual act, Tillich is
able to describe the relationship as one of both 'identity and tension.
Because the spiritual act essentially intends its fulfilment, its essential
form is to express this intended identity. Because the individual spiritual
act is also an act of existence, it experiences the relation between subject
and object, and thought and being, in terms of tension and even incom-
mensurability or estrangement.[14] The inadequacy of a naive realist theory
of knowledge is that it comprehends the spiritual act only as a meaning-
receiving act; while the idealist theory of knowledge comprehends it only
as a meaning-bestowing act. In terms of the meta-logical method, he
wishes to speak of the spiritual act as meaning-receiving, meaning-
bestowing and meaning-fulfilling. The ultimate intended fulfilment of
meaning becomes the norm by which the limits of either the naive realist
or idealist approach is judged since, 'Every spiritual act is an act of meaning . . . spirit is always [the medium for] the actualisation of meaning
[Sinnvollzug], and the thing intended by the spirit is a systematic interconnection of meaning' (*WR* 56). Hence the task of a meta-logical
account of meaning is to give an analysis of the principles of meaning
and a theory of the elements of meaning. But to attempt to explain the
meaning of meaning is paradoxical and may lead to an infinite regress.
Instead, one must try to develop metalogically an account of the elements
contained in every concrete actualisation of meaning.

There are three elements in any awareness of meaning. First, an
awareness of the interconnection of meaning in which every separate
meaning stands and without which it would be meaningless. Second,
an awareness of the ultimate meaningfulness of the interconnection
of meaning and, through that, of every particular meaning, i.e. the
consciousness of an unconditioned meaning which is present in every
particular meaning. Third, an awareness of the demand under which
every particular meaning stands, the demand to fulfill the unconditioned meaning. (*WR* 57)

With this account of Tillich's three meta-logical criteria of meaning we
effectively complete the outline of his metaphysics of meaning. His theory

of meaning, as we have stressed throughout, is developed with a double purpose: to meet the intellectual demand for a coherent theory, and to meet the demand for a new *Weltanschauung*. Tillich interprets his remit in such a way that the two demands become one. The intellectual demand is to be satisfied by the vision of a unified theory of meaning, that is, an essentially ideological world-view rather than a discursive semantic theory. The demand for an approach that is existentially relevant is to be met by the religious character of his theonomous metaphysics of meaning. The unconditioned ground of all being and meaning is the proper object of man's ultimate concern.

3. *Tillich's metaphysics of meaning*

The limitations of Tillich's metaphysics of meaning are partly the limitations of the metaphysics and partly those of the theory of meaning that he inherits from Kant. However, there are also difficulties with the apparatus of categories and distinctions inherited from Fichte, Schelling and Hegel.

As we have seen, Tillich enthusiastically adapts Kant's transcendental method to his purposes. He follows Troeltsch in seeing it as a means of clarifying the constitutive and regulative principles of meaning in different universes of discourse. However, he is also anxious to avoid the charge of formalism that the application of the transcendental method tended to provoke. His way round this is to suggest, in a manner reminiscent of Wittgenstein, that Kant's analysis of form, while not committing him to *saying* what being is, can nevertheless be interpreted as a way of *showing* or exhibiting the essential structures of being. The principles that are constitutive of a universe of discourse cannot simply be assumed to be constitutive of reality, but may be taken as indicating the essential structures of being, that is, as the intended substance or import of meaning. This position is well summarised by Guyton Hammond:

> The 'finitude of reason' means to Tillich that reason cannot rise to knowledge of being-itself, that it cannot establish the existence of God through rational proof. Here he does in fact agree with Kant, but Tillich departs from the explicit position of Kant in maintaining . . . that *an essential ontology of finitude is possible*. Tillich follows Martin Heidegger's interpretation of *Kant's philosophy as at least implicitly containing the attempt to formulate an ontology of the structures of finitude as experienced by man himself*.[15]

An objection to the transcendental method of clarifying questions of meaning, which applies to Kant as it does to Tillich, is that it treats each universe of discourse as complete in itself and capable of being analysed from above, as we might analyse the formation and transformation rules of an axiomatic system. One may wonder to what extent different universes of discourse are actually separable from one another and, more particularly, whether it is not necessary to begin with the meaning of words and sentences in ordinary language before considering the metaphysically loaded question of the principles presupposed in and necessary to the formulation of ethics or aesthetics. Characteristically, Tillich's theory of intentionality is concerned not with explaining how ordinary words mean but with the relationship between thought, being and the spiritual act. It may provide an interesting vision of the unity of all things in being-itself, but it does not provide us with criteria for determining the meaning or truth of particular words or utterances. In general, Tillich uses the fact that he has given a transcendental metaphysical account of meaning as an excuse for not dealing specifically with theological semantics. What he has to say about the need for 'semantic rationality' (*ST1*, 61–2, 136–9) confirms this: a theonomous metaphysics of meaning is enough, empirical linguistics and formal semantics do not interest him.

Tillich's treatment of ambiguity is open to many objections, from the charge of equivocation to that of cosmic pessimism. On the one hand, he is vague about what he understands by a term or a symbol's being ambiguous. He uses 'ambiguity' to express the vague sense of dissatisfaction felt by man at the incompleteness of his knowledge. This comment is less illuminating than it might be if he distinguished semantic, rational and metaphysical senses of ambiguity. On the other hand, he links ambiguity to the state of human estrangement. He comes so close to identifying finitude with the state of estrangement (*ST2*, chapter xv) that, apart from the pessimism about human nature that this entails, it does not explain what he means by ambiguity; for by contrast with what do we know that something is ambiguous? To suggest that only a theological answer is possible either devalues the experience of ambiguity as an existential state, or devalues theology by making it a kind of semantic panacea.

There is a sense, too, in which Tillich uses the transcendental method as a technique of 'one-up-manship'. When challenged to defend his theory of meaning, he does not come down to earth and explain the intentional relations of sign-user, sign and thing signified; he goes 'one-up' and suggests a higher-order level of analysis. For example, in relation to ethics we have, first, the philosophy of ethics, the history of ethics, and the normative science of ethics. These are comprehended within the systematic of culture in general: the philosophy of culture, the history of culture and the normative science of cultural values. This, in turn, is comprehended within the science of the functions of meaning in general and the religious functions of meaning in particular: the philosophy of religion, the history of religion, and theology as the theonomous metaphysics of meaning. Finally, these subordinate levels are brought under the systematic of meta-logic that considers the relations of thought, being and the spiritual act.

It may be objected that it is unfair to apply this criticism to Tillich's work, since he drops many of these distinctions in his later work. This is only partly true. He jettisons many of the unnecessary dialectical distinctions, but he retains the dialectical method, and the heart of the theory underlies his definitions of philosophy and theology in the *Systematic Theology*; besides, he never abandons the tendency to analyse everything into dialectical triads (see, e.g. *ST1*, 21–32).

More serious is the danger implied in reading off ontological conclusions from the distinctions derived from transcendental analysis. Tillich criticises idealists for seeking to deduce ontological conclusions from the *a priori* logical forms of reason, but he does not recognise the same danger in his interpretation of the Ontological argument as a 'rational description of the relation of our mind to Being as such', or in his argument from the logical demand for an unconditional validity of truth to the existence of that which is unconditioned in being and meaning. The fact is that Tillich does reify the logical fictions of his dialectic and attributes to them a quality of being superior to the being of ordinary finite things. The logical beings of reason become normative for the categorisation and evaluation of finite being. Although Tillich tries valiantly to reinvest being-itself with its primitive realistic ontological meaning, he is drawn by the inner logic of his own dialectic towards ontologism, that is, towards an idealistic doctrine of being based on the categories of an idealist logic. In general, Tillich hesitates to admit fullness of being to finite beings, because he wishes to reserve the perfections of being to God or being-itself, and because finite being is characterised by estrangement: essence and existence are separated under the conditions of existence. Thus logical and theological considerations combine to reinforce the tendency to ontologism.

A typical example of this tendency is the way he exploits the systematic ambiguity of the term *Unbedingt* in the key phrase *das Unbedingt seiendes*. The noun form is used as cognate with 'the unconditioned', 'the ultimate', 'the absolute' and, 'the infinite'. The adjectival form *unbedingte* is used as a synonym for 'unconditional', 'necessary' and 'imperative'. Just as 'must' in English can be used as equivalent to 'is logically necessary', 'is ultimately necessary' and 'is morally necessary', so Tillich uses the German term *unbedingte* with the same range of connotations. For example, it is impossible to understand how he gets from the notion of the unconditioned as the ground and abyss of meaning to his description of the three related elements in the structure of meaning, unless we understand how he exploits these ambiguities in the term *unbedingte*. The three elements that he describes as necessary in the structure of meaning are: universal interconnection – the logically necessary; ultimate meaningfulness – the metaphysically necessary, and necessary fulfilment of meaning – the unconditional moral demand (see *WR* 57).

In combining the logical, metaphysical and moral connotations of the term *unbedingte*, Tillich is only following the example of Kant who exploits the ambiguity of the term, in the *Groundwork to the Metaphysics of Morals*, by implying the logically necessary and metaphysically founded character of the unconditioned imperative. This may make Tillich's usage respectable but it doesn't make it right or provide the ultimate legitimation for his theory of meaning that he hopes it will. It is a favourite device of Tillich's, to substitute for argument poetic licence or allusive suggestion. To follow the train of suggestion is genuinely fascinating, as in the case of his theory of meaning, but the real business remains that of translating his insights into workable theories.

Much of what passes as dialectic in Tillich's thought is vulnerable to Nietzsche's satirical comments on Kant and the post-Kantians: 'Perhaps it was only *some popular superstition* of time immemorial (for example the soul-superstition which in the *guise of subject- and ego-superstition*, has not ceased doing mischief even today); perhaps it was *some play upon words, some seduction on the part* of grammar, or *some reckless generalisation* of very narrow, very personal, very human-all-too-human facts'.[16] He remarks on Kant's inordinate pride in his table of categories and his discovery of a new faculty in man: 'How are synthetic *a priori* judgements possible, Kant asked himself. And what was actually his answer? *By virtue of a virtue* – but unfortunately not in five words but so complicatedly, respectably, with such a show of German profundity and sinuosity, that one failed to hear the funny German simple-mindedness inherent in such an answer'.[17]

He describes with almost malicious pleasure the tendency of the age to take the game of dialectic with ultimate seriousness; to define realities into being and then christen them as offspring of the absolute. He describes how 'all the young theologians of the *Tübinger Stift* went beating the bushes for "virtues"', and what they couldn't find they invented.

In a different context, he speaks of the predilection for dichotomous divisions and antitheses as the disease of metaphysics, particularly endemic amongst idealist philosophers. 'This type of valuation stands back of all their logical methods; this is the "faith" that enables them to struggle for what they call "knowing" – a something which at last they solemnly christen "truth". The basic faith of all metaphysicians is *faith in the antithetical nature of values*.'[18] In spite of his determination to doubt everything, this is one thing the idealist metaphysician does not doubt. 'But we may indeed doubt: first, *whether antitheses exist at all*, and second, whether those popular valuations and value-antitheses upon which the metaphysicians have placed their approval are not perhaps merely superficial valuations, *merely provisional perspectives . . .*'.[19]

The key question is whether antitheses exist at all, whether they are not artificial creations of thought reflecting on itself. Tillich never seriously asks this question. In fact, his account of logic is unclear because he lacks distinction between ordinary vocabulary and the logicians second-order vocabulary, that is, between what mediaeval logicians called first intentions and second intentions. The consequence is that Tillich does attribute real existence to antitheses, and fails to see that they are mere logical beings of reason.

These ambiguities in Tillich's metaphysics and theory of meaning are partly attributable to Kant. This tendency to dichotomous division is related to the somewhat inadequate class-logic he inherits from the same source.

Tillich conflates the relations of subject and object, and thought and being, and treats the identity between the first pair as of the same kind as the identity between the second pair. The same can be said of the relation of identity between finite and infinite. The epistemic, logical and meta-physical senses of identity are conflated. He assumes that arguments that establish identity at one level will do so at another. This is a weakness inherent in the idealist logic that he inherits.

This logic makes several related assumptions: that all propositions are reducible to propositions of the Subject-Predicate form; that all such propositions concern either individuals and their properties, that is, class-membership relations, or class-inclusion relations; that all relations are reducible to dyadic relations; that subject and predicate are related as antecedent and consequent; and finally, that all affirmative propositions express relations of identity.

What particularly concerns Tillich's metaphysics of meaning is that this logic, in identifying subject and predicate as antecedent and con-sequent, fails to distinguish between logical consequences and causal consequences. The two are conflated, and the relations of subject and object, thought and being, and finite and infinite are assimilated to one another. Inferences that apply to the principle of identity as a purely formal principle, signifying a dyadic logical relation, are taken to be valid for reality as a whole. By asserting a relation of antecedent and con-sequent between God or infinite subject and nature or finite object, a causal connection between them is inferred.

In spite of these criticisms, it cannot be denied that Tillich's theono-mous metaphysics of meaning has an impressive coherence, but it is the coherence of a picture or vision rather than that of a philosophical sys-tem. In his excellent critical treatment of Tillich's theology, David Kelsey has suggested that Tillich understands the Biblical account of Jesus as the Christ as a picture, and that Tillich implicitly advocates the adoption of aesthetic criteria for the evaluation of theology.[20] Whether or not this is desirable in general, it is pertinent to ask if aesthetic rather than logical criteria would not be appropriate to the assessment of Tillich's system. We do not intend to follow this suggestion but the analogy is illuminating. Because Tillich's system is presented in a discursive and purportedly rational manner we shall continue to explore its internal logic, but in speaking of its character as a belief and value system that offers man a meaning for life, we also wish to do justice to its character as a vision of the possibility of a unified system of meaning.

We have seen that Tillich distinguishes, in its presentation, three distinct levels of intentionality: the general metaphysical sense in which the spiritual act intends an identity between thought and being, while presupposing a structural interdependence between them in reality; the general theory of the intentionality of cultural acts as providing the basis for the distinguishing of the cultural sciences *nach Gegenständen und methoden*; and the intentions of individual acts and judgements express-ing the relations between existing subject and existing object in their engagement with one another.

The general application of this theory to epistemology and logic will be discussed in the remaining chapters, but we turn now to a specific application of the theory in Tillich's account of signs and symbols and the nature of religious symbolism.

4. *The ultimate meaning of signs and symbols*

Paul Tillich's theory of symbolism is a natural extension of his theonomous metaphysics of meaning. It is primarily intended not as a general semiotic theory, but as an attempt to make sense of religious and mythological symbols, which are the symbols of man's ultimate concern. If we are to do justice to this theory we must understand it as an attempt to provide concrete theological and cultural applications for his general metaphysics of meaning. Although Tillich says 'The centre of my theological doctrine of knowledge is the concept of symbol . . .' (*TPT* 333) it would be a mistake to assume that he gives us a fully developed theory of symbolism. His specific interest is in religious symbols.

Tillich responded to the fashionable interest in symbolism in a number of articles and chapters.[21] What is striking about these is that there is little in them that was not expressed in his first paper on the subject 'Das religiöse Symbol'. He reworks the same ideas and distinctions and provides different illustrative material. He makes no significant progress towards the clarification of the relationship of religious symbols and ordinary signs and symbols. The theoretical content of his explanations hardly justifies the enormous amount of attention that has been given to the doctrine. If it ever was necessary to discuss the theory in detail in order to demonstrate its incoherence, this has been done very competently, at some length, and with a show of logical virtuosity by William L. Rowe.[22]

In general, we agree with Lewis S. Ford who, in his generous attempt to make sense of Tillich's account of symbols, maintains that these are employed in Tillich's thought with two main functions: 'To fulfill its religious function, the symbol must be capable of representing that which ultimately concerns us . . . [and] In its metaphysical function the religious symbol must be capable of designating that which is ontologically prior to all beings and beyond the categorical requirements of the structure of being'.[23] Having examined the three main criteria offered by Tillich for the definition of religious symbols, namely, that they dialectically negate their literal meaning but affirm their self-transcending meaning, that they must be transparent towards their ultimate ground, and that they must participate in the unconditioned that they symbolise, he concludes: 'We find, then, that Tillich's three strands, whether taken singly or jointly, constitute an adequate theory for the religious use of symbols to articulate our ultimate concern, but that their metaphysical use, on the other hand, remains problematic'.[24] This is meant not to be dismissive of the theory, but to stress that its real value can be appreciated only if it is seen in terms of Tillich's attempt to give expression to religious faith.

The same general point is made by Battista Mondin, who says of Tillich's doctrine that 'it is a theological and not a philosophical doctrine, i.e. it is the doctrine of a theologian, not of a philosopher; it is a doctrine asserted in the circle of faith and not the product of philosophical reason'.[25]

A proper interpretation and criticism of Tillich's theory must begin with a clear recognition of his metaphysical and theological purpose. It is easy to caricature what he has to say, if we assume that his intention was to develop a general semiotic theory or that he was specifically concerned with symbolism in language. These interests may have been paramount in the minds of his contemporaries but they were not Tillich's. He was concerned with the bearing of symbols on our fundamental beliefs and attitudes and with the demonstration of the relevance of fundamental Christian symbols so as to affect the beliefs of his contemporaries. His method is closer to that of the exegetical preacher than to that of the philosopher. He stands, as Mondin has correctly asserted, in the tradition of Augustine and Bonaventura, who use symbolism, allegory and myth to interpret Scripture and to express the hidden meaning of ordinary human experience.

Tillich himself gives an admirably brief account of his doctrine of the religious symbol.

> A religious symbol uses the material of ordinary experience in speaking of God, but in such a way that the ordinary meaning of the *material used is both affirmed and denied.* Every religious symbol negates itself in its literal meaning, but it affirms itself in its self-transcending meaning. It is not a sign pointing to something with which it has no inner relationship. It *represents* the power and meaning of what is *symbolised through participation.* The symbol participates in the reality which is symbolised. Therefore, one should never say 'only a symbol'. This is to confuse symbol with sign. Thus it follows that *everything religion has to say about God,* including his qualities, actions and manifestations, *has a symbolic character* and that the meaning of 'God' is completely missed if one takes the symbolic language literally. (*ST2*, 10)

Apart from the distinction which Tillich draws between the literal and the symbolic, which does have primary application to language, his other criteria are based, we suggest, not on the paradigm of linguistic symbolism, but on the way symbols work in art, in politics and even in depth psychology.[26] It is not accidental that, in almost every paper devoted to the subject, he uses illustrations taken from art as primary examples of symbols.[27]

> Works of art express levels of reality which remain hidden in our ordinary encounter with reality. In relation to these levels they are symbolic even if they try to be as naturalistic as possible. The tree in a picture by Ruysdael is symbolic for treehood, but it is not the beautiful copy of a possibly real tree. It is the impression of a level of experience which may be provoked by an actual tree. But the picture does not depict the actual tree. It transforms it into a symbol.[28]

The picture is not simply a copy or imitative sign of an actual tree. It both is and is not a representation of the tree. It denies or edits out certain features of the empirical tree in order to affirm or highlight other features that point beyond this tree to the transcendent form or essence of tree-hood that it attempts to express. It is, however, intrinsically related to that which it represents. The spiritual act that unites subject and object in the act of creation, and that the work of art attempts to express, is the participation of the artist and the work of art in the reality represented. Finally, the medium that arrests attention in itself, that does not point beyond itself, that is not transparent towards that which it ultimately signifies, fails to be a work of art. In Tillich's terms, unless it satisfies all these functions, the work of art fails to qualify as a genuine work of art. If it satisfies these criteria, it becomes what he calls a symbol.

There is a formal and a metaphysical aspect to Tillich's choice of art as a paradigm for the interpretation of symbols. The formal aspect concerns the type of symbolism that he has in mind. There is an important difference between discursive symbolism such as we employ in language and the presentational forms that we use in art and music.[29] In language, we use verbal signs in sign complexes in which, by setting out the signs sequentially, we create patterns of meaning. The words in a sentence are strung together like clothes on a clothes-line. In a picture, it is only the total configuration of related parts simultaneously presented, that can be said to be meaningful or to represent something to us symbolically. What is required is that the picture be grasped as a single *gestalt*, like the image of a man fully dressed, a single entity clothes and all.

Part of the difficulty we have in making sense of Tillich's distinction between signs and symbols is that his examples are nearly all presentational forms, such as national flags, paintings, poems, psychological archetypes, the power of the king and religious objects; but he applies the term 'symbol' to the analysis of religious *language*. This is doubly confusing because it first overlooks the distinction between discursive and presentational forms and then applies the latter in the interpretation of the former.

This difficulty is further compounded by the fact that Tillich fails to distinguish, as philosophers have done since the time of Aristotle, between natural signs and conventional signs or symbols. The fact that logicians have always referred both to ordinary words and to the artificial signs of mathematical and logical notation as 'symbols' is not recognised by Tillich.

If we are to comprehend both discursive and presentational forms within the same symbolic system we need to distinguish between types of natural sign and types of conventional sign. Of natural signs we need perhaps to distinguish between indices, which literally indicate other things, and images or iconic signs, which directly imitate what they represent. Conventional signs have traditionally been referred to as *symbols*, that is signs made significant by convention; these include archetypes, paradigmatic individuals, words and artificial symbolic notation.

Now it is obvious that Tillich wishes to reserve the word 'symbol' for a special class of symbolic forms, that is, those with religious or meta-physical import. Unfortunately, he does not give us sound theoretical grounds for such a restriction; instead, he offers argument by legislative definition. What appeals to him about art is that a picture, by its very nature, seems to express something metaphysical. His fondness for examples from Expressionist painters, the school of Rembrandt, and representatives of the New Realism, confirms this. 'Art without meta-physics is without style. It is either abstract formalism or formless arbitrariness' (*DSW* 251).

The other key areas from which he culls examples, namely, politics and depth psychology, are loaded, for Tillich, with metaphysical significance. Only a German living in the first part of this century could choose the national flag as an important symbol and invest it with metaphysical significance as Tillich does. He was caught up in a view of politics in which the alternative claims of Nazism and Religious Socialism were meta-physical claims. Likewise, his fascination with the archetypes and sym-bols of depth psychology reflects both a religious and a metaphysical interest in the essential structures and dynamics of being, and in the un-conditioned ground and abyss of being and meaning. This interest is already evident in his paper 'The Religious Symbol', but continues into his *Systematic Theology* and *The Courage to Be* not to mention his many articles on depth psychology.[30]

His general purpose is indicated by his concept of a theology of culture. For example, in *The Interpretation of History* he says, 'in religion the sub-stance which is the unconditioned source and abyss of meaning is desig-nated, and the cultural forms serve as symbols for it' (*IH* 50). Cultural forms express this ultimate import indirectly:

> The import is not this or that individual psychological element, nor is it biographical or sociological or national. All these factors are co-determinative. They provide the subjective possibilities of the style, just as the forms determine the objective possibilities. But a possible basis is not a real basis. The essence of the import lies beneath all these subjective factors. It is a certain attitude toward reality. It is an interpretation of ultimate meaning, the profound apprehension of reality. It is the functioning of the Unconditioned which supports every conditioned experience, colours it and prevents it from plunging into the void of nothingness.[31]

This is how he understands the function of symbols, or cultural forms, in service of a theology of culture.

To describe Tillich's account of symbols as a covert attempt to restrict the meaning of 'symbol' to 'religious symbol' explains the perspective from which he approaches the problem of the nature of symbolism, but it does not really indicate the value or the limitations of his theory.

Discussing symbols of faith, he lists six points that he considers import-ant in explaining what he means by symbols. i) Symbols and signs have in common the fact that they point beyond themselves to something else. ii) Symbols, unlike signs, participate in the reality of that to which they point. iii) Symbols 'open up levels of reality' that are otherwise closed to us. iv) They 'unlock dimensions and elements of our soul' that correspond to the dimensions and elements of reality. v) They cannot be produced intentionally, because they function within a complete social and cultural setting. vi) Symbols live and grow, and can be discarded and die.[32] In 'The Meaning and Justification of Religious Symbols', Tillich adds a seventh point: vii) Symbols have an 'integrative and disintegrative' power over individuals and groups.

That signs and symbols are said to point beyond themselves explains very little, because the expression 'point beyond' merely translates what the word 'sign' literally means. Unless we distinguish the various senses in which signs can be said to point beyond themselves, for example, by ostensive definition, by imitation, or by abstract convention, it is impossible to get much further. What is particularly confusing is that Tillich suggests that all signs are conventional signs and can be replaced at will, whereas symbols cannot be. His preference for the word 'symbol' is surprising, as it might seem natural for him to use the biblical term *semeion* or sign for what he means. The fact that he does not is indicative of idealist influence in his thinking, that is, of the tendency to consider metaphysical meanings as normative for the interpretation of ordinary meanings, rather than the reverse. It is also indicative of the difference between the theory of symbolism and the doctrine of *analogia entis*, which would more naturally speak of signs in this context.

Although Tillich believed his doctrine to mean the same thing as the doctrine of *analogia entis* there are, as Gustave Weigel has pointed out, important differences between the two.[33] Relativism and subjectivism are necessary concomitants of Tillich's theory of symbols because he links the symbol so directly to the meaning-creating and meaning-fulfilling spiritual act: 'This subjective act takes on special importance in a system such as Tillich's where "meaning", or being in relation to us, is given almost the importance which is attributed to the simple concept of being in Scholastic Philosophy.'[34] By contrast, St Thomas is concerned with being as the publicly real; the foundation for inter-subjective communication in the truth. The structures and dynamics of being are not mystically intuited in some special personal experience but are part of the shared reality in which we participate. The analogies that link the different orders of beings and different modes of be-ing are real independently of our experiencing them. God, too, as the prime analogate is posited as the independently existing ground of these analogies: 'All that was needed to constitute the reality of those analogies was the reality of the term to which they were related and by which they are designated'.[35] Tillich's stress on the experience of be-ing involves emphasis on an important necessary condition of our knowledge of being-itself, but is not sufficient to establish its independent reality. His method involves making symbols not the means but the end of religious knowledge, with the result that he must conclude that 'symbols provide no objective knowledge'.[36] Symbols, as the products of revelatory experience, do not reveal to us the nature of God but mirror the experience of the reality of the depth of being. Weigel concludes that, 'without a vigorous conception of the intrinsic reality of the analogy of proper proportionality and of the radically analogous character of being itself', it is impossible to reach a doctrine, like St Thomas's, that objective knowledge of God is possible.

Tillich explains the fact that signs may be replaced at will, whereas symbols cannot be, in terms of the participation of symbols in that which they symbolise. This is again confusing because we would ordinarily say that the defining characteristic of a natural sign is that the sign signals its significandum in virtue of some direct relation of imitation, spatiotemporal proximity, or causal connection. Once again, this is a cue that Tillich is concerned to emphasise something else. For him, the crucial thing about symbols is that, on the objective side they open up new levels of reality to us, and on the subjective side they unlock dimensions and elements of our soul. The symbol becomes a simple synonym for the spiritual act, the act of faith, which is meaning-receiving, meaning-creating and directed towards its meaning-fulfilling ultimate import. Because he identifies the symbol with the act or process of symbolising, Tillich readily falls into metaphors of participation, and being transparent to the ground of meaning. This also explains why he insists that symbols cannot be produced intentionally and that they have a life of their own. Spiritual acts are, for Tillich, the expression of our belonging to a circle of commitment to shared beliefs and values, and therefore symbols are something like Lévy-Bruhl's 'collective representations,' which signify the modes of figuration by which a group expresses its conception of, and its relation to reality. 'The collective representations and interconnections which constitute such a primitive mentality are governed by the law of participation and in so far they take but little account of the law of contradiction.'[37] He also uses the term 'symbol' to mean archetypal images or, in some instances, paradigmatic individuals. In the case of a paradigmatic individual such as Jesus as the Christ, Tillich's various descriptions of symbols make sense. Again, Kelsey's point about pictures and aesthetic criteria applies.

Kelsey makes another fascinating observation that goes a long way to explaining why the notion of symbol and the act of faith are intrinsically connected in Tillich's mind. Tillich's account of symbols corresponds almost point for point with his account of miracles as elements in revelatory events: 'It may be that "religious symbol" is just another term for "miracle". At the very least the class of "religious" symbols includes all miracles. This means that analysis of revelatory events, and especially of the way miracles function in them, provides the warrants for judgements about religious symbols'.[38] If this is granted it helps to explain Tillich's claim that symbols have an integrative and disintegrative power over individuals and groups, and the related point that religious symbols have healing power.

When Tillich discusses religious symbols that are also words, such as the name of God, and statements about Jesus as the Christ, he makes use of the distinction between ordinary or literal language and symbolic or figurative language. In general, statements about God or about Jesus as the Christ must be interpreted symbolically, for if they were interpreted literally the resulting statements would be idolatrous. There is one exception however: 'The statement that God is being-itself is a non-symbolic statement. It does not point beyond itself. It means what it says directly and properly; if we speak of the actuality of God we first assert that he is not God if he is not being-itself. Other assertions about God can be made theologically only on this basis' (*ST1*, 264–5).

Leaving aside the literal absurdity of the assertion that the statement 'God is being-itself' does not point beyond itself (it could not mean at all unless it referred beyond itself *qua* statement), there is an inherent difficulty in Tillich's theory of language to which we must refer briefly. The point is made tellingly by Donald Keefe.

> Behind the method of correlation which Tillich employs is a point of view which forces that method. This point of view has to do with the meaning of ordinary, as opposed to theological language. The ordinary function of language, in which words are governed by the laws of formal logic, is the description of appearances, of phenomena. In this ordinary usage language is categorical and logical; it deals with the appearances of things as though these appearances were identical to the reality, as though phenomenal descriptions were definitions of essences.[39]

While this language may be satisfactory for the purposes of physical science, it is inadequate when applied to theology. 'In short, if the ordinary, non-dialectic use of language is taken to be philosophically and theologically valid, the world of existential ambiguity is resolved into a coherent system of essences, and the distinction between existence and essence vanishes.'[40] The conclusion is that ordinary language is inadequate to the needs of theology, and it is only by the dialectic of affirmation and negation that symbols can express the unconditioned meaning and import of theological statements.

Tillich's view of the relations of the literal and the figurative is not coherent. That he recognises this is shown by his assertion that at least one theological assertion must be literally true if we are to secure significance for symbolic statements. However, the difficulty is really more general. If every theological statement but one is symbolic, how are we to relate them to the rest of ordinary discourse? The problem is that Tillich concedes too much to literal discourse, and does not explain the difference between ordinary literal and ordinary figurative discourse. The lack of any theory of metaphor in Tillich's account of language parallels the lack of a theory of analogy in his doctrine of being.

Ironically, it is the nominalist view that takes factual statements to define literal meaning and regards all non-factual statements as symbolic, figurative or metaphorical. This point of view assumes that it is transparently clear what we mean by 'facts', and that when language is not concerned with the expression of facts it is engaged in flights of fancy or merely emotive expression.

In classical and mediaeval thought 'literal' meant 'the literary meaning' or 'the meaning intended by the author'; 'figurative' meant 'of the figure' or 'of the mode of figuration'. Thus we can be sure about what words mean because we invent the conventions and rules that govern their use. But the significance of things, facts and events is ambiguous because the same phenomena can be figured in a variety of ways, and the same figuration can have multiple significance for us.[41]

A less uncritically Kantian view of ordinary language might have allowed Tillich to explore more sensitively the nuances of ordinary language in its literal and figurative modes, and to realise that within scientific language itself there is both factual and metaphorical symbolism. The recognition that metaphysical symbols play a fundamental part in the constitution of our universe of meaning is an important insight of Tillich's that applies to both religious and secular symbols, and, in particular, to those that express our basic collective representations of reality.

Given such a re-interpretation of the literal and the figurative, Tillich might have been able to develop a more positive theory of our knowledge of God. Again, the difference between St Thomas's theory and that of Tillich is illuminating:

> It is clear then that symbolism and analogy do not solve the problem of theological language in the same way. According to the symbolical theory of theological language everything can be predicated of God symbolically and only symbolically. According to the analogical theory some names are predicated literally, some symbolically and some neither literally nor symbolically. For example, the analogical theory refuses to apply to God names like *accident, potentiality, sinner*, etc., even symbolically, but maintains that the perfection signified by names like *person, goodness, wisdom*, etc., applies to God literally. The symbolic theory does not make any distinction between these two classes of names and applies all of them to God as symbols.[42]

In conclusion, we reiterate that the value of Tillich's theory of symbolism lies in its attempt to illuminate the nature of religious symbols. It is not intended as, nor does it succeed as, a general semiotic theory. He approaches the theory of symbolism, as he approaches the metaphysics of meaning, from the standpoint of a theologian seeking a theology of culture that will yield a comprehensive Christian *Weltanschauung*.

5. *Theology as a paradigm of meaning and method*

Tillich's systematic theology raises in a challenging way the question of the nature of theological method and its relationship to the methods of other sciences. This question, which is the central concern of *Das System der Wissenschaften* remained central throughout his life. His confidence in methodological solutions to theoretical problems is both a virtue and a limitation of his work. It is a virtue in the sense that his greatest contribution to theology may well have been that his work provoked a searching re-examination of methodological questions in theology. It is a limitation in that he was too easily content to prescribe general methodological solutions rather than to work out appropriate semantic, epistemological and logical theories. He not only gives a new emphasis to the importance of philosophical and ontological considerations in defining theological method, but he sets up theology as a paradigm of meaning and method: 'We must understand that thought itself is rooted in the Absolute as the ground and abyss of meaning. Theology takes as its explicit object that which is the implicit presupposition of all knowledge' (*OB* 56).

Tillich is not a theologian who seeks to give an account of science and culture in which theology is presented as one science among others. This approach he explicitly rejects in the form of Troeltsch's ethics of cultural values. Theology cannot survive if it simply attempts to accommodate itself to scientific method. On the contrary, it must challenge the adequacy of natural science as a universal paradigm of method. The normative cultural sciences must be recognised as sciences in their own right, and theology must be given its proper place among the *Geisteswissenschaften*.

Also, Tillich is not just another philosopher offering us an idealist analysis of the respective domains of, and relations between, the philosophy of logic, the philosophy of nature and the philosophy of spirit. The account of the *Geisteswissenschaften* is radically qualified for Tillich by his theistic belief in the paradoxical immanence of the transcendent; by his Christian faith that the unconditioned and transcendent Absolute has been revealed in immanent human experience as a concrete historical *kairos*.[43]

The first approach, which sees theology as one science among others, tends to be dominated by a conception of scientific method in which theoretical physics serves as the paradigm of method; a view that was strengthened by Kant's canonisation of Newtonian physics as the ideal science. From this point of view, it appears that the problem for theology is to conform itself to this ideal or be dismissed as unscientific. This leads to a positivisitic relativism or scepticism, or to rationalistic deism or a return to neo-orthodox supranaturalism.

The second approach, based on idealist dialectic, adopts Kant's model of the transcendental method as the method of philosophy and extends it to all the philosophical disciplines, including theology. This approach tends to subordinate theology to philosophy by making it into either a sub-department of philosophy or an instance of the application of philosophical method to a specific range of problems. Either way, theology tends to become synonymous with the philosophy of religion, in strict analogy with for example, the philosophy of science. The result is a kind of theosophical gnosticism.

Tillich rejects both approaches, not only because they lead to unacceptable theological conclusions, but also for two other reasons. Firstly, both of these reductionist approaches result in a misrepresentation, a caricature, even, of the nature of theology: 'because of its panlogistical tendency, neo-Kantianism could not comprehend the experience of the abyss and the paradox' (*OB* 53). And, secondly, we venture to suggest, he adopts theology itself as his paradigm of method. Theology becomes the paradigm science in terms of which other sciences are classified and judged. The methodology that Tillich elaborated in the formative works produced between 1920 and 1930[44] is, we submit, largely unintelligible unless we recognise this.

In his posthumously published lectures on nineteenth- and twentieth-century Protestant theology, he discusses the various strategies that theologians have adopted since 'the breakdown of the universal synthesis' of idealism, under the heading 'New Ways of Mediation' (*P* 208–45). The first strategy involves the attempt to accommodate theology to some other paradigm of method: science (the neo-Kantian Ritchlian school), philosophy (the neo-idealist school), or psychology (the Erlangen school's emphasis on experience, and Schleiermacher's stress on feeling). However, he rejects these forms of reductionism as leading essentially to the 'theology of retreat'.

The second strategy involves the attempt to treat religion *sui generis*, in terms of its own categories and methods. He identifies this approach with phenomenology, and particularly with the work of Rudolf Otto and his epoch-making book, *The Idea of the Holy*. He rejects this approach because it is too abstract: in attempting to characterise the universal features of religion it does not do justice to the specific character of religious commitment.

The third strategy he identifies with the attempt of Harnack, in his massive work the *History of Dogma*, to disentangle the specifically Christian from the Greek aspects in Scripture and the tradition of the Church. While he admits the value of such an approach and the liberation it brought 'from the necessity of identifying Hellenistic concepts with Christianity itself', he rejects the tendency to dismiss philosophy and the intellectualising influence of Hellenism as if Christianity could do without these. 'My criticism of the whole liberal theology, including Harnack, is that it had no real systematic theology; it believed in the results of historical research in the wrong way' (*P* 223).

Tillich's own way is to define philosophy as the science of the functions of meaning and their categories; to define metaphysics as the attempt to express the unconditional in terms of rational symbols; and to define theology as theonomous metaphysics. By this series of moves, theology becomes the theonomous science of the norms of meaning. Tillich's approach can be compared to Schelling's attempt to develop a distinctively Christian philosophy of existence. As Erich Przywara observes: 'The thought of Paul Tillich in its innermost intention is directed to the examination of Christian root-terms. This focus emerges early in his interpretation of Schelling who himself had sought for a "philosophy of revelation", not for the purpose of taking up revelation into a final philosophical concept (as did Hegel), but rather to understand revelation in terms of its own immanent concepts'.[45]

Tillich accepts the identification of certain concepts as distinctively Judeo-Christian and as definitive of the world-view that Judeo-Christian culture entails. These not only define the subject-matter with which theology deals but, in a more profound sense, are the concepts in terms of which he philosophises; they provide the conceptual frame of reference in terms of which he undertakes a re-interpretation and critique of contemporary philosophy. Yet he does not accept the alternative of a 'Christian philosophy', argued for by the Neo-Calvinist Dooyeweerd; who, with Kuyper and other Ritschlians of the Dutch school, accepts Troeltsch's religious '*a priori*'.[46]

As has been pointed out in our discussion of Troeltsch, Tillich refused to accept that religion is merely another cultural function alongside science, morality and art. He explicitly rejects the idea of a Christian philosophy:

> There is nothing in heaven and earth, or beyond them, to which the philosopher must subject himself except the universal *logos* of being as it gives itself to him in experience. Therefore, the idea of a 'Christian philosophy' in the narrower sense of a philosophy which is intentionally Christian must be rejected. The fact that every modern philosophy has grown on Christian soil and shows traces of the Christian culture in which it lives has nothing to do with the self-contradicting ideal of a 'Christian philosophy'. (*ST1*, 32)

However, this discussion points to a central difficulty in Tillich's theology. He rejects the subordination of philosophy to theology typified by early mediaeval thought and Protestant neo-Orthodox theology; this leads to the destruction of philosophy by subjecting it to the heteronomous authority of church or scripture. He rejects also the attempt, characteristic of the Enlightenment in general and Hegel in particular, to subordinate theology to philosophy; this leads to a caricature of the Gospel and the idolatrous apotheosis of autonomous reason. He also rejects the attempt to maintain the distinctive characters of philosophy and theology that posits a divorce between truths of faith and truths of reason; this was exemplified in the thinking of the late Middle Ages, British empiricism and theological Kantianism (see *WR* 27–30). This can only lead to cultural and personal schizophrenia. He continues: 'only the synthetic solution remains ... The way of synthesis alone is genuine and legitimate. It is required, even if it fails again and again. But it is not necessary that it fail. For there is a point in the doctrine of revelation and philosophy at which the two are one. To find this point and from there to construct a synthetic solution is the decisive task of the philosophy of religion' (*WR* 30).

However, he says elsewhere that no synthesis is possible: 'Thus there is no conflict between theology and philosophy, and there is no synthesis either – for exactly the same reason which ensures that there will be no conflict. A common basis is lacking. The idea of a synthesis between theology and philosophy has led to the dream of a "Christian philosophy" ...' (*ST1*, 31).

It is not satisfactory to say simply that in the earlier paper Tillich was still under the spell of Schelling and Hegel and of the ideal of the high Middle Ages that a synthesis between philosophy and theology was possible, and that the later statement represents the position of his later 'theology of correlation'. His belief in the possibility of mediation was based on the conviction that at a higher level, in the philosophy of religion, it is possible to see the systematic inter-relations between philosophy and theology in a way that preserves the integrity of each. The resulting synthesis cannot be described as a 'Christian philosophy' because the philosophy of religion serves a different methodological purpose from either philosophy or theology. It is, rather, the theory of the categories and the forms of meaning in their relation to the unconditional; whereas philosophy is concerned with the categories and forms of meaning in general, theology is concerned with the concrete normative expressions of the ultimate in the history of religions.

The reasoning that lies behind the argument of *Systematic Theology*, Volume 1, is rather different. Here, Tillich is concerned to stress the difference between theology and philosophy. The method of correlation purports simply to set the answers derived from revelation alongside the questions that reason formulates in its quest for the meaning of being, essence and existence; but it is nevertheless a type of synthesis too. It is not a direct synthesis of philosophy and theology, such as might yield a Christian philosophy, but an intellectual synthesis at a higher level where, in the courage of faith, the questions of philosophy and the answers of theology are affirmed as belonging together because of an affirmed identity between the universal *logos* of reality and experience and the concrete *logos* revealed in Jesus as the Christ.[47]

There are two sides to Tillich's conception of systematic theology, neither of which must be confused with the attempt to construct a Christian philosophy. On the one hand, the method of systematic theology involves a theonomous theory of meaning, that is, the norm of ultimacy is introduced into the theory of meaning and, as the Protestant principle, is applied equally to the critique of autonomous philosophical forms and to heteronomous religious forms in which the attempt is made to express the meaning of being. In this sense, Christianity, in its various forms, and different philosophies are subjected to the same systematic critique. On the other hand, Tillich not only subjects fundamental Judeo-Christian ideas to philosophical examination, but, more importantly, employs fundamental Judeo-Christian concepts in developing his philosophical ontology, epistemology, ethics, aesthetics and even logic: concepts that have been seriously neglected in modern philosophy, such as personality and community, guilt, alienation, love, fate and destiny, kairos and history, the holy and the demonic (see *IH* parts 2 and 3, and *PE* chapter 1).

Ultimately, Tillich rejects the idea of a Christian philosophy because it is not bold enough. A Christian philosophy alongside other philosophies is merely one among many, this leads either to relativism or to an elitist and esoteric view of truth. For Tillich faith in the ultimate identity of the universal *logos* and the concrete *logos* revealed in Jesus as the Christ, is the basis of a much more ambitious view of systematic theology as comprehending both philosophy and religion in the normative theonomous theory of meaning. Although he appears, in *Biblical Religion and the Search for Ultimate Reality*, to employ the same distinction between Greek and Hebrew thought that was fundamental to the school of Harnack, he makes profoundly different use of it. He uses biblical concepts to criticise and expand traditional ontology and, using ontological analyses, is able to exhibit in a new way the universal relevance of biblical teaching about man, sin and salvation. Similarly, in his account of the method of correlation (*ST1*, 67f., *ST2*, 14–18), we do not simply have an artificial meta-logical approach that transcends the dichotomies between faith and reason, theology and philosophy, and personalism and ontology. Instead, we have a sensitive transformation of traditional, rational ontology in the light of categories drawn from the biblical world-view, and a re-interpretation of the traditional biblical concepts in terms that are designed to fulfil the demand for a rationally consistent ontology. To the philosophers, Tillich appears to be importing alien theological concepts into philosophy; to the orthodox he appears to dissolve Christianity into ontology. Both points of view are, in a sense, correct. The *raison d'être* of the method of correlation and of the earlier philosophy of religion synthesis, is the same: a new, ontologically-based, normative and theonomous theory of meaning.

In a different way, we may say that rather than advocating a Christian philosophy, Tillich offers, in terms of his biblical categories, a critique and re-interpretation of philosophy. In this sense, he may be said to be doing something analogous to the work of St Augustine in adjusting Platonism to the demands of the Christian Faith, or that of St Thomas in modifying Aristotelian hylomorphism to make it compatible with, for example, the biblical doctrine of *creatio ex nihilo*. What Tillich does recognise is the inadequacy of accepted paradigms of theological method, as well as the fact that these paradigms entail world-views that may not be compatible with the Christian world-view. Therefore, what may be required for the full expression of Christianity is an entirely new world-view that transcends both established world-views and the time honoured, but culturally dependent, forms that Christianity has taken in the past.

Even more interesting is his recognition that within each such ideology or world-view we operate with different paradigms of, for example, reason, knowledge, persons and things. Families of related words have different meanings within these different world-views. Tillich's sensitivity to this point brings us to a most important part of his philosophy: his recognition that if we are to distinguish adequately between revelation and reason, theology and philosophy, and biblical religion and the search for ultimate reality we must acknowledge that they are based on different paradigms of knowledge. Further, we cannot simply rest in the acceptance of this fact but we have to recognise the relativities involved and, subjecting both theology and philosophy to critical judgement, strive to formulate a more adequate theory that will comprehend both.

Tillich is not prepared to accept only a defensive role for theology. His metaphysics of meaning is a theonomous metaphysics of meaning. For him, religious symbolism is paradigmatic for the theory of symbolism generally. Theological systematics is normative for the classification of the other sciences. The fact that Tillich is, so to speak, methodologically aggressive in theology has to do with his kerygmatic and existential purpose: to communicate a Christian philosophy of life that is both theoretically and practically relevant to the situation of man in the twentieth century.

Chapter 5

The Metaphysics of Truth:
Tillich's 'Ontology of Cognition'

1. *Why an 'Ontology of Cognition'* ?[1]

While it is undoubtedly correct that 'the key problem of [Tillich's] whole system [is] the question of truth',[2] this does not mean that Tillich is concerned with epistemology in a conventional manner. He does not set about the analysis of specific cognitive acts, nor does he have much to say about the determination of the truth of specific statements. He is concerned with the metaphysical foundations of truth.

Because he questioned the basis of traditional ontology, Kant's critical idealism raised in an acute form, the question of the ultimate reference of truth, and the possibility of knowledge of God. Like Fichte, Schelling and Hegel, Tillich was concerned first and foremost with what he called 'theological epistemology', that is, with the relation of truth and ultimate reality. Dorothy Emmet reaches the heart of the matter when she emphasises that Tillich's work is important 'because he puts the problems of epistemology and the idea of revelation in the centre of his thinking'. In the same passage, she says, 'Here I believe that Tillich's main contribution to epistemology lies in what he has seen about the way in which reason can work in *theology*, when he describes the interrelation of the "technical" with the "ecstatic" reason, and the combination of both with a sense for what he calls the "depth of reason"' (*TPT* 199). Tillich was chiefly interested in the grounds of theological knowledge (see *TPT* 331); he was less concerned with epistemology than with the attempt to formulate the general metaphysical principles that are presupposed in and necessary to the formulation of any body of objective knowledge (*TPT* 199). In terms of a characteristically transcendental approach, he believes that the question of the possibility of knowledge in general has to be decided before we can determine the truth of specific judgements. This somewhat paradoxical belief underlies and explains the method of approach adopted in part 1 of the *Systematic Theology* and the epistemological aspects of his other writings.[3]

In 'Kairos und Logos: Eine Untersuchung zur Metaphysik der Erkenntnis' Tillich sets out what he regards as the metaphysical foundations of a characteristically Protestant theory of knowledge. He describes the constitutive and regulative principles governing the notion of truth. Among constitutive principles he identifies the concepts of truth, being, fate, history and the personal. Among regulative principles he identifies the concepts of standpoint, attitude, decision, dialectics and the critical Protestant principle that guards against the identification of the absolute with anything finite and contingent.

'Participation and Knowledge: Problems of an Ontology of Cognition' is more like conventional epistemology, in that he considers the roles of detachment and participation in the act of knowledge. However, he is still more concerned with the phenomenological investigation of the structures and dynamics of cognitive experience than with the specification of the truth conditions of particular judgements.

Given our claim that the question of truth is central to Tillich's thought, it may seem strange that we commenced our discussion of his work with an exposition of his metaphysics of meaning. The explanation of this apparent anomaly is partly historical and partly methodological. It is a matter of fact that Tillich first attempts to answer the problems raised by Kant's critical idealism by elaborating an alternative Christian world-view. This world-view is presented as the concrete, normative expression of a new philosophy of meaning; the problem of truth is part of the onto-logical and existential problem of meaning. For him, the metaphysics of knowledge and the ontology of cognition, together with the metaphysics of logic and meta-logic, fall within the wider category of the metaphysics of meaning. These all form subordinate parts within the total structure of his 'Theonomous Systematics' (see *WR* 32–7, 156f., and *DSW* 111, 116f., and *passim*). As we have suggested, Kant tends to subordinate the question of truth to the question of meaning. By asking what are the con-stitutive and regulative principles of each universe of discourse, Kant effectively places discourse about knowledge, ethics and aesthetics on the same level, and at the same time, questions of the metaphysics of meaning become paramount. Like Schelling and Dilthey, Tillich takes up the question first at the level of the metaphysics of meaning, and this suits the interests of his philosophy of religion well; for, it becomes possible to relate all universes of discourse to the ground of all being and meaning, namely, Being-itself or God.

However, Tillich offers two other reasons for subordinating the ques-tion of truth to that of meaning. Firstly, the question of truth, although capable of the widest ontological connotation, primarily concerns man's cognitive encounter with reality and not his whole being, nor does it do justice to man's pre-reflexive participation in and intuition of being. Secondly, he emphasises the primary ontological sense of intentionality; namely, the given structural bond between self and world. It is within this ontological polarity that the dialectic of concrete existence, in which man discovers the meaning of his being in thought and action, is played out; and it is this meaning-of-being that constitutes the truth for man. Because man is for Tillich the being who is ultimately concerned about his being and meaning, he places the primary emphasis on the experience of be-ing and the discovery of its meaning. He sees the quest for the true, the good and the beautiful as embraced within the quest for the ultimate in being and meaning, that is, the quest for the Holy.

Tillich is reacting to the nominalist tendency to abstract the question of truth from the question of being. This tradition ignores the fact that every form of human cultural activity, rational and non-rational, is expressive of man's ultimate and existential concern with meaning. Man is concerned to comprehend the meaning of his own being, to create meaningful structures within his own world, and above all to reach fulfilment of meaning in the unconditioned and unconditional ground of all being.

That Tillich does not provide us with a developed statement of his epistemology has provoked comment from a variety of authors. Dorothy M. Emmet and John Herman Randall, Jr, both complain that Tillich does not adequately explain such key notions as objective reason and participation (*TPT* 198–214, 132–61). Part of the difficulty is that the distinctions used in the *Systematic Theology* rest on arguments worked out in his earlier and less accessible German writings. Insofar as Tillich does explain the theoretical foundations of his thought, it is in such early works as *Der Begriff des Übernatürlichen, Das System der Wissenschaften* and 'Religionsphilosophie'. However, even when he discusses supranaturalist epistemology he avoids giving a detailed account of the theory of knowledge and tends to take as definitive the analyses given by Kant. He seeks simply to qualify the more extreme interpretations based on Kant's doctrines, and defends his comparative neglect of epistemology in the following terms:

> Many contributors ask me about my epistemology, some of them with misgivings about the lack of a developed doctrine of knowledge. Again I answer, first, with a biographical comment: I come from 'the age of epistemology', and from a country in which, since the rise of neo-Kantianism, the doctrine of knowledge had completely obscured the question of being. In reaction to this state of affairs I have followed those who made it clear that every epistemology has ontological assumptions, whether hidden or open. And I decided that it is better to have an open, critical and constructive ontology than a surreptitious one. That in spite of this attitude I did not mean to neglect epistemology is proved by the First Part of my *Systematic Theology*, which contains under the title 'Reason and Revelation' my theological epistemology. (*TPT* 331)

But that Tillich came from the age of epistemology in Germany, and that every epistemology has ontological presuppositions, do not absolve him from the task of dealing with the logical and epistemological problems raised by his own philosophical theology.

Tillich's remarks illustrate a tendency, at work throughout his system, to translate ordinary philosophical questions into metaphysical ones. The first-order epistemological problems are not solved by translating them into questions about the metaphysics of knowledge. Whatever the value of his theological epistemology, it does not answer the ordinary problems about the relation of sense-experience and intuition to cognition and judgement. Such terms as 'experience', 'intuition' and 'cognition' are frequently used by Tillich but their relations remain opaque, unless we assume that he is using them, as he often does, in a Kantian manner. His discussions of technical and ontological reason, of subjective and objective reason, of the depth of reason, and of the logical and ontological object are suggestive. but of such generality that they have limited value in actual philosophical debate.

In Tillich's defence, it must be stressed that what he is concerned with is the question of our general philosophical orientation; the *Weltanschauung* that determines our philosophical and theological method in the most profound and subtle way. Oppressed as he is, by sterile controversy arising from the uncritical acceptance of a nominalistic world-view, which forces theology in the direction of an other-worldly, subjective and pietistic fideism or supranaturalism, his predominant concern is ideological, that is, to re-orientate philosophy and theology in a direction where these discussions may be more constructive, fruitful and relevant to contemporary cultural and political life.[4]

Part of the difficulty is illustrated by Tillich's characterisation of the nineteenth century as the age of epistemology. This is simply not true insofar as it implies that this was an age of searching and critical examination of different epistemologies. Rather, it was the age of one great epistemology, namely, Kant's; almost everything written, in Germany at least, consisted in critical refinement, and baroque elaboration, of the theory of knowledge developed in Kant's first *Critique*. The unconscious tendency of the age was to assume that Kant had done for philosophy in general, and epistemology in particular, what Newton had done for physics, Euclid for geometry and Aristotle for Logic; and in this respect Tillich was no different from his contemporaries and predecessors. It is not that he lacks an epistemology but that his is an uncritical and oversimplified version of the general position of Kant. It is necessary to mention two parts of the Kantian legacy that had a particularly fundamental effect in determining the course that theological discussion took in Tillich's day; namely, the stress on the strictly limited character of finite reason (leading to scepticism with regard to knowledge of God), and the stress on the primacy of practical reason.

Kant, in the *Critique of Practical Reason*, finds that, in order to secure the coherence of moral discourse it is necessary to postulate God, freedom and immortality as principles; that is, as regulative and not constitutive principles of morality. This follows from his conception of the radical finitude of human reason and the fact that while it is possible to know *that* we know and can legitimately enquire *how* we know, we cannot give final answers to the question *what* it is that we know. If things-in-themselves remain essentially unknowable by human reason, the same conclusion applies *a fortiori* to God. Questions concerning the essence of things become impermissible since we cannot ultimately say *what* it is that is constitutive of reality. However, it is permissible to speculate concerning the unconditional grounds of possible experience!

The Copernican revolution here involves a shift away from concern with the intentional objects of knowledge, to a focus on the forms and modes of knowing – to a focus on the intentionality of acts of conscious-ness. The concern with the regulative principles that make knowledge and action possible is a concern with the intentionality of human experi-ence, that is, of human acts conceived as the dynamic experience of being in encounter with reality. The central questions concern not so much the nature of reality, as the unconditional grounds of meaning *in* this active encounter with reality.

Similarly, in Tillich's theological epistemology, he rejects the possi-bility of proofs of the existence of God, with their implication that reason can reveal the existence or the nature of God to us, and, beginning with man's ultimate concern with his being and meaning, he seeks to intuit the unconditioned grounds of possible being and meaning. His approach is phenomenological in so far as it begins with the human experience of ultimate concern, rather than with the object of that concern, and seeks to comprehend what makes this concern with ultimates, which is definitive of human experience, possible.

Tillich's central concern with truth is not a straightforward concern with the question, 'What is Knowledge?'. It is, more specifically, a con-cern with the question, 'How is knowledge of God possible?', or 'What are the principles presupposed in, and necessary to, any talk of God?'. Hence, in his ontology of cognition, we are always concerned with two questions that, for him, are intimately related: 'What are the ontological grounds of possible knowledge in general?' and 'What makes ultimate concern possible?'.

2. *The ontological foundations of knowledge:*
logos, ontos *and identity*

In giving an account of Tillich's theory of knowledge, it would be mis-leading to follow the order of exposition in the *Systematic Theology*, for his most fundamental concepts and basic methodological principles are not those expressed in part I ('Reason and Revelation'). That discussion presupposes the categories and distinctions that are expressed in part II ('Being and God'), especially chapter 7.[5] Underlying his definition of knowledge as a form of union between subject and object, for example (*ST1*, 105) is his discussion of the self/world polarity as characterising the dynamic structure of reality, and of the subject/object dichotomy as belonging to the cognitive comprehension of that structure (*ST1*, 181–206).

The section 'Being and God' is of central importance for another reason: it demonstrates that Tillich views the principle of identity differ-ently from the philosophers of identity, and offers different grounds for postulating it. He does this by an emphatic reassertion of the connection between being and God, based on what he called 'the Augustinian solu-tion': 'They coincide in the nature of truth. *Veritas* is presupposed in every philosophical argument; and veritas is God' (*TC* 12f.). In the light of the Augustinian mystical tradition Tillich claims that the ontological

Argument must be seen not so much as an argument for the existence of God as 'The rational description of the relation of our mind to Being as such. Our mind implies *principia per se nota* which have immediate evidence whenever they are noticed: the transcendentalia, *esse, verum, bonum*. They constitute the Absolute in which the difference between knowing and known is not actual' (*TC* 15).

a) *Identity and being itself.* In the first instance then, the identity that makes truth possible is not some abstract identity between thought and being, but the identity between being and God'. 'God is being-itself'. 'Therefore, God is the answer to the question implied in being' (*ST1*, 261, 181). This Augustinian principle may be called the ontological principle of truth-in-general, and is formulated by Tillich in the following terms: 'Man is immediately aware of something unconditional which is the *prius* of the separation and interaction of subject and object, theoretically as well as practically' (*TC* 22; cf. *MSA* 80–3). God is the unconditioned power of being that is the *prius* of everything that has being:

> It precedes all special contents logically and ontologically. It precedes every separation and makes every interaction possible, because it is the point of identity without which neither separation nor interaction can be thought. This refers basically to the separation and interaction of subject and object, in knowing as well as acting. This *prius* of subject and object cannot become an object to which man as a subject is theoretically and practically related. God is no object for us as subjects. He is always that which precedes this division. (*TC* 25)

While Tillich (like Fichte, Schelling and Hegel) responds to Kant's criticism by seeing the basic problem to be that of the ontological foundations of a possible identity between thought and being, he sees God, as being-itself, to be the answer to the question of being, rather than as a philosophical synthesis of thought and being. We will return to this point, for it is the source of the concept of the ground and the abyss of Being, that is, the dimension of depth that calls in question every philosophical synthesis, and this emphasis is distinctively Tillich's.

b) *Identity and the essential structures of being.* The second question concerns the essential structures of being that make knowledge and understanding possible. 'The ontological question presupposes an asking subject and an object about which the question is asked; it presupposes the subject-object structure of being, which in turn presupposes the self-world structure as the basic articulation of being. *The self having a world to which it belongs – this highly dialectical structure – logically and experientially precedes all other structures*' (*ST1*, 183. Italics added). The analysis of this ontological polarity of self and world is the basic task in determining the essential nature of knowledge.

Tillich's use of the Principle of Identity differs from that of the idealists. When discussing the essential structures of being that make understanding possible, and that make it possible to grasp the world of becoming as a world, he is at pains to stress that the categories are categories of finitude (*ST1*, 90–2). Causality, substance, quality and quantity are unconditionally necessary forms of possible experience, but they cannot serve as a foundation of our knowledge of God or of the Unconditioned; similarly, with what Tillich calls forms of perception (space and time), ontological polarities (individualisation and participation, dynamics and form), and states of being (essence and existence, finite and infinite): these are principles presupposed in and necessary to the formulation of objective knowledge (*ST1*, 181–6). With Kant, Tillich would assert that while these principles are regulative for knowledge and our concept of reality, we are not entitled to claim that they are constitutive of reality. It is this qualification that is lacking in all the idealists.[6]

c) *Identity and existence*. The third question concerns the distinction between the essential identity of thought and being, and subject and object; and their actual separation under the conditions of existence.[7]

There are two levels at which Tillich draws the distinction: the first concerns the dialectic of the act of knowing in its usual form, and the second has to do with this dialectic under the conditions of alienated existence.

His frequently repeated definition of knowledge stresses that knowledge is necessarily an act of union *and* separation for finite beings. The knower and the known stand in a dialectical relationship of opposition.

> Knowing is a form of union. In every act of knowledge the knower and that which is known are united; the gap between subject and object is overcome. The subject 'grasps' the object, adapts it to itself, and, at the same time, adapts itself to the object. But the union of knowledge is a peculiar one; it is a union through separation. Detachment is the condition of cognitive union. In order to know, one must 'look' at a thing, and, in order to look at a thing, one must be 'at a distance'. Cognitive distance is the presupposition of cognitive union. (*ST1*, 105)[8]

The detachment and separation here are cognitive in that they are necessary to the act of knowledge as a reflexive judgement about the relation between subject and object. They are also existential in that there is a variety of factors that affect the act of knowledge; in particular, anxiety, guilt and despair affect the subject's capacity to know reality,[9] and alienating conditions of social and economic life affect a man's perspective on reality.[10]

It is with reference to the first kind of distinction between union and detachment that Tillich objects to the comparison of his philosophy to the philosophies of identity:

> About 20 years ago I tried to elaborate an *ontology of encounter* on the assumption that it is possible to derive the subject-object relation from the phenomena, while it is impossible to make forms of encounter like love or knowledge understandable by starting either with pure objectivity or pure subjectivity or by starting, as Spinoza and *Schelling* did, with a preceding identity. *What precedes is not identity but polarity, and, in the actual process of life, encounter.*[11]

However, Tillich does tend to confuse the two kinds of separation

(*Entfremdung*) involved by insisting, against some existentialists and Marxists, that man's state of self-alienation is total. The result is a conflation of two things that he maintains are necessary features of our experience: the kind of separation that characterises the cognitive process, and the kind of self-alienation that results in the distortion of our perception of truth. Tillich shies away from drawing this conclusion about truth, but if he insists that self-estrangement is total in the moral and political spheres, then it seems that he must opt for a modern version of the doctrine of total depravity in the theory of knowledge as well![12] The ambivalence he manifests at this point affects his treatment of our knowledge of finite objects in particular; and the realism that demands that we recognise the estrangement as a factor in knowledge is in conflict with the demand of a philosophical realism that it must be possible for reason to grasp the essential natures of things.

3. *Evaluation and discussion of the systematic implications of Tillich's ontology of cognition*

a) *Being-itself and Truth-in-general.* George F. McLean has summarised Tillich's doctrine aptly:

> The dynamics of the system of Paul Tillich are those of dialectical motion. They order the various elements of his thought, playing one against the other. As a type of *thesis* one finds idealistic elements of identity with the divine. These are both continued and contradicted in an *antithesis* which is the existence described by the existentialists. Both elements, the 'Yes' of identity and the 'No' of existential estrangement, interact to bear man toward a synthesis where estrangement is overcome and God is 'all in all'.[13]

The great merit of Tillich's metaphysics of knowledge is the single-mindedness with which he has sought to establish the foundations of an essentially Christian theological epistemology and has adapted and profoundly modified the principle of identity as expressed in the philosophies of identity; nevertheless there remain certain inherent weaknesses which pertain to his retention of the principle of identity.

His most fundamental statement of the principle of identity, in the *Systematic Theology*, illustrates some of the difficulties:

> Being is inseparable from the logic of being, the structure which makes it what it is and which gives reason the power of grasping and shaping it. 'Being something' means having a form. According to the polarity of individualisation and participation, there are special and general forms, but in actual being these never are separated. Through their union every being becomes a definite being. Whatever loses its form loses its being. (*ST1*, 197)

Unfortunately, like many of Tillich's general assertions, this statement is somewhat opaque. He exploits the ambiguities of 'logic' in the phrase 'logic of being'. It refers variously to formal logic, to the immanent structure of being-itself (the logos) and to the special form of particular beings. This is inexcusable equivocation. It is also baffling, because of the seeming univocity that Tillich attributes to terms like 'being' and 'logic'.

On the one hand, maintaining that terms like 'thought' and 'being' are univocal, when in fact they are analogical, is essential to the easy dialectic that establishes their 'identity'. This trick is used by Fichte, Schelling and Hegel. Hegel's *Logic*, in particular, could not have been constructed without it. It is also fundamental to the 'deduction' by which Tillich establishes the division of the sciences in *Das System der Wissenschaften* (*DSW* 117–20). On the other hand, it must be said in Tillich's defence that this idealist dialectic becomes more and more qualified by criticism as the years go by.

It might also be said that exploiting an implied univocity of such terms is Tillich's way of insisting that they are *systematically* ambiguous, that is, that their different meanings are related. It is, however, a serious fault that he does not demonstrate systematically the connections between the cognate meanings of systematically ambiguous terms, for it would have greatly enhanced the rigour of his system and avoided some ambiguities. He relies, instead, on our ability to intuit the common ultimate reference of his terms. His style, like that of a poet or a propagandist, relies on the provocative juxtaposition of cognate meanings and paradoxical suggestion; by the mutual 'interinanimation'[14] of words, we are pointed towards the deeper ground of being and meaning in which the disparate meanings meet. The connections are exhibited ostensively rather than discursively.

These remarks apply with special force to Tillich's manifold uses of the term logos. Not only in his theology (which owes a great deal to the Johannine tradition) but also in his philosophy, he uses the term logos to link the use of the principle of identity to bridge the gap between subject and object in epistemology, and its use to bridge the gap between finite and infinite in ontology and the philosophy of religion. Here he makes full use of the wide range of associated meanings that the term logos has in the history of Western thought, from Heraclitus and Plato to the Stoics, from Philo Judaeus and the Johannine corpus to St Augustine, and from the mediaeval Franciscans to Schelling and Hegel.

Another term that Tillich uses as if it were univocal, in order to exploit its ambiguities in the service of a systematic construction, is the term 'identity' itself. In addition to his tendency to conflate logical and ontological identity, he uses the principle of identity to refer to the disparate relations between knower and known at the existential level, thought and being at the abstract theoretical level, and finite logos and infinite *logos* at the ontological and theological level.[15] This does not necessarily mean that his conception of identity is incoherent, but it is misleading in as much as arguments used to defend the principle at one level do not suffice to establish it at another level.

Part of the difficulty lies in the inadequate logic on the basis of which the principle was developed by his idealist predecessors. They presupposed that all propositions, which, following Kant, they mistakenly called 'judgement',[16] are, or can be reduced to, propositions of the subject-predicate type, and that the relations of subject and predicate are synonymous with the relations of antecedent and consequent. As a result, the relations of subject and object, and finite and infinite are assimilated to simple relations of the dyadic type; and, instead of the correlative character of these terms, *qua* relational terms, being realised, they are reified by considering them as the *relata* between which some now mysterious relations obtains. Further, by the related tendency to conflate formal and causal implication, subject and object are identified as standing in the relation of antecedent and consequent mutually determining one another by a kind of reciprocal causality. Similarly, inferences that apply to the principle of identity as a purely formal principle signifying a certain kind of dyadic logical relation, are taken to be valid for reality as a whole, and a causal connection between God, as subject and antecedent, and Nature, as predicate and consequent, is invalidly inferred.[17] Many of the limitations of Tillich's ontology of cognition are due to the fact that he never wholly succeeded in disentangling his thought from the idealist matrix in which it was given its first formal expression.

There is, however, another more basic, criticism. Tillich's theory, which equates being-itself, truth and God, is not only modelled on that of St Augustine[18] but is open to the basic objection formulated by St Thomas Aquinas in the *Quaestiones disputatae de Veritate*.[19] Considering St Augustine's claim that 'truth' and 'being-itself' are convertible terms, he argued that while this states a necessary formal condition that truth must satisfy in order to be truth, it is not sufficient as a criterion of truth because it is not specific enough to enable us to distinguish between the true and the false. In this sense it is an essentialistic and formalistic statement that, even if it is given content by a mystical experience of the ultimate identity of truth and being-itself, remains empty in that it provides solutions to none of the practical problems of science or epistemology.

As is evident particularly from the argument of *Das System der Wissenschaften*, Tillich is sensitive to the charge of formalism, and tries to deal with the problem of truth and verification (see *ST1*, 112–18). However, as we shall see, he does not succeed in providing us with a specific formal criterion of truth, and his abstract statement of a necessary correspondence between the *logos* structures of mind and reality is open to the objections advanced by St Thomas.

b) *Ontological Structures and Understanding.* We turn now to consideration of the merits and weaknesses of Tillich's account of the absoluteness of ontological structures for understanding and of the dialectic of encounter in the act of knowing. His contribution in this area, which is highly original, has great general philosophical importance, as well as being the most thoroughgoing attempt to develop a theory that does justice to those dimensions of reality that a Christian philosophy of life must take into account and that most philosophies ignore. As George F. McLean expresses it:

> His interests centre on God and this has directed his work towards the construction of a theonomous philosophy. He seeks and organises traces of the divine in all reality and thus every field of human

enquiry becomes a mirror for the revelation of God to man in the present age. But if it is theonomous it is also genuine philosophy with an epistemology and even a great stress on the importance of being.

... Since all this is presented in his rigorously systematic fashion there can be no doubt that it holds a place of honour among the most forceful and impressive presentations of modern thought.[20]

i) What is distinctive about Tillich's theory is that, among so-called existentialist thinkers, he is the most consistent and thoroughgoing in working out the implications of existentialist principles for metaphysics in general, and for the metaphysics of knowledge in particular.

This is shown in his profound existential interpretations of certain conceptions: the self-world polarity and its tensions; the existential relevance of the categories of substance, causality, quantity and quality; space and time as forms of perception; the distinctions between essence and existence, and finite and infinite, as modes of being. Finally, it is shown in his dynamic view of the polarities of individualisation and participation, dynamics and form, and freedom and destiny.[21]

Perhaps the most important point is Tillich's distinction between the abstract subject of traditional epistemological analysis, which somehow exists outside space and time, and the actually existing ontological subject whose knowing takes place within the co-ordinates of a definite spatio-temporal situation (see *IH* 129–36, *ST1*, 186–90). Paralleling this is his distinction between the logical and the ontological object (*ST1*, 190–3).

Tillich rightly points out that, since Descartes, philosophers have prescinded from any discussion of the ontogenetic and historical order in which knowledge takes place; they have concentrated attention exclusively on the knowledge relation and have ignored the knowledge situation. This not only results in a caricature of actual knowledge, which either is assimilated to timeless and eternal truths *more geometrico*, or collapses into a subjectivist atomism of discrete and discontinuous sense data, but, more seriously, it becomes regulative for the conduct of science and all related human enquiries. At a theoretical level, this means that the intentional co-ordinates of the act of knowing are ignored: the fact that a judgement intends both a knowing subject and an object known is overlooked. This establishes a hiatus between cognitive and other intentional acts, creating a painful dichotomy between theory and practice. At a practical level, it means that the ontological restraints that limit intellectual free creation are ignored, creating the dangerous illusion that there are no limits to the expression of the intellectual will-to-power in science and politics, leading to the totalitarian will-to-dominate both Nature and other men.[22]

In emphasising the relevance to epistemology of the existing historical subject and of the ontological status of the object known, Tillich is not only giving expression to an existential theory of knowledge and implying the necessity for an adequate intentionalist theory of human acts, but he is also taking issue with the method of 'bracketing out existence' that Husserl describes as the great merit of Descartes' new method.[23] And, while he has some sympathy with the phenomenological intuition of essences as necessary to ontology, he rejects this method in the theory of knowledge.

The upshot of Tillich's emphasis on the existing historical subject is that we are obliged to recognise that in the account of knowledge we cannot ignore the concerns of the subject, since *qua* existing being he is concerned to participate meaningfully in being together with all other beings. The knowing subject is 'ultimately concerned with his being and meaning' and his knowledge is an expression of that fact.

ii) The second area in which Tillich makes an original and provocative contribution is the analysis of the act of knowing as a form of encounter, directed towards union with the thing known but also involving detachment from it.[24]

It is important to emphasise how revolutionary this approach was when first formulated, and how it still challenges some of the most deep-seated prejudices of philosophers, whether rationalists, empiricists, idealists or positivists, who abstract knowledge from its intentional context and seek purely extensional definitions of truth. The notion of 'encounter' draws attention to the fact that knowing is an existential engagement between beings of different kinds, and to the fact that the meeting of persons with persons will produce a kind of knowledge different from that yielded by the encounter of persons with the rest of the living and inorganic universe. The implications for his philosophy of this fact are taken very seriously by Tillich, but it has profound consequences, in particular for his account of our knowledge of God. The language he uses is strongly reminiscent of that used by Aquinas when, for example, he says, 'Knower and known are not agent and patient to one another, they are two things from which one principle of knowledge results,[25] and, 'in speaking of the known as actual we imply a distinction between the things known and its being known'.[26] In echoing this earlier, mediaeval, realist tradition Tillich is concerned to undercut the nominalist presuppositions of the entire post-Cartesian tradition, and to escape from the charmed magic circle of idealist and essentialist notions on which he and his generation had been reared. There are, however, elements of exaggeration in Tillich's existentialist account that undermine this realism and bring it dangerously close to subjectivism: in particular, there is the tendency to make the dialectical encounter definitive for the nature of reality as well as for knowledge, and, therefore, to call in question the existence of a reality independent of thought. Related to this is a tendency, perhaps inherited from the romantic tradition, to make emotion a *conditio sine qua non* for true knowledge (on the analogy, frequently used by Tillich, between *gnosis* and sexual love).[27]

On the first point, Tillich's confusion is partly due to the fact that he lacks a clear distinction between the intelligible species and the thing's essence. These, though identical in the act of consciousness, are distinct in reality, and are, in fact, of different ontological types *qua concept and qua fundamentum in re*.[28]

On the second point, Tillich does not distinguish clearly between the ontological *inter-esse*, that is, the condition of contingent finitude essential to man *qua* man, and the different *interests*, appetitive and intellectual, that necessarily arise in him because of his ontological condition. Further, his argument, while rightly emphasising the connection between knowledge and desire, misrepresents their relation to one another and to man's nature as a contingent being. Because man exists in a state of contingent *inter-esse*, he has a necessary interest in other beings. The necessity that governs his appetitive desires is physical and related to his creaturely needs. The necessity that operates in the desire for knowledge is different, for it arises simply from man's capacity for reflexive awareness of himself *qua* contingent being, and the consequent need to comprehend his own being and meaning.

Tillich tends too easily to conflate the various meanings of 'love' and 'desire' in his use of the term 'concern', and to interpret man's essential concern with his being and meaning as having an appetitive character and an ultimately utilitarian purpose. The philosophical *eros* is certainly a kind of passion, but it is easy to be misled by the analogies that support this metaphor, for ordinary desires and intellectual passions have different logics in terms both of the needs that fire their appetites and the objects that satisfy them. And, while knowledge may usually be directed towards more effective and meaningful participation in being, it does not necessarily serve utilitarian ends.

A further consequence of his doctrine is a tendency to exaggerate the separation between subject and object that has to be overcome by the unitive act of *gnosis*: the object is known only mediately in its relation to the subject, and the subject is the discrete consciousness of a Cartesian *res cogitans* (*ST2*, 76).

George F. McLean comments:

> To Tillich's element of subjectivism St Thomas would reply with a still more profound consideration of why the object of the knowing mind must be the thing itself. He would accompany this with a metaphysical demonstration of the possibility of such knowledge . . . This would greatly change the nature and function of the categories of the mind and narrow the exaggerated dichotomy of subject and object. This in turn would reduce the essential role given to the emotions in all meaningful knowledge. Reality would then be freed from the necessity of participating in the categories of the mind and place would be made for a truly transcendent reality which is still a being.[29]

Part of the difficulty with Tillich's use of expressions such as 'love', 'union', 'separation', 'detachment' and 'estrangement', is that his ideological purpose – the recommendation of a new world-view – produces a rhetoric aimed at persuasion rather than precision. While this detracts from the theoretical consistency of his thought in a way that perhaps undermines its practical impact, it would be a mistake to underestimate the Christian and existential insights that Tillich adds to our understanding of the kinds of encounter involved in our knowledge of person and things, and of the kinds of alienation that can operate in these encounters.

The plain fact is that Tillich is not primarily interested in giving a text-book anatomy, as it were, of truth; he is concerned, rather, with the possi-bility of a living truth. To continue the medical metaphor, he seeks the physiology and pathology of such a truth, and an aetiology of its mal-functions as well as an explanation of the dynamics of its normal life. He is concerned with healing and saving truth. 'Knowledge is more than a ful-filling; it also transforms and heals; this would be impossible if the know-ing subject were only a mirror of the object.[30] He offers men a directive philosophy for life, one that will provide a man's life with some ultimate meaning, and will supply him with unconditional principles on which to base his value-judgements and moral decisions.

iii) Tillich is also concerned with the alienations that frustrate the translation of truth into life. He emphasises three kinds of alienation: ontological, moral, and intellectual or spiritual. These correspond to three kinds of realisation of the truth: namely, 1) the ideal congruence of being and truth, that is, the ideal of being in the truth; 2) the conformity of what one is existentially, here and now, to what one essentially ought to be; and 3) the agreement of the intellectual form and the real form of truth.

1) the forms of alienation that may be called 'ontological' concern those anxieties that arise in man as a result of his awareness of his finitude and the 'threat of non-being', and that can seriously distort man's perception of reality if they are not overcome by a self-affirming 'courage to be'. These are described in classic terms in *The Courage to Be*:[31] the anxiety of fate and death in the face of the threat of non-being to man's ontic self-affirmation; the anxiety of guilt and condemnation arising from the threat of non-being to man's moral-self-affirmation; and the anxiety of meaninglessness in the face of the threat of non-being to man's spiritual self-affirmation. Such anxieties are structural and ontological, Tillich maintains, and not to be confused with pathological forms of the same anxieties.

'Pathological anxiety is a state of existential anxiety under special con-ditions.'[32] This is characterised by specific forms of self-affirmation that fail to resolve the anxiety threatening the individual in his sometimes unique and tragic circumstances of suffering or vulnerability: 'He who does not succeed in taking his anxiety courageously upon himself can succeed in avoiding the extreme situation of despair [only] by escaping into neurosis. He still affirms himself, but on a limited scale. Neurosis is the way of avoiding non-being by avoiding being.'[33] Not only are neurotic individuals withdrawn from reality, they are afraid to face the truth about themselves and reality, afraid, that is, of the process of healing, 'because it throws them out of the limited but safe house of their neurotic self-seclusion'.[34]

However, even for the normal individual, 'Our anxiety puts frightening masks over all men and things'. This is due, he explains with reference to the *libido moriendi* of Seneca, to our uncontrolled desires: 'Desire as such is not unlimited. In undistorted nature it is limited by objective needs and is therefore capable of satisfaction. But man's distorted imagination transcends the objective needs ... and with them any possible satisfaction. And this, not the desire as such, produces the "unwise tendency toward death".'[35]

And, because the Stoics understood that 'One cannot remove anxiety by arguing it away',[36] so they understood that this is achieved only by the expulsive power of a deeper affection or a more ultimate concern: 'Stoic courage pre-supposes the surrender of the personal centre to the Logos of being; it is participation in the divine power of reason, transcending the realm of passions and anxieties'.[37] Ultimately, Tillich's theory of truth owes much to the Stoic doctrine, particularly his concept of the courage to be as the expression of the rational will to be in the truth and to overcome the illusions and fantasies that are the creations of our anxiety. Faith is, for Tillich, 'being grasped by a power that is greater than we are, a power that shakes us, and turns us and transforms us and heals us'.[38]

2) The forms of alienation that are moral in character concern the distortion of the truth in a man's self-understanding and perception of reality, when he is guilty of moral error and acts in a way that contradicts his humanity. Crimes of inhumanity not only have depraving and destructive effects, but are commonly associated with a distorted grasp of reality.

What Tillich does is to raise again, in a provocative way, the neglected question of the relation between knowledge and virtue, that is, the relation of the theoretical distinction between truth and falsity to the practical distinction between truth and error.

> Error becomes dangerous if it means union with distorted and deceiving elements of reality, with that which is not really real but which only claims to be. Anxiety about falling into error . . . the tremendous reactions against error in all cohesive social groups, the interpretation of error as demonic possession – all this is understandable only if knowledge includes union. (*ST1*, 108)

Or, to put it another way, he is concerned to distinguish between the epistemic and the existential uses of 'belief'.[39] In the epistemic sense, opinion, belief and knowledge form a hierarchy, in which belief is a lower-grade form of knowledge to which we give qualified assent, and opinion is characterised by the fact that it is a matter of indifference whether we give or withhold assent. In the existential sense, belief represents the faith by which a man lives, the system of absolute presuppositions that provide his primary orientation to reality and that, by defining the meaning of being for him, also suggest his basic criteria of truth and value. A system of beliefs of this kind need not be explicitly religious, although we may agree with Tillich that it performs an implicitly religious function insofar as it expresses a man's ultimate concern.

In this second, existential, sense of belief, it matters profoundly what a man believes, because there is an intimate and intrinsic connection between belief and action. It is at this level that the great ideological battle for the mind and allegiance of man is fought out. Liberal humanism, communism, nationalism, democratic socialism, and the great religions, insofar as they purport to offer man a practical way of life, compete in offering man ideals and values by which to live and to achieve fulfilment, but even more in offering their diagnoses and explanations of the pathology of error, and the aetiology of the various forms of individual, social, economic, historical and political alienation.

In his Religious Socialist phase, but also throughout his entire life, Tillich was concerned to attack not only the subjectivist and epistemological theories of Western philosophers since Descartes, but also the individualistic and bourgeois philosophies of life that have dominated popular thought since the Industrial Revolution and the rise of capitalism. The latter, by prescinding from the objective sociopolitical and economic dimensions of life and ignoring the ontological structures and dynamics of being, produce philosophies that are egocentric and moralistic, in that they are obsessed with the sexual peccadilloes of men and women in their private lives, and ignore the social and structural problems of institutionalised evil and injustice. This is the basis of his concern with moralism and morality, his analysis of sin and estrangement, and his concern with the possibility of a theonomous ethics and the achievement of a 'trans-moral conscience'.[40] Since morality is concerned with man's self-integration as a total person, the forms of estrangement that have a moral character are grounded in the 'structures of destruction' in personality, society and world (see *ST3*, 36–47, *ST2*, 69f.). 'Only man has a completely centred self and a structured universe to which he belongs and at which he is able to look at the same time' (*ST2*, 69). The truth about evil is that it involves not only estrangement from other people but, more fundamentally, 'self-loss' and 'world-loss', that is, the distortion of the dialectic that governs both truth and man's being-in-the-world:

> Self-loss is the loss of one's determining centre, the disintegration of the unity of the person. This is manifest in moral conflicts and in psycho-pathological disruptions, independently or interdependently. The horrifying experience of 'falling to pieces' gets hold of the person. To the degree in which this happens, one's world also falls to pieces. It *ceases to be a world*, in the sense of a *meaningful whole*. Things no longer speak to man; they lose their power to enter into meaningful encounter with man, because man himself has lost this power. (*ST2*, 75)

3) The forms of alienation that are intellectual or spiritual concern the kind of intellectual attitude adopted towards truth, or the existential stance a man adopts towards 'his' truth. Scepticism and doubt relate to the first, and idolatry to the second.

The notions of attitude and stance play a very important part in Tillich's account of truth, and both in his earlier work and in the *Systematic Theology* are critical elements in his account of the relationship between faith and reason.[41] For example, in 'Religionsphilosophie', he uses the concept of stance in this crucial passage:

> We find therefore in any particular stance of the knowing act on the

one hand an awareness of the infinite reality of all being, striving as it does against thought and at the same time providing a basis for thought, and on the other hand the demand for a universal knowledge of being, a demand driving out beyond the particular, the individual. It is now possible for the spirit to orient itself to the infinity of the particular claims to knowledge and their achieved unity, or to the unconditioned being that is the basis for everything particular and yet transcends everything particular. The first directedness is the cultural one, the second is the religious. (*WR* 66)

Very important for the interpretation of an attitude is what Tillich has to say about the element of decision involved in the choice of method, whether in the empirical, the formal or the normative sciences, including philosophy and theology: 'Whoever wants to understand knowledge through analysing the single act, must necessarily divide it into a technical side (which can be expressed in scientific genius) and a moral side (which can be enhanced as far as asceticism). He cannot see the third element, the quality of freedom and fate belonging to knowledge' (*IH* 145). This third element of knowledge, and 'its decisive character, its genuine historic quality, its position in fate and in the Kairos', cannot become an object of ordinary knowledge. This is because the acceptance of a world-view is constitutive of our world in a formal sense, and regulative for the determination of our procedures and objects of knowledge. 'It can become an object only for the metaphysics of knowledge' (*IH* 146f.).

That is, the adoption of an attitude is a matter of pre-philosophical faith, and cannot be justified at a first-order level by means of the very criteria it helps to establish. The conscious commitment to such a point of view is, however, an act of courage and involves the acceptance of responsibility. Even the unconscious acceptance of a world-view carries certain responsibilities towards truth and values: 'the responsibility on both becomes infinite and direct: the (scientific) responsibility towards the true is as great as the (moral) responsibility towards the good, rather it is one responsibility' (*IH* 146). This has a bearing on Tillich's discussion of ultimate concern in which he seeks to distinguish philosophy from theology according to differences in 'the cognitive attitude of the philosopher and the theologian': the former adopts the attitude of 'detached objectivity' while 'the attitude of the theologian is "existential"' (*ST1*, 25). However, he also distinguishes between them according to a difference in affective disposition between 'the philosophical *eros*' and the theological 'love which accepts saving, and therefore personal, truth' (*ST1*, 26). The cognitive attitude combined with the particular affective disposition of a given individual serve to define his particular concern with, or 'stance' in relation to, truth. Tillich would deny that complete affective neutrality is possible in any sphere of human endeavour, for man cannot be entirely indifferent to truth. His concept of ultimate concern, 'the first formal criterion of theology' (*ST1*, 15; cf. *WR* 65–6), is the criterion by which he judges the fundamental beliefs of men. The test is not only whether a given belief is ultimate in the sense of enjoying logical priority

over all other beliefs for that individual, and commanding his unconditional love and loyalty; ultimate concern is the touchstone of an
authentic attitude to truth and the criterion of whether a man's stance in
relation to truth is idolatrous or not, according as the object of his concern
is really ultimate or not.

This can be seen in his analyses of scepticism and faith as attitudes to
truth, and of idolatry and ultimate concern as two kinds of stance with
respect to the unconditional validity of truth.

What is distinctive about Tillich's analysis of scepticism and doubt is
that he does not regard them as being necessarily forms of alienation from
the truth. Methodological doubt[42] is the expression of a kind of scepticism in the service of truth, and is always a means to greater certainty,
clarity and unconditional validity. Scepticism for its own sake would be
wilful abrogation of responsibility for, or unwillingness to be obedient to,
the truth. This wilful unbelief would be the alienated form of the intellectual attitude to the truth.[43] Existential doubt however, is the expression
of an ultimate concern with being and meaning and, as such, is comparable to faith; it is justifying (and perhaps justified) scepticism. This is a
constant theme in Tillich's work from the publication of 'Rechtfertigung
und Zweifel' in 1924 to *My Search for Absolutes* in 1967. Existential
doubt is the expression of awareness of the risk involved in every commitment to truth, that is of the ambiguity and incompleteness of every
expression of truth in word, thought or action. In the ultimacy of its concern with truth, this attitude is implicitly religious. 'It does not reject every
concrete truth, but is aware of the element of insecurity in every existential
truth. At the same time, the doubt which is implied in faith accepts this
insecurity and takes it into itself in an act of courage. Faith includes
courage. Therefore, it can include doubt about itself.'[44]

The alienated form of existential doubt with respect to the truth would
be the inability to commit oneself to any truth, because of a lack of faith,
or obsessive anxiety about the insecurity of all truth; such an attitude
would be identical with despair. An analogous form is the fanatical
adherence to some expression of truth, which lacks unconditional
validity as if it were ultimate. This is the stance of the idolater, who
through lack of courage, cannot accept the relativity and insecurity of
every human expression of truth.[45]

In earlier sections,[46] we have sought to combat the popular view that
Tillich never escapes from the spell of Schelling, and that what we are left
with at the end of the day is a restatement of an idealist ontology. What
ultimately gives the lie to this view is Tillich's profoundly realistic and
Christian interpretation of these three types of alienation from the truth,
and his doctrine of the holy and the demonic in nature and knowledge
that underlies this ontological analysis. It is Tillich's willingness to take
the epistemological significance of sin seriously that marks him out from
all idealist philosophers. 'In theology one must distinguish not only ontological from technical reason, but also ontological reason in its essential
perfection from its predicament in the different stages of its actualisation

in existence, life and history' (*ST1*, 83).

R. Allan Killen is one of the few commentators to emphasise this particular aspect of Tillich's thought, although he, too, is eager to prove
Tillich's dependence on Schelling: 'Tillich's views of nature and man's
participation in it have an influence upon his view of nature and sin . . .
Nature is the "finite expression of the infinite ground of all things". It
gives a revelation of the divine-demonic conflict within the creation and
needs salvation just like man, and it can also become transparent to the
divine'.[47] Thus, he concludes that Tillich's doctrine of union and detachment in knowledge is intimately related to his doctrine of Salvation, since
Tillich uses 'union' and 'detachment' univocally for the relationship
with the thing known in the knowledge act, and for union and separation
from God: 'But separation is also used for the estrangement and conflict
between God and man, between man and man, and even within man.
Taken in this sense, separation is sin and reunion is salvation' (*TPT* 344).
Similarly, in speaking of the role of decision and commitment in knowledge, Tillich employs a paradigm of philosophy that confuses his critics,
for it has more to do with religious and ideological belief-systems, than
with the systematic constructions of theoretical knowledge. Such belief-
systems are related to peoples' deepest commitments. They embody
choices and metaphysical attitudes: 'What is meant is the *attitude
towards the Unconditioned*, an attitude which is freedom and fate at the
same time, and *out* of which action as well as knowledge flows' (*IH* 145;
italics added).

In Tillich's view, it is characteristic of modern philosophy that it uncritically ignores these attitudes and beliefs that constitute our world-
views and determine our entire perspective on man and reality; for they
are matters of pre-philosophical faith, and are often held with passionate,
dogmatic and even fanatical conviction on the part of self-styled,
critical, objective and dispassionate thinkers.

Because such belief-systems have a religious or quasi-religious character, in any period dominated by such a belief-system, 'the will-to-truth is
subject to a special and outstanding responsibility quite independent of
the moral one. And no moral greatness can balance defection from the
truth in such a period: the defection from the truth is not equal to
immorality but a conscious devotion to the demonic in practice' (*IH* 145).

In his paper 'Das Dämonische' (*IH* 77–122) he goes much further in
discussing the relationship of nature and knowledge to the demonic and
the holy. It is characteristic of Tillich that he is prepared to consider the
philosophical relevance not only of such positive religious concepts as
'the holy', but also the negative concepts of 'sin', 'the demonic' and 'hell',
when most modern theologians would be too embarrassed to mention
them. Sin and the demonic are related to essence and knowledge, and
transcend a narrow individualistic and moralistic view of sin:

> The demonic is the perversion of the creative (in knowledge and
> action), and as such belongs to the phenomena that are contrary to
> essential nature, or sin . . . Sin does not always appear in demonic

form . . . Normally it remains within the limits of uncreative weakness. That does not change its character as sin. It is contrariness to essential nature and therefore is plainly to be denied as contrary to meaning, the separation from absolute being; and it is this, no matter whether it appears as weakness or as ecstatic strength. (*IH* 93)

For Tillich, the demonic is connected not only with essential nature, but also with the inexhaustibility of being-itself, the abyss, and this in polar dependence with the notion of the infinite creative ground of all being and meaning. 'Form of being and inexhaustibility of being belong together. Their unity in the depth of essential nature is the divine, their separation in existence, the relatively independent eruption of the "abyss" in things, is the demonic' (*IH* 84).

This translation of the concept into the broadest ontological terms disturbs Killen who, writing shortly after the publication of the first volume of the *Systematic Theology*, claimed that, under the demands of an idealist ontology Tillich is driven to abandon the Demonic in favour of the concept of the *Me-on* or non-being. However, he might have been reassured by the more concrete analyses of sin and estrangement in Volume 3, where it is clearly connected with the paradigmatic character of the personal in Tillich's thought: '"Heaven" and "Hell" are symbols of ultimate meaning and unconditional significance. But no such threat or promise is made about other than human life' (*ST3*, 326). Or again: 'The background of the imagery of a twofold destiny lies in the radical separation of person from person and of the personal from the sub-personal' (*ST3*, 434). Finally, as an earnest of the eternal truth that Tillich takes so seriously, he sees the solution to the conflict between such absolute threats and promises as 'being lost' and 'being saved' in terms of a symbol taken from cognitive experience: 'The conceptual symbol of "essentialisation" is capable of fulfilling this postulate, for it emphasises the despair of having wasted one's potentialities yet also assures the elevation of the positive within existence (even in the most unfulfilled life) into eternity' (*ST3*, 434). What this means, he explains in speaking of eternal blessedness, is that 'all things – since they are good by creation – participate in the Divine Life according to their essence . . . The conflicts and sufferings of nature under the conditions of existence and its longing for salvation, of which Paul speaks (*Romans*, chapter 8), serve the enrichment of essential being after the negation of the negative in everything that has being' (*ST3*, 432).

c) *Essences, Existence and Rational Discourse.* It is obvious from the preceding that, in developing his account of the self-world polarity, Tillich stresses the ontological structures presupposed in and necessary to understanding, and the dialectics of union and detachment in the act of knowing. He strives to develop systematically the implications of an existential account of the relation between knower and known, and to incorporate into this account the insights that a Christian emphasis on 'doing the truth' and 'knowledge through love'[48] add to our understanding of living in the truth and being alienated from the truth. And, in spite of weaknesses in his account of the relationship between knowledge and desire, the ambiguities in his use of 'concern', 'unity', and 'separation', and the tendency to make the dialectic of encounter definitive for reality as well as for the act of knowing, there is no doubt that Tillich's account of the essential nature of knowledge represents an important criticism of modern epistemological discussion; much of the latter has ignored the ontological foundations of knowledge, and has led to either empty formalism or subjectivism, because it fails to recognise the unconditional validity of the ontological structures that make experience possible. Further, his account of the dialectic of union and detachment in knowledge, under the conditions of existence, adds a dimension of existential realism to his Christian and socialist account of authentic knowledge and estrangement from the truth, correcting the tendency to ignore these questions in academic philosophy.

Tillich's account of our knowledge of essences and their necessary function in making knowledge and rational discourse possible, highlights a number of problems in, and unique features of, an existential theory of knowledge. In *My Search for Absolutes*,[49] for example, he discusses how the power of abstraction enables man to grasp universal qualities in things and to express these universals in language; how this enables him to classify things into *genera* and *species*, and, finally, to communicate with other men about the things around him. This is a fairly standard and unexceptionable account, but it illustrates some typical preconceptions about knowledge in Tillich's thought, and, since it was the last work he prepared for publication, it is rather significant.

Firstly, it shows a typically traditional preoccupation with substantives and adjectives as definitive for our understanding of universals or essences, and a total indifference to Russell's and Wittgenstein's criticisms of the name theory of linguistic meaning,[50] with their far-reaching implications of our understanding of relations and relational words. Tillich's examples of essences are, 'Redness', the species 'Pine', the genus 'Tree'. Some of the difficulties he gets into in trying to make essence equivalent to potentiality, in order to make essences dynamic, are due to his inadequate understanding of relations and relational concepts.

Secondly, his account suffers from his uncritical acceptance of the connotation-denotation theory of meaning, and the crude class logic on which it was based (*MSA* 72; cf. *ST1*, 136–7). Unfortunately, his use of that theory was based on a deficient understanding of it. While he employed a rough-and-ready distinction between the expressive function of language and denotation (which does duty for a sense and reference distinction), his use of these distinctions is vague and confused. He does not distinguish between denotation and extension, and hence tends to use the word 'denotation' and its cognates in a way that is indistinguishable from the usual meaning of 'connotation': 'The denotative power of language is its ability to grasp and communicate *general* meanings' (*ST1*, 137; italics added). Likewise, since he fails to distinguish between connotation and intension, he cannot make his point clear when he uses the term 'expressive power' as a substitute for both in formal contexts: 'The expressive power of language is its ability to disclose and to communicate *personal* states' (*ST1*, 137; italics added). Because Tillich does not work out formally the requirements of a logical and semantic theory that would do justice to what Grice has called 'utterer's meaning and intention',[51] and does no more than hint at the need for an intentional logic to do justice to the communicative aspects of language, his own account remains very unsatisfactory.

Thirdly, this account leads to confusion between the essence instantiated in the individual and the essence as conceived by the mind. On the one hand he wants to emphasise the dynamic character of essences: '"*Redness*" as an essence is not a thing beside other things. It is the *transtemporal potentiality* of all red things in the universe' (*MSA* 73). On the other hand he wants essences to be 'absolute': 'It is absolute in the sense of independent of any particular moment in which "redness" appears and even of a situation in which cosmic events could produce its complete disappearance' (*MSA* 73). His concern to bridge the gap between the contingency of actual existential experience and the essential character of knowledge leads him to attempt to 'existentialise' knowledge, and to flirt with the idea that, because individuals can acquire symbolic significance, it must follow that there are universal individuals or essences of individuals, and hence that there can be direct knowledge of individuals. While this latter argument can be shown to be based on confusion, some of the other insights that emerge from Tillich's analysis are genuinely illuminating.

Chapter 6

The Metaphysics of Truth: Existential Aspects

There are three kinds of problem that arise for an existentialist theory of knowledge, and that Tillich is obliged to examine although he might question the label 'existentialist' as applied to his metaphysics of knowledge. In this chapter, we shall examine his attempts to deal with these problems, for his solutions define more clearly the nature of his theory of knowledge.

The problems are:

1. Is knowledge of individuals *qua* individuals possible, or is all knowledge general (essentialist) in spite of the fact that the knowledge encounter is between individuals? (cf. *MSA* 74–5 and *ST1*, 224–7)

2. Is there an alternative to the doctrine of abstraction that does not prescind from the intentionality of the act of knowledge considered as a meaning-creating and meaning-fulfilling directedness towards being? (*WR* 56–69)

3. Is a non-essentialist hermeneutic of being[1] possible, that is, is there a literary or philosophical style that is evocative of the dynamic character of existence and does not incarcerate it in static categories?

1. *Knowledge of individuals and knowledge of essences*

Tillich believes that the traditional doctrine that knowledge is of universals does less than justice to two basic human experiences: our knowledge of persons is immediate in the experience of love and encounter; our knowledge of ourselves as individuals is also immediate, in the act of self-awareness.

In his classic paper, 'The Two Types of Philosophy of Religion', Tillich stated and illustrated the principles upon which his epistemology had been based from the beginning, and which are particularly important for the argument of 'Kairos and Logos: A Study of the Metaphysics of Knowledge'.

As we saw in chapter 3, Tillich subordinates cosmological interpretations of being to ontological ones, and sets out to demonstrate that cosmological arguments for the existence of God are valid only to the extent that they are subject to ontological re-interpretation. The argument by which he reaches this conclusion is of decisive importance in illustrating his views on the difference between our knowledge of persons and our knowledge of things.

Following Augustine,[2] Tillich argues that there is one thing that the sceptic cannot doubt, namely his self-certainty of his own existence, for it is the *conditio sine qua non* of his being able to doubt at all; so God, as the unconditioned ground of all being and meaning, is the truth presupposed in the sceptic's doubt, for 'Man is immediately aware of something unconditional which is the *prius* of the separation and interaction of subject and object, theoretically as well as practically' (*TC* 22). Self-certainty and immediate awareness of the unconditioned ground of all being and truth are, for Tillich, the necessary grounds for the possibility of our knowledge of objects and of God. The cosmological approach, in Tillich's words, represents 'the way of meeting a stranger'. To the subject conditioned by scepticism, the object is an alien thing, and God, by analogy, is a strange and unfamiliar object whose existence must be demonstrated. If we are separated from the certainty of our own existence in doubt, then *a fortiori* we are alienated from objects, and God *qua* object, becomes an inaccessible, abstract, hypothetical cause or purpose.

Thus, the ontological approach underlines the precedence of personal knowledge over knowledge of things, and underlines the fact that the reversal of this order of priorities leads to scepticism not only with regard to knowledge of God, as historically it led to deism, but also with regard to knowledge of the world of objects, as it did historically in rationalism and empiricism.

Although it was Tillich's concern with the possibility of knowledge of a personal God that drove him to stress the priority of our knowledge of persons, acceptance of this doctrine has profoundly important implications for epistemology in particular and philosophy in general.[3]

Following his order of exposition we will examine briefly the consequences of the doctrine for: i) ontology and philosophical theism; ii) our conception of the relative importance of space and time for the identity of individuals; iii) our choice of paradigms of method in the sciences and philosophy; iv) the theory of knowledge in particular; and v) the doctrine of Revelation and the Christ.

i) It is a curious fact, that when philosophers use 'being' it is usually as a gerund or substantive, with the entitative sense of a being, rather than as a verb participle, descriptive of the process of be-ing. This is because, as Heidegger has observed,[4] they have tended to follow Aristotle in taking the being of natural objects as the paradigm for the being of all beings. 'To be' is associated with the 'Is' of substantial being. In consequence, 'Any problem that arises in traditional ontology is in advance understood in the horizon of substantiality'.[5] As Heidegger maintains:

> This idea of being . . . is too narrow and restricted to be able to explain all the ways and senses in which we can understand being. Above all, it is incapable of explaining the distinctively and uniquely human way of being. Man exists so that his being is *manifest* to him, and it is manifest to him as his own. That is why each of us must say

of himself: I am . . . the whole meaning and structure of the being we express by the AM is totally different from the real existence of a thing.[6]

In other words, not only is it surprising that the 'Is' of substantial being is taken as our paradigm of being, when the 'I am' of personal being is immediately accessible to us, but there is a danger that we will become alienated from our personal being by understanding it by analogy with the being of objects, that is by abstracting the personal form of 'To Be' as 'I am' into the 'Is' of *Da-sein*, the there-being of things.

Now Tillich, without much formal acknowledgement, has thoroughly assimilated these conclusions into his own thinking and, having the purpose of employing them in the elaboration of a Christian personalism, adapts them to his own ends. In his version, these views are closely linked to his insistence on the primacy of our knowledge of persons and the immediate *self*-certainty of our knowledge of our own existence. This is obvious in his subordination of the cosmological approach to the ontological approach (*TC*, chapter 2). Since the whole argument implies that in our experience of being we are immediately aware of our own existence and of being-itself as the unconditioned ground of being and meaning, and hence that we understand the being of things by analogy with our own being. From this follows Tillich's second objection to the cosmological approach; namely, that it turns God into an object or substance, whereas He is pre-eminently self-communicating personal being: 'The prius of subject is theoretically and practically related. God is no object for us as subjects. He is always that which precedes this division' (*TC* 25).

Discussing the personal character of the experience of the holy, Tillich significantly remarks: 'It is meaningless to ask whether the holy IS personal or whether its bearers ARE personal. If "is" and "are" express an objective, cognitive assertion, they certainly are *not* personal. But this is not the question. The question is what becomes of them as elements of the religious encounter? And then the answer is clearly that they become personal'.[7] He uses Buber's I-Thou distinction to say, of the experience of the holy, 'All the gods of the myths are personal; they all are "thou's" for a human ego'.[8] Our highest conception of being is not substance but the personal being whose name is 'I am that I am'. This is not a nature or an object, to which we are externally related by causal or teleological principles, but a self-affirming, self-communicating personal being who is experienced as the power of our own power of being. 'It is the unconditional character of the biblical God that makes the relation to him radically personal. For only that which concerns us in the centre of our personal existence concerns us unconditionally. The God who is unconditional in power, demand, and promise is the God who makes us completely personal and who, consequently, is completely personal in our encounter with him.'[9]

ii) An important consequence of this change of focus from things to persons is a profound change in our understanding of the relative importance of space and time, that is to say, of physics and cosmology on the one hand and history on the other. Spatial location and dimension are of paramount importance for Aristotle in defining the identity of any entity, including man. For Augustine, on the other hand, 'time is the mode of being of creatures'.[10] In other words, a thing's identity is inseparable from its history, that is, its perdurance in time and its occupation of space throughout the act of its existence. And for Tillich, who is developing a personalist and existential ontology, time and history are of essential importance in defining the nature of man's being. Here there is a parallel with Heidegger, and his fundamental concerns in *Sein und Zeit*.

Tillich not only develops an interpretation of history that forms an integral part of his ontology, but also finds it necessary to introduce the concepts of history and fate into the theory of knowledge.[11] However, what is of most profound philosophical significance is Tillich's analysis, in the *Systematic Theology*, of the relative importance of space and time as categories of being. Here, he asserts unequivocally, 'Time is the central category of finitude' (*ST1*, 214). Man's awareness of time and of his finitude are linked with his realisation that he has to die: 'It is anxiety about *having* to die which reveals the ontological character of time. In the anxiety of having to die non-being is experienced from "the inside"' (*ST1*, 215). History is the record of man's courage to be; of his affirmation of himself in spite of the threat of non-being: 'He affirms the present through an ontological courage which is as genuine as his anxiety about the time process. This courage is effective in all beings, but it is radically and consciously effective only in man, who is able to anticipate his end' (*ST1*, 215). Time is related to space, for Tillich, as for Augustine,[12] in what Tillich calls 'presence'. 'The present always involves man s presence in it, and presence means having something present to one's self over against one's self (in German, *gegenwaertig*). *The present implies space. Time creates the present through its union with space*' (*ST1*, 216; cf. *TC* 30–40).

iii) This shift of emphasis from things to persons, and from physics to history, in the interpretation of being and knowledge, was anticipated in idealist philosophy, especially by Schelling and Hegel. In Schelling's distinction between the philosophy of nature and philosophy of spirit, and in Hegel's analysis of the relations of the logical idea, nature and spirit in *The Phenomenology of Spirit*, we may observe the gradual modification of Cartesian subjectivism into an ontology of the being of subjects, and a stress on the priority of our knowledge of persons.

In Tillich's case, this is reflected in the stance from which he approaches the whole question of human culture. For instance, his famous formula that: 'Religion is the substance of culture and culture the form of religion' (*PE* 63) is reached only by a fundamental change of the perspective that has dominated secular culture since Galileo and Descartes; by an emphasis on human culture as the discovery, creation and transformation of the forms of meaning.[13]

It is also fundamental to his revolutionary proposals in *Das System der Wissenschaften*, where he not only proposes a new classification of the sciences in terms of the distinction between *Seinwissenschaften, Ideal-wissenschaften* and *Geisteswissenschaften*, but also, in his searching discussion of the crucial importance of history in the human sciences, anticipates much later discussion of the inadequacy of mathematical and physicalist models for scientific method. In an argument that foreshadows the discussion prompted by Wittgenstein's analyses of 'language games',[14] he objects to attempts to force the *Geisteswissenschaften* onto the procrustean bed of mathematical or physical models and contends that all the sciences, from a human point of view, need to be re-interpreted in the light of intentionalist and historical categories.

The rationale for this lies in Tillich's realisation that while Descartes' *Cogito, ergo sum* appears to enshrine the principle of the priority of personal knowledge, paradoxically, it is put in the service of a formalist mathematicism and a subjectivist rationalism that lead in the opposite direction from Augustine's *Si fallor, sum*, and subordinates ontology to a mechanistic cosmology and an entirely utilitarian science. This is because Descartes, in his method of systematic doubt, consciously prescinds from the discussion of the ontological presuppositions of truth and consciousness, and leaves science without objective ends. Also, he abstracts the self-conscious subject from the historical and onto-genetic order; the resulting cosmology cannot deal with the organic in nature, let alone with the historical mode of being of self-conscious agents. In reviving an Augustinian personalist ontology, Tillich seeks to reverse this Cartesian order of priorities. His ontology and epistemology are, as a result, more open than those of any other major theologian to the serious consideration of the categories of personal being, history, time, freedom, fate and decision. From this perspective, it was possible for him to contribute a personalist and ontological emphasis to the discussion of depth psychology, and to attempt an ontological interpretation of the foundations of axiology.[15]

iv) The exploration of the radical consequences of this change of perspective was first attempted in 'Kairos und Logos: Einer Untersuchung zur Metaphysik der Erkenntnis'. Since we have discussed subjective interest and decisions, attitudes and methods in the previous sections, we shall here examine mainly the emphasis on subjectivity in the problem of truth, and its connection with decisions and history.

The first sub-section is significantly titled 'The Absolute Subject and History'. Further to his distinction between two opposed but complementary traditions in Western philosophy, the critical methodical and the contemplative mystical approaches, Tillich distinguishes between the asceticism of scientific detachment and the *eros* or subjective interest that the existing subject brings to bear on any enquiry no matter how he tries to abstract himself from the picture.[16] Physics and cosmology seek the absolute object; Tillich following Schelling, seeks the unconditioned absolute that transcends the subject-object split, but employs the paradigm of our knowledge of persons, which gives a central place to love that overcomes the estrangement between knower and known. '[This] is the attitude of pure theory: asceticism towards the Kairos, Eros towards the Logos; . . . the opposite attitude, namely pure practice, can be defined with analogous formulae. It would be asceticism towards the Logos and Eros toward Kairos' (*IH* 130). These attitudes are complementary, neither position can be made absolute without serious inconsistency in knowledge resulting. This consequence can be recognised only when we emphasise the irreducible element of subjectivity in knowledge.

The reality and ontological objectivity of subjective existence is the reality and objectivity of history; the reality and objectivity of personal knowledge is grounded in the fact that, alone among existing beings, man is capable of critical, reflexive self-consciousness. This contrasts with the subjectivism of philosophy in the Cartesian tradition, which treats the perceiving subject as timeless, 'not in the sense that it should step out of the current of passing time, but in the sense that it could be without qualitative time, "a kairos"' (*IH* 132). When the knowing subject is abstracted from his historical situation he becomes an isolated disembodied consciousness contemplating his own private mental contents. Philosophy in this tradition leads to egocentric subjectism, because it denies the objective historical situation of the knowing subject, and tends to deny the ontogenetic basis of human critical rationality. Both empiricism and rationalism tend towards subjectivism in knowledge because, in Tillich's terms, they are *a kairos*.

Tillich identifies the Protestant attitude with three personalist emphases in the theory of knowledge: the emphasis on the vital contribution of the knowing subject to the act of knowledge; the emphasis on the historical nature of knowledge; and the emphasis on the critical principle that guards against the absolutisation of knowledge, and that expresses man's spiritual nature as a being orientated towards the infinite and unconditioned.

> The question of the knowing subject became more serious only when historical thinking penetrated into the sphere of supernature through Protestantism, and into the sphere of nature through humanism.
>
> The fundamental Protestant attitude is to stand in nature . . . to make decisions in concrete reality. Here the subject has no possibility of an absolute position. It cannot go out of the sphere of decision. Every part of its nature is affected by these contradictions. Fate and freedom reach into the act of knowledge and make it an historical deed: the Kairos determines the Logos.
>
> There is a religious attitude from which the absolute position of the subject is attacked. This attitude is the consciousness of standing in separation from the Unconditioned, and in the sphere of cleavage and decision, without being able to evade this situation even in knowledge. (*IH* 133–5)

Tillich's claim that these emphases are characteristically Protestant may be disputed. He does not produce historical evidence to substantiate it, and we suggest that this is an example of persuasive definition. This is in keeping with Tillich's rhetorical style and his tendency to indulge in historical generalisations. He is more concerned to characterise the mood of philosophies than to document them accurately.

One could point to Catholic thinkers in whom these emphases are present, from St Ignatius and Erasmus to Vico and Pascal, but this would be beside the point. What is important is that, within its own history, Protestantism has been concerned to defend the importance of personal knowledge against the charge of subjectivism; to defend the importance of historical knowledge against the charge of relativism; and to defend the Protestant principle against the charge of arbitrariness and arrogance. These emphases relate to three key issues in the rhetoric of the Protestant / Catholic debate; the authority of conscience versus the authority of the church; the authority of the historical Scriptures and tradition versus the authority of the Pope and defined dogma; and the authority of the prophetic principle versus the judicial authority of the organised Church. These antitheses are based on an oversimplified view of the nature of the complex social, political and theological interaction between the Protestant and Catholic traditions. What is of importance is that Tillich seeks to isolate and restate these underlying principles of the Reformation, and to build them into a coherent Protestant world-view. The historical argument is less important than the fact that Tillich uses it as the basis for prescribing a Protestant epistemology.

Characteristically, he overstates the case. While the emphasis on the contribution of the knowing subject is important and counterbalances the popular myth that scientific knowledge is based on objective consciousness and affective neutrality, he fails to explain how subjective knowledge can become inter-subjectively valid. Here, detailed epistemological analysis is essential if his thought is to be saved from subjectivism. Generalised ontological assertions are not sufficient to establish the important point he is making. In attempting to emphasise the historical nature of truth, Tillich fails to distinguish adequately between the existential and propositional senses of 'truth'. That all experience is historical is a position which can hardly be denied. Equally, the non-historical character of propositional truth cannot be denied unless we ignore the distinction between existence and thought. To make all thought historically contingent is to reduce knowledge to relativistic nonsense. Tillich does not adequately explore the logical grounds for the possibility of the trans-historical validity of truth. His defence of the Protestant principle is characterised by a tendency to conflate two kinds of critical principle inherent in human thought. The first concerns the possibility of criticising particular items of knowledge on the basis of other knowledge taken as established, or even questioning the validity of some fundamental theory on the basis of a suggested alternative. This type of criticism, associated with what Whitehead called 'provisional realism', does not undermine the possibility of objective knowledge; on the contrary, it describes the public criteria by which we establish the publicity of truth. The second kind of critical principle, which Tillich calls 'the guardian position' with respect to the ultimacy of ultimate truth, represents rather an attitude of agnosticism towards all systems of truth that claim ultimacy than a denial of the possibility of objective truth. This position can be maintained as a consistent attitude only on the basis that certain beliefs are taken for granted as objectively true, for example, that there is an unconditioned ground of all being and meaning. Tillich has no need to conclude that Protestant thought must lead to the denial of the objectivity of knowledge. It is sheer exaggeration, and confusion of ordinary knowledge and knowledge of the absolute that lead him to say: 'There is no Protestant conception of knowledge. It has to be irrational and dynamic' (*IH* 135). Fortunately, Tillich does not mean what he literally says, for this statement would vitiate his epistemology. By 'irrational' he surely means 'antirationalistic', and by 'dynamic' he merely means 'opposed to static systems of truth or dogma that are not open to criticism'. The valuable emphasis on subjectivity, history and criticism in the theory of knowledge, whether or not peculiarly Protestant, needs to be recovered, shorn of exaggeration, and based on careful elaboration of the philosophical distinctions that are necessary to bring their significance to light.

v) Finally, a very important consequence of the emphasis on the primacy of our knowledge of persons is the effect this has on Tillich's doctrine of revelation. It means that revelation is understood by analogy with communication between persons and knowledge of persons by persons. This is fundamentally different from the analogy of the contemplation of objects or knowledge of the Divine *qua* object or substance.

The comparison with Augustine is illuminating. Although St Augustine employs arguments to justify belief in god,[17] all such arguments are *ex post facto* in relation to what he regards as the datum: the reality of God to faith. He begins from a theocentric position, and to *believe* God is the pre-condition of *believing in* Him. The point of his famous doctrine, I believe in order that I may understand, as the context shows, is less that faith is an act of will than that it is a personal response to a personal confrontation and challenge, that is, to the act of self-communication of the incarnate Word of God.[18]

Even the type of demonstration that we associate particularly with Augustine, that is, the argument that leads from the fact of the self-certainty of our own existence to God as the ground of all being and truth, is the expression of a highly personal understanding of truth. This is admirably expressed by Vernon J. Burke:

> Two things should be observed concerning it. The thinking starts from conscious (personal) experience and not from the physical world. Augustine considers the mental (spiritual) to be at once more real than the physical and nearer to God: hence, the mind is a superior point of departure for his argument. In the second place, this 'demonstration' is not an exercise in logic; rather, it is one person taking another person by the hand and guiding him so that he may eventually see God for himself. Human reason needs to be exercised and directed (in this a human teacher may help), but, in the final

analysis, my reason must see for itself. No other person can see for me; no other person can or will understand for me. To grasp a truth is a highly personal experience. Augustine's argument is not intended to substitute for that experience, but to lead to it. In the long run, one either sees that God is – or one does not. The second part of the alternative seems almost incredible to Augustine: that a thinking person could fail to understand that there must be a highest Truth, Beauty and Goodness.[19]

Mutatis mutandis, almost identical remarks may be applied to the theological programme of Paul Tillich, who is quite categorical that there is no revelation in general: 'Revelation, as revelation of the mystery which is our ultimate concern, is invariably revelation for someone in a concrete situation of concern. This is clearly indicated in all events which traditionally have been characterised as revelatory. There is no revelation "in general" (*Offenbarung ueberhaupt*) . . . There is no revelation if there is no one who receives it as his ultimate concern' (*ST1*, 123; of *ST2*, 113). The objective event Tillich, following tradition, calls 'miracle', and the subjective reception he calls 'ecstacy' or 'enthusiasm'. The meaning of 'miracle' is treated by Tillich as having particular significance because it emphasises the importance of personal vision – that one must see for oneself, as in the experience of great art. Creative art had for Tillich great personal significance, for he saw it (particularly Expressionist and Mystical Realist art) as effecting a disclosure of ultimate reality, and hence of new dimensions and possibilities for finite being. This is brought about through the artist's act of self-revelation by which he communicates his experience of the depth of being. What is more, Tillich explicitly attributes his doctrine of revelation to his personal experience of the impact of great art.[20] However, it is the analogies of personal self-disclosure, of 'seeing it for oneself', and of 'opening of the eyes' to perceive the infinite depth revealed in the finite, that are of material importance in this context.

Further, Tillich, like Augustine, felt that there was something essentially peculiar about trying to prove the existence of a person, and, *a fortiori*, of God. He took profoundly seriously the argument, which derives in part form Kant, that even if the validity of the traditional proofs is taken for granted, they do not suffice to establish the existence of the kind of being that Christians or theists call God. They may prove the existence of a divine abstraction such as a First Cause, but they fail to prove a divine person.[21]

Even if we could prove the existence of an object (and there is something peculiar about wanting to prove the existence of *anything* unless, for example, it is something we know existed in the past and we want to know if it still exists) the question arises, how do we prove the existence of a person? We may be able to prove that a certain body, say, with human attributes, exists at a particular time and place, but how would we prove that the body was inhabited by a person or that a person existed in that body? The person must act to express himself, to reveal and communicate his personal be-ing to us; we must believe that he exists before we can prove him.

This is the point that underlies Augustine's claim that we must first believe God in order to believe in him. His argument that a man would be a fool if he refused to love his parents on the ground that he had no definite proof that he was their son, is intended to illustrate this fact. For, he argues, children palpably do regard their parents as their parents and show them filial devotion, not on the grounds of logical or empirical proof of being their progeny but on the testimonies of their mother and father, nurses and friends, whose words only serve to reinforce a deeper conviction based on a life-time (however brief) of communication and sharing of being with them. The certainty that one's mother is one's mother, and one's father is one's father, rests ultimately on one's confidence in their integrity, communicated as they have shared their life, their love and their being with one.[22]

Tillich emphasises again and again the decisive importance of the Biblical emphasis on communication and love to our discovery of what it means to be a person. In man's encounter with objects he may become aware of himself as a self-conscious subject, but it is only in a person to person encounter, that he becomes aware of himself as a person; becomes aware, that is, of the unconditional demand and promise, as well as the threat and judgement that the other person represents to him, a free being capable of self-affirmation and self-expression. This is what Tillich understands by spirit.[23]

This emphasis on the word is intimately linked then with Biblical personalism, but it is also a peculiarly Protestant emphasis. It is through the word that man becomes a person in community with other persons; the word is peculiarly suited as a symbol for Revelation, that is, for the acts of self-disclosure of a personal God. In 'Nature and Sacrament', Tillich shows how there is ultimately no opposition between Word and Sacrament; rather, the incarnation of the *logos* is the paradigm for our understanding both of the hearing and receiving of the Gospel Word and of our touching and tasting of the sacramental elements (*PE* ch. 7; *ST1*, 135–9). While he criticises the nominalism that turns the Protestant emphasis on the word into an empty verbalism and an abstract intellectual culture, and emphasises the importance of seeing, touching and tasting for personal experience and a realistic grasp of the sacramental reality (*ST1*, 46; cf. *HCT* 206) he nevertheless constantly emphasises the role of language in making human life and society possible and of Communion in the Word as making the community of the Church possible (*ST3*, 159–72).

Finally, Tillich's doctrine of faith as ultimate concern is intimately linked with his emphasis on the personal experience of God as the ground of the personal. This is emphasised with great clarity in a passage quoted earlier: 'The God who is unconditional in power, demand and promise is the God who makes us completely personal and who consequently, is completely personal in our encounter with him'.[24] Here God is the object of our ultimate concern and the ground of the possibility of our

being ultimately concerned; like the Spirit 'which itself maketh interces-
sion for us with groanings which cannot be uttered' (*Romans* 8). Further-
more, the spirit of ultimate concern evinced by Tillich throughout his work
is itself an expression of apostolic *caritas* towards the world and an invitation to become involved, to experience ultimate concern for ourselves.
'Taste and see, the Lord is good. Blessed is he that trusteth in him.'[25]

2. *Critique of the doctrine of abstraction*

The second issue that arises as a problem for an existentialist theory of
knowledge is the traditional theory of abstraction, which sustains the
doctrine that all knowledge is of essences, and is the basis of the semantic
theory that identifies the meanings of terms with universals. An abstrac-
tionist may concede that knowledge of the essence 'dog' presupposes
acquaintance with individual dogs, in the sense that someone must have
been directly acquainted with dogs; nevertheless, he denies this 'acquaintance' the status of knowledge. Direct acquaintance may be a necessary
condition for knowledge, but it is not a sufficient condition. According
to the theory of abstraction, it is essential that the defining attributes of a
class should be intuited and expressed in an abstract concept and then that
this concept should be predicated of an individual or class in the reflexive
act of judgement. Only then, may we be said to have knowledge. Names,
according to this view, either refer to individuals or express the abstract
essences of things. The name denotes the individuals in a class and con-
notes the defining characteristics of the class. Naming and judgement are
essential to knowledge.

Now Tillich, and several of his contemporaries, notably Heidegger,
Ernst Cassirer and Peirce, attack this doctrine on metaphysical, epistemological and semantic grounds. Tillich specifically attacks its serious, even
dangerous, consequences for our conception of being. The doctrine of
abstraction is responsible for 'the static ontology behind the logical
system of Aristotle' (*STl*, 63).

It may be seriously disputed that Aristotle's ontology was static, and
that the doctrine of abstraction in this form can fairly be attributed to
him, but this would be beside the point. What Tillich and his contemporaries were attacking was the form that the doctrine had taken during the
Enlightenment; a form that was historically associated with the tendency
to reify essences and to treat being-itself as timeless and static. However,
this was due to the radically a-historical method of philosophising of the
post-Cartesians,[26] and to the simplistic class logic on which their ontologies were based,[27] rather than to anything that could be strictly attributed to Aristotle. Tillich's attack on static ontologies, inspired as it was
by Hegel's *Logic* and his dialectic, has more to do with the deficiencies of
eighteenth- and nineteenth-century logic and metaphysics than with
either classical or mediaeval philosophy.

Nevertheless, with these qualifications, Tillich's criticisms of the doctrine of abstraction, are important both in their own right and as laying
the foundations for his own theory of knowledge. He contends that the

traditional Aristotelian doctrine of abstraction is nominalistic in effect, if not in intention, in that it emphasises the reality of individuals at the expense of the essences they instantiate, and ignores the groundedness of finite beings in being-itself. This results in both the being and the meaning of things remaining ultimately mysterious and inexplicable.[28] Further, instead of seeing the verbal or conceptual essences as the functional means by which we grasp the reality of things or apprehend the being of individuals, we are encouraged by the doctrine to reflect on a world of reified essences and words in abstraction from being; for essences as concepts and words are not distinguished from essences as 'powers of being' of the 'transtemporal potentialities' of things. Such a distinction is basic to Tillich's definition of truth: 'Truth, therefore, is the essence of things as well as the cognitive act in which their essence is grasped. The term "truth" is, like the term "reason", subjective-objective. A judgement is true because it grasps and expresses true being; and the really real becomes truth if it is grasped and expressed in a true judgement' (*ST1*, 113; cf. *MSA* 73).

Throughout his life Tillich was concerned with 'the ambiguities of abstraction' (*ST3*, 75, 271) and its negative implications for our understanding of thought, language and philosophical method. The limitations of the doctrine are the basic problem in the epistemological discussions that preface his two earliest works on Schelling, and it is explicitly referred to in *Der Begriff des Übernaturlichen* as the cause of the subject/object split in conscious thought (*DBU* 76ff.). In 'Religionsphilosophie', while he allows that we abstract, he explicitly rejects abstraction as an adequate basis for philosophical method. Such a method, insofar as it presents the unity of the forms of meaning, abstracts from their import, traces out purely logical or dialectical relations and, not surprisingly, finds itself in possession of a system of forms that are absolutely empty. This method 'involves only the one element inherent in all consciousness of meaning, namely, the *form* of meaning, while it misses the *import* or *substance* of meaning. The import of meaning is the ground of reality presupposed in all forms of meaning, upon whose constant presence the ultimate meaningfulness, the significance, and the essentiality (*Wesenhaftigkeit*) of every act of meaning rest' (*WR* 43). Finally, he discusses the ambiguities of abstraction in relation to language and thought, or, as he puts it, 'the ambiguity of the self-creation of life in the cognitive function of culture' (*ST3*, 75). On the one hand, 'Abstraction gives us the power of language, language gives us freedom of choice, and freedom of choice gives us the possibility of infinite technical production' (*MSA* 74; cf. *ST3*, 73). On the other hand, ambiguity enters into this process because 'the word, while creating a universe of meaning, also separates the meaning from the reality to which it refers. The act of grasping objects by the mind, on which language is based, opens up a gap between the object grasped and the meaning created by the word. The inherent ambiguity of language is that in transforming reality into meaning it separates mind and reality' (*ST3*, 73).

In developing his constructive alternatives to the doctrine of abstraction, Tillich makes use of arguments that are strikingly similar to those we find in Heidegger, Cassirer and Peirce. To begin with, what they have in common is their mutual indebtedness to Kant and their appreciation of the revolutionary significance of his doctrine of concepts. They grasped that his doctrine, which postulates that concepts are formulae rather than a class of abstract things,[29] represents not only a fundamental critique of the doctrine of abstraction, but a positive alternative to it. This, together with the doctrine that the understanding exhibits, in its grasp of the *a priori* necessary forms of reason, the pre-reflexive intuition of the categorial structure of being, suggested a way out that is rich in epistemological and semantic, ontological and theological possibilities. That Tillich's solutions were developed in critical dialogue with Heidegger and Cassirer, makes it necessary to examine their theories.[30] In the case of Peirce, we have an independent agent working along similar lines, and coming to conclusions similar to those we find in Tillich.

Tillich and Heidegger share a critical attitude towards Western man's nominalist ontology. This is characterised by a preoccupation with substance and the being of material things. It ignores being-itself as the unconditioned ground of the unity of experience and of all being and meaning. Both see this as connected with Aristotle's doctrine of abstraction and derived from his attempt to define and classify things, for scientific purposes, into a *scala naturae*. The concept of a class becomes determinative for our concept of being, and classes, as the reified products of the process of abstraction, become the abstract essences that thought attempts to manipulate instead of to contemplate; scientific-technical thinking depends upon this technique of reducing things to abstractions. This is the basis of man's technical mastery of nature, but also of his simultaneous alienation from his own natural being and nature itself.[31]

Heidegger's influential doctrine of the immediacy of our pre-reflexive grasp of being, and his poetic and mystical views of the primaeval, creative function of language in articulating the modalities of being and beings, have their counterparts in Tillich's more practical and methodical development of the doctrine of *das Unbedingt Seiendes* in the theory of meaning and truth, and his use of the critico-dialectical meta-logical method as the basis for a more adequate method in metaphysics and the philosophy of religion. This concern with method distinguishes Tillich's work from that of Heidegger, even his treatment of art and poetry, although based on a religious faith that the being-itself that is the unconditioned ground of consciousness is God, is more realistically concerned with the transformation of socio-political reality.[32]

Tillich's thought is also more explicitly theological, and it may be that the critique of the doctrine of abstraction is necessitated by theological considerations. For Tillich, it is impossible to proceed by abstraction from knowledge of finite individuals to knowledge of God. On the other hand, the anti-nominalist assertion that the pre-reflexive intuition of being-itself is the ground of the possibility of our knowledge of finite things, and therefore the basis for grasping the meaningfulness of abstract meanings, suggests the theological conclusion that God is being-itself. Whether Tillich is consciously developing ontology as a basis for Christian theology, or simply drawing out the epistemological and ontological implications of Christian theology, the conclusion is the same: the doctrine of abstraction is inadequate for his purposes. The alternative dialectical method he espouses is demanded by his conception of the Trinity: 'The doctrine of the Trinity . . . describes in dialectical terms the inner movement of the divine life as an eternal separation from itself and return to itself'. This dialectical form 'transforms the static ontology behind the logical system of Aristotle and his followers into a dynamic ontology, largely under the influence of voluntaristic and historical motives rooted in the Christian interpretation of existence . . . It posits in a new way the question of the relation of the structure of thought to the structure of being' (*ST1*, 63).

What Tillich and Cassirer have in common is that they developed the Kantian critique of the doctrine of abstraction, and the Kantian doctrine of concepts into a comprehensive philosophy of symbolic forms.[33] Both view language and myth, science and art as expressive forms that are reflections of man's awareness of himself and his world. Both consider the principle of intentionality essential to understanding man's forms of cultural self-expression. In Cassirer's words, 'The content of [cultural forms and linguistic] concepts, and the principle which determines their structure become fully intelligible only if beside their abstract *logical* meaning we consider their *teleological* meaning'.[34] Both criticise the nominalistic presuppositions of the doctrine of abstraction, for example, the idea that a purely extensional theory of meaning, which makes no reference to human intentions or to the context of co-operative human activity in which meanings are formed and grasped, is possible. Cassirer's emphasis is on the way that language pre-forms our conception of things; Tillich emphasises the pre-reflexive intuition of being as the ground of the meaningfulness of all meaning. Both depend heavily on Sigwart's critique of abstraction in his *Logik*. Cassirer quotes him directly, while Tillich appears to quote him without acknowledgement: 'Abstraction presupposes an awareness of that which is to be acquired through abstraction. For without such an awareness the range of phenomena on the basis of which abstraction is to take place would be vague and arbitrary'.[35]

Sigwart suggests that the theory that concepts are formed by comparison and abstraction has meaning only if, as is often the case, the problem is to indicate the common factor in things that general linguistic usage actually designates by the same word, and thus to elucidate the true signification of the word. He concludes: '[A]ny attempt to form a concept by abstraction is tantamount to looking for the spectacles which are on your nose, with the help of these same spectacles.'[36] Cassirer follows the same general line, and develops a genetic theory of concept- and class-formation in language in which meaning is predetermined by the structural demands of language as a whole – the demands for objectivisation, and for attribution of intrinsic signification to particular contents within the unity of the linguistic and conceptual manifold. This must necessarily precede the generalising process and the subsuming of one concept under another. Related to this is the special subjectivity that expresses itself in different languages. Cassirer admits that 'although philosophical analysis can never claim to grasp completely the special subjectivity that expresses itself in the different languages, still the universal subjectivity of language remains within the scope of its problems. For while languages differ in their perspectives of the world, there is a perspective of language itself which distinguishes it from the other cultural forms'.[37]

While sympathising profoundly with Cassirer's claim that a language embodies particular intuitions of being that have a meaning and value in themselves, independent of considerations of their truth, Tillich strenuously resists the implication that we have many universes of discourse, each with its own internal validity and beauty, and no criteria for determining their truth. He agrees with Cassirer that 'the essential impulsions [of linguistic concept formation] are not taken solely from the world of being but are always drawn at the same time from the world of action'.[38] However, he considers Cassirer's theory of intentionality inadequate insofar as it lacks an objective criterion of truth and thus leads to scepticism. His own doctrine of symbolism bears striking resemblance to Cassirer's, –[39] however, he opts for a realist epistemology, and rejects Cassirer's 'critical-idealistic' metaphysics and the 'pan-symbolism' he believes this generates.[40]

Tillich seeks, by his doctrine of belief-ful realism, to ground the meaning of symbols in the unconditioned. Being-itself, as the ultimate source of meaning in every perspective of the world, grounds every language and cultural form in a common reality that 'brings the principles of meaning into a unified and necessary relationship'; it is the substance or import of their meaning. The unconditioned and unconditional ground of all being and meaning is the common reference point of all conditioned expressions of meaning, and the criterion by which their truth is judged. Tillich identifies being-itself with the Divine Word, as the power that overcomes the ambiguities of abstraction and the alienation between men encapsulated in their own diverse languages. The Incarnation of the Word is the ultimate theological answer to the ambiguities and conflicts of man's cultural life. 'This makes it understandable that in biblical thought the word is united with power in the Creator, that it becomes a historical personality in Christ, and that it is ecstatic self-manifestation in the Spirit. In these symbols the word not only grasps encountered reality; it is itself reality beyond the split between subject and object' (*ST3*, 74).

It is interesting to note again in this context that Tillich is led by the rejection of the nominalist presuppositions of the doctrine of abstraction to a restatement of a realist and intentionalist theory of symbols that owes a great deal to Scotus. Tillich, like Peirce, follows Scotus in maintaining that essences are dynamic 'transtemporal potentialities' of things. However, what is more controversial is that as he moves closer to an existentialist position, he is inclined, like Heidegger, to move away from the Kantian denial of the knowability of finite things-in-themselves to a doctrine of the *per se* intelligibility of singulars. Having discussed other Scotist elements in Tillich's thought, we must now examine more closely his attempt to make sense of our knowledge of particulars. He was greatly influenced in this direction by his discovery of art, in which individual things exemplify transtemporal potentialities. Tillich's answer to Kant's scepticism is a mystical theory according to which we intuit the essence directly. The individual existent becomes intelligible *per se, qua* exemplar of a transtemporal potentiality. This doctrine is perhaps less important and less fully exploited in his epistemology than it is in his theory of symbolism. In his epistemology, he tends to equivocate, either because his Kantian doubts returned or because he didn't appreciate the full implications of a Scotist theory of intentionality.

In *My Search for Absolutes*, Tillich finds it possible to take a more positive view of abstraction, because he is there concerned to emphasise the absoluteness of essences, which are given prior to experience as the transtemporal potentialities of things, and which make language possible. The power of abstraction, possessed by man alone among the beings we know, gives us the power to create universals in terms of language: 'abstraction liberates us from bondage to the particular by giving us the power to create universals' (*MSA* 73).

Now this view may not be wholly consistent with his earlier strictures on abstraction, but the more positive emphasis is due to the new stress he places on two realist principles: firstly, that the basic datum is the given absoluteness of the essence, instantiated in the individual and experienced directly as its power of being; and secondly, that it follows that the individual must be intelligible in itself, insofar as being acquainted with this individual being means being acquainted with its power of being. This is the real point of his somewhat misconceived arguments that there are essences for individual human beings, and that individual essences of men are expressed in personal names.

There are obvious objections to both arguments. To the first, it may be objected that the concept of essence becomes incoherent if for every man there is an individual essence: every man must be a species in himself,[41] and no general knowledge of man or human nature would be possible. Similarly his account of names confuses logically proper names, which have no connotation and refer uniquely to one individual, and quasi-proper names which, in practice, may denote one individual, but connote characteristics applicable to several individuals. The facts that some names have a meaning and that some individuals are chosen as paradigmatic examples of particular attributes, have nothing to do with the logical function of proper names nor do they necessitate the modification of the distinction between existence and essence, matter and form, and potency and act.

Tillich fails to draw a clear distinction between the functions of these terms in the cognitive order, in which we attempt to give a theoretical explanation of the categories and modalities of being, and in the order of existence, where existence and essence are experienced in their dynamic inter-dependence. It only adds to confusion to oppose the cognitive and existential orders as static and dynamic respectively, and then suggest that the cognitive order really ought to be dynamic as well. It doesn't make sense to speak of static and dynamic ontologies.[42] It makes sense to speak of the different characters of first-order experience of being and second-order reflection on that experience, to distinguish between the existential order and the cognitive order, and to attack the tendency in philosophy first to reify ontological categories and then to re-import these into experience in a way that falsifies it.

In this context, Tillich is concerned to maintain that the individual beings with which we are acquainted are, under the conditions of existence, a unique combination of form and matter. The essences we grasp in knowledge and express in the universals of language, are experienced as the unique expressions of the power of being of particular individuals, for whom that trans-temporal potentiality of being is realised in a distinctive way. The interest of poetry and art, is that they seek to communicate the experience intact; to exhibit the essence as experienced under the conditions of existence. They emphasise the paradigmatic and symbolic possibilities of individual experiences, things or persons, without abstracting the forms from the context of their instantiated concrete existence in the way that an analytic and classifying science of knowledge must do.

Whether it is possible to build a critico-dialectical method or a dynamic ontology on such foundations may be seriously doubted, for the purposes of method and ontology are specifically discursive and analytic; but the almost inevitable tendency in philosophy to reify ontological concepts, and for theoretical knowledge to be interposed between the individual and his experience in such a way as to alienate him from it, is a justified matter of protest. On both subjects Tillich must be taken seriously.

The fact remains that Tillich made considerable capital out of his attack on the static ontologies based on the 'demonry of abstraction' (*ST1*, 63 and *ST3*, 271). He complains that cognition, in trying to reach the essence of an object, is compelled to abstract from many particulars and thus, as more and more inclusive abstractions are sought in the vain attempt to comprehend the inexhaustible being of the object, it is farther and farther removed from the original existent. In the impact of world-historical individuals such as Jesus, Socrates and Buddha, Tillich sees paradigms of the way in which, at a more prosaic level, the encounter with a particular individual may be decisive for knowledge, and at the same time open a vista onto the inexhaustible and unconditioned ground of all being and meaning.

Tillich's fascination with art is related to this epistemological and ontological insight. Because of the limited practical and the theoretical ends of scientific knowledge, and the inherently limited possibilities of finite philosophical reason, we tend to prescind from the inexhaustible and infinite in human experience, for it evokes not only the unconditioned ground but also the abyss of all human knowledge and experience. Tillich identifies himself with the Neo-Platonic-Augustinian tradition, and with artists, who are 'a special category of people who acknowledge an essence for the individual, [who acknowledge] something absolute in him. They don't always do this philosophically, but they do it through their works. They are the artists who create essential images of individuals in paint or stone, in drama or novel, in poetry or biography' (*MSA* 75).

Following Schelling, Tillich thought that he had discovered in art a form of knowledge that is non-discursive and yet expresses, in individual form, insights that have a symbolic, universal and essential meaning. Related to this is his comment on the shift of emphasis at the Reformation 'from the predominance of the eye to the ear', or from 'seeing the sacramental embodiment of the reality', to 'hearing of the word' and 'preaching of the word' (*HCT* 206). Rejecting nominalism, and the verbal and abstract culture it generates, Tillich seeks to return to Scotus and the mystical realism of the Middle Ages: '[Mediaeval] realism sees the essences of things. "Idea" comes from *idein*, "seeing". Eidos, "idea", means picture, the essence of a thing which we can see in every individual thing. Of course, this is an intuitive spiritual seeing, but it is still seeing, and is expressed in the great art. The great art shows the essence of things, visible to the eye' (*HCT* 206).[43] However, to attempt to extrapolate from this pictorial account of immediate experience to an explicit doctrine of the *per se* intelligibility of singulars is to be guilty of equivocation in the treatment of things and concepts. His quest for essences of individual human beings, based as it is on the analogy with the expressive and symbolic character of individual works of art, ignores the fact that works of art are not individuals that have somehow become universals, but represent, rather, a class of signs, different from words, that are nevertheless universal *qua* works of art, and universal *qua* paradigmatic or symbolic images. There is a simple confusion between the work of art as work of art and the work of art as individual thing; it is not an individual and universal in the same sense, any more than the word 'dog' is both an individual and a universal. (In the first sense it is a word, in the second it is the essence dogginess.)

3. *A possible non-essentialistic hermeneutic of being*

The third problem raised by an existentialist theory of knowledge concerns the possibility of expressing existential truth in a form that does not essentialise it. If a constructive alternative to the nominalistic doctrine of abstraction is possible, and if knowledge of existence is possible in the sense that immediate knowledge of individuals is possible, then this would seem to demand a radically new method of exposition for such existential knowledge.

In rejecting essentialism and the rationalising tendencies of idealism, all existentialists face the same problem. Kierkegaard experimented with a variety of styles of indirect communication, for example, dialectical lyrics, dialogues, novelettas and polemical treatises, but finally rejected anonymous and maieutic communication for the sermon and direct proclamation of the Gospel. Nietzsche used a variety of poetic forms and proverbial and sibylline utterance. Dostoevsky and Kafka, like Camus in this century, were self-styled writers rather than philosophers, but use the novel and the play for the exposition of existential truth. Heidegger and Sartre initially adopted the phenomenological method: Heidegger rejected it in favour of a crypto-poetic style of utterance that allowed language to effect its own disclosure of being; Sartre experimented with plays and finally adopted a Marxist dialectic as the medium for the exposition of existentialist ideas.

In considering Tillich we have to say that, for him, the most appropriate instrument for the hermeneutic of being was art; yet his massive *Systematic Theology* is a standing monument to his efforts to find a method appropriate to the exposition of existence in the light of Christian truth. He was not capable of presenting his theology on canvas, and it is tempting to suggest that he simply fell back on the idealist model of a system. Kenneth Hamilton's critique[44] may be somewhat simplistic, but highlights an unresolved ambiguity in Tillich's understanding of what constitutes a system. Despite his denial, in *Systematic Theology*, Volume 2, that he operates with the model of a deductive system, the weight of the evidence suggests that he does. While he argues, in the introduction to Volume 1, that his work is half way between an essay and *summa*, its structure is dictated by the logic of his theological ontology, even if the content attempts to do justice to the existential aspects of human experience.

Tillich himself experimented with a variety of styles. In his earlier work he was clearly still influenced by idealist and phenomenological models. Later, he became disillusioned with phenomenology and increasingly critical of its method. In its place, he formulates what he calls the critico-dialectical or meta-logical method (*WR* 41–50). This is still rather abstract, but is soon modified by a radical new emphasis on history, so that 'dialectics as the art of determining the relation of ideas to one another and to existence' has to be considered in relation to fate and concrete historical existence. Dialectics must take account of the 'inner inexhaustibility of the idea'. The task and demand that future dialectics must face is 'to grasp the relationship of ideas, the structure of the essential, in such a way that the ambiguity of every solution becomes visible in the solution itself' (*IH* 168).

This historical emphasis takes on an even more decisive character in *The Religious Situation*, and in the articles on belief-ful realism and Religious Socialism in the years 1927 to 1933. In 1933, with the publication of *Die Sozialistische Entscheidung*, we reach a watershed in Tillich's life and thinking. The development of a dialectical exposition of his ideas that owed a great deal to the historical realism of Marxist thought, combined with existential analysis and personalist emphases from the Christian tradition, marked the emergence of a method distinctively his. This method, which he came to call 'the method of correlation', formulates questions that are based on an historical, existential analysis of human existence and culture, and purports to develop these in strict correlation with answers derived from reflection on Christian revelation (*ST1*, 67f).

One additional component that enters into Tillich's method is a profound appreciation of depth psychology and the light it throws on the alienated forms of human existence. However, there is a methodological reason for this, as there is for his several autobiographical essays. He appreciates, like Kierkegaard, that autobiography is the most obvious means by which the individual can provide us with a hermeneutic of existence, a psychological means of access to contingent existence, and an ontogenetic rather than static and phylogenetic account of being. It is perhaps surprising that he did not make more direct use of depth psychology, as Nietzsche, Kierkegaard, and even Sartre did. But we must not forget Tillich's sermons, for they are crucial to the understanding of his use of depth psychology to illuminate and express his doctrine of existence; not to mention his use of it as an instrument of Biblical exegesis.

In attempting to understand the full scope of Tillich's concern with the communication of existential and theological truth, we must not only understand the rationale for his 'answering' and 'Apologetic' theology but also see the system and the sermons in their strict systematic correlation with each other. It is the purpose of the sermons to attempt a hermeneutic of existence. They exhibit the grandeur and misery of human existence, and communicate directly the Word of God as incarnated in Jesus as the Christ, in its personal and historical immediacy.

The rhetoric governing *Systematic Theology* is different – it is a sustained dialectical account of 'the relationship of ideas, the structure of the essential' that is both ontological and philosophical; but it is also existential insofar as it seeks 'to bring out the ambiguity of every solution in such a way that it becomes visible in the solution itself'. He is faithful to his conception of dialectic as an 'attempt to comprehend the fate of the ideas from our Kairos, from the fate of our period' (*IH* 69). His dialectic is not essentialist; nor is it simply existentialist, for his object is to develop a new ontological synthesis in which the structural relationships of essence, existence and being-itself can be grasped in a new and more relevant way for our times. This task is ontological and theological at the same time, for the *ministerium verbi divini* involves opening our eyes to see the inexhaustible ground and abyss of all being and meaning in every meaningful encounter with another finite individual being, and to interpret our perception of the eternal truth of such experience in historical and personal terms that make sense of our existential experience here and now (Cf. *ST1*, 3).

Systematic Theology has this double aspect: it aims to provide a coherent rationale for religious belief and it aims at an actual disclosure of the unconditional as ground and source of our being. It is, in other words, both apologetic and kerygmatic. There is a complete unity of purpose between Tillich's sermons and his systematic theology: both aim to proclaim the Word of God; both aspire to be media through which an actual revelation of God himself, as Being-itself, as New Being and Spirit, can be effected. Tillich's theology is a work of piety and evangelical passion in spite of its formidably intellectual appearance.

That Tillich was concerned to communicate the existential truth of faith in terms that are at the same time intellectually coherent and perceived to be relevant to one's existence, is evident in his earliest papers on the idea of a theology of culture and on the philosophy of religion. Underlying the discussion of revelation and myth in 'Religionsphilosophie', and the corresponding discussion in *Systematic Theology*, Volume 1, is a concern with this apologetic and kerygmatic purpose of theological communication.

Revelation and myth are not discussed simply as abstract theoretical categories in the philosophy of religion. Tillich is constantly concerned with their existential significance for those who stand within the theological circle, and for whom these are objects of ultimate concern. He does not attempt to give a detached outsider's view of revelation and myth, rather, he makes us feel what it is like to stand within the theological circle or the sphere of 'unbroken myth'. What is distinctively existential about his standpoint is his attempt to adopt the 'participant-observer' method of approach to the hermeneutic of revelation and myth. By contrast, his method of correlation is either a somewhat contrived and self-conscious literary device for presenting his hermeneutic of being in a philosophical and dialectical manner, or it is, as Mahan has recently suggested, an expression of ultimate optimism: of tension overcome, ambiguity resolved and the separated reunited.[45]

The task of the Christian theologian is to be both existentially involved and concerned to show which categories are constitutive for religious objects in the various spheres: 'A philosophical theory of the categories of religion must accordingly concern itself with the appearance of the religious element in the individual spheres of meaning' (*WR* 101). Insofar as it attempts to do justice to the element of commitment in religious faith, the philosophy of religion cannot be content with a theoretical and phenomenological investigation of the essential characteristics of religion in general, nor with a merely empirical investigation of the history of religions, but must be prepared to make judgements and evaluations on the basis of the theologian's own concrete and, for him, normative religious commitment.

Tillich uses the term 'revelation' to apply to the form in which the religious object is immediately apprehended in religious faith: 'We speak of revelation wherever the unconditioned import of meaning breaks through the form of meaning. Faith is always based on revelation, for it is an apprehension of the unconditioned import through conditioned forms' (*WR* 105). In contrast, myth is the concrete-normative expression of the content of revelation for a particular individual or community of faith: 'In *myth* the logical and the aesthetic apprehension of the Unconditional come together. The myth is not only aesthetic: it aims to give expression to the true and the real. And it is not only logical: it aims to apprehend intuitively the import of the Unconditional. The two are united in the original myth' (*WR* 102). There is thus a tension in religious faith between commitment to the particular symbols that are, for the believer, bearers of unconditional import, and fidelity to the unconditioned, which is the ultimate ground of their import. A hermeneutic of existence that does justice to human existence *qua* religious existence must take account of the tension.

In 1930, in an article on myth in *Die Religion in Geschichte und Gegenwart*,[46] Tillich introduced a vital distinction between 'unbroken' and 'broken' myth. In the former, the tension between commitment to mythic forms as bearers of unconditional import and fidelity to the unconditioned has not been disrupted by autonomous criticism or by prophetic protest against the identification of the unconditioned with conditioned forms. In the latter stage of broken myth, the critique of demonic elements in the original myth that is based on the protest of the unconditioned against the contingent, has disrupted the uncritical faith in specific mythopoeic forms, but this does not mean that mythopoeic forms are dispensable. On the contrary, every experience of faith requires concrete-normative expression in some kind of mythopoeic or symbolic form. In this sense, Tillich both agrees and disagrees with Rudolf Bultmann's programme of demythologisation. On the one hand, demythologisation 'can mean the fight against the literalistic distortion of symbols or myths' (what Tillich calls 'deliteralisation'). In this sense he agrees with Bultmann's programme. On the other hand 'demythologisation can also mean the removal of myth as a vehicle of religious expression and the substitution of science and morals'. This latter view he firmly rejects: 'It would deprive religion of its language; it would silence the experience of the holy' (*ST2*, 175–6). In this sense, Bultmann's attempt to translate the kerygma into existential form necessarily involves what Tillich calls 'remythologisation'. As Klaus Rosenthal has observed:

> It should be noted that the definition of disruption in myth is almost identical with the definition of the substance of revelation, as disruption of the conditional by the unconditional. *Revelation, therefore, is neither identical with myth nor radically opposed to myth.* Revelation, rather, is the act of disruption of the unreflected, unbroken myth by the reflected, broken myth. It is the death of the unbroken myth, and the lasting and supporting presupposition of the broken myth. Myth and revelation are interdependent: not only does broken myth depend on revelation, because the latter protects the former from relapse into the demonic sphere, but also revelation depends on myth, because myth in itself is 'the form of expression for the content of revelation'.[47]

In other words, Tillich attempts to do justice to the irreducible element of myth in all human thought, to the extent that it seeks to express man's ultimate concern with being and meaning. He presents, in the form of a triad, the way in which all real things and their ideal unity are apprehended from the point of view of the unconditional: 'Myth presents itself in a threefold tendency: as a myth of being, a myth of history, and a myth of the absolute idea, or in the language of myth itself, as creation, redemption and fulfilment' (*WR* 105). The three broad divisions of Tillich's *Systematic Theology* correspond to these tripartite divisions, and in this broad sense his system is an attempt to do justice to the concrete-normative 'myth' that expresses the content of revelation for Christian faith. Its object, like that of his original paper 'Religionsphilosophie', is to express 'the immediately existent on the one hand and the meaning-fulfilling spirit on the other, and finally the perfected unity of being and meaning. The absence of any one of these is a sign of declining mythical power. Only in their unity does the relation of the Unconditional to the conditioned come to complete expression, and only then is a true symbolism achieved' (*WR* 105).

In Tillich's sense of 'Myth' and 'symbol', his *Systematic Theology* is itself to be understood as a symbol expressing faith in the unconditioned ground and abyss of all being and meaning; as a mythic expression, in concrete-normative terms, of the content of revelation for Christians. It attempts to be adequate to its subject matter, but built in to its form is the critical principle that recognises the inadequacy of all conditioned forms as expressions of the unconditional. It seeks 'to bring out the ambiguity of every solution in such a way that it becomes visible in the solution itself'. To the extent that Tillich manages to express the ultimate ambiguity of the answers and solutions of the System, he succeeds in his task, and his hermeneutic of existence is authentic and convincing. To the extent that he becomes fascinated by his own dialectical constructs and the working out of an inevitable series of schemata dictated by those constructs, his thought becomes wooden, unconvincing and inauthentic. Both forces are at work in his system, and at least part of the explanation for the incomplete success of his attempt is that he fails to subject his theoretical insights to properly rigorous criticism.

Our discussion of Tillich's account of the knowledge of individuals, of the doctrine of abstraction and of the hermeneutic of being, in this chapter, has shown that while he throws out many stimulating suggestions and provokes us to re-think these issues, he does not always reconcile his conflicting insights, relying instead on the broad thread of his dialectic to knit up and conceal the holes in his argument. In addition to his impatience with sustained logical argument, his arguments on all three topics are characterised by vagueness and an element of romantic anti-intellectualism. It is not sufficient to complain of the essentialist characters of the traditional doctrine of essences and the doctrine of abstraction, for, paradoxically, the deficiency of his theoretical analyses leads to an overemphasis on the dialectical component in the system as a whole. The machinery of the system at the macro-level has to carry a greater burden because of the inadequacy of the machinery at a micro-level.

However, while Tillich's argument may not always stand up to close examination, this is not because he was mistaken in his beliefs rather, it is because his rationalisations of these were inadequate. The vision as a whole remains impressive whatever the objections to details, and he cannot be faulted at the level of his personal piety and concern to inspire men with a vision of God as Being-itself, as the answer, that is, to man's anxious quest for the ultimate meaning of his being.

Chapter 7

The Metaphysics of Truth:
The Question of Truth and Verification

In this study of Tillich's ontology of cognition the last major issue that remains to be examined is that of the adequacy of his criteria of truth, and particularly their adequacy for determining truth in practice. He has been criticised by many philosophers for vagueness on this score. Even sympathetic critics, such as J. H. Randall Jr and Dorothy Emmett, chide him for being less than specific in explaining his epistemological criteria, and those concerned with theology and verification in the 1950s tend to dismiss him as muddle-headed (*TPT* 146f., and 212–14).[1]

Tillich was sharply critical of positivism and tended to dismiss rather contemptuously the view that every meaningful proposition must be either analytic or empirically verifiable. On the one hand he displays a fairly typical, romantic, anti-mathematical bias in dismissing the efforts of such philosophers as Carnap, Russell and Wittgenstein to provide rigorous extensional and truth-functional criteria for scientific truth: 'The principle of semantic rationality must not be confused with the attempt to construct a pan-mathematical formalism. In the realm of spiritual life words cannot be reduced to mathematical signs, nor can sentences be reduced to mathematical equations' (*ST1*, 61). On the other hand, he was inclined, with some justification, to dismiss as naive and uncritical the view that empirical verification is straightforward and unproblematic. In a variety of contexts, he points out how positivism begs the question of the scope and limits of experience: uncritically adopts an empiricist ontology and then legislates on the basis of its reality principle; proscribes discussion of being-itself while imposing its own view that the application of the term 'being' must be restricted to atomic facts or individuals; and fails to answer the question of the validation of its own criterion of truth (see *ST1*, 112–14, 206, 255–6).

While his criticisms have considerable force, they display a typically patronising attitude to positivism, and a tendency to content himself with generalisations rather than the critical analysis that would clarify the basis of his objections. He fails to take sufficiently seriously the challenge of logical empiricism to theology. Had he not so failed, he would have produced a more universally relevant apologetic theology, and would have been forced to spell out his logical and epistemological theories in a more systematic way.

It is perhaps surprising that he didn't adopt, and adapt to his own ends,

Moritz Schlick's famous formula. 'The meaning of a proposition is the method of its verification',[2] for it would have suited his purposes admirably. Without accepting the naive empiricism that Schlick advocated, we can agree that the formula states with admirable simplicity a principle that underlies Tillich's illuminating discussion of the variety of methods and forms of verification in the various sciences; namely that the *Denkwissenschaften, Seinswissenschaften* and *Geisteswissenschaften* have different subject matter and methods and that therefore the rules for determining meaning in each and, *ex hypothesi*, the methods of verification in each, must differ (see *DSW*). This view, which owes more to Aristotle's pragmatic realism than to a Wittgensteinian idealist view of different language games each with its own rules, is reflected in the argument of *Systematic Theology*, Volume 1, but it is not developed into a comprehensive logical and epistemological theory. However, this does not mean that we cannot attempt to spell out some of its implications.

Tillich's theory of truth, in the narrower sense found in modern epistemological discussion, has three parts. There is a version of the correspondence theory of truth, namely, a requirement that there be a correspondence between the *logos*-structures of mind and reality. There is a theory that the diverse cultural purposes served by the different sciences imply a variety of criteria of truth, in order to do justice to the intentionality of these different meaning-creating and meaning-fulfilling human activities. And there are discussions of the relations between truth and judgements, between the cognitive act and the essence *qua fundamentum in re*, and between the three absolutes in the act of knowing.

1. *The correspondence between the* logos-*structure of mind and the* logos-*structure of reality*

Tillich lays the foundations for his discussion of criteria of truth in an inquiry into the structure of reason (*ST1*, ch. 3). Here, he argues that unless we begin by questioning the concept of reason that is presupposed in scientific-technical thinking, then so far as philosophy and theology are concerned, the game is lost before we begin. This is because this concept of reason, which he calls 'technical reason', prejudges the nature of being by its assumptions of an empiricist metaphysic and utilitarian values; and the adequacy of these assumptions cannot be discussed without introducing another concept of reason that he calls 'ontological reason' (*ST1*, 80f.). Ontological reason embraces technical reason in a form of contemplation that includes reflection on the nature of reality as well as on the ends that should govern knowledge and action. Such a concept of reason is required for the explicit criticism of the ontological and axiological assumptions of our culture, without which theological apologetic cannot begin.

The definition by which he seeks to express the giveness of being, the subjective and objective character of reason and truth, and the fact that ontological and technical reason are both expressions of, and means for, man's intelligent participation in being is given in the succinct formula,

'Ontological reason can be defined as the structure of the mind which enables it to grasp and to shape reality' (*ST1*, 83).

Not surprisingly, he turns to the classical *logos* doctrine as a means for developing his discussion of the structure of reason, for it embraces a variety of meanings that are necessary for the theory he wishes to develop. Firstly, it embodies the concept of an intelligible order, common to the logical structure of the mind and the *logos*-structure of reality, and based on the self-world polarity of experienced be-ing. Secondly, it embraces the technical and ontological functions of reason in a view of knowledge and culture in which language, art, science, technology and religion are related as different forms of man's meaning-creating and meaning-ful-filling participation in reality. Finally, it relates finite reason to the infinite ground and depth of all being and meaning, that is, the *mysterium fascinans et tremendum*.

The correspondence that he affirms as basic to the doctrine of know-ledge, value and being, is the correspondence between 'the rational struc-ture of the mind and the rational structure of reality' (*ST1*, 84). However, this is based on his *logos* doctrine, and cannot be discussed apart from it. Those who see this formula as a restatement of the Hegelian formula that 'the real is the rational and rational is the real', fail to take seriously both the philosophical and the theological grounds on which such an inter-pretation cannot be attributed to Tillich.[3]

The *logos* doctrine, as he expresses it in 'Kairos and Logos' (*IH* 123–175) is clearly directed towards solving the dilemmas created by the idealist treatment of the relations of subject and object, and of finite and infinite. It is expressed in terms of a belief-ful realism that combines a revolutionary philosophy of history and a radical interpretation of revela-tion in his doctrine of *kairos*. Although his treatment in the *Systematic Theology* is more abstract, it is none the less evident that he rejects Hegel's dialectic and his theory of the identity of the rational and the real (*ST1*, 83). However, he recognises that idealism is one of four possible ways in which the relations of subjective and objective reason can be described; the others being realism, dualism and monism. Somewhat paradoxically, 'The theologian is not obliged to make a decision about the degree of truth of these four types. However, he must consider their common pre-suppositions when he uses the concept of reason' (*ST1*, 84). The clear implication of all Tillich has written is that his doctrine of being over-comes the antithesis between realism and idealism and dualism and monism. Belief-ful realism transcends the alternatives, realism and ideal-ism, by pointing realism towards self-transcendence in the perception of the spiritual meaning of the real, and stressing that idealism must trans-cend its idealisation of the real, in the power of faith. 'For' he continues, 'faith implies an absolute tension and cannot be united with any attitude in which the tension is weakened. Idealism relativises, self-limiting real-ism denies, but self-transcending realism accepts the tension' (*PE* 77). What he means by 'self-transcending realism' is shown in his develop-ment of the *logos* doctrine in his writings in the period from 1924 to 1939.

They are marked by an air of excitement and discovery as ideas from a variety of sources begin to coalesce and develop into a doctrine with revolutionary new systematic and critical possibilities. This doctrine combines idealist, existentialist, Marxist and Christian elements and, not surprisingly, finds its systematic expression in Volume 1 of the *Systematic Theology*, which he commenced writing in 1925. It was the excitement of these discoveries that moved him to embark on this ambitious work of theological creation and synthesis. In fact, the chapter with which we are concerned, namely 'The Structure of Reason', is virtually a straight reworking of 'Ueber gläubigen Realismus', published in 1928.

The point at which Tillich's realism demands faith or self-transcendence is the point where fidelity to the *logos* structures of mind and reality requires us to admit that reason in its objective and subjective structure, points to something that appears in these structures but transcends them in power and meaning; namely, the unconditioned ground and abyss of reason, to which finite reason can respond only with ecstacy or despair. 'The Depth of Reason' and 'Ecstatic Reason' are correlative aspects of this transcendent reality in which the divine *logos* is manifest and the contingency and finitude of human reason revealed.

This correlativity becomes the critical and constructive principle of Tillich's systematic theology. It is the integrating principle of ontology and theology. It is also the principle in terms of which idealism can be criticised for its failure to take account of man's existential and historical relation to the *logos*. It is the basis from which scientific-technical realism can be criticised for 'making the thinking subject bearer of all power' and failing to recognise his contingency and finitude. It is the basis from which 'positivism can be criticised for its radical reduction of the power of being of things to their theoretical calculability and practical utility'. It is the basis from which mystical realism can be criticised for its denial of the tension between the finite and the infinite *logos* of being, that is, for seeking union with the one through the contemplation of the eternal essences, without regard to their instantiation in space and time. It is the basis for the criticism of historical realism for stopping short of the affirmation 'of the ultimate ground and meaning of an historical situation and, through it, of being as such' (*PE* 78–85; cf. *ST1*, 79–92).

The first and most decisive sense in which the *logos* doctrine provides us with a criterion of truth, transcends epistemological argument as ordinarily understood. It is the sense in which beliefs must be subjected to the test of their authenticity and ultimate validity. It is only by being in a relation to truth, by standing as a knowing subject in a truthful relation to being, that the correspondence between the *logos*-structures of mind and reality can be realised. The validity of this relationship can be tested only in the experience of an existing historical subject, who in the contingency of a particular situation, grasps the ultimate meaning of being and, subjecting that experience to the judgement of the divine *logos*, the unconditionally ultimate, finds it confirmed as authentic.

Tillich emphasises that truth is an existential relationship before it is a cognitive one; the truth of the latter depends on the truthfulness of the former. This is no simple affirmation of existential truth over against abstract, theoretical knowledge, but the affirmation of an important ontological truism: truth is a disposition of one's being before it is a form of knowledge. Particular truths express aspects of the relationship of the existing subject to being-itself. The contingent, historical person standing in a particular relationship to being itself is the datum, the condition and ground of the possibility of truth, and truth, in the first instance, is the expression of the intentionality of this relationship.

This is distinct from the conscious striving to *be* in the truth. The truth is not created by this striving, but is affirmed in the act of striving and the act of realisation. It also emphasises the sense in which Tillich takes with ultimate seriousness the epistemological implications of the Augustinian doctrine that *fides praecedat intellectum*. This is no fundamentalist or irrationalist view that one must believe Scripture or Christian doctrine before one can understand the truth, nor does it mean that faith is an act of will or of naive trust. It means that the truthful correspondence between finite existence and the demands implicit in the structures and dynamics of being is the object of knowledge and the test of its truth, before it is abstracted as a formal relationship between cognitive experience and reality, or more narrowly, between facts and propositions. Truth in this sense demands, simultaneously, recognition of the givenness of the ontological relationship of finite being to being-itself as the ground of the possibility of truth and recognition of the historical and contingent character of every specific relationship and every specific expression of the truth.

> [T]his eternal truth, this logos above fate, is not at man's disposal; it cannot be subjected as Hegel thought it could, to the processes of human thinking; it cannot be described or presented as the meaningful world process . . .
>
> [T]his unconditional truth is not in our possession. It is the hidden criterion of every truth that we believe we possess. There is an element of venture and of risk in every statement of truth. Yet we can take this risk in the certainty that this is the only way in which truth can reveal itself to finite and historical beings. (*PE* 15)

Tillich is fully aware of the charges of relativism and subjectivism to which such a theory exposes him. He first points out that the relativism involved is an irreducible element in any and every theory of truth, and to deny it involves self-deception and unjustified dogmatism, for no theory of truth is self-verifying. The commitment to a particular theory of truth is a matter of humility and faith, and an acknowledgement that the justification of any theory of truth involves a meta-theory; beyond that, one is involved in an infinite regress. The alternative is to uncritically assert one's theory of truth as true and to be guilty of a *petitio principii*. After outlining his meta-theory, that is to say, his ontology of cognition, Tillich opts for an agnostic position that, paradoxically, involves an affirmation of the ultimacy of truth by an epistemological version of the doctrine of Justification by Faith (*IH* 169–75).

He openly admits the element of decision in the commitment to a theory of truth. This makes it irredeemably relative and subjective, but only in a somewhat uninformative and tautological sense; namely, that the truth must always be true for some subject and relative to some subject, for without an existing subject to stand in an actual relation to being itself, there would be no truth. Consequently, the only unequivocal judgement is the judgement concerning the relation of the unconditioned and the conditioned; namely, 'that our subjective thinking can never reach the unconditioned truth, that it must always remain in the realm of ambiguity . . . The absolute standpoint is therefore a position which can never be taken; rather it is the guard which protects the Unconditioned, averting the encroachment of a conditioned point-of-view on the sphere of the Unconditioned' (*IH* 170–1).

This ultimate relativism of all theories of truth, and the subjectivism (if such it be) involved in affirming that truth is always truth in relation to an existing subject, need not, and in practice does not prevent us from affirming a particular position that we believe expresses adequately the relationship of conditioned to unconditioned being. Such philosophical reservations need not prevent us from affirming particular truths, nor need they lead us to total scepticism – because the truth that we can grasp is necessarily partial, conditioned, and relative to our historical situation as existing subjects.

If Tillich's theory resembles any other it is not so much that of the idealists as that of the mediaeval realists, and perhaps especially that of Aquinas. It is strikingly similar to St Thomas's in several respects, although it also differs significantly. Aquinas similarly adopts an agnostic attitude towards the truth of different philosophies, although there is no doubt which he prefers and why: we can give reasons for preferring one theory of truth to another, and in that sense can demonstrate its superiority, but we cannot provide irrefutable proof. Again, Aquinas's statement that truth consists in the 'adequatio intellectus et rei' is rather similar to Tillich's assertion of a correspondence between the *logos*-structures of mind and reality. Both recognise that there is a simple 'Third Man Argument' against correspondence theories: if we are to confirm a correspondence between two things then there must be a third position from which we can inspect them; and this is impossible for the relationship of mind and reality since we cannot get outside our own minds to compare them with reality.

The differences between Tillich and St Thomas at this point are very interesting, because they opt for very different methods of justifying their realist presuppositions and the correspondence theory these entail. St Thomas develops Aristotle's empiricism into a subtle theory in which sense perception, conceptual abstraction and judgement play a part. In this theory, the correspondence between mind and reality is tested by referring back to sense-experience for further confirmation the second-order abstractions derived from the intuitions of sense-experience, and expressed in judgements. Judgements become the *tertium quid* in terms of which the correspondence can be tested, because the abstract essences expressed in the words of a judgement stand in relation to first-order experience as second-order reflections on that experience, and we may compare these reflections with past experience in memory and test them in future experience. But in any event the confirmation is indirect; the only direct confirmation would be the exact replication of the identical experience in the identical situation (which science mimics in abstract experiments), but this, *ex hypothesi*, is impossible.

Tillich opts for a metaphysical solution, in affirming the fundamental ontological truism that truth is identical with being and that this identity is the *prius* of all knowledge as well as the *prius* of the sceptic's doubt of that which makes it possible for him to doubt anything at all (*TC* 22–6).[4] The correspondence is established 'from above', as it were. In one sense, it involves a formal statement of a necessary condition that any theory of truth must satisfy; namely, that truth must agree with being. In another sense, it involves the statement of a concrete condition that is necessary for the correspondence between the *logos*-structures of mind and reality to be realised; namely, that the relation of truth and being must be expressed in a truthful existential relationship between a particular historical being and being itself. In a third sense, it refers to the necessary attitude of ultimate concern, in which alone the identity of truth and being can be cognitively affirmed.

Tillich is right to emphasise these much neglected necessary conditions for the realisation of truth, but, even taken together, they are not sufficient to determine the truth in a specific case. What is required is a specification of the practical means and ends of knowing, as well as its formal causes or theoretical conditions.

Aquinas developed a critique[5] of the doctrine of Augustine that truth is convertible with being, and in the process developed a theory of the intentional relations between causes, means and ends that was valuable in clarifying the nature of cognitive acts and of different truth-theories also. In discussing Tillich's logic, we hope to show that there is in principle no reason why he could not have adopted a similar theory of intentionality and a thoroughgoing intentional logic. That he failed to do so is a weakness of his system in general and of his theory of knowledge in particular.

What is lacking in Tillich's theory of truth can be made clearer by scrutiny of St Thomas's discussion of different theories of truth in terms of the relations between causes, means and ends. On the basis of this structure he classifies three types of theory, which we may call formalist, verificationist and pragmatist. However, he considers each inadequate insofar as it emphasises one aspect of the intentionality of cognitive acts at the expense of others. Only if we consider causes, means and ends together, he suggests, can we provide a set of truth conditions that is both necessary and sufficient for the determination of the truth or falsity of judgements in particular cases.

Under the heading 'Causes', he considers the theories of Augustine, Avicenna and Anselm as theories in which truth 'is defined according to that which precedes truth and is the basis of truth'. However, such theories, while stating formal and necessary conditions for truth, fail to provide us with a specific criterion of truth.

Now the three things that Tillich emphasises as necessary conditions for the realisation of truth are just that – formal and necessary conditions – and, without further specification, remain empty. He is concerned with the objective ontological and subjective existential conditions that are necessary for the realisation of truth as such, but they are not sufficient to provide either the content of truth in a particular case or the means for verifying it.

Tillich tries to overcome this deficiency by means of his distinction between 'receiving knowledge' and 'controlling knowledge', and a stress on the complementarity of the 'experiential verification' associated with the former and the 'experimental verification' associated with the latter (*ST1*, 108–9, 114).[6] Unfortunately, he discusses this distinction in principle only, and does not spell out how it would be applied in practice. He is too eager to emphasise the limitations of empirical verification as a means to truth, and weak in his defence of its indispensable importance.

Under 'means' St Thomas considers some examples of what we may call 'verificationist' theories, pointing out their limitations. His examples are the theory of Isaac Israili, and a formula of Anselm's and Aristotle's, who define truth 'according to that in which its intelligible determination is formally completed'. Such theories demand recognition of a practical requirement of all theories of truth, namely, that they should provide criteria that can serve as means for the verification of judgements. It is the lack of a specific criterion of truth in this sense that is the chief weakness of Tillich's epistemology and correspondence theory of truth, rather than any inconsistency or invalidity in his general position.

He is too ready to endorse the general criticisms that St Thomas advances against theories that confuse their practical criteria of verification with the theoretical definition of truth in general, and that thus beg the question of the validity of the verification principle employed. Additionally, both would reject the nominalist attempt to provide extensional criteria of truth, which abstracts propositions and facts from the ontological order, obscures the importance of causes and ends, and misrepresents the intentionality of cognitive acts.

Finally, under 'effects' or 'ends' St Thomas considers what we may call 'pragmatist' or 'utilitarian' theories of truth. His examples are the theory of Hilary, and two formulae of St Augustine's from the *De vera religione*, which define truth 'according to the effect following upon it'. His criticism of all such theories is not that they are false in themselves, since they emphasise an essential component in knowledge, but that the protagonists of these views err when they take one aspect of the intentionality of cognitive acts as definitive of truth in general.

Tillich criticises pragmatism and utilitarianism in a variety of contexts, while commending their emphasis on meaningful participation in being as a practical goal of the act of knowing. However, he lacks a formulated doctrine of intentionality in terms of which to give a coherent account of theories of truth, including his own; although, as we shall see, the outlines of such a theory are discernible in his writings.

2. *Varieties of criteria of verification in the different sciences*

The second part of Tillich's theory of truth, developed in *Das System der Wissenschaften nach Gegenständen und Methoden*, and paraphrased in summary form in 'Truth and Verification' in *Systematic Theology*, Volume 1, points to the variety of criteria of truth required by the formal, empirical and normative cultural sciences. The argument is based on a theory that distinguishes the different sciences according to the cultural purposes they serve and the intentionality of each of these meaning-creating and meaning-fulfilling human activities. However, apart from emphasising how the unity of the sciences is ultimately guaranteed by the fact that they point beyond themselves to that which is unconditional in power and meaning the theory is tantalisingly sketchy.

In *Das System der Wissenschaften*, he develops some interesting criteria for distinguishing the different sciences according to subject-matter and method, but his ultimate object is apologetic: to demonstrate how all the sciences ultimately point to their ontological and religious foundations in that which secures the universal interconnection of meaning, grounds the unconditioned meaningfulness sought in every meaningful act, and ultimately satisfies the demand for an unconditional fulfilment of meaning (see *DSW* 113–24, 235–8, 284–93, and *WR* 57–8). In the same work, he refers briefly to empirical verification when discussing the physical sciences and the attempts of psychology to adopt the experimental method (*DSW* 145f., 167). However, it would be a gross mistake to imagine that that is all he has to say about verification. The very idea of a system of the sciences arises because all the sciences seek truth, and, 'Because all Science stands in the service of the one Truth, each science is disrupted when it loses its connection with the rest' (*DSW* 11). Further, 'Every cognitive act strives for truth' (*ST1*, 112). If we are to do justice to the various senses in which the sciences seek truth it does not help to speak about verification directly, for the methods of justifying the truthfulness of the insights of different sciences are so various; and to use experimental verification as a paradigm of all verification is as misleading as it is to set up the criterion of truth in mathematics as normative for all truth. To speak of empirical verification, as he is at pains to point out, is to beg the questions of what scope we allow to the term 'experience', what aspect of experience we are concerned with, and with what intention or criterion of relevance we approach it.

Consequently, he tends to speak of the forms of justification appropriate to the different subject-matters investigated and methods employed. In particular, he insists that there are at least four different aspects of the method of each science that require justification. Firstly, there is what he calls the *Erkenntnisziel*.[7] This may loosely be called the aim of the science. It is illustrated in the sorts of questions it asks. It is the determining principle or intention that defines the science's criteria of relevance and dictates its manner of concept formation. (Differences in *Erkenntnisziel* would be most clearly illustrated in the differences between the physical and the historical sciences, but are also illustrated in the differences between physics and chemistry.) Secondly, there is the *Erkenntnisstellung*. This is the attitude required of the knowing subject towards the object known. It determines the degree of subjective involvement that the subject-matter and the *Erkenntnisziel* permits, and is illustrated in the differences between the pure sciences and the human sciences such as psychology. Thirdly, there is the *Erkenntniswege*, that is, the course or working procedure followed by a particular science; or, in the narrowest and strictest sense, its method. The differences here between the sciences are obvious – for example, the diverse ways in which the mathematician, chemist, historian, and anthropologist go about testing their hypotheses – yet we tend to neglect them in generalised discussions of verification. The nub of the debate about verification centres on these differences, and demands an exact phenomenological description of each, if we are to do justice to the richness of the term 'verification', or to illustrate its systematic ambiguity. Finally, there is the *Erkenntnisgrad*, the grade of knowledge produced by the investigations of a particular science, which determines the degree of certainty and significance that it has for us. The point is comparable to Aristotle's belief that it is the mark of an educated man that he attributes only that degree of certainty to a branch of study that its subject-matter allows.[8] Tillich remarks that the degree of certainty of a science is not related to its degree of significance for us. Mathematics or logic may reach a high degree of exactness but have little existential significance. Philosophy and theology may have very limited certainty but still be of the greatest significance for us. 'Knowledge stands in a dilemma; controlling knowledge is safe but not ultimately significant, while receiving knowledge can be ultimately significant, but it cannot give certainty' (*ST1*, 117).

It is in terms of this distinction between controlling and receiving knowledge that Tillich discusses, in the *Systematic Theology*, the differences between forms of verification in the physical, biological, human and historical sciences, and also in philosophy and theology. His basic contention is that controlling knowledge and receiving knowledge are involved to different degrees in all the sciences, and this is his answer to what he regards as a simplistic version of the verification principle. Positivism is right to insist that 'The verifying test belongs to the nature of truth', and that 'Every cognitive assumption (hypothesis) must be tested' (*ST1*, 114). However, while the safest test may be the repeatable experiment, he comments that the repetition is achieved at the cost of abstracting those elements that can be repeated from the totality of the experience, which is not itself strictly repeatable. The process of applying quantitative tests to the qualitative data of experience conceals the artificiality of the procedure by which we make the data amenable to treatment by the inferential techniques of mathematics, and actually edit out significant parts of our experience. The experiential and experimental do not coincide, and physics must admit that it does not investigate the whole of nature, but attempts only to describe, predict, verify and control those aspects of reality that are amenable to treatment by its methods. The paradigm case of experimental verification, namely mathematical physics, reveals a limited truth about the nature we experience and know, and *mutatis mutandis* similar remarks apply to the other sciences.

Tillich points out that the biological and historical sciences require different paradigms and methods, and that the attempt to reduce them to the model of the physical sciences is foredoomed to failure; he thus anticipated by 40 years the critique of reductionism in positivist philosophy of science. He further remarks that if positivism tends to caricature the sciences this is *a fortiori* true of its treatment of philosophy. An adequate understanding of method in philosophy involves recognition of the parts played by the criteria of coherence and consistency (emphasised by the idealist and rationalist stress on the analogy of mathematical demonstration), by practical goals (emphasised by pragmatism's stress on the technical character of science), and the part played by empirical verification (as stressed by logical empiricism in the analogy of the physical sciences). However, none of these methods of justification does full justice to the experientially based, receiving knowledge that is the basis of our knowledge of knowledge, of meaning, and of value, all of which are comprehended in our knowledge of being.

As far as theology is concerned, Tillich set out to establish that we cannot begin with something like the positivist verifiability principle and end with anything like a positive theology. This is the main burden of his complaint against those who, without subjecting the presuppositions of empiricist theories of knowledge to radical criticism, try to adduce deductive or inductive proof for the existence of God. What he had learned from Hume and Kant is that, on such presuppositions, no valid proof is possible and we are led inevitably to scepticism or irrational fideism on the one hand or to a formalistic Deism, based on a kind of *via negativa*, on the other hand. The nearest to proof we can get is something like Kant's conclusion that God, freedom and immortality are necessary postulates that guarantee the coherence and intelligibility of practical reason and moral experience.

Tillich would see any proofs for the existence of God as accessories after the fact; unless we can accept *a priori* that *Deus est Veritas* or *Deus est Esse-ipsum* serves as the objective ontological ground, and *ultimate concern* as the subjective existential ground, of the possibility of any knowledge of God whatever, empirical verification of items of religious experience is beside the point. The risk that faith must accept is inherent in the contingency and finitude of human reason, and the necessary inconclusiveness of all verification that this entails. 'Verification is threatened by the possibility of final meaninglessness . . . It is significant in what it tries to verify, but it is not secure in its verification' (*ST1*, 117). He concludes that if we can accept the limitations inherent in all knowledge and in every human quest for meaning, then we may be able to recognise the truth expressed in revelation: '[F]or revelation claims to give a truth which is both certain and of ultimate concern – a truth which includes and accepts the risk and uncertainty of every significant cognitive act, yet transcends it in accepting it' (*ST1*, 117).

The evidence that verifies this revelation, or the kind of demonstration that establishes it, is exhibited in the experience of faith: in the discovery that man's ultimate concern with being and meaning corresponds to the pre-reflexive intuition of being-itself as truth, that is, as the unconditioned ground, source and abyss of all being and meaning. With this, all theology must ultimately agree.

While we should agree with Tillich in principle, we should say that, in practice, the reception of the truth is a matter of experience. A coherent theology demands that we make sense of empirical experience and our knowledge of finite beings, as well as of our knowledge of being-itself and our experience of the unconditional as the ground of all possible meaningful experience.

Tillich refers rather dismissively to St Thomas's 'sense bound epistemology' and its concern with our knowledge of individual substances and the nature of sense-experience (*TC* 18f.). We are not concerned to defend St Thomas against this implied criticism, but in the final section of this chapter we shall examine Tillich's alternative; it will become obvious that he cannot escape these questions himself, and that his criticism of St Thomas is ill-founded.

3. *The relationship between truth and judgements*

The final part of Tillich's theory of truth concerns the relationship between truth and judgements, or between the cognitive act and the essence *qua fundamentum in re*.

Tillich defines truth in this specific sense in the following terms: 'Truth therefore, is the essence of things as well as the cognitive act in which this essence is grasped. The term "truth" is, like the term "reason", subjective-objective. A judgment is true because it grasps and expresses true being; and the really real becomes truth if it is grasped and expressed in a true judgement' (*ST1*, 113). Once again, it is obvious that Tillich is concerned to stress a dialectical concept of truth that entails both the truth-value of judgements and the concept of true being, since 'The truth of something is that level of its being the knowledge of which prevents wrong expectations and consequent disappointments' (*ST1*, 113). Unlike Von Neurath, who would assert that truth consists in the coherence of all true judgements, or Hegel, who would identify truth as the identity of the rational and the real, Tillich maintains not only that it is the correspondence between the *logos*-structures of mind and reality that characterises truth essentially but also that, in actual existence, the predicate 'true' appertains to judgements on the basis of a correspondence between a judgement and being.

Tillich never gets down to the prosaic level: 'sense bound' or not. What we have spelt out in St Thomas's epistemology is a blank in Tillich's.

Aquinas attempts to say how knowledge is knowledge, and Tillich does not. It is the *how* of the process of knowing as distinct from the *what* of knowledge that he fails to specify. He deals with the essential nature of knowledge at the levels of formal and final causality with great penetration but at the levels of material and efficient causality the nature of knowledge is left vague and unsatisfactory.

This appears to be because of the boundaries within which he conceives the problem of knowledge. In particular his constant preoccupation, which almost amounts to an obsession, is with the problem of absolutism and relativism in knowledge. Conceived in this way, that is, from the standpoint of the *ultimate* justification of knowledge, the type of apologetic required is necessarily formal and essentialist. If he had posed the question differently – for example, how do we justify the particular judgement *p*, (where *p* is say, an observational report, historical assertion or doctrinal statement) he would have been forced to give content to his formal statements about knowledge as an act of union and detachment, involving subject and object in a dialectical relation. The greatest single limitation of Tillich's philosophical theology is his failure to appreciate the need for apologetics to comprehend such particular judgements and their justification, as well as the general questions of the justification of philosophies and epistemologies. His courage is shown in his willingness to develop an ontology of cognition, in which he could deal with those most abstruse of metaphysical questions relating to the foundations of truth and knowledge. His failure, whether it is one of judgement or of nerve, consists in his not demonstrating how his epistemology would actually make sense of the process of knowing. He was certainly capable of doing it, but he did not do it.

Now the formalistic character of his epistemology does not make him an idealist, for even if the solutions he works out are worked out only in principle, they are realistic by intention. Similarly, although his method is essentialist, that doesn't make his ontology essentialist, for he is concerned to spell out in principle how existential knowledge is possible.

Perhaps the most revealing thing about Tillich's works is the way he returns in his last publications to the concerns of his earliest. However, that *Systematic Theology* Volume 3 returns to the themes of his earliest works on Schelling is interesting, but it does not show that he returns to an idealist position, if, indeed, he ever occupied one. What it does mean is that the same concerns dominated his life from beginning to end; but the various solutions he proposed differ considerably, and there is a marked development of his ideas. A specific example is the affinity between his last publication, *My Search for Absolutes*, and the early work, particularly *Das System der Wissenschaften* and 'Religionsphilosophie'. In this last work Tillich worked out, in more detail than ever before, some of the specific theoretical problems that underlay his treatment of truth, morality and religion in his earlier works. It is interesting that just before his death he should have returned to consideration of the absolutes entailed in the act of knowing that enable us to transcend and overcome the split between subject and object. Anxiety about this division has characterised Western philosophy since Descartes; Tillich inherits from Schelling and the post-Kantians these twin preoccupations with absolutism and relativism, and the subject/object dichotomy.

Part of the difficulty, as Tillich realised, is the confusion in Western philosophy of the existing subject with the abstract subject of epistemological analysis, and the substitution of the logical object for the ontological object. He is trying to solve these problems in the discussions entitled 'Subjective and Objective Reason' (*ST1*, 83–7) and 'The Logical and the Ontological Object' (*ST1*, 190–3). However, what is missing is a clear distinction between first- and second-order discourse and between what the mediaeval logicians called first and second intentions. It is lack of clarity in his theory of intentionality that undermines the force of his criticisms. While he does distinguish between the senses in which 'truth' applies to the essence of the thing known and to the act by which it is known, his characteristic move is to play on the ambiguities involved rather than systematically clarify them.

He poses his question regarding the absolute in the act of knowing in a characteristic manner: 'Does the idea of truth presuppose something absolute and unconditional, and, if it does, can the absolute be found in the process of knowing?' (*MSA* 67). He then restates his view that knowledge is based on an original unity, and involves a separation and a reunion of subject and object; it is comparable to the relationship of love and, like the Greek *gnosis*, is analogous to the knowledge of essences and mystical union with the divine that supposedly accompanies knowledge through sexual union.

This model of knowledge as involving an immediate union between knower and known is particularly appealing to Tillich for, to a greater degree than even aesthetic awareness, the act of sexual communication is direct and not mediated through pictures or words or symbols. That this is true may be doubted. What matters is that Tillich is always looking for something that gives direct access to reality and immediate certainty and knowledge at the same time. This is due partly to his realistic instincts. It is also due to the kind of scepticism, inherited from Descartes, that demands that certainty must be absolute. Like the Scotists and Cartesians, Tillich cannot bring himself to affirm that incomplete knowledge is nevertheless real knowledge. It must be absolute knowledge to be trustworthy. St Thomas also maintained that being is inexhaustible and that human knowledge is always in the process of trying to grasp it better and never completely succeeds. Nevertheless, he could embrace the paradox that real knowledge *is* this partial grasp that we have of reality.

The act of knowing, then, for Tillich, must be immediate, certain and of absolute or unconditional validity. The theory has two parts.

Firstly, the ambiguity of the subject/object structure of the human mind is necessary 'to make it possible for me as a subject to look at you as an object and even at myself as an object'; secondly, it is necessary 'in order to have truth as actual reality. It is necessary for the existence of truth' (*MSA* 68). Once again, he stipulates, as necessary conditions of truth, that the subject / object polarity should exist and that this relationship must be discovered in experience and is not given *a priori*. This original unity of subject and object, of truth and being is intuited immediately in pre-reflexive experience, and mediately in cognitive knowledge.

The question of the absolute in knowledge is identical, he contends, with the question, 'How is the unavoidable split between subject and object overcome in the act of knowing?' (*MSA* 68). The answer he gives is that the three absolutes in the act of knowing by which the split between subject and object is overcome, are the immediate certainty of sense-experience, the immediate certainty of the logical *a priori*, and the immediate self-certainty of one's own existence. Many philosophers have appealed to these alleged immediate certainties in an attempt to establish the trustworthiness of knowledge: the empiricists to the first, the rationalists and idealists to the second, and Augustine, the Scotists and Descartes to the third.

We shall not give a detailed analysis of each, but it must be pointed out that all are susceptible to the same objection: either they stipulate necessary *conditions* for knowledge and thus are not forms of immediate knowledge or, if treated as knowledge, they involve tautological judgements such as 'immediate experience is experienced immediately by the knowing subject', or 'there is a logical form presupposed in every form of logical theory', or 'one can be certain that one exists because of the self-certainty of existence'.

The fact that construed as judgements these immediate certainties are tautologies does not make them unimportant. They exhibit the form of our experience, and show what ontological principles are presupposed in the act of knowing, but it is an illusion to suppose that we can get from such formal statements to any kind of substantive knowledge.

The seductive model of the self-evident truths of mathematics and logic plays a decisive role here, and Tillich is caught in an ambivalent position: on the one hand he wants to demonstrate absolute foundations for knowledge and experience, and on the other hand he recognises that in the formal disciplines we achieve certainty at the cost of triviality. The dilemma is: 'controlling knowledge is safe but not ultimately significant, while receiving knowledge can be ultimately significant, but it cannot give certainty' (*ST1*, 117). How one bridges the gap between the subjective certainty and immediacy of private sense-experience and the publicity of knowledge, or how one relates the certainty of logical and mathematical knowledge to the probabilities of science, or how one builds a philosophical ontology on the contingency of the subject's experience of his own being, these are questions that Tillich never answers satisfactorily. With respect to the first, he lacks a clear distinction between the formal sign and the instrumental sign in the act of knowing. With regard to the second, he lacks a clear distinction between first intentions and the second intentions of logical, semantic and mathematical meta-discourse. As to the third, he lacks a clear distinction between the copulative and existential senses of the verb 'to be'.

These weaknesses account for a general ambiguity in his treatment of experience. He asserts categorically that experience is one of the sources of knowledge and the medium of revelation: 'The sources of systematic theology can be sources only for one who participates in them, that is, through experience. Experience is the medium through which the sources "speak" to us, through which we can receive them' (*ST1*, 46). At the same time, he equivocates about our knowledge of finite things and falls back on a mystical doctrine of our immediate pre-reflexive intuition of being itself as the unconditioned and unconditional ground of knowledge and experience. Scepticism and mysticism are mixed in his account of experience. The doubts of Descartes and Kant are only partially met by the faith of Augustine and Scotus.

If we are to sum up the merits of Tillich's epistemology in the narrower sense, we must stress the following elements: a) his illuminating discussion of the meta-epistemological questions of the ultimate justification of truth criteria; b) his discriminating discussion of the different modes of verification in the formal, empirical and normative cultural sciences, and the implied distinctions between logical, scientific and existential truth; c) his suggestive treatment of 'true' and 'false' as evaluative terms; d) his related treatment of the evaluative elements in perceptual experience (based on his experience of art) and the consequent suggestion of a phenomenological account of perception that undermines the empiricist dogma of the privacy of sense-experience; also his discovery that the eye and the ear have their own logic (cf. *PE* 74–92; *HCT* 206f. and *TC* chs 2, 3 and 6); e) his stress on the contribution of the knowing subject in the meaning-creating and meaning-fulfilling activities of human culture, and on science and technology, as forms expressive of man's self-awareness of himself and his world; f) his re-discovery of mediaeval realism; and g) his emphasis on the progressive, evolutionary character of knowledge, including theology, and the implication of this for an ontology that is concerned less with the hierarchical structure of being than with be-ing as a process and the 'multi-dimensional unity of life' (*ST3*, 11–32).

We have consistently tried to defend the view that Tillich's metaphysics of truth in its three parts – the ontology of cognition, existential aspects, and truth and verification – is based on ontological realism and an intentional logic that has more in common with mediaeval mystical realism than with idealism. However, it would be perverse to deny the idealist influence on Tillich; the similarities between his thought and that of Schelling or Hegel are at times so close that our distinction between his realism and their idealism may appear to be a distinction without a difference.

However, we maintain that the distinction is a significant one; although his rhetoric owes a great deal to Schelling and Hegel, we must attempt to do justice both to his explicit concern with realism and his equally explicit rejection of central doctrines in idealism. The same ambiguities and tensions arise, as we shall see, in Tillich's metaphysics of logic.

Chapter 8

The Metaphysics of Logic:
Logic, Meta-logic and Theology

It may seem strange that we have left the discussion of Tillich's Metaphysics of Logic till last. For those who emphasise the kinship of Tillich's thought with idealism, and particularly his dependence on Schelling and Hegel, it would be natural to begin with this topic. After all, he formulated most of his ideas on the subject very early in his career. However, we have chosen to treat it last for three reasons. Firstly, we take seriously Tillich's attempt to formulate a realist philosophy, and his consequent denial that ontological categories can be deduced from logical ones. Secondly, we believe that his metaphysics of logic is a product of his metaphysics of meaning rather than *vice versa*. Thirdly, the practical and rhetorical character of his system means that he neglects the theoretical concerns of a more dialectical study of thought forms, and it also accounts for the insignificant proportion of his writing that is devoted to philosophical logic.

The influence of Hegel on Tillich's thinking about logic is considerable. Nevertheless, it is equally true that he reacts against Hegel's idealist dialectic; however much he retains of the distinctions basic to Hegelian logic, we must do justice to the seriousness of his critical stance.

It is possible to argue that Tillich's logic owes more to popular Aristotelianism and mediaeval realism than it does to the idealist tradition. This is because he believes that being-itself is directly intuited as the basic datum, and that it serves as the *prius* of the subject / object distinction and as the foundation of any possible correspondence between the *logos*-structures of mind and reality (*ST1*, 181–2). Further, human logic simply expresses in cognitive form the given, absolute, structures that are inherent in being and prior to thought (*ST1*, 182–4). Finally, he never confuses the finite subject and the Absolute Subject as Hegel does, nor does he see the categories simply as moments in the dialectic whereby the Absolute Idea realises itself in history. He agrees with Kant that 'the categories are categories of finitude' (*ST1*, 91f.).

Then too the internal evidence of Tillich's discussion of logic suggests that he was influenced to a great extent by the critical and realist character of the logical writings of Lotze and the great Tübingen scholar Sigwart. The brief account of Logic that Tillich gives, in *Das System der Wissenschaften*, virtually paraphrases the arguments for the autonomous character of formal logic as the science of the norms of unconditional validity that we find in the introduction to Sigwart's *Logic* from which Tillich also borrows some criticisms of the doctrine of abstraction.[1]

On the other hand, it is possible to draw many parallels between the distinctions used by Hegel and those used by Tillich. For almost every criticism he directs against Hegel he borrows some concept or distinction from him. There is, for example, striking resemblance between the divisions of Hegel's *Enzyklopädie* and the major divisions among the sciences that Tillich draws in *Das System der Wissenschaften*,[2] and many examples could be produced to support the general impression. However, closer attention to the details of Tillich's argument shows that the resemblances are in most cases apparent rather than real, and that there are important differences of purpose behind his and Hegel's systematic constructions.

1. *Logic, meta-logic and the system of the sciences*

It is not without significance that *Das System der Wissenschaften* is dedicated to Ernst Troeltsch, for Tillich perhaps owed more to the immediate inspiration of Troeltsch's work and its neo-Kantian categories than to Hegel. Tillich's enterprise is closer to the spirit of the *Groundwork to the Metaphysic of Morals* than it is to Hegel's *Enzyklopädie* or his *Logic*. Like Troeltsch, he is concerned to identify the constitutive and regulative principles of the various universes of discourse of the formal, empirical and normative cultural sciences. However, for an explanation of the relations of the three kinds of sciences, he tends to fall back on the Hegelian architectonic.

The purpose of Hegel's system is to demonstrate the fundamental importance of logic and to prove that the philosophy of nature and spirit are ultimately derived from logic by the immanent dialectical movement of Absolute Spirit. The Absolute is first posited in thought, to which nature is op-posited as its antithesis. Finally, in the synthesis of the realised Absolute Idea, thought and nature are '*aufgehoben*', that is, negated, transcended and the dichotomy between them overcome.

Tillich certainly does not agree with Hegel's fundamental presupposition that logic is the all-important source for our knowledge of being. Logic is severely restricted in what it can indirectly disclose about being through its revelation of the form of thinking. Logic takes its place among the *Denkwissenschaften* along with mathematics, and possibly phenomenology, as a science with a proper but limited validity.

The ultimate purpose of Tillich's system of the sciences is more practical. Hegel's logic, in essence, was the translation of a theology into philosophical terms. Tillich's logic subserves his theology. If it is the presupposition of his theology, it is a logic that is transcended in the direction of an explicit Christian theology. In *Das System der Wissenschaften*, he is primarily concerned with the questions, How is theology as a science possible? and, How does it stand in relation to the other sciences? His attempted classification of the sciences shows a regard for the distinctive characteristics of the sciences rather than any tendency to force them into a preconceived scheme.

Again, if we compare the structure of Tillich's *Systematic Theology* with Hegel's *Science of Logic*, as set out in the *Enzyklopädie*, the structural features are surprisingly similar. This early work of Hegel's divides into three parts:

1) Logic / Metaphysics: the science of the being of the Idea in and for itself.

2) Philosophy of Nature: the science of the Idea in its existing otherness.

3) Philosophy of Spirit: the science of the Idea in its essential realisation, come back to itself out of otherness.[3]

Apart from its first and last sections, which have some similarity to Hegel's *Phenomenology of Spirit*, and his *Philosophy of History*, the main sections of the *Systematic Theology*, 'Being and God', 'Existence and the Christ', and 'Life and the Spirit', could be said to correspond to the division of Hegel's *Logic* into 'Being and the Absolute Idea', the 'Absolute Idea in its Existing Otherness', and the 'Absolute Idea in its Essential Spiritual realisation'.

There are other important Hegelian triads that have parallels in Tillich's thought. For example:

Hegel	*Tillich*
1) *Aspects of Logic*	*Methods of Thought*
Abstract Thinking	Reflective-Rational or Formal Logic
Dialectical Thinking	Dialectical-Rational or Dialectic
Speculative Thinking	Critico-Dialectical or Meta-logical[4]
2) *Categories of Logic*	*Metaphysics of Knowledge*
Being (Quality, Quantity, Degree)	The absoluteness of the structures of Being, which makes understanding possible
Essence (Ground, Appearance, and Activity	The absoluteness of Essences, which makes language possible
Idea (Subjective Notion, The Object, the Idea)	The absoluteness of Being-itself – which makes Truth possible[5]
3) *Modes of Thought*	*Theory of Knowledge*
Immediacy – The Notion implicit and in germ	The pre-reflexive intuition of Being-itself
Alienation in Reflection, Mediation in Dialectic (the appearing of the idea, the being-for-self)	The act of Knowing as involving Detachment and Union
Reconciliation in Synthesis (the idea in its return to itself and developed abiding in itself)	The ontological synthesis: transcending the Subject / Object dichotomy[6]

These parallels are striking and cannot be ignored, but it must be insisted that closer examination of Tillich's account of meta-logic, dialectic and formal logic reveals important differences in the characters and emphases of Tillich's logic and that of Hegel.

In any case, it would be a mistake to place too much weight on the similarity of these triadic distinctions, for their use is not peculiar to Tillich and Hegel. The whole Platonic and Augustinian tradition relies on such distinctions, and their use amounts almost to a compulsory literary convention. However, use of the same literary form does not prove identity of content, as is perhaps shown by the widely contrasting uses made of Plato by Hegel and by Kierkegaard.

Tillich explicitly attributes the distinction between *Denkwissenschaften, Seinswissenschaften,* and *Geisteswissenschaften* to Fichte, and even compares it to the Stoic distinction between logic, physics and ethics (*DSW* 120, 122). He makes the point that if one begins the analysis of knowledge with the assumption of a duality of act and object, then this distinction commits one to a particular kind of analysis, and a particular mode of representing acts of knowledge. 'In each act of knowledge a duality is contained; the act and that upon which it is directed, the referring and that which is referred to. If we call the act through which consciousness directs itself to something in the interest of objective comprehension, 'Thought'; and that upon which it is directed, 'Being', then we have determined the two basic elements of knowledge as thought and being' (*DSW* 118). Given such an analysis, the relationship between thought and being, considered in the abstract, can be described only in terms of three kinds of relations:

1) Being is posited in thought as the grasped, the understood, as the determination of thought.

2) Being is sought out by thought as the foreign, the incomprehensible as that which resists thought.

3) Thought is present to itself in the act of thought, it is directed upon itself and turns itself into a being.

The first statement can read: Being is the determination of thought. (The Principle of Absolute Thought.) The second statement can read: Being is the contradiction of thought. (The Principle of Absolute Being.) The third statement can read: Thought itself is being. (The Principle of Spirit) (*DSW* 118–19).

The division of the sciences into *Denk- oder Formwissenschaften, Seins- oder Realwissenschaften* and *Geistes- oder Normwissenschaften* is derived from this schema.

It is characteristic of the *Denk- oder Formwissenschaften* that

Thought seeks every object – a bit of nature, an historical person, a movement of the soul, a form of society – in order to integrate it into the sphere of absolute consciousness with the aid of Concepts, Laws and Connections. The object is translated into these until nothing dark or strange remains. But Concepts, Laws and Connections are the creations of thought appearing in knowledge. Then all knowledge dissolves into a net of determinations of thought, until all being is gathered into the unity of thought, and being itself has been dissolved into thought. (*DSW* 119)

By contrast it is characteristic of the *Seins- oder Realwissenschaften* that:

[I]n every thought more is intended than mere thought: something beyond the process of thought, something which 'is' in itself, without reference to any consciousness, and before which every consciousness stands as before something Insoluble, which thought, being unable to be taken up into Infinity, just has to accept. (*DSW* 119)

The *Geistes- oder Normwissenschaften* arise because of

the strange fact that thought is not only directed towards being but also towards itself; that it is, so to speak, its own spectator while it is thinking. Thought thus turns itself into an object amongst other objects. Thought places itself under all the determinations and conditions proper to being and into which thought has dissolved being. Thought becomes a piece of existence. If we now ask *where* this existing thought is to be found, we can only answer: 'Inside' the conscious being, that is for us, in the spiritual life of human beings. (*DSW* 12)

These extensive quotations have been given because they are basic statements of Tillich's thought. Fundamental, ontological, epistemological, logical and semantic principles are contained by implication in them. What they illustrate, in spite of their striking similarity to analogous distinctions in Fichte and Hegel, is that Tillich refuses to take the fatal step towards absolute idealism, and translates these distinctions into instruments for a basically realist philosophy of being. Perhaps the sharpest contrast is his substitution of the realist principle of 'the inner inexhaustibility of being' for the idealist principle of 'the inner inexhaustibility of thought' (cf. *DSW* 123 and *IH* 168). Like Kant, he emphasises the radical finitude of human thought, although he believes thought can exhibit, within itself, its dependence upon the unconditional as the ground of its validity, and thus point beyond itself to the unconditioned as the ground and abyss of meaning and truth.

For Tillich, the system of sciences is not based on logic as foundation and source of its constitutive and regulative principles, as it is for Hegel. His position is closer to Fichte's *Wissenschaftslehre*, which gives logic a subordinate place in a general philosophy of meaning founded on *das Unbedingt*, that is, the unconditioned and unconditional. Idealism drew the radical consequences of a position that sought to establish universally valid foundations for science:

If we think, as in common life we tend to think, that the proofs of science are valid unconditionally, when the truth is that they rest upon the assumption of certain unverified conditions, then we are obviously under an illusion. And if these conditions are the absolute conditions of the very possibility of scientific method itself, then it is not science, but only logic, which can save us from that illusion. Such at any rate is the task which Kant himself in his logic undertook and handed down to the Idealist logicians after him.'[7]

Fichte considers logic fundamental in its demonstration of the universally valid conditions of science, but he doesn't consider it the source of all being and meaning. Tillich likewise emphasises the unconditioned and the unconditional, but concludes that the universal and necessary ground of the science of sciences is being-itself. Because being-itself is inexhaustible, it is also the abyss of all being and meaning, and hence not identical with the subject matter of logic.

With these critical reservations, Tillich is able to distinguish his own meta-logic from Hegel's *System of Logic* and the logicism it generates; and also to distinguish his theistic philosophy of meaning from the closed system of absolute idealism of Fichte's *Wissenschaftslehre*. However, he is also able to appreciate the positive insights and emphases of idealist logic.

His basic and most revealing statement concerning the relationship of the various sciences to being itself is the following:

> *The approach to being can be made equally well through the logical as through the aesthetic, ethical, social and religious functions.* For each of these functions being is somewhat different, and yet the same thing is intended by all – it is the Unconditionally real which gives content to all forms. *The basic question for logical thinking is whether it can allow each of these approaches to being to make its own impact*, of finding forms which, without prejudice to logical accuracy, will express the fulness of ontological content as seen from all these points of view. We call this method 'meta-logical' in analogy with 'metaphysical'. (*DSW* 122; italics added)

This recognition of the variety of approaches to being entails a modification of the limited meaning of 'Being' in idealist thought, which tends to make the logical conception of being normative for other universes of discourse. Similarly, the recognition of cognitive functions other than reflection, such as contemplation, intuition and believing, emphasises that 'Thought' has to be qualified to include more content-orientated cognitive acts. Meta-logic demands a dynamic reinterpretation of the antithesis of thought and being. 'Pure logic seeks to grasp everything real in an unchanging rational form. It is static and must be so, because the highest rationality is the abiding and immutable identity of "A=A"' (*DSW* 123). The inspiration for such a meta-logical method comes from Hegel. However, a chief limitation of Hegel's logic is that 'The logical in it swallowed up the meta-logical and dynamic, and that at some point or other of its logical and chronological development the Dynamic was abandoned. Thought seeks to completely subjugate Being, but Being cannot be subjugated . . . There are no empty categories (and there are also certainly no other things of a higher order), but rather there are different meaning-elements of reality, grasped by the different mental functions which must be set out scientifically in systematic order' (*DSW* 123). While Tillich thus criticises and ultimately rejects Hegel's logic, he admits his indebtedness to Hegel and gives credit to idealist logic for a number of revolutionary insights that, radically transformed and modified, are taken up into his own thought.

The first concerns the Hegelian critique of traditional formal logic and the divorce between logic and metaphysics brought about by the combination of formalism and scepticism in the rationalist tradition.[8] Tillich agrees that there must be an intrinsic connection between logic and ontology, but refuses to accept Hegel's conclusion that logic and ontology must be identical.

Secondly, Hegel criticises the doctrine of substance as the paradigm of being that underlies traditional logic and ontology. Tillich agrees with his demand for a logic and ontology that is suited to the expression of the dynamic and active life of spirit.[9] He also agrees that our knowledge of persons is more fundamental than our knowledge of things, and that a logic adapted to the 'material mode of speech' will be unsuited to characterise the dialectic of man's inner life. However, he does not agree with Hegel's pantheistic absolute idealism, which sees the rational activity of finite subjects as simply movements of the inner life of Absolute Spirit.

A related matter is Hegel's demand that we distinguish between ordinary formal logic and philosophical logic, or dialectic.[10] The former is concerned with the modes of proof proper to the natural sciences; dialectic is intended to reflect the self-expressive forms of the life of spirit. Tillich endorses this demand for a logic of communication as distinct from the prevailing logic of calculation.

The fourth point to be emphasised in idealist logic is the importance of intentional and teleological concepts in our explication of knowledge.[11] Knowledge is to be understood not by analogy with impersonal physical processes but as an activity of the knowing subject. While agreeing with this emphasis, Tillich is careful to qualify the absolute subjectivism by which Hegel makes all knowledge the self-expression and self-reflection of Absolute Spirit.

Finally, Tillich takes very seriously Hegel's treatment of the 'unhappy consciousness', or the analysis of the forms of self-alienation in thinking.[12] However, while Hegel sees the alienation as an inevitable part of the historical dialectic of evolving consciousness, going through its successive stages of thesis, antithesis, and synthesis, Tillich rejects Hegel's deterministic and rationalistic historicism, and in its place emphasises man's historical contingency and existential freedom and offers us a much more realistic account of historical evil and tragedy. The dialectic by which this alienation is overcome is no inevitable rational process. It is the struggle of existing persons to realise their historical destiny in freedom, and to participate in the redemption of time and the realisation of the Kingdom of God.

2. Tillich's critique of traditional formal logic

The exalted view of logic in the rationalist tradition from Descartes to Leibniz, and the reservations about the value of deductive reasoning in the empiricist tradition from Locke to Hume, both stem from a formalist interpretation of logic. In the former, logic is literally constitutive of reality: in the latter, the forms of deductive proof-logic are rejected as empty. The empiricists are led first to explain inference in terms of association. Later they develop a radically empiricist relational logic: the extensional and truth-functional logic of *Principia Mathematica*. Kant, however, took a different course and it is with his heirs and successors that we are mainly concerned.

Kant's main problem was to explain how knowledge of the material-object world is possible. He rejects the doctrine that we can deduce the nature of reality from the structures of logic. However he does assume the completeness of Newtonian physics, Euclidean geometry, and Aristotelian logic, and is driven to the conclusion that insofar as physics and geometry reveal the way in which the *a priori* forms of intuition (space and time) operate in our grasp of the material object world, the laws of logic reveal the laws of thought. By this he means that the laws of thought, the forms of judgement and the rules of inference reveal the *a priori* necessary and universally valid categories of reason, and these categories are the *conditiones sine qua non* for knowledge. The categories, in Kant's terminology, are regulative of our knowledge of nature and not constitutive of nature itself. Because reason is finite, the categories cannot say anything directly about the nature of reality, but it is an open question whether they may not exhibit or show the possible form of reality.

Fichte, Schelling and Hegel are dissatisfied with this account as it leaves the nature of reality undetermined, and the universal validity of scientific truth is thus called in question. 'Historically then the Idealist logic sets out on its course with two fundamental tenets. First, that the old logic is inadequate to explain modern science; secondly, that empirical psychology cannot produce an adequate theory of thinking – and therefore logic must set its own house in order by the use of a method of its own, distinct from that of psychology'.[13]

There are three distinct steps by which Hegel reaches his distinctive view of philosophical logic as the science of sciences. The first is to see formal logic as restricted in its scope and validity to the material mode of speech and thought: 'The Aristotelian logic is in Hegel's view a natural history of finite thought; (or of thought as appearance only), i.e. it presents a set of fixed thought-forms elicited by the reflection of the Understanding upon the thinking of natural science and common sense'.[14] The second step involves the recognition that, on the Kantian model, logic is not merely illustrative of, but *is* the transcendental method *par excellence*. The third step involves distinguishing formal logic, and other possible logics, from philosophical logic or dialectic, which is concerned with the systematic justification of their validity. 'Kant is convinced that formal logic, by successfully eliciting all the formal relations in which concepts *qua* united in judgement can stand to one another, has shown that the Understanding itself is a system ... But he cannot tell us how formal logic was able to discover and exhibit this systematic connection.'[15] This

it is the task of the dialectic to establish: 'It is par excellence as a logician
. . . that man exemplifies the highest phase of Absolute Spirit, philosophy . . .' The categories, from this perspective, become 'partial self-
definitions of Absolute Spirit', or, as he prefers to call them; 'Denk-
bestimmungen'.[16] Tillich refuses to accept that in philosophy we have
privileged access to the inner life of Absolute Spirit or that we are equip-
ped to speculate *sub specie aeternitatis.* He agrees, however, with Hegel
that formal logic is nothing more than the natural history of finite reason,
and insists, with Kant, that the categories are categories of finitude. The
categories are indispensable for all coherent thinking, however sceptical;
and, from the standpoint of finite human reason,

> We live in the structures they give us. They provide us with the onto-
> logical safety without which neither thinking nor acting would be
> possible . . . These basic structures make possible our excursions of
> thought into the unsafe flux and relativity of encountered things.
> *They give us the structure of thought as well as the structure of reality.*
> (*MSA* 77)

However, Tillich is careful to qualify this position, which sounds so
like Hegel's, for he insists that our group of categories is relative: 'I admit
that our group of categories and our knowledge grasp of the character of
categories are relative' (*MSA* 78). Nevertheless, in the process of clarifying and distinguishing categories we are constantly reminded that they
are the indispensable grounds and conditions for our knowledge of being; yet we can never claim to comprehend them entirely or exhaust their
meaning, for we do not have direct access to the be-ing of being-itself, but
only to our own be-ing and perhaps to the be-ing of other finite things.

The Hegelian view that formal logic is a logic adapted to the explication
of the material object language, with the double implication of its limited
validity and the possibility of other logics that embody other perspectives
on being, is heartily endorsed by Tillich as we have already stressed.[17]

Tillich appreciated the significance of Hegel's attempts to escape the
naive formalist and reductionist views of formal logic and to do justice to
the pluriformity of logics in different sciences. Long before Wittgenstein's
Philosophical Investigations, Tillich accepted the view that different
universes of discourse presuppose different logic, and that attempts to
force them to fit the Procrustean bed of traditional formal logic could
lead only to caricature and misrepresentation. Long before Goedel provided a formal proof of the incompletability of logico-mathematical
systems, Tillich argued, in *Das System der Wissenschaften*, that if we
attempt to provide a formal justification for formal logic as such, we need
a meta-logical doctrine concerning the nature of logical truth, that is, a
metaphysics of logic. Tillich became so committed to defending his own
account of the logic of theological discourse, that he was unable to
appreciate the ground he shared with the 'linguistic theologians' who
sought to apply the insights of Wittgenstein and Goedel to the explication
of the logic of religious language in general and theological discourse in
particular (cf. *ST2*, 104–7).

The sense in which Hegel sought to introduce change into logic has been a source of confusion and controversy. Kierkegaard attacked Hegel in the most sarcastic manner for committing the absurdity of trying 'to make movement explain logic, when as a matter of fact logic cannot explain movement'.[18]

It was convenient for Kierkegaard's anti-Hegelian and anti-essentialist polemic to imply that Hegel attempts to introduce change and movement into traditional formal logic, and that he reifies the categories of formal logic in the manner of the rationalists. This disregards the fact that Hegel distinguishes between formal logic and the higher logic or meta-logic of philosophical dialectic, and that he distinguishes between change and becoming, suggesting that it is possible at this meta-level to develop a logic that can include the concept of 'becoming' as a category. There are two perfectly intelligible senses in which change can be introduced into logic, although the bombastic and equivocal language of Hegel obscures his meaning. The first is the sense in which logic itself is subject to change, growth and development in the history of thought: traditional formal logic is not a closed and finished science, nor does it exhaust all the possibilities. Rather must our understanding of the historical dimension of human thinking include a recognition of the fact that 'Logic must be an open-ended science'. Human thinking is not only concerned with knowledge of the material world but is also 'a living, growing activity, in pursuit of the truth about the nature of thinking and the nature of mind'.[19] The second is the sense in which Hegel does recognise a distinction between change as a first-order phenomenon of our experience and becoming as a category of second-order reflection on that experience. In this sense, his antics in dialectics apart, he is making a valid and important distinction and it is doubtful whether he means that becoming itself must change. Mure puts it well: 'Hegel's "Becoming" is not change, for change is *temporal* and Time is not a category but a phase of Nature. Becoming is a pure thought, as it is, of course, a category operative in the experience of change'.[20]

Tillich's view is that human culture is a dynamic, evolving process in which human activity expresses, in a variety of forms, man's developing consciousness of himself and his world. This account, which finds its fullest expansion in *Systematic Theology* Volume 3 is based on a view of human thought and logic that owes a great deal to Hegel's concept of the historical evolution of human consciousness. However, there are crucial differences between them; for Tillich, this evolution is subject to the capriciousness of human freedom; we do not know history's *denouement* in advance, or know the mind of the Absolute Spirit; and human history and the realisation of the Kingdom of God stand in an ambiguous and uncertain relation to the other.

Tillich accepts the Hegelian view that becoming is a necessary category of thought and being:

The dynamic character of being implies the tendency of everything to transcend itself and create new forms. At the same time everything tends to conserve its own form as the basis of its self-transcendence. It tends to unite identity and difference, rest and movement, conservation and change. Therefore, it is impossible to speak of being without speaking of becoming. Becoming is just as genuine in the structure of being as is that which remains unchanged in the process of becoming. (*ST1*, 200; cf. *ST3*, 26–7, 430–3)

However, the striking thing is that Tillich locates the source of the impulsions to change in being-itself and not in thought. It is also significant that while Hegel's main criticisms are directed against the static logics of the past, in Tillich's thought, these become strictures against static ontologies of the past.

Now it is arguable that Tillich meant by 'ontology' simply what Hegel meant by 'logic': namely, second-order reflection on the categories. Structurally considered, Tillich's meta-logical method and Hegel's dialectic would appear to be identical. The methodological purposes they serve seem to be the same; namely, to provide an ultimate justification for the *a priori* necessity and unconditional validity of the categories employed in all forms of human thought, and to provide the frame-work for a system of the sciences. 'Dialectical thinking is not in conflict with the structure of thinking. It transforms the static ontology behind the logical system of Aristotle and his followers into a dynamic ontology . . . This change in ontology opens up new vistas for the task of logic in describing and interpreting the structure of thought. It posits in a new way the question of the relation of the structure of thought to the structure of being' (*ST1*, 63).

Tillich contends that, in the doctrine of 'the cunning of the idea' Hegel grasped that there is a dynamic interaction between the ideas and history. This is the greatness of the Hegelian dialectic: 'to grasp the idea dynamically', that is, to grasp that ideas not only express man's conception of reality but help to shape that reality.

> The theory of the cunning of the idea is no myth; rather is it a paradoxical expression for faith in providence, but in its idealistic metamorphosis. The believer in the traditional idea of providence also knew that the ways of providence are dark, contradictory and obscure; nevertheless he believed in it and was certain that it would arrive at its goal. Hegel goes one step further. He knows of the ways in which the idea develops; he is aware of its cunning and of the true meaning of the devious and roundabout course which history follows. He stands at the end and can look back upon the whole development. Thus it is in his, the final philosopher's thought that philosophy finds its full realisation and achieves its freedom from fate. Every external necessity disappears in the 'absolute' system. (*PE* 13)

The relationship of logos and kairos to one another is, as we have seen, central to Tillich's theology and ontology, but it is central to his understanding of logic, in the sense of dialectics, also. However, what distinguishes his dialectic from Hegel's is that he uncompromisingly insists that the dialectic must be a dialectic of *existence*, and must embrace fate and contingency, since they characterise not only man's historical existence but also his rational life: '*Dialectics is observation of the essence, insofar as essence is in the hands of fate; not of the essence as it remains without fate*' (*IH* 165).

There is grave risk of confusion here if we do not distinguish the precise sense in which this is intended as an indictment both of formalist logic and metaphysics and of idealistic dialectic and metaphysics. This double critique illustrates once again Tillich's ambivalence towards idealism. He maintains that these logics ultimately isolate themselves from social and historical reality. They fail to see how the doctrines of being that they generate express and reinforce particular types of social order and reify particular types of historical reality. Traditional formal logic and rationalistic metaphysics sought to reify the socio-historical reality of Enlightenment Europe and the idealised world of its cultural elite. Hegel's dialectic ultimately absolutised the subjective idealism of the nineteenth-century bourgeoisie and, in its baroque and decorative form, embodied their optimism and belief in rational progress. Tillich would see the empiricist logic of this century as grounded in the scientific-technical world-view of contemporary man and as expressing both his fate (*Geschick*) and the meaning of his history (*Geschichte*).

In emphasising the relationship between dialectics and fate, Tillich does not wish to be understood as suggesting that the propositions of formal logic, for example, are temporally contingent. He is well aware that the abstract and formal character of logic expresses itself in the fact that the propositions of logic are timeless, neutral and context-independent. However, even formal logic acquires a relation to time and history when it is put to service in other spheres of human cultural activity. Logic inevitably has an expressive and symbolic value as well as a functional application. It is not a matter of indifference which logic we choose, for logic tends to function as a powerful paradigm of method and can dictate the form of the ontology we develop on its foundation. For example, Tillich would maintain that the static ontology of Leibniz is the result of his choice of traditional subject-predicate logic as the model for his ontology. He echoes, in rather more pompous terms, Aristotle's caution that we should adapt our logic to the form of our experience and not vice versa: 'Our task is to serve the logos out of the depths of our new kairos, a kairos that is emerging in the crises and catastrophes of our day. Hence, the more deeply we understand fate – our own personal fate and that of society – the more our intellectual work will have a power and truth' (*PE* 17). This is a protest against *a priorism* in philosophical logic and a plea for a metaphysics of truth and logic that is aware of historical reality and includes it in its systematic constructions. Logic is as much a self-expressive form of human activity as art and music are, and it is subject to the same ambiguity, that is, it has the same potential to be read and used in a variety of ways. This is the secret of its power and the fascination it exercises over men's minds.

This broad, symbolic and metaphorical sense of 'ambiguity' plays a crucial role in the thought of Paul Tillich and is a vital part of his philosophy of meaning. 'Ambiguity' is not confined to its narrow semantic connotation. In Tillich's metaphysics of meaning, it is a key instrument in the hermeneutic of human culture, and the *Geisteswissenschaften* in particular. It signifies that in every meaning-creating human activity there is a manifest and a latent intention. The manifest intention is to express the specific thought or feeling or volition required by the context; the latent intention is expressed in the goal of all meaning-creating activity, namely, to achieve meaning-fulfilling unconditionality and universality. For Tillich, the possibility of a theology of culture or a philosophy of religion rests on the possibility of making this distinction between the contingent acts of finite beings and the directedness of these acts towards the unconditional ground of all being and meaning.[21] Tillich's central point is that unless we distinguish these levels of intentionality we cannot make sense of the symbolic and expressive forms of human culture, nor, ultimately, of physical science and formal logic, for they are human activities expressive of man's view of himself and his world.[22]

The correlate to contingency in Tillich's ontology is the concept of ambiguity in his account of meaning, truth and logic. He brings to bear on logic a double critique: of its naive assumption of the ideal of unequivocal logical truth, and of its related attempt to erect an unambiguous ontology on the basis of excluded contradiction and the ideal of a coherence theory of truth.

Like Hegel, he appreciated the ambiguity of ideas and in particular, of the idea of essence, both as a category of formal logic, and as a symbol for the power of being of things. Both attack traditional philosophy and formal logic for canonising the ideal of certainty; an ideal based on the rejection of the analogical and symbolic element in ordinary language and on the demand for a language of univocal terms that excludes all ambiguity.[23] Both are concerned to develop a dialectical logic that will do justice to human discourse in all its forms. Not only must such a logic of discourse accept the symbolic and expressive, and thus ambiguous, element in all human communication; it must attempt to give intelligible explanations of the use we make of univocal, equivocal and analogous terms, and show how we can make sense of both literal and figurative discourse. If we admit this broader concept of ambiguity as philosophically important then we will recognise its relevance to the interpretation of the whole of man's social activity and cultural history.

Tillich can say of Hegel: '(His) employment of ambiguity as a principle of historical dialectics is an intellectual achievement of decisive importance'. However, 'Hegel's limitation at this point consists in this, in that in his thought the ambiguity is removed if we look at it from the point of view of the total process, the contradiction thus losing seriousness . . . History is taken into the synthesis of syntheses, but it is not a challenge to every conceivable completed synthesis' (*IH* 167–8).

In his own *Systematic Theology*, therefore, Tillich tries to avoid the premature synthesis and to give due weight to the element of ambiguity in all human thought and historical cultural activity. He tries to stick to his own precept concerning the demand that any future dialectics must fulfil: '[I]t must try to grasp the relationship of the ideas, the structure of the essential, in such a way that the ambiguity of every solution becomes visible in the solution itself' (*IH* 168). Thus, Tillich's dialectical method employs the concept of ambiguity both as a principle of his philosophy of meaning and hermeneutic of human culture, and as a means of expressing the incompleteness and fragmentariness of his system. In this sense, the principle of ambiguity is central to Tillich's logic.

In *Systematic Theology* Volume 1, Tillich employs the principle mainly as a means of emphasising the relativity and finitude of human knowledge and our empirico-rational structures of thought (*ST1*, 90–4). In Volume 2 it is used as correlative to the meaning that is revealed in 'Jesus as the Christ as the New Being' and applies to the ambiguity of human self-estrangement, of the creative and destructive impulses in human life and of the greatness and tragic contradictions of human culture (*ST2*, 4, 86, 152–4). In Volume 3, it becomes the central category in the interpretation of the relationship between human life, culture and the life of the spirit, and between human history and the Kingdom of God. It is the constant correlate to 'the quest for unambiguous life', and the indispensable foundation of Tillich's theory of symbolism and the dialectic of the whole work (*ST3*, especially chapters xxiii, xvii–xxx and xxv).

We shall have more to say about the limitations of this structural concept of ambiguity in the concluding section of this chapter, but in this context it is sufficient to note the various senses in which Tillich has identified sources of ambiguity in logic and shown us how that ambiguity can be exploited or ignored with serious consequences for logic and ontology.

3. *Tillich's own account of the nature of logic*

As we have seen, Tillich distinguishes formal logic and dialectic, considers the kinds of logic appropriate to different universes of discourse, examines the relation of logic to ontology and stresses the importance of intentional categories in logic. However, in the introduction to *Das System der Wissenschaften*, he has some brief but revealing things to say about the nature of formal logic itself. In addition, what he has to say about semantic, logical and methodological rationality in *Systematic Theology* Volume 1, chapter 2 is important for the understanding of his conception of formal logic.

In the former, he begins by characterising the *Denkwissenschaften*, and distinguishing the functions of logic and mathematics: 'In the cognitive formal sciences, scientific inquiry directs itself towards those forms which are essential to Thought, [considered] apart from their connection with Being – although it does not exclude the possibility of such a connection. There are two sciences to which these characteristics apply: Logic and Mathematics' (*DSW* 124).

Logic has a connection with the normative cultural sciences that parallels the relationship between mathematics and the empirical sciences, for 'Logic considers Thought divorced from all content, but is determined in the nature of its Objects (*Objekten*) by the possibility of grasping contents in a cognitive manner. Mathematics equally considers Thought divorced from all content, but it is determined in the form of its subject matter (*Gegenständen*) by the possible factual existence (*Daseins*) of a content-ful Reality' (*DSW* 124). Chronologically, mathematics precedes logic because thinking directs itself first onto being, and only thereafter reflects upon itself; whereas in order of priority, logic stands on the first rung of knowledge, because mathematics presupposes the logical as its foundation and not vice versa.

There are several important points here. The first is that Tillich, in emphasising the formal character of logic and mathematics, reflects the views of late nineteenth-century logicians such as Lotze and Sigwart, who see mathematics as a branch of logic.[24] However, he does not accept the position of either Hegelian or Russellian logicism, which would claim that mathematics is actually reducible to logic, for mathematics, he maintains, is concerned with the forms of our knowledge of possible objects, whereas logic is concerned merely with the logical possibilities of thought.

A more controversial view is the suggestion conveyed in the expression that logic and mathematics are concerned with 'those forms which *are essential to* Thought': The suggestion is that logic and mathematics prescribe the forms that are essential to the normative and empirical sciences respectively. The relation in which logic stands to the other sciences has to be carefully qualified if we are not to revert to Hegelianism. It is tempting, on the basis of this kind of expression, to suggest that logic is a kind of ethics-for-thought; that it is proleptic for thought in the way that ethical values and rules are for human action.

Tillich rejects as dangerous the position that makes logic normative for the *Geisteswissenschaften*, for this involves importing elements of meaning and value into a discipline that is purely formal. However, he does not have at his disposal the notion of pure syntax and the distinction between syntax, semantics and pragmatics, nor does he use the mediaeval definition of logic as the science of second intentions. Thus it is difficult for him to explain the relation between logic and the other sciences if he rejects the 'all-controlling position of formal logic' in rationalist thought and the Hegelian alternative.

His solution, which is a sensible one, is to subordinate logic to the categories of his theory of meaning, in terms of his meta-logical method. His main attention is devoted to the possible application of logical terms such as 'necessity', 'universality' and 'validity' in the metaphysics of meaning and truth. Logic is interpreted very generally as imposing requirements of consistency and systematic order on all the sciences, and as illustrating *par excellence* the meaning-fulfilling universality, necessity and unconditional validity sought by all the sciences:

Validity is a primitive function; it means nothing else but that

Thought seeks to realise the Absoluteness of its form in each existing thing, but no existing thing is dressed in pure form. Validity reveals that the thought-form is at the same time the opposite of reality and the necessary pre-condition and forming principle of everything real – as it corresponds to the original congruity [identity] between Thought and Being. The concepts of Denkwissenschaften are thus concepts of validity. (*DSW* 125)

He explains that logical and mathematical concepts are thus both 'gestalten' and 'gesetzen', that is, essential forms and laws or principles. However he is most insistent that when we speak of consequences (*Folge*) in logic and mathematics we exclude the temporal and historical connotations of the word 'because pure thought-forms have no relation to time'. Also he uncompromisingly rejects the view that *formal* logic can include the concept of temporal change. If thought is to deal with these logically it must do so within a dialectical logic. On the other hand – 'Logico-mathematical concepts . . . are expressions of ideal gestalten and their structural laws. However, ideal *gestalten* are not genuine *gestalten* and ideal laws are not genuine laws. Both expressions are used only in an analogous sense in the formal cognitive sciences (*Denkwissenschaften*)'. For, as he explains, 'A genuine law is decisive for all the individual cases, only *the* individual case, the ideal instance governed by its definition.' He concludes: 'Instead of speaking of *gestalten* we do better to speak of *gebilden* (or constructs),' and thus 'Logico-mathematical concept formation is therefore directed towards these constructs, and formulae about these constructs' (*DSW* 125–6).

Because of the overall methodological standpoint from which he approaches logic, the details of logic and the critical testing of arguments are given the most superficial treatment. This means that the particular function of logic in clarifying the relations and uses of concepts, judgements, and arguments is inadequately understood. These traditional topics of logic are given only a passing mention in *Das System der Wissenschaften*. This is unfortunate, because his *Systematic Theology* lacks the critical rigour that more attention to matters of logic would have given it; also, his ontology could have been given useful reinforcement had he considered the logical basis of the distinctions between being, essence and existence, especially, as we shall see, in terms of the kind of intentional logic that derives from Scotus and John of St Thomas.

His discussion of logic and mathematics in terms of the distinctions between *Erkenntnisziel, Erkenntnisstellung, Erkenntniswege* and *Erkenntnisgrad* is interesting because it illustrates the difficulties inherent in an approach that seeks to define them according to subject-matter and method ('nach Gegenständen und Methoden'). He avoids the extreme realism of Meinong; logical propositions are not about any kind of things. In using the word 'objekt' in conjunction with logical expressions, he has in mind that which a proposition expresses rather than a specific class of referents for logical propositions. Here, he comes close to the mediaeval doctrine of *suppositio*; but could equally well be said to have been working with a distinction similar to that of Wittgenstein's between showing or exhibiting logical concepts and operations in use, and saying something about occult logical entities. Curiously enough, he uses the word '*Gegenständen*' of mathematical expressions, because he considers that mathematics has the relation of intending a possible reality.

He describes the *Erkenntnisziel* of logic and mathematics as corresponding in this case to the *Erkenntnisstellung*. In other words, the *aim* or *determing principle* that defines their criteria and manner of concept-formation is identical with the attitude or disposition required of the knowing subject towards the object known, for the aim is intuition, and the required attitude is intuitive. However, the intuition involved in logical thought is not the psychological intuition of empirical experience, but the 'methodological intuition' of reflexive self-consciousness, that is the critical and intuitive self-examination of the structures of thought. It is the means by which we characterise the *a priori* rational forms that are constitutive of and regulative for rational thought: 'In both the Formal and Normative Cultural Sciences it is in fact not upon being that knowledge directs itself, but upon thinking – sometimes as pure form, sometimes as norm. That is the problem of ideal and normative concept formation' (*DSW* 125).

In the process of exhibiting the ideal forms or structure of thought, logic implicitly supplies the criteria by means of which we evaluate rational thought. It is these implicit structural criteria to which all disciplines, including theology, must conform if they claim to be rationally intelligible. 'The second principle determining the rational character of theology is *logical rationality*. This principle refers first of all to the structures which determine any meaningful discourse and which are formulated in the discipline of logic. Theology is as dependent on formal logic as any other science. This must be maintained against both philosophical and theological protests' (*ST1*, 62–3). The criteria embodied in the principle of logical rationality are criteria of validity. However, Tillich does not use the concept of validity in a purely formal sense, that is, in a sense applicable only to words, or to thought divorced from being. Although it is a formal concept, it is implicitly ontological in significance. In reflexive intuition:

> Thought directs itself on being which is not yet in being – a Paradox – for which the conventional logical expression is: Validity. There is no more precise definition of 'Validity', as each definition of the term would either have to employ the term 'being' or the term 'validity'. Validity is a primitive function; it means nothing else but that Thought strives to realise the Absoluteness of its form in each existing thing. (*DSW* 125)

We will have more to say about the use Tillich makes of this concept of validity in developing the ontological basis of his theology in the final section of this chapter; in this context, it is important for the further development of his ideas about logic.

Although he qualifies what he has to say about logico-mathematical '*gestalten*' and suggests that it is preferable to call them '*gebilden*' (or constructs), he is committed to the view that the structures of being are implicit in the *a priori* logical forms of reason, for he would not concede that these *gebilden* are arbitrary constructs or fictions of thought. This fact explains two attributes of Tillich's logic that have been remarked upon critically by J. Heywood Thomas, namely, his fondness for 'legislative definitions' and his tendency to equate formal logic with deduction of a rather narrow kind.[25]

On the one hand, he maintains that 'The logico-mathematical gestalten ... are not formed from within, but from without, by definition, and they are therefore inter-definable and interchangeable' (*DSW* 126). On the other hand, he tends to regard such definitions as revealing the true nature of things. Thus, like Husserl and the phenomenologists, he is inclined to believe that definitions express intentions of essences and so reveal the essential structures of being. However, this line of argument, while designed to emphasise the intrinsic connection between thought and being, leads to confusion when it fails to distinguish between real beings and the beings of reason. The fact that logic is concerned with second intentions and the structural relations between beings of reason means that definitions derived from reflection on logical entities and the structure and dynamics of thought cannot reveal anything about the real world. When he says, of logical expressions, 'Instead of speaking of "gestalten" we do better to speak of "gebilden" (constructs)', he does so in order to emphasise the inadequacy of formal logic. 'In this way we can pinpoint the deficiency of its arrested conception of being'. He is aware that 'Logico-mathematical concept-formation is directed towards these "gebilden" (constructs) and formulae about these constructs' (see *DSW* 16), but he implies always that there is a more embracing view in which the ontological significance of logical forms can be revealed, that is, where logic is free of the self-imposed limitations of its *Erkenntnisziel*.

The limitations of this view of formal logic are shown, too, in his treating formal logic as synonymous with deduction. He not only ignores non-demonstrative types of inference, but he also has a very restricted view of deduction and virtually equates it with syllogistic argument. Tillich tends, like Kant to regard the propositions of mathematics and logic as synthetic *a priori*, that is, as universally valid and true prior to experience but also as informative. He lacks a clear definition of logical truth and tends to conflate formal validity and truth. A curious consequence of these views was that he regarded tautologies as logical mistakes. It is not surprising therefore that he tended to resent Heywood Thomas's suggestion that the systematic form of his theology was deductive in character, and that many of his fundamental statements are reducible to tautologies.[26]

His view of the deductive character of Formal Logic derives from his rather simplistic stress on form, and a tendency to equate thought with form and experience (or being) with content. He is led by the inexorable 'logic' of his own figurative language to define formal logic in terms of the explication of logical forms. Deduction reduces itself to this tautology: formal logic is the analysis of logical forms. This emphasis on form is derived from Kant and Husserl, and he explicitly identifies himself with the latter's rejection of psychologism in logic (*OB* 53). The influence of Husserl's *Logische Untersuchungen* is equally obvious in his treatment of phenomenological method, and the nature of logic in *Das System der Wissenschaften*. Like Husserl, he regarded symbolic logic as nominalistic. Unlike Husserl, he did not make any serious attempt to explore the realist and intentional logic of the mediaeval tradition from Scotus to John of St Thomas. Instead, it suits his apologetic interests to represent formal logic as exclusively concerned with validity, necessity and the uncon-ditional. Hence he argues that the grade of knowledge (*Erkenntnisgrad*) with which formal logic is concerned is 'evident knowledge' and 'cer-tainty': 'Just as the limitless (infinite) distance between Thought and Being does not exist here, since Thought is directed upon itself, so there is no probability, only certainty. In every logico-mathematical formula the unconditional absoluteness of the pure thought-form finds its expression, that is its value but also the expression of its alienation from true being' (*DSW* 127).

The fact that Tillich ignores induction, the probability calculus, modal logics and non-demonstrative inference is very revealing, for it shows how much investment he has in maintaining this view of formal logic as the science of logical forms. A great deal of the emotional attraction of his appeal to the unconditional, universal validity, and absolute necessity is lost if formal logic is demythologised and treated either as a study of inferential techniques in the modern sense or as an art in the Aristotelian sense. It is rather important to his argument that logic should be a science; that it should have a subject-matter and not be mere method. And even if it is purely formal it has an important paradigmatic significance as being about *das Unbedingt*, universal necessity and knowledge that is in some sense certain. The question Tillich never dared to ask himself was Witt-genstein's – whether Logic achieves certainty at the cost of triviality, at the cost, that is, of dealing in tautologies. It is not surprising, therefore, that when he comes to deal directly with logic he does not discuss the various parts of logic, but is concerned, rather, to defend his definition of formal logic. He represents the main alternatives to his view as the attempt to make logic into an empirical science and the attempt to reduce it to a cultural art.

His chief argument against empiricism and those who make psycho-logy the foundation for logic, is that 'The sort of validity which is deriv-able from the sphere of observation and human factual knowledge lacks absolute certainty and demonstrable self-evidence' (*DSW* 128). It is not clear whom he is attacking. It may be Hume and Mill, as the arguments he borrows from Kant would suggest; it may be Husserl and Brentano, as the paraphrase of arguments from Sigwart would suggest. Whichever it is, it is not clear that he grasps what is at issue, for instead of providing an explanation and justification of his view that 'logic precedes all other science as unconditionally valid form-science', he contents himself with some rather lame criticisms of empiricism. These are that the empiricist cannot satisfactorily explain the difference between natural necessity and logical necessity, that empiricist logic must be relativistic and limited in validity to human thought only, that empiricism provides no adequate basis for distinguishing between factual truth and logical truth and, similarly, that the empiricist cannot avoid confusing judgements of existence and judgements concerning the meaning of propositions.

What Tillich failed to anticipate was that empiricism would develop a thorough-going truth-functional and extensional logic that would make it possible to distinguish natural necessity and logical necessity, factual truth and logical truth, and semantic and syntactical functions of propositions, without compromising the universality of logical laws and without committing the empiricist to belief in the existence of a special kind of non-empirical and unconditional meaning and truth that it was the purpose of logic to reveal. By insisting that logic merely exhibits inferential techniques in use and does not have a special metaphysical subject-matter, modern logical empiricism has sought to demythologise the Kantian view of logic and to demonstrate the prosaic sense in which logical laws are universally valid and how, *qua* analytic statements or tautological expressions, their truth is purely formal. Tillich holds to the Kantian view that logical laws are synthetic *a priori* judgements, and fails to see that logical empiricism undermines the credibility of this view and demands a different form of apologetic if his own philosophical position is to be defended. Only on the basis of a thorough-going intentional logic is it possible to maintain the intrinsic connection between logic and ontology, and give coherent expression to the kind of realist epistemology that Tillich espouses.

In discussing the attempt to associate logic with the cultural arts, Tillich is mainly concerned with popular contemporary misconceptions of logic rather than with serious philosophical theories. Two bear some resemblance to theories of Fichte's; these are attempts to derive logic from the theory of knowledge, and to equate logic with the theory of method in general. A third equates logic with drill in the practical art of thinking. The form in which these theories are expressed and the kind of criticisms raised against them trivialise what are potentially important criticisms of the modified Kantian position adopted by Tillich.

He falls prey to two popular idealist misconceptions of Aristotle: that his logic is deduced from his metaphysics and epistemology, and that he considers logic a mere technique for the regulation of thinking. 'Validity and utility are two quite different concepts' says Tillich, considering that this disposes of the crass pragmatic empiricism of Aristotle! What he fails to understand is that there is no simple deductive relationship between either metaphysics and logic or epistemology and logic in Aristotle's thought. Nor does he recognise that logic is not a mere technique but is an art – what Aquinas calls an intellectual virtue or habit by which the soul expresses what is true.[27] Consequently, he fails to do justice to the intrinsic relation between logic and metaphysics, and thus tends to exaggerate the autonomy of logic.

> Now it is doubtless possible and necessary to interpret logical laws metaphysically, but it is not legitimate to ground them on this or to find their interpretation in this, for the formulating of any principle and the interpretation of and logical expression resulting from such a principle always pre-supposes the validity of the laws of logic. It must always remain true of Formal Logic that it cannot pre-suppose anything – not even the distinction between a knowing subject and a known object, not even the existence of a world to be explained. Precisely for this reason everything depends on the formal character of Logic, as that by means of which it becomes a pure Thought-science, equally to be distinguished from a necessarily incomplete Empirical account of things as from the concrete-individual Cultural sciences. (*DSW* 129)

Similarly, Tillich is so concerned with defending formal logic as the source of the crucial concepts of unconditioned validity, necessity and certainty, and so concerned with maintaining his definition of Formal Logic as the paradigmatic *Ideal- oder Denkwissenschaft* in order to defend the architectonic of his System of the Sciences, that he almost completely ignores the technical and practically useful aspects of logic. The prosaic side of logic, that is, its development of techniques for the analysis of concepts, propositions and arguments, does not appeal to Tillich's high-flying metaphysical mind.

The great merit of *Das System der Wissenschaften*, as we have repeatedly emphasised, is that, in considering the different sciences according to subject-matter and method, it emphasises the diversity of logical forms required for the explication of different universes of discourse. However, its greatest limitation is its inadequate account of formal logic itself. He fails to consider the possibility that not all sciences have a subject-matter and by exaggerating the autonomy of logic as the paradigmatic form-science, he fails to do justice to the insight of the tradition of *Methoden-lehre*, which, although it made the mistake of equating logic with the study of method, had the virtue of seeing that in studying the different methods of the arts and sciences logic lays bare their different logical forms.

4. *Intentional logic and the critique of Tillich's logic*

Tillich's opposition to nominalism included rejection of its logic, but his criticisms of nominalist logic are directed at the metaphysical pre-suppositions of nominalism rather than at the details of its logic. This is unfortunate, since logic is concerned with the theory of signs and their functions, and Tillich's lack of clarity about different semiotic theories not only means that he retains elements of nominalist logic in his own system, with resulting ambiguity and ambivalence in his treatment of logic, but more specifically it leads to confusion in his theory of signs and symbols and his theory of intentionality.

Tillich, along with Peirce, Ernst Cassirer, Heidegger and others, has emphasised how nominalist presuppositions contribute decisively to the formation of the modern scientific-technical world-view. As we have seen,[28] he attacks the cult of scientism, and the cult of the calculus that are characteristic of this secularist ideology. Not only are his metaphysics of meaning, metaphysics of logic and metaphysics of truth designed as an answer to nominalist metaphysics and the supranaturalist theology that goes with it, but his attempt at a realist doctrine of signs and symbols and the elaboration of a theory of intentionality are designed to meet the inadequacies of nominalist logic. However, his efforts are only partially successful for he fails to carry through his programme with sufficient logical rigour. If, in the critique of nominalism, Tillich had shown the logical acumen of Peirce, or Peirce had displayed the metaphysical perspicacity of Tillich, the resulting system would have been a truly formidable one. As it is, Tillich's thought takes refuge in vagueness and generalisation when it comes to deal with matters of logic and semantics.[29] Peirce, on the other hand, gets lost in an intricate web of abstractions as he attempts to work out the metaphysical implications of his theory.[30]

The task that confronts us here is to clarify the senses in which Tillich's thought may be said to be based on an intentional logic, and to clarify the theoretical basis of the theory of signs.

As has been pointed out,[31] intentional logics are to be contrasted with logical systems modelled on mathematical calculi or formal axiom systems. Intentional logics are concerned with the expressive functions of human acts and with the logic of communication. This does not mean that intentional logics cannot be formalised, but rather that this must be done without abstracting the communicating subject from the situation to be analysed. The crucial difference, as Peirce pointed out, is that the sign-using function is not reduced as it is in nominalist logics, to the dyadic relation of word and thing, or proposition and fact, but the relationship is recognised to be a triadic one involving interpretant, sign and thing signified.[32] Intentional logic is characterised, then, by its inclusion of the existing subject as a factor in the analysis of the meaning of words, statements and arguments; hence it can consider other functions of discourse besides the informative and it does not have to artificially establish the relationship between logic and ontology, because the ontological dimension is included within its scope.

Theories of intentionality and intentional logics are not new. The logic of Aristotle and the mediaeval Scholastics may be said to be intentional in the broad sense specified above. In a more specific sense, the logic of Scotus and John of St Thomas is an intentional logic because they explicitly maintain that logic is concerned with intentions and formal logic with the structural relations of second intentions. However, before we examine this theory further, it is important to summarise what Tillich understands by intentionality and to discuss in what sense his logic may be said to be an intentional logic.

Tillich owes his use of the term 'intentionality' to Brentano and Husserl, who derive the term partly from mediaeval sources and partly from Kant and Hegel. In this tradition, it is emphasised in the analysis of cognitive acts that consciousness is always consciousness *of* something. The act of consciousness intends an object, whether this object is a substance, an event or a goal. It is not clear whether this is a dyadic or triadic relation, and this ambiguity creates further ambiguities for the logics derived, as is Tillich's, from this tradition.

The term 'intentionality' is a term with a variety of applications both in mediaeval philosophy and in its more recent usage. It can be said to be a systematically ambiguous term or an analogical term, since there are systematic or analogical connections between its various uses. This is no less true of Tillich's uses of the word and its cognates.

We can distinguish at least four different uses of intentional concepts in Tillich: a) There is structural or ontological intentionality; b) There is intentionality of cultural forms in general; c) Human acts are intentional in a specific sense; d) There are intentional distinctions between forms of discourse.

a) By structural or ontological intentionality we refer to the presupposition that the structural interdependence of self and world provides the horizon within which all particular meanings are expressed or articulated. 'The self having a world to which it belongs – this highly dialectical structure – logically and experientially precedes all other structures' (*ST1*, 183). 'Man is aware of the structures which make cognition possible. He lives in them and acts through them. They are immediately present to him' (*ST1*, 187). He explains that by virtue of his use of language and 'the power of universals' man is capable of reflexive self-consciousness, and thus, 'because man has an ego-self, he transcends every possible environment. Man has a world'.[33] The self-world structure that is presupposed is both ontological and intentional in character: 'This structure enables man to encounter himself. Without its world the self would be an empty form. Self-consciousness would have no content, for every content, psychic as well as bodily, lies within the universe. There is no self-consciousness without world-consciousness, but the converse also is true' (*ST1*, 189). It is this general meaning of intentionality that underlies its more specific senses in the discussion of human acts, discourse, and cultural forms. He makes the point explicitly in discussing the polarity of dynamics and form in relation to man:

> The polarity of dynamics and form appears in man's immediate experience as the polar structure of vitality and *intentionality* . . . Ordinarily one speaks of the vitality of men, not of animals or plants . . . Vitality, in the full sense of the word, is human because man has intentionality. The dynamic element in man is open in all directions; it is bound by no *a priori* limiting structure. Man is able to create a world beyond the given world; he creates the technical and the spiritual realms. (*ST1*, 199)

b) This leads straight to the intentionality of human cultural forms in general. As we have seen, the fundamental premise of Tillich's metaphysics of meaning is that underlying man's conscious awareness of the self-world structure of experienced being is an immediate and pre-reflexive awareness of being-itself as the unconditioned ground and source of all being and meaning (*TC* 22). Human activity and cultural creation takes place, according to Tillich's meta-logical theory, within the context provided by ontological intentionality, but against the background of this metaphysical intuition of being-itself. Human cultural forms thus explicitly express man's self-awareness of himself and his world; but they are also implicitly expressive of his quest for the unconditioned and unconditional ground of all meaning. Ontological intentionality is this meaning-creating and meaning-fulfilling activity of man (see *WR* 56–72).

c) The third meaning of intentionality embraces the general teleological concepts that he uses in the analysis of human acts into causes, means and ends, and also the specific Husserlian point that consciousness is always consciousness of something. He nowhere critically analyses these distinctions and their relations. In general, the relationship between purpose and meaning remains vague in Tillich's thought. This may be due in part to the tendency in idealism to make cognitive acts paradigmatic, and to understand acts of making and doing by analogy with these, rather than to follow the realist tradition, in which the paradigmatic sense of 'act' is to do or to make, and thus to speak of cognitive processes as 'acts' involves a metaphorical extension. It may also be due to the tendency to understand consciousness as a two-term relation between consciousness and object, where 'object' can mean either the goal or the *terminus ad quem* of an action. Tillich uses the term '*Gegenständen*' to avoid this ambiguity by emphasising the correlativity of subject and object'. However, since 'subject' and 'object' are terms of the logician's second-order vocabulary, it is easy to conflate 'subject' and 'consciousness', and 'object' and 'intentional object'. Because of these ambiguities, it is doubtful that Tillich maintains a consistent realist doctrine of intentionality.

d) Finally, there are the various intentional distinctions that Tillich draws between different forms of discourse. First, there are the distinctions between the informative or denotative function of language, its expressive function, and its communicative or revelatory function:'The denotative [or informative] power of language is its ability to grasp and communicate general meanings. The expressive power of language is its ability to disclose and to communicate personal states' (*ST1*, 137). The communicative or revelatory function of language is its power to reveal the unconditional and ultimate, which is the ground of all meaning and truth, but which cannot be consciously intended in the ordinary usage of language: 'The word as a medium of revelation points beyond its ordinary sense both in denotation and in expression . . . Language with this power is the "Word of God" . . . something shines (more precisely, sounds) through ordinary language which is the self-manifestation of the depth of being and meaning' (*ST1*, 137–8).

In *Systematic Theology* Volume 1, these distinctions are introduced in order to explain his doctrine of revelation, that is, to explain how the pre-reflexive and immediate awareness of being-itself is expressed in linguistic and cultural forms (*ST1*, 137–9). The same distinctions are used in developing his doctrine that the divine spirit overcomes the ambiguities inherent in finite human language and cultural forms: 'The word which bears the Spirit does not grip an object opposite to the speaking subject, but it witnesses to the sublimity of life beyond subject and object . . . Whereas the ordinary symbol is open to an interpretation which throws it back into the subject-object scheme, the Spirit-created symbol overcomes this possibility and with it the ambiguities of language (*ST3*, 269).

This revelation of the unconditioned norm of all meaning is both particular and universal: 'Every language is particular because it expresses a particular encounter with reality, but the language which is a bearer of the Spirit is at the same time universal because it transcends the particular encounter which it expresses in the direction of that which is universal, the Logos, the criterion of every particular logos' (*ST3*, 270). According to his meta-logical theory, theology as the theonomous science of the norms of meaning is pre-eminently the study of this communicative or revelatory function of language. The denotative and expressive functions of language 'the first result of the self-creation of life under the dimension of spirit' are the province of logic and semantics:

> Meaning pre-supposes a self-awareness of life which has trans-psychological validity. Something universally valid is intended in every meaningful sentence, even if the subject spoken about is particular and transitory. Cultures live in such meanings. The meaning-creating power of the word depends on the different ways in which the mind encounters reality, as expressed in language from the mythical to that of daily life and between these, as expressed in the scientific and the artistic functions. All this is continuous activity of the self-creation of life in producing a universe of meaning. Logic and Semantics deal scientifically with the structures and norms through which this universe is created. (*ST3*, 73)

Corresponding to the kinds of intentionality of the denotative, expressive and communicative functions of language are the disciplines of logic, semantics and meta-logic that study them, and the reflective-rational, dialectical-rational and paradoxical attitudes. Superficially, these distinctions appear to be similar to those in traditional intentional logic between formal logic, dialectic and rhetoric, but there are important differences that are based partly on different metaphysical presuppositions, partly on different conceptions of the scope of logic, and partly on the curious conflation of rhetoric and dialectic that takes place in post-Kantian philosophy.

Tillich's realism, like that of Scotus, is based on the paradoxical claim that we have an immediate pre-reflexive intuition of being itself that cannot be expressed in ordinary language; literal discourse is concerned with the world of appearances and the really real can be expressed only by figurative or symbolic language. In practice, this extreme realism approximates so closely to idealism as to make the distinction appear to be one without a difference, for both maintain that we cannot know or express the being of things directly or immediately; substances are *sensibile per accidens* not *sensibile per se*, and it is only the pre-reflexive intuition of being-itself that gives us the confidence to infer the existence of substances from their phenomenal appearances. So, in the case of Kant, things in themselves are not directly knowable but can only be inferred from sense experience. Tillich admits the similarity of Scotist realism and post-Kantian idealism, (*STI*, 197n) but does not recognise the criticisms to which both have been subject from the standpoint of moderate realism and the intentional logic of the Aristotelian tradition and John of St Thomas.

These criticisms relate to the distinctions between *ens* and *ens in se*, the supposed dilemma of nominalism versus extreme realism, and the parallel distinctions between *sensibile per accidens* and *sensibile per se* and between instrumental and formal signs in the theory of intentions.

On the first point, the argument is that by creating a hiatus between *ens*, which can be known only by inference from phenomenal experience, and *ens in se*, which is supposedly the object of immediate intuition and certainty, extreme realism drives inevitably towards mystification or nominalism. On the one hand, being-itself becomes the object of an increasingly mysterious metaphysical intuition divorced from our knowledge of being, and on the other our knowledge of being becomes the subject of increasing scepticism in a doctrine of the epistemologically mediate and instrumental function of sense experience and language. This ambivalence is characteristic of Tillich's thought, but is it unavoidable?

It is unavoidable if one assumes that extreme realism and nominalism are exhaustive alternatives, that is, that either essences are conventional devices for the logical manipulation of the data of sense, or that in themselves they are real and universal. But it is possible to maintain, as St Thomas did, that the distinctions between essences are real in the sense that they are based on distinctions that have a *fundamentum in re* in the world of particulars, but that, in the cognitive order, essences take on the characteristic of universality *qua* abstracted being.

> The escape from this dilemma lies in a clear recognition of the fact that in themselves essences are neither universal nor particular, but in coming to be or exist they take on characteristics which as such and in themselves they do not possess at all. Thus, in coming to be really and *in rerum natura*, essences become individuated and associated with other essences; on the other hand, in coming to be known, or in becoming objects before the mind, essences become universal and predictable of many.[34]

Thus, as Aristotle insisted, the distinction between form and matter is based on a real distinction between modes of being in things, but form and matter can never exist in themselves in separation from one another, except in the world of mental abstraction. Categorical distinctions and universal terms are thus intentions, the objects which it is the peculiar task of logic to study, but *qua* intentions they cannot become an independent source of knowledge about reality. As the essence or nature becomes one when abstracted from the many and considered in a universal concept, so universal concepts give fundamental expression to relations of identity between the one nature or essence abstracted and the many particulars from which it has been so abstracted, and in which it exists as a real multiplicity.

Unfortunately, Tillich, like the idealists, is tempted to attribute real being to these beings of reason and to make metaphysical capital out of speculation on the nominal value of terms such as being, existence and essence, matter and form, act and potency and so forth, and to erect an ontological 'stock-exchange' on the notion of identity. We have examined the metaphysical implications of this tendency in preceding chapters, but here it is our task to examine its implications for his view of logic.

The basic question concerns the scope of logic and its relation to rhetoric on the one hand and to dialectic on the other. Because of Tillich's view that the only real alternatives are nominalism and mystical realism, he is constantly inclined to undervalue the technical side of logic and to exaggerate the metaphysical aspect of dialectic. His view of logic is both too broad and too narrow. It is too narrow in that his Kantian-type scepticism makes opaque the relation between the first-intentional concepts of ordinary knowledge-relations and the second-intentional concepts of logical analysis and ontological speculation; hence formal logic must be restricted to being a 'pure form science'. It is too broad in that in place of the prosaic study of the relations between epistemic and logical concepts, we have to substitute the *quasi* mystical, metaphysical and meta-logical dialectical study of ontological relations; thus dialectic is inflated into a science of being-itself.

Tillich does not distinguish between rhetoric and dialectic in the traditional manner, and often uses the word 'dialectic' for the science of theological communication in general as well as in the exalted metaphysical sense in which dialectic is the instrument for the disclosure of true being. In practice, he distinguishes literal or ordinary language from, and contrasts it unfavourably with, symbolic or revelatory communication (*ST3*, 61–5, 73–4). In this context, theological dialectic becomes an exercise in the translation of these cryptic, symbolic statements into statements that answer the questions arising out of man's existential predicament. Tillich tends to conflate rhetoric and dialectic, and consequently lacks a clear distinction between preaching, or first-order religious communication, and theology, or the second-order analysis of religious language. The distinctions he draws between the philosophy of religion and theology are very tortuous because he lacks such simple but important distinctions.

One must say quite directly that Tillich was confused about the role of dialectic in philosophy, and about the proper domain of logic. Because of this, Maritain's criticisms of Hegel are very apt when applied to Tillich, in spite of the latter's attempts to repudiate idealist influence. What Maritain says is the following:

The Real introduced forcibly into the logical Being of Reason does violence to Logic.[35]

Kant refers to the classical conception of dialectics (logic of controversy). But for him dialectics becomes consubstantial with the activity of Reason. It is the only way judgements can be formulated on the subject of the Ideas of Reason, and this way leads to fundamentally necessary and inevitable antinomies.

With Hegel these antinomies are no longer mere antinomies of Reason, they belong to the Real itself (which is Thought). Whence the Hegelian revolution: dialectic is no longer identified simply with philosophical knowledge as in Plato, it passes over to the object, becomes the essence of Reality, which is logical self-movement.[36]

Tillich takes as paradigmatic of intentionality the fundamental unconscious tendency that underlies all thoughts: to reveal being-itself. Somehow, we have to work back to the ordinary and prosaic intentions of everyday thought. It is not surprising that we do not reach clarity about their nature or their relations to the fundamental metaphysical sense from which he begins. From the point of view of Aristotle or St Thomas, he puts the cart before the horse. He makes meta-logic normative for logic rather than recognising that meta-logic is an abstraction from the distinctions of ordinary logic.[37] He makes the logical categories of thought (second intentions) normative for the interpretation of the ordinary objects of thought (first intentions) instead of seeing the former as derived from our knowledge of the latter. However, the primary source of his confusion is the mishandling of the distinction between formal signs and instrumental signs.

As Veatch points out, it is common for intentions to be referred to as formal signs. What is meant by this distinction can be made clear by considering the triadic relation between knower, sign and thing signified. The distinction between natural and artificial signs is based on the different ways in which a sign can be related to its significance: relations of natural causality may justify speaking of clouds as signs of rain, or of pain as a sign of organic malfunction; human conventions determine how signals, guideposts and words signify their objects. By contrast, the distinction between instrumental and formal signs is based on the different kinds of relations between the sign and the knower. An instrumental sign is one that signifies its significatum to a possible knower only by being first apprehended itself. Both natural signs and artificial signs are instruments by which we gain mediate knowledge of things. By contrast, 'A formal sign is one whose whole nature and being are simply a representing, or a meaning, or a signifying of something else. Such signs, in other words, are nothing but meanings or intentions'.[38] Thus concepts, propositions and arguments, which embody different kinds of meanings, are examples of formal signs. To have a concept is to understand what it means. A concept or proposition or argument signifies its significatum immediately. In other words it is tautological to say: I understand what the concept means. To have a concept of x is to know what x means, otherwise you cannot be said to have a concept of x. (The same applies *mutatis mutandis* to know-ing propositions and arguments.) Now Veatch argues that it is funda-mental to nominalism, and to the empiricist and rationalist traditions that stem from it, that it treats all signs as instrumental signs.

As a matter of fact, it is significant that the decline of realism in mod-ern philosophy has been accompanied by a tendency on the part of philosophers either to deny, or at least to ignore, any such thing as a formal sign. Thus with Descartes, and particularly with Locke, even concepts or ideas became transformed into instrumental signs. Locke, for example, opens Book IV of his *Essay* with the proclama-tion that 'the mind, in all its thoughts and reasonings, hath no other immediate object but its own ideas, which alone it does or can con-template.' In other words, an idea for Locke is no longer to be regarded as an *id quo*, but rather as an *id quod*, of knowledge.

Or, as he immediately continues: 'An idea, instead of being something which *immediately* represents its object to a knowing power, is rather something which has to be known in itself first; and then from this know-ledge one has to make some *sort of inference to the object* of which the idea is presumably *a copy or resemblance*, and hence an instrumental sign'. He concludes that this position leads to serious inconsistency: 'One no sooner declares that we know not objects, but only our own ideas, than the same problem emerges all over again regarding this knowledge of our own ideas . . . unless one recognises formal signs at some stage of the game or other, the explanation of knowledge will involve an infinite regress'.[39] The nub of the argument is that while instrumental signs are often a necessary condition of our knowledge of objects, they are never a sufficient condition of that knowledge.

Nominalism and empiricism are driven to reduce the sign-using relation to a dyadic one because of their treatment of signs as instrumental signs, and of words and propositions as conventional signs. The problem of the nature of intentionality is suppressed by ignoring the question of the logical status of concepts, propositions and arguments, and concentrating on the relation between language and reality, where the intentional con-cepts remain implicit in the overall concepts of a language that is un-critically presupposed.

From the realist point of view, because the relation is a triadic one, the articulated word, sentence or piece of reasoning points in two ways: towards the intending subject and towards the intended object. The empiricist, however, attempts to ignore both these kinds of intentional relations and strives to de-intentionalise language, thereby reducing all meaning relations to syntactical ones. Rationalism, by contrast, tends to confuse the intension of a word (its connotation) with its intentional relations. In particular, there is a tendency to reduce the sign-using relation to the dyadic relation between subject and sign, and to con-centrate on the subjective intension rather than the objective intentional-ity that governs the meanings of words. By using Husserl's concept of intentionality, Tillich attempts to correct this subjective emphasis in rationalism and idealism, but he merely substitutes one kind of nominalism for another insofar as he is stuck with a view of intentionality as a two-term relation.

The corrective to idealism that is required, if Tillich's realism is not to collapse into either sceptical nominalism or idealism, is a bold recognition that concepts, propositions and arguments do give us immediate knowledge, and that it is only on the basis of that knowledge that we can understand the intentional relations in which instrumental signs stand relative to their objects. From concepts, propositions and arguments, understood as instrumental signs, we can never get to immediate or certain knowledge of things. This is why it is necessary for Tillich to introduce the '*deus ex machina*' argument that we have a pre-reflexive knowledge of being-itself, in order to secure the credibility of ordinary empirical knowledge.

The realism of St Thomas by contrast is based on the twin assumptions that there are beings that are, and are what they are, independently of anyone's knowledge of them, and that these beings are capable of being known, even if, in practice, our knowledge is incomplete. Thus he would maintain that our knowledge of contingent things is real knowledge, in spite of its inadequacies, and whether or not we can attain to knowledge of the infinite. However, on the basis of the doctrine of the analogy of being, we reach out tentatively towards knowledge of being-itself. By the agnosticism of the *via affirmativa*, it is possible to develop a theory of knowledge that includes knowledge of finite being and knowledge of being-itself within the same view. It remains possible for the gulf between finite and infinite to be bridged from the God-ward side in revelation, and also, in principle, from the manward side by the analogy of being.

In contrast, Tillich offers us a kind of gnosticism based on a mystical and pre-reflexive intuition of being-itself as the unconditioned ground and source of all being and meaning. Not only can the gap between infinite and finite be bridged from the God-ward side only, but even the possibility of knowledge of finite things rests ultimately on this mystical intuition of being-itself. Whether one finds Tillich more plausible than St Thomas depends in part on what one finds least incredible: the distinction between instrumental signs and formal signs, and possibility of real but finite knowledge of contingent things; or the necessity of grounding all knowledge on a metaphysical intuition of being-itself. As C. W. Morris was to point out in a classic paper in which he elaborated on the doctrines of Peirce,[40] the realist doctrine of signs requires that an adequate semiotic theory, that is, one that takes account of the triadic nature of the sign-using function, must include not only syntax or the study of the formal relations between signs in a sign-system, but also semantics or the study of the projective relations between signs and things signified, and pragmatics or the study of the relations in practice between sign users, signs and things signified. None of these is given adequate treatment by Tillich, who certainly failed to understand the theoretical relationships between them, in part because he was operating with an inadequate logic and an incomplete theory of intentionality. One's disappointment with Tillich is ultimately a disappointment with the inadequately systematic character of his system. He raises important questions, but he fails to follow through his theoretical insights and tends to take refuge in obscurity and mystification. All the ingredients of a realistic ontology on the basis of a thoroughly intentionalist logic are present in his system, but he hesitates to commit himself to a radically realist position. It is difficult to say with confidence why this is so. It is partly due to the sceptical element he inherits from Kant, but it is also undoubtedly due in part to a tendency so to emphasise the transcendence of God as primary cause, that the efficacy of secondary causes, both as causes of knowledge in the human mind and as possible means of grace, is undermined.

The consequence is that Tillich seems to commit us to the view that, apart from the immediately mystical intuition of being-itself, we cannot know being and its categories and modes without first knowing the intricacies of meta-logical theory and ontology. In practice, it is certainly the case that, in *Das System der Wissenschaften* and the *Systematic Theology*, one has to master the dialectic before one can begin to master the ontology. But is knowledge of the real dependent on knowledge of the logical (of Tillich's meta-logical in particular), or is knowledge of the logical dependent on knowledge of the real? It may be objected that they are obviously interdependent, but it seems equally necessary that knowledge of ordinary, real, finite beings must be possible and must precede the development and refinement of logical categories. However, the discussion of the relationship between logic and metaphysics requires to be demonstrated not from above, from the standpoint of unconditioned and infinite being-itself, that is, *sub specie aeternitatis*, but from below, *sub specie mortalis*, and in relation to our knowledge of finite and contingent beings. It is perhaps surprising that Tillich did not recognise this or appreciate that in traditional logic, there are the means of establishing the links between the modes of being and the logical forms. Provided that concepts, propositions and arguments are recognised to be formal signs that immediately express relations of identity *qua* intentions of the real, they can be seen to correspond to the different modes in which we know or apprehend other beings. Concepts correspond to the mode of knowing in which we seek to express what things are, hence concepts are precisely formal signs or intentions of essences. Propositions correspond to the mode of knowing in which we seek to express whether in fact things exist, hence propositions are intentions of acts of existence. Arguments correspond to the mode of knowing in which we seek to express why things are as they are, hence arguments are intentions of causes or reasons.[41]

If we must know our instruments of knowledge and their reliability before we can hope to know anything of the real we seem to be led into an impossible *cul-de-sac* of knowledge. If however we start from a realist basis, admitting the possibility that human beings do grasp the real in their cognitive operations, then the justification for a genuinely intentional logic, for an insistence that logical instruments are formal signs or intentions of the real, lies in the fact that through them the real comes to be known without distortion and as it is in itself.

5. *Tillich's metaphysics of logic and his theology*

Tillich's metaphysics of logic is the product of his attempt to press logic into the service of theology. It has been the burden of this chapter to argue that Tillich would have done greater service to theology by applying the techniques and distinctions of logic in its ordinary form to the task of clarifying arguments and maintaining higher standards of consistency and rigour. Instead of a logic adapted to our knowledge of finite being, he offers us a meta-logic that takes its point of departure from *das Unbedingt* or the infinite: the unconditioned and unconditional ground of necessity, validity and certainty. Instead of St Thomas's argument from contingent to necessary being, we have something like a meta-logical version of the ontological argument: an argument from necessary to contingent and finite being.[42]

He describes the ontological argument as not so much an argument for the existence of God as a description of the relation of the essential structure of the mind to the divine substance:

> It is the rational description of the relation of our mind to Being as such. Our mind implies *principia per se nota* which have immediate evidence whenever they are noticed: the transcendentalia, *esse*, *verum*, *bonum*. They constitute the Absolute in which the difference between knowing and known is not actual. This Absolute as the principle of Being has absolute certainty. It is a necessary thought because it is the pre-supposition of all thought. (*TC* 15)

Tillich tries to redeem this argument from being a series of purely tautological, meta-logical observations about the relations of thought and being by insisting that 'They constitute the Absolute in which the difference between knowing and knower is not actual'. Their connection under the conditions of existence requires faith.

> The immediate awareness of the Unconditioned has not the character of faith – but of self-evidence. Faith contains a contingent element and demands a risk. It combines the ontological certainty of the Unconditioned with the uncertainty about everything conditioned and concrete.
>
> The risk of faith is based on the fact that the unconditional element can become a matter of ultimate concern only if it appears in a concrete embodiment. (*TC* 27–8)

These formulations are typical of the ambiguities in Tillich's logic and illustrate the way in which he is forced to maintain that faith, in the religious sense of ultimate concern, is necessary not only to affirm a particular instantiation of the Absolute in human experience, but also to overcome 'the uncertainty about everything conditioned and concrete'. Thus religious faith is required even to guarantee our knowledge of everything 'conditioned and concrete'. The alternative would be to admit that religious faith and the logical faith in the certainty of self-evident propositions are identical, or to capitulate to the philosophical gnosticism of Hegel who would simply identify logic and ontology and deduce conclusions about reality from the logical beings of reason.

Tillich tries to avoid the Hegelian position by stressing ambiguity and alienation in finite human experience and thought. Quoting Alexander of Hales, 'The divine substance is known in such a way that it cannot be thought not to be,' he continues: 'The fact that people turn away from this thought is based on individual defects but not on the essential structure of the mind. The mind is able to turn away from what is nearest to the ground of its own structure. This is the nerve of the ontological argument' (*TC* 15).

The difficulty with this notion of alienation of the mind from its essential ground is that it is almost indistinguishable from the alienation of thought from being that is said to be *necessary* to achieve the pure form-science of logic (*DSW* 122–3, 124, 127–8) and that is said to be *necessary* to the dialectical process. The principles of Absolute Thought, Absolute Being and Spirit describe in meta-logical terms, the dynamic dialectical movement of thought in its relation to being under the governance of spirit (*DSW* 118). The difficulty is that Tillich equivocates upon the notions of ambiguity and alienation in logic. He is in danger of trivialising the tragic effects of the self-alienation of man from himself, from other men and from God, by conflating alienation in the sense of sin, and alienation in the sense of intellectual detachment. Conversely, he attributes too great a metaphysical significance to the detachment that is a necessary part of the process of reflection. Is reflexive self-consciousness the sin of Adam? Tillich comes pretty close to this view, because he fails to distinguish which meaning of alienation is primitive and paradigmatic and which is metaphorical for theology on the one hand and logic on the other. The important and great insights Tillich communicates about human alienation and the irreducible element of ambiguity in all finite human thought are devalued and trivialised when they are artificially constrained into harmony with the meta-logical dialectic that he seeks to impose on the whole. The almost irresponsible way Tillich plays upon the many meanings of 'alienation' for example, shows the difference between the punster such as St Augustine who puns with a nice sense of the proportions of creaturely existence and the analogical principles to which the proper use of puns is subject, and someone who in all seriousness obscures the relations between different meanings and becomes trapped in the web of his own dialectical creations.

At first glance, Tillich's use of paradox seems to be a redeeming feature in this tendency to take the essential structures of thought as if they were identical with the structures of being. In Volumes 1 and 2 of the *Systematic Theology* (*ST1*, 63–4; *ST2*, 104–7), Tillich introduces the concept of paradox to point to the limitations of logical and dialectical thinking. For example: 'That is paradoxical which contradicts the *doxa*, the opinion which is based on the whole of ordinary human experience, including the empirical and the rational' (*ST2*, 106). However, his handling of paradox shows his inclination to idealism; for he suggests implicitly that, from the higher vantage point of his dialectic, the paradoxes can be transcended (*aufgehoben*) and understood. If he had been content to point out that paradoxes arise in any system when we try to make it self-validating, then he would have made an important point about the limits of all philosophical systems. He would have emphasised that we cannot give a justification of our absolute presuppositions without either begging the question or stepping outside the system of presuppositions. However, he uses this logical point to try to make an analogous theological point about the Christological paradox: 'Historically and systematically, everything else in Christianity is a corroboration of the simple assertion that Jesus is the Christ. This is neither irrational nor absurd, and it is neither reflectively nor dialectically rational; but it is paradoxical, that is, against man's self-understanding and expectations. The paradox is a new reality and not a logical riddle' (*ST2*, 107). There are, of course, paradoxes that are logical puzzles, for example, the Liar Paradox or Russell's Paradox, and their resolution requires a clear distinction between first- and second-order discourse, and between the primary and secondary occurrences of logical expressions. The new reality disclosed in the case of logical paradoxes is the distinction of logical types at the point of intersection of two universes of discourse. Tillich would appear to mean that paradoxes in general reveal a new reality in this way. However, the Christological paradox is not a logical paradox and logical paradoxes do not reveal new ontological realities. Once again, Tillich equivocates. It is almost as if he considers that a logical remark can be transformed, if uttered in the appropriately solemn manner, into a kerygmatic utterance, and kerygmatic utterances can be included in meta-logic if the latter is expanded enough to blur the distinction between logic and metaphysics. Alternatively, we can come to grasp the new reality of the Christological paradox from the higher vantage point of the philosophy of religion. If so, then theology is subordinate to the philosophy of religion, in spite of Tillich's insistence that it is rather, the concrete-normative part of theonomous systematics that judges the formal and historical parts. There is an unresolved tension in Tillich's thought between the universal and formal requirements of the philosophy of religion, and the concrete and normative demands of theology with its fundamental paradoxes. He tries to have it both ways: the paradoxes of faith and the solutions of dialectical reason. Ironically, we must admit that he succeeds because he effects a kind of apotheosis of both dialectic and paradox in his concept of the unconditioned as the ground and abyss of the conditioned: the object of our ultimate concern.

Having marshalled what evidence is available to show that in Tillich's writings we have the outlines of a coherent metaphysics of logic, and having considered some of the many criticisms which can be directed against the theories he advocates, we must admit that his ramshackle logic does have some plausibility. Its weaknesses are not so much major errors or inconsistencies as the result of over-hasty generalisation on the basis of inadequate analysis, and superficial theoretical understanding of the traditions of Western logic.

His impatience with analysis and proof is the product of impatience to get his message across. He was personally involved in the crises facing Western man in the twentieth century, and was consciously concerned about the urgency of the issues that demanded an answer. We may legitimately complain of the deficiencies of Tillich's logic, and at the way his somewhat crude dialectic dictates the form of his thought. We cannot complain at the logic of his searching attempt to identify the deepest concerns of contemporary man, and his courageous attempt to find answers to some of contemporary man's questions. The logic of his system as a whole is consistent with the pursuit of this aim. His method of correlation is successful to the extent that he succeeds in communicating with contemporary man; it is also a monument to his own 'ultimate concern with being and meaning'.

Chapter 9
Conclusion

In our Introduction to this study of Paul Tillich's theory of meaning, truth and logic, we remarked on the importance of style for the interpretation of an author's work, and on its peculiar importance in the case of Tillich. What he says about artistic style is true of himself: 'I would say that every style points to a self-interpretation of man, thus answering the question of the ultimate meaning of life. Whatever the subject matter which an artist chooses, however strong or weak his artistic form, he cannot help but betray by his own style his own ultimate concern, as well as that of his group, and his period' (*TC* 70). Tillich's metaphysics of meaning, truth and logic is in a real sense an expression of his personal quest for meaning, truth and logical coherence. This is what gives it its distinctive form and style. It is an urgent, serious, driving quest for saving truth and a relevant philosophy of life. It is also the expression of the quest of his generation for a meaningful self-interpretation of man: a quest for meaning at a time of global upheaval and chaos; a quest for logical coherence when fundamental philosophical categories were being fundamentally questioned.

We have argued, on the basis of a general interpretation of Tillich's style, that he was primarily concerned with practical rather than theoretical ends. He was concerned with the articulation of a new Christian *Weltanschauung* for his times, and not with the construction of a theoretical system for its own sake. The main value of his *Systematic Theology* consists in the way it serves as a practical belief and value system. The theoretical deficiencies of the system are due to the fact that, in general, theoretical concerns are subordinated to practical ones, and to the fact that no clear methodological distinction is maintained between them.

We have argued, for instance, that his definition of man as that being who is essentially concerned with his being and meaning is central to his thought. It gives his thinking its practical and existential character. However, his tendency to regard the existential state of being ultimately concerned as necessary and definitive for the determination of meaning and truth tends to make his theory of meaning, truth and logic subjectivist and relativist, and leaves many important theoretical questions unanswered, for example, questions, concerning the exact nature of the relations between the existential and theoretical orders in knowledge.

Tillich's popularist concerns, his disregard of the canons of exact scholarship and his canonisation of the spirit of criticism are all linked, we have argued, with his concern to change the world rather than contemplate it. His style is rhetorical in the positive sense, that is, it is concerned with communication rather than knowledge. His thought lacks a clear distinction between the rhetorical and the dialectical, and in his use of 'dialectic' he tends to conflate religious language and theological language, moralising and moral philosophy, and ideological speculation and philosophical analysis.

This means that while methodological questions may be confused and theoretical answers are often unsatisfactory, Tillich's thought illuminates, in a practical way, the relations between sermons and systematic theology and between ideologies or 'fighting creeds' and philosphy. The correlations that he attempts between theology and philosophy, and between religion and culture may be contrived and in some cases unconvincing, but the questions that his work provokes about the nature of these human creations and their relations with one another are of abiding importance.

His critique of supranaturalism and nominalism was a natural extension of his quest for a new Christian world-view that would embrace the whole of modern culture. His critique of supranaturalism (like his later critique of neo-Orthodox theology) was based on the demand for a metaphysics of meaning, truth and logic that would overcome the dualism between religion and culture, as it was also intended to point up the inadequacies of idealist philosophies of identity that subordinated religion to morality, art or philosophy. Similarly, his critique of nominalism is not incidental to his central theological and philosophical concerns. On the contrary, he demonstrates how nominalism, as a subtly pervasive attitude of modern man, predisposes us to regard questions of meaning and value as merely subjective and ontological questions as irrelevant. He attacks the spirit of scepticism, not as a disciplined attitude to the quest for truth, but as an attitude of indifference, cynicism or despair that denies the objectivity of the structures of being and meaning that alone make significant human life and culture possible. Scepticism in this sense underlies both supranaturalist theology and nominalistic naturalism in science and philosophy, and frustrates both individual man's ultimate concern with being and meaning and any attempt at a constructive philosophy of life or theology of culture.

We have discussed Tillich's critique of scepticism, supranaturalism and nominalism in some detail, not merely to illustrate the genesis of his own metaphysics of meaning, truth and logic but also because we believe it represents an important and neglected part of his construction of a Christian world-view for our time. It is at least as important, for ideological purposes, to identify what needs to be attacked as it is to identify what needs to be affirmed. This Tillich does in a penetrating and often illuminating way.

One thing of crucial importance that emerges from his critique of scepticism, supranaturalism and nominalism, is his conviction that it is only on the foundation of a new ontological realism that any adequate theology of culture can be based.

A central problem throughout Tillich's work is what he means by realism, whether it be belief-ful realism, mystical realism or just realism. His typical approach is from above, that is, from the transcendental point of view; he begins with being-itself rather than the being of finite beings. While his work clarifies in a most illuminating and provocative way the constitutive and regulative principles of ontology, it is frustratingly vague about the relation between being and beings, and about our knowledge of finite beings. For this reason, in spite of his strenuous attempts to defend the realistic principle that our primary and prereflexive intuition is of being-itself, we must ultimately conclude that his ontology is closer to that of the idealists than to that of the mediaeval realists to whom he compares his thought.

This tendency is reflected in his metaphysics of meaning, where his unashamedly theocentric position, and his desire to provide a meaningful philosophy of life for modern man, combine to produce a theory that is preoccupied with the unconditioned ground and abyss of meaning rather than with the explanation of the prosaic forms of ordinary meaning. Tillich offers us a theonomous metaphysic of the norms of meaning rather than a semiotic theory. Even his theory of symbolism subserves his ultimately theological and metaphysical interest.

On the constructive side, we must say that Tillich's symbolist approach to meaning forms an intelligible part of his overall ideological worldview. It is in character with his kerygmatic or rhetorical purpose. In this respect his situation was analogous to that of St Augustine and his strategy for dealing with it much the same. Confronted with a situation of encompassing irrationalism, both realised that what was required was a new vision for the contemplation and consolation of men, a new vision of the relations between the *Civitas Dei* and the *Civitas Terrena*. What was required was a new ideology, that is, a strategy of a moral and psychological kind for bearing up against the universal confusion, rather than systems of abstract philosophical knowledge. Just as Augustine committed the Church to centuries of symbolism and analogy when he sought to adapt the neo-Platonic and Stoic concept of the *logos* to Christian revelation, so Tillich's *logos*-theology seeks to re-introduce this symbolic, mythological and paradoxical element into our thinking about man and his relation to the unconditioned ground and abyss of all being and meaning.

The success of Tillich's system is measured by the success with which this symbolist vision of being and meaning in relation to the unconditioned, appealed to many people, and seemingly helped to sustain and reconstruct the psychological and moral structure of their inner world. On the other hand his theonomous metaphysics of meaning lacks the corroborative support that a worked-out semiotic theory would have given it. In the absence of such a theory and in view of the inability of his system to make sense of ordinary semantic problems, his talk of symbols, myths and paradox invites the charge of mystification and obscurantism.

Tillich's metaphysics of truth is impressive at the level where he discusses the general questions of the relations of thought and being, and of subject and object. In discussing the absolutes that make knowledge possible, namely, the absoluteness of being itself that makes truth possible, the absoluteness of the categories and structures of being that make understanding possible and the absoluteness of essences that make language possible, he follows very much the tradition of Kant and the Transcendental Idealists. One is tempted to think that this is his natural milieu, and in a sense it is. He moves with assured confidence when he is speaking the language of idealist dialectic. However, as we have insisted, he cannot simply be described, or dismissed, as an idealist. Any serious attempt to deal with his metaphysics of truth must take account of his experience of the crisis and abyss of idealism out of which he sought a new belief-ful realism. His attempt to develop his dialectic on a realist base has a double aspect: the attempted restatement of ontological and epistemological realism, and the attempt to do justice to the demands of an existential and social realism.

It is easy to cavil at Tillich's metaphysics of knowledge, and say that he does not answer the problems that are the real concern of philosophers, but this is not fair since his explicit purpose was to demonstrate the metaphysical grounds for a possible knowledge of God. Much of his discussion of the ontological grounds of knowledge in general is of genuine philosophical interest to all but purblind anti-metaphysicians, and what needs to be criticised is not so much glaring errors as his disconcerting vagueness and impatience with sustained analysis and proof. His realism, which he ascribes in part to mediaeval sources, could have been made more plausible if he had bothered to develop or apply the subtle epistemological and logical theories that were developed by Bonaventura, Duns Scotus and John of Salisbury, for instance.

While Tillich makes use of the distinction between experimental and experimental verification, he never clearly distinguishes between the existential and the theoretical aspects of science and knowledge. His emphasis on existential aspects of the knowing-act as an actual engagement between an existing subject and object is important, but he lacks the theoretical means of distinguishing between necessary and sufficient conditions in knowledge, and ends up with an inadequate doctrine of theoretical knowledge, and flirting with an unilluminating subjectivism and relativism.

This subjectivism also characterises, in his later thought, the move away from a social realist base to a greater pre-occupation with depth-psychology and man's interior life. The Marxist criticism of Western realism, that it simply diagnoses man's social predicament and provides analyses of the dynamics of alienation without emphasising the way by which man can be helped back to participation in a common social and political reality, is also applicable to Tillich's thought. As religious and existentialist concerns come to predominate over political and socialist ones in Tillich's later life, so his thought moves away from a realist to a more idealist position. His failure to engage seriously with scientific and technological realism, and his extreme defensiveness towards the pragmatist and empiricist traditions of Anglo-American philosophy, meant that he effectively alienated himself from a tradition that (as in the case of Peirce's realism) might have provided him with some of the theoretical answers he needed to make his philosophy more complete and consistent.

Tillich's metaphysics of logic illustrates best, perhaps, his struggle to find an adequate intentional logic to express his philosophical and theological doctrines. Although he shares much of the heritage of idealist philosophy, he also made use of the late mediaeval realists. We have suggested that intentional logic, particularly that of John of St Thomas, would have been a natural extension and application of the ideas that he expresses in his cryptic and suggestive remarks on the foundations of logic and the applications of logic in knowledge. The fact that he contented himself with the most superficial and general remarks on logic, and never made a serious attempt to study it, meant that his understanding and application of logic was based on inadequate knowledge. It also meant that, in spite of the promising suggestions contained in his discussion of the *Denkwissenschaften*, he tended to fall back on idealist categories and distinctions for lack of an adequate alternative. We have argued that such an alternative exists in intentional logic, and Tillich's metaphysics of meaning, truth and logic is poorer for not having made use of it.

In his paper, 'Protestantism and Artistic Style', Tillich discusses Picasso's masterpiece 'Guernica', and describes it as a great Protestant painting, saying that 'it is not the Protestant answer, but the radicalism of the Protestant question' that characterises it. Paradoxically, this is true of Tillich's *Systematic Theology*. If it is a masterpiece, it is so because of the questions it provokes and the stimulus it gives to new lines of research and discovery, rather than because of any answers it gives. Tillich is dead, but his system remains. Whether or not it will be finally regarded as a masterpiece, perhaps as a weapon (in the sense in which Picasso spoke of 'Guernica' as a weapon) we cannot ignore it, for it is surely one of the greatest constructive contributions to Christian thought in this century.

Notes and References

CHAPTER 1. Introduction: Paul Tillich's Rhetoric

1 'Kierkegaard as Existential Thinker', 5-7.
2 cf. E. D. O'Connor in *Paul Tillich in Catholic Thought*, ed. O'Meara & Weisser, 25-6, and J. Heywood Thomas in the Introduction to *On the Boundary* (v), (vi), as well as *The Theology of Paul Tillich* (x), (xi) and W. Leibrecht *Religion and Culture*, 3-4.
3 This and the previous quote from the *Times Literary Supplement* 31 January 1975, 98.
4 Etienne Gilson *The Christian Philosophy of St Augustine*, 236-7.
5 cf. *Ultimate Concern: Dialogues with Students*, 7, 8, *The Dynamics of Faith*, 22, *The Shaking of the Foundations*, 57.
6 Alan Watts *Beyond Theology or The Art of Godmanship*, 218-19.
7 See, for example, *The Theology of Paul Tillich*, 87, 248 and 299, R. Allan Killen must be the only commentator to suggest that Tillich had a 'good sense of humour' *The Ontological Theology of Paul Tillich*, 11.
8 *The New Being*, 141-52.
9 John Henry Newman *Grammar of Assent*, 117.
10 ibid., 116.
11 Paul Holmer's introduction to S. Kierkegaard *Edifying Discourses*, 12-13.
12 *The Journals of Kierkegaard 1834-1852*, 238.
13 See J. Heywood Thomas's introduction to Paul Tillich *On the Boundary* (v); Kegley & Bretall *The Theology of Paul Tillich*, ix-xiv; W. Leibrecht *Religion and Culture*, 3-5; *Paul Tillich in Catholic Thought*, ed. O'Meara & Weisser, 25f.
14 Leonard F. Wheat *Paul Tillich's Dialectical Humanism*, 1-47.
15 *The Theology of Paul Tillich*, x and xi.
16 cf. the discussions of EPHISTEMI in Plato's *Theaetetus* and of inspiration in his *Phaedrus*.
17 Dietrich Bonhoeffer *Letters and Papers from Prison*, 108-9.
18 Søren Kierkegaard *Concluding Unscientific Postscript*, 1801.
19 See, for example, the detailed record in *My Travel Diary: 1936*.
20 Rollo May *Paulus*, 109.
21 'Rechtfertigung und Zweifel'.
22 *The Dynamics of Faith*, 22.
23 cf. *ST1*, 14 and *The Dynamics of Faith*, 2-3.
24 cf. George Tavard in *Paul Tillich in Catholic Thought*, ed. O'Meara & Weisser, 85-96, and *Paul Tillich and the Christian Message*, 2 and 3.
25 See *The Rhetoric of Aristotle* Book 1, chs 1, 2 and 4 and his *Prior Analytics*, 1.1.
26 cf. *ST1*, 3-9, 67-73 and 74-6.
27 *Rhetoric*, Book 1, ch.1, p.9.
28 loc. cit.
29 In the commentaries of Alexander of Aphrodisias in the third century A.D.
30 A useful summary account is given in *The Development of Logic* by William and Martha Kneale.
31 See particularly Plato's *Phaedrus*; cf. also F. M. Cornford *Plato's Theory of Knowledge*, and R. E. Cushman *Therapeia*.
32 *The Theology of Paul Tillich*, xii.
33 David Kelsey *The Fabric of Paul Tillich's Theology*, 1.
34 Louis Racine O.P. *L'evangile selon Paul Tillich*. See the review by J. Heywood Thomas in *Journal of Theological Studies*. New Series vol.22, 1971, 675-6.
35 *Rhetoric*, Book 1, ch.2, 1.10.
36 See *Das System der Wissenschaften nach Gegenständen und Methoden*.
37 See *ST1*, 59-67 and 112-17.
38 *Rhetoric*, Book 1, ch.2, 1.12.
39 Nauen *Revolution, Idealism and Human Freedom*.
40 This is reflected in the Autobiographical Introduction to *The Interpretation of History*.
41 See *My Travel Diary: 1936*, 40.
42 Quoted by Anthony Clare in *Psychiatry in Dissent*, 64.
43 Both Tillich and Heidegger point out that Western philosophers, in developing their ontologies, have been preoccupied with the notion of substance. In this they have followed the example of Aristotle whose analyses concentrate attention on substantial being, because he is more concerned with 'being' as a substantive rather than as a verb-participle standing for the process or experience of being. Adopting the convention used by several writers on Heidegger, we use 'being' for the former and 'be-ing' for the latter. For further

discussion of the implications of this distinction for ontology and theology, see ch.6.

44 Intentional logic is so called because in this tradition logic is understood as the science that studies the logical instruments of thought and these are traditionally referred to as formal signs or intentions. The three classes of intentions in intentional logic are concepts, propositions and arguments. Each of these is an instrument by means of which we seek knowledge of the real: essences by means of concepts, the facticity of existence by means of propositions and conditions or causes of states by means of arguments. Intentional logic presupposes a realist ontology. This implies two related assumptions: (i) that things exist and have distinct natures of their own independently of anyone's knowledge of them, (ii) that such things are intelligible, and can be known as they are in themselves even though such knowledge may be imperfect and incomplete. Intentional logic distinguishes between first intentions, which refer directly to existing things (e.g. 'cow') and second intentions, which express the mode of being of a subject (e.g. 'substance', 'accident', 'cause', 'subject', 'predicate', 'relation'). Formal logic is the science that studies the relations of second intentions.

The distinction between intension and extension, i.e. roughly the distinction between connotation and denotation, is one that can be used equally in an intentional logic or a mathematical logic. The extensional and truth-functional logic devised by Russell represented an attempt to develop a purely formal syntactical system in which questions about the meaning of identity, for example, would not arise – for its function would be illustrated in the contexts in which it was used. Thus the dispute about intensional or extensional definitions in logic is independent of the question whether a logic is intentional or non-intentional. The latter distinction, however, involves a dispute about the logical status of logical instruments and the question whether concepts reveal to us immediately the nature of the things we know. Realist and intentional logic maintains that they do; mathematical logic sees concepts and other logical instruments as technical means by which we infer knowledge of things we cannot know directly as they are.

It is arguable that Aristotle's logic is intentionalist. The observations of St Thomas Aquinas on logic were crucial in giving impetus to the development of intentional logic. (See, for example, Robert W. Schmidt, s.j. *The Domain of Logic According to St Thomas Aquinas.*) This tradition persisted in the logical writings of Duns Scotus (Johannes Duns Scotus *Commentaries on Aristotle*, 26 vols. Paris 1891-95 Pars 1-11) and more particularly in John of St Thomas (*Ars Logica*, ed. a B. Reiser Taurini 1930). This tradition was revived in the last century by Brentano, and some aspects of the mediaeval theory of intentionality were taken up in the *Logische Untersuchungen* of Edmund Husserl. More recently Jacques Maritain (*Introduction to Logic*) and Henry B. Veatch (*Intentional Logic*) and W. A. Wick (*Metaphysics and the New Logic*) have restated the essentials of the logic of John of St Thomas in terms that have relevance to contemporary issues in philosophical logic. C. S. Peirce (*Collected Papers*, ed. C. Hartshorne & P. Weiss) however, independently made considerable use of mediaeval intentional logic in developing his own controversial logical theories.

45 *STI*, 25-8.

46 G. K. Chesterton *Introduction to the Book of Job*, xxii.

47 *Paul Tillich in Catholic Thought*, 26.

48 ibid., 37.

49 George Tavard *Paul Tillich and the Christian Message*, 32-3, 50-1.

50 ibid., 23.

51 Laswell, Casey and Smith *Propaganda and Promotional Activities*.

CHAPTER 2. The Critique of Naturalism and Supranaturalism

1 In his early works he often speaks of 'theonomous systematics'.

2 *Christianity and the Problem of Existence*, 4.

3 e.g. *STI*, 27-8, and chs 4 and 7.

4 op. cit., 7-8.

5 *Love, Power and Justice*, 18-19.

6 See R. Allan Killen *The Ontological Theology of Paul Tillich*, 13; Kenneth Hamilton *The System and the Gospel*, 135; Kenan B. Osborne *New Being – A Study on the Relationship between Conditioned and Unconditioned Being according to Paul Tillich*. See also David H. Hopper 'Towards Understanding the Thought of Paul Tillich' *Princeton Seminary Bulletin*, Vol.LV, no.3 April 1962; D. J. O'Hanlon *The Influence of Schelling on the Thought of Paul Tillich* Gregorian University, Rome, Thesis 1957, and Jerry H. Gill Paul Tillich's Religious Epistemology' *Religious Studies*, vol.3, 1967/8, 477-98.

7 See 'Existential Philosophy' *Journal of the History of Ideas*, vol.5.

8 op. cit., 98-120.

9   See *On the Boundary*, 52. Cf. *The Theology of Paul Tillich*, 12-16, and the indirect confirmation given in Hannah Tillich's bitter-sweet biography *From Time to Time* in which, with the mixture of resentment and idealisation of the bereaved, she speaks of their difficult life together, particularly in the period following the First World War.
10   op. cit., 24-34.
11   See 'Religionsphilosophie' and *Das System der Wissenschaften*.
12   See J. K. Feibleman *An Introduction to Peirce's Philosophy*, 11f.; also C. S. Peirce *Collected Papers*, 1.4, 1.560, and 2.113.
13   See *On the Boundary*, 46, and *Mystik und Schuldbewusstsein*, 18, 51.
14   *Collected Papers*, 3.487.
15   Immanuel Kant *The Critique of Pure Reason*, Analytic of Concepts, ch.1.
16   cf. Ayer *The Revolution in Philosophy*.
17   Michael Dummett *Frege: Philosophy and Language*.
18   cf. *Der Begriff des Übernatürlichen* with the argument of *A History of Christian Thought*, 137-42.
19   These are the terms used by Tillich in *STI*.
20   Reinhard *Dogmatik*, 83.
21   See above 72-3.
22   Schelling *Philosophical letters on Dogmatism and Criticism: Werke*, I, 208.
23   Copleston *History of Philosophy*, vol.7, 132.
24   Schelling *Werke*, IV, 234 (Copleston's translation).
25   One exception might appear to be D. J. O'Hanlon, who in his dissertation *The influence of Schelling on the thought of Paul Tillich*, part 2, chapter 1, does discuss the work; but he is too inclined to see it simply as a defence of Schelling and as a preparation for the argument with Troeltsch regarding the possibility of a religious *a priori*. He does not analyse the arguments themselves or consider their significance for the definition of Tillich's own stance.
26   cf. J. Luther Adams *Paul Tillich's Philosophy of Culture*, 43f. 'Criticism of supernaturalism might be said to be the beginning of all criticism'.
27   *The Religious Situation*, 181-219.
28   cf. Carl E. Braaten's introduction to *Perspectives on Nineteenth and Twentieth Century Protestant Theology*.
29   op. cit., 42.
30   Erik H. Erikson *Young Man Luther*, 20.
31   Robert P. Scharlemann *Reflection and Doubt in the Thought of Paul Tillich*.
32   Particularly in 'Über die Idee einer Theologie der Kultur', 'Rechfertigung

und Zweifel', 'Religionsphilosophie' and 'Kairos und Logos: Eine Untersuchung zur Metaphysik der Erkenntnis'.
33   Etienne Gilson *The Unity of Philosophical Experience*, 113-22.
34   R. Allan Killen *The Ontological Theology of Paul Tillich*, chapter 4.
35   *Reflection and Doubt in the Thought of Paul Tillich*, xxviii-xix.
36   T. S. Eliot *Four Quartets*.
37   *The Dynamics of Faith*, 19.
38   ibid.

CHAPTER 3. The Critique of Nominalism
1   Etienne Gilson *Being and Some Philosophers*.
2   See C. S. Peirce *Collected Papers*, 1.19 and 5.61, and Jacques Maritain *The Degrees of Knowledge*, para.2.
3   Alisdair M. Macleod *Tillich: An Essay on the Role of Ontology in his Philosophical Theology*, 154-5.
4   ibid., 155.
5   cf. *The Courage to Be*, 61, 95, 129-30; *STI*, 196, and *Masse und Geist*, *GW* II, 37f.
6   The expression is J. L. Talmon's (see his *Origins of Totalitarian Democracy*), but the thought is Tillich's.
7   See *Love, Power and Justice*, 11-13 and ch.2.
8   ibid., 14.
9   ibid., 108-9.
10   *The Courage to Be*, 130.
11   See 'On the idea of a Theology of Culture', 'Art and Ultimate Reality' and 'Das religiöse Symbol'.
12   James Luther Adams *Paul Tillich's Philosophy of Culture, Science and Religion*, 91f.
13   Typical of this approach, in the discussion of secular ideologies, is the argument of *Ultimate Concern: Dialogues with Students*. A similar approach to the critique of other world religions occurs in *Christianity and the Encounter of World Religions*.
14   cf. Kenan B. Osborne *New Being*, 194-6.
15   See *The Courage to Be*, 129f., and *Perspectives on Nineteenth and Twentieth Century Protestant Theology*, 244f.
16   Quoted by J. K. Feibleman in *An Introduction to Peirce's Philosophy*, 60.
17   cf. *Love, Power and Justice*, 18f., and *The Courage to Be*, 129.
18   See 'Kairos und Logos: Eine Untersuchung zur Metaphysik der Erkenntnis' and 'Participation and Knowledge: Problems of an Ontology of Cognition'.
19   *The Courage to Be*, 129; cf. *A History of Christian Thought*, 187, and the remarks of Carl E. Braaten in *Perspectives on Nineteenth and Twentieth Century

Protestant Theology, xxiii-xxiv.

20   See C. S. Peirce *Collected Papers*, 2.220f. Cf. Feibleman *An Introduction to Peirce's Philosophy*, ch.3.
21   William L. Rowe *Religious Symbols and God*, 53f.
22   *The Courage to Be*, 61, 129-30; cf. *Perspectives*, 194 and *A History of Christian Thought*, 191, 142.
23   *The Courage to Be*, 172; see also 171-8. Cf. *The Dynamics of Faith*, ch.11.
24   *The Courage to Be*, 95-6.
25   *The Protestant Era*, 105-25, and also 74-92.
26   *The Dynamics of Faith*, 41-55.
27   op. cit., 264-8; cf. *ST2*, 9-11.
28   *The Courage to Be*, 32f.
29   See Rollo May *Existence: A New Dimension in Psychology and Psychiatry*; Erich Fromm *The Fear of Freedom, The Sane Society*; R. D. Laing *The Divided Self*; and Frank Lake *Clinical Theology*.
30   E. Gilson *The Unity of Philosophical Experience*, 40f. (my italics).
31   This is why Tillich is so anxious, in *Das System des Wissenschaften* and elsewhere, to rebut the charge of formalism.

CHAPTER 4.
The Metaphysics of Meaning
1   See ch.16 Michael Dummett *Frege: Philosophy of Language*.
2   See James Luther Adams *Paul Tillich's Philosophy of Culture, Science and Religion*, 56-7.
3   *The Courage to Be*, 46f.
4   See *Der Sozialismus als Kirchenfrage* and *Die religiöse Lage der Gegenwart* (*GW* II).
5   James Luther Adams *Paul Tillich's Philosophy of Culture, Science and Religion*, 122.
6   ibid., 122.
7   op. cit., 58.
8   Schelling *Werke*, II, 349 (tr. F. Copleston *A History of Philosophy*, vol.7).
9   *Werke*, III, 402.
10   Ernst Troeltsch *Christian Thought: Its History and Application*, part III.
11   This is the general argument of 'Religionsphilosophie', and of 'Ernst Troeltsch: Versuch einer geistesgeschichtlichen Würdigung' in *Kant-Studien* xxix, no.3/4 (1924).
12   cf. Troeltsch *Christian Thought: its History and Application*, 114-17; and *What is Religion?*, 157.
13   Kirkegaard *Concluding Unscientific Postscript*, 112.
14   In one piece of hyperbole he speaks of 'the infinite contradiction between thought and being' (*Das System der Wissenschaften*, 210). See also the discussion in 'Participation and Knowledge:

Problems of an Ontology of Cognition'.
15   Guyton B. Hammond *Man in Estrangement*, 54 (my italics added). Cf. *Perspectives*, 215-16.
16   Friedrich Nietzsche *Beyond Good and Evil*, xi (italics added).
17   ibid., 11.
18   ibid., 2.
19   ibid. (italics added).
20   David H. Kelsey *The Fabric of Paul Tillich's Theology*, 147f.
21   The chief of these are: 'The Religious Symbol'; 'Symbol and Knowledge: a Response'; 'God as being and the knowledge of God' (*ST1*, ch.10); 'Theology and Symbolism'; 'Religious Symbols and our Knowledge of God'; 'Existential Analyses and Religious Symbol'; 'Symbols of Faith' (*The Dynamics of Faith*), ch.3; 'The Word of God' in *Language: an Enquiry into its Meanings and Function*, ed. Ruth Nanda Anshen, and 'The Meaning and Justification of Religious Symbols'.
22   William L. Rowe *Religious Symbols and God*.
23   'The Three Strands of Tillich's Theory of Religious Symbols' *Journal of Religion*, XLVI, no.1, part II, 124.
24   ibid., 127.
25   Battista Mondin, s.x. *The Principle of Analogy in Protestant and Catholic Thought*, 133.
26   See *Religious Experience and Truth*, ed. Sidney Hook, 301-21.
27   See *On the Boundary*, 28, but compare also: 'The Word of God' in *Language: an Inquiry into its Meanings and Functions*, 132; 'Theology and Symbolism' in *Religious Symbolism*, ed. F. Ernest Johnson, 109; 'The Nature of Religious Language' in *Theology of Culture*, 56-7; and 'Existential Aspects of Modern Art' in *Christianity and the Existentialists*, ed. Carl Michalson, 128-47.
28   'The Word of God' in R. N. Anshen, op. cit., 132. Cf. *The Theology of Culture*, 68-75.
29   See S. Langer *Philosophy in a New Key*.
30   See especially 'Psychoanalysis, Existentialism and Theology'.
31   'Religiosen Stil und religiöser Stoff in der bildenden Kunst'. (Translated and quoted by James Luther Adams in *Paul Tillich's Philosophy of Culture, Science and Religion*, 80.)
32   *The Dynamics of Faith*, 41-3.
33   See Gustave Weigel, s.J. 'Myth, Symbol and Analogy', and Paul Tillich 'An Afterword: Appreciation and Reply' in *Paul Tillich in Catholic Thought*, ed. O'Meara & Weisser. Cf. *ST1*, 266.
34   *Paul Tillich in Catholic Thought*, 177.

35   ibid., 180.
36   'Symbol and Knowledge: A Response', 204.
37   L. Lévy-Bruhl *How Natives Think*.
38   David H. Kelsey *The Fabric of Paul Tillich's Theology*, 40.
39   Donald J. Keefe, s.j. *Thomism and the Ontological Theology of Paul Tillich*, 129f.
40   ibid.
41   See, for example, *Summa Theologiae*, 1a.1.10.
42   Mondin, op. cit., 144-5.
43   cf. The 'coincidentia oppositorum' of Nicholas of Cusa: see *Mystik und Schuldbewusstsein*, *GW*, I, 256, and *What is Religion?*, 15, 82-4, 92-8.
44   Notably, 'Über die Idee einer Theologie der Kultur', *Das System der Wissenschaften*, 'Religionsphilosophie', and *Religiöse Verwirklichung*.
45   Erich Przywara, s.j. in *Paul Tillich in Catholic Thought*, 197.
46   H. Dooyeweerd *A New Critique of Theoretical Thought*, vol.I, 69, 524.
47   See Tillich's remarks on the transition from the method of synthesis to the method of correlation in *The Protestant Era*, xli-xlii.

CHAPTER 5. The Metaphysics of Truth: Tillich's 'Ontology of Cognition'
1   See 'Participation and Knowledge: Problems of an Ontology of Cognition' *Sociologica* 1955, and *The Interpretation of History*, part 2.
2   R. Allan Killen *The Ontological Theology of Paul Tillich*, 2.
3   See 'Religionsphilosophie', *Das System der Wissenschaften*, 'Kairos und Logos: Eine Untersuchung zur Metaphysik der Erkenntnis', and 'Participation and Knowledge: Problems of an Ontology of Cognition'.
4   See chs 2 and 3 above.
5   Knowing that Tillich commenced work on his *Systematic Theology* in 1926, it is instructive to see what were his main concerns at this time. The most relevant works published about this time are: *Das System der Wissenschaften*, 'Religionsphilosophie' and 'Kairos und Logos: Einer Untersuchung zur Metaphysik der Erkenntnis'. In all these works, as in his preceding studies of Schelling and supranaturalism, he was concerned with the most general ontological questions: the relations of thought and being, the principle of identity and the abysmal character of being. It is clear that if one of these sections (*ST1*, parts 1 & 2) was written at this time it was almost certainly part 2. This is the burden of the historical evidence, but the order, part 2 then part 1, is also, within the overall

structure, the correct logical order. Cf. *My Search for Absolutes*, 70-83.
6   The tension between the *Infra Lutheranum* and the *Extra Calvinisticum*, in Tillich's thought, is particularly conspicuous at this point. Cf. *The Theology of Paul Tillich*, 4-5, 9-11.
7   cf. Kierkegaard: 'The Systematic Idea is the identity of Subject and Object, the unity of Thought and Being. Existence on the other hand, is their separation' in *Concluding Unscientific Postscript*, 112. That Tillich endorses Kierkegaard's position at this point, constitutes the decisive objection to those who would characterise his thought as idealist and essentialist without reservation.
8   This stress is perhaps not quite so marked in *Das System der Wissenschaften* (*GW*, I, 117-20) in the discussion of the nature of knowledge. It is present nevertheless. Cf. also: *Interpretation of History*, 129-36, where he discusses Eros and Asceticism in relation to knowledge: *The Protestant Era*, 76; 'Participation and Knowledge: Problems of an Ontology of Cognition' *Sociologica*, vol.1, 1955, 202-3; and *My Search for Absolutes*, 67.
9   See *The Courage to Be* and 'Kairos and Logos'. Cf. *ST1*, 92-104; *ST2*, 14 and 15; and *ST3*, ch.23.
10   See e.g. *The Protestant Era*, 241f. and 279-80; 'Estrangement and Reconciliation in Modern Thought' *Review of Religion*, IX, no.1 (Nov. 1944), 5-19; *Christentum und Soziale Gestaltung* (*GW*, II); *Die Sozialistische Entscheidung*, 281-9 and passim. Cf. the discussion of alienation in the *Systematic Theology* and Tillich's other writings on alienation; see the excellent discussion in Guyton B. Hammond *Man in Estrangement*.
11   See 'Participation and Knowledge: Problems of an Ontology of Cognition', 202.
12   See Hammond *Man in Estrangement*, 15; cf. *ST2*, 85-6.
13   George F. McLean *Man's Knowledge of God According to Paul Tillich*, 1 (italics added). Cf. the fuller discussion in D. J. O'Hanlon *The Influence of Schelling on the Thought of Paul Tillich*, part 2, ch.3.
14   See I. A. Richards *The Philosophy of Rhetoric* Lecture 111.
15   This is not unlike Berkeley's argument, which purports to establish, with reference to objects known by us, that 'esse est percipere', but which is extended to mean 'esse est percipi', with reference to the contingency of our being on *God's* continued perception of us.
16   This conflation of propositions and judgements blurs the distinction between

logical and ontological identity; between syntactical forms and semantic content, between Logic and Being.

17 As in Fichte's *Grundlage der ge-sammten Wissenschaftslehre* (a work that had a profound effect on Tillich, as can be seen from *Das System der Wissen-schaften*).

18 See pp.65-6, 73-4 and 77-81 above.

19 St Thomas Aquinas *The Disputed Questions on Truth*, translated by R. W. Mulligan, 3-9.

20 G. F. McLean *Man's Knowledge of God according to Paul Tillich*, 13.

21 *ST1*, 182-4 and ch.VIII; *My Search for Absolutes*, 70-83; *ST2*, 77-86; *ST3*, 333-47, and indirectly, in chapters 22 and 23.

22 It is no accident that leads Des-cartes and Hobbes to describe the object of philosophy as being to enable man to subject nature to the control of his will, and Francis Bacon to say that 'Know-ledge is Power' (a frightening inversion of the Socratic 'Virtue is Knowledge'). Cf. Nietzsche's caustic exposure of the will-to-power underlying the apparently dispassionate and objective philosophy and science of the modern world since Descartes, in *Beyond Good and Evil*, Article I and II.

23 Edmund Husserl *Cartesian Medita-tions*.

24 Tillich 'Participation and Know-ledge', 202-3. Cf. *ST1*, 105-12.

25 *Disputate de Veritate* 7, ad 2.

26 *Summa Theologiae* 1a. LXXXV 2, ad 2.

27 See *ST1*, 107f., 'Participation and Knowledge', 208f.; *My Search for Absolutes*, 67.

28 cf. Aquinas *Disputate de Veritate Quodlibet* 4 'The intelligible species is the likeness of a thing's essence, *and is*, in some manner, *the very essence and nature of that thing existing consciously*, not physically' (italics added).

29 McLean *Man's Knowledge of God according to Paul Tillich*, 16.

30 See *ST1*, 106, 107. This explains his success as a preacher and his life-long concern with healing and the ministry of healing. See especially; *ST1*, 129-30, *ST2*, 185-6 and *ST3*, ch.30; also *The New Being*, ch.5 and *The Shaking of the Foundations*, 117.

31 op. cit., 40-54. Cf. *ST2*, ch. 14 and ch. 15.

32 ibid., 65.

33 ibid., 66.

34 *The New Being*, 38.

35 *The Courage to Be*, 13-14.

36 ibid., 13.

37 loc. cit.

38 *The New Being*, 38.

39 *The Dynamics of Faith*, 30-5, 74-98.

40 On moralism see *ST2*, 58, 66; *ST3*, 42 and 171, and *The Theology of Culture*, 133-46. On sin and estrangement see *ST2*, chapters 14 and 15, and 'Estrange-ment and Reconciliation in Modern Thought'. On the trans-moral con-science, see *The Protestant Era*, ch.9 and *Morality and Beyond*.

41 e.g. in *Das System der Wissen-schaften*, 116, 124-5, 'Religionsphilo-sophie'; *What is Religion?*, 34-6, 47-9 and *passim*; also 155-60; *The Interpreta-tion of History*, 146-51. In *Systematic Theology* it is expressed in Tillich's doctrine of 'Ultimate Concern'.

42 *The Dynamics of Faith*, 16-22.

43 See *The Dynamics of Faith*, 19.

44 ibid., 20.

45 *The Dynamics of Faith*, chs 1 and 2; *ST1*, 16, & *passim*.

46 See ch.2, sections 2 and 4.

47 R. Allan Killen *The Ontological Theology of Paul Tillich*, 13-14.

48 See *The Shaking of the Foundations*.

49 op. cit., 72-5; cf. *ST1*, 136, 137, *ST3*, 61-9.

50 B. Russell 'On Denoting' in *Logic and Knowledge*. Cf. Ludwig Wittgenstein *Philosophical Investigations*.

51 *Philosophical Review* 1969, vol. 78.

CHAPTER 6. The Metaphysics of Truth: Existential Aspects

1 The phrase is Heidegger's; see *Sein und Zeit*.

2 St Augustine *De Civitate Dei* XI, 26; cf. *De Trinitate* XV, 12. 21-2. The argu-ment that God is the ground of all truth and being is developed in *De Libero Arbitrio* II, 12, 15, 16.

3 cf. Marthinus Versfeld *Persons*.

4 In *Sein und Zeit* (see *Being and Time*, tr. J. Macquarrie & E. Robinson).

5 Magda King *Heidegger's Philo-sophy*, 16.

6 loc. cit. The question is whether it is not Heidegger who makes Tillich turn again to Augustine and Aquinas and so attempt to resurrect a personalist onto-logy.

7 *Biblical Religion and the Search for Ultimate Reality*, 24.

8 ibid., 25.

9 ibid., 27.

10 *Confessions* XI, 30.40; cf. *The City of God* XII, 15.

11 This concern underlies the argu-ment of *The Interpretation of History*, in particular, part 2.2, 'Kairos and Logos', in which he undertakes an enquiry into the metaphysics of knowledge.

12 See St Augustine *Confessions* XI, 14, 17-30, 40; cf. *The City of God* XI, 5, 6, where he defines being in time in terms

of duration, and the eternity of God in terms of his simultaneous presence to His entire creation.

13   See his two epoch-making papers to the Kant Gessellschaft, 'Über die Idee einer Theologie der Kultur' and 'Die Überwindung des Religionsbegriffs in der Religionsphilosophie', as well as 'Religionsphilosophie'.

14   See *Philosophical Investigations*.

15   On depth psychology, see especially *The Courage to Be*. On axiology, see *ST1*, 23, and *ST3*, 17 and 29-31.

16   See *The Interpretation of History*, 129. In the argument of this section there are strong echoes of Nietzsche's *Beyond Good and Evil* and of the critique of philosopher's prejudices – in particular the myth of 'objective consciousness'.

17   In fact, we find in his writings anticipations of most of the arguments later employed in natural theology.

18   'For believing in one thing, and understanding another; and we must first believe whatever great and divine matter we desire to understand. Else would the Prophet have said in error *nisi credideritis non intelligetis . . .* nor does anyone become prepared to find God who does not first believe that which he is afterwards to know.' *De Libero Arbitrio* II, 2, 6. tr. Carroll Mason Sparrow *St Augustine on Free Will*, 35-7.

19   Vernon J. Bourke *The Essential Augustine*, 122.

20   See *On the Boundary*, and cf. 'Art and Ultimate Reality' *Cross Currents* x, no.1, Winter 1960.

21   This, we suggest, is the real reason for his insistence that it is as atheistic to attempt to prove, as it is to try to disprove, the existence of God: 'God does not exist. He is being-itself beyond essence and existence. Therefore to argue that God exists is to deny him' *ST1*, 227. Cf. his frequently repeated claim that if, *per impossibile*, one were to prove the existence of God, one would reduce Him to an object among objects. See e.g. *ST1*, 82.

22   See St Augustine *De Utilitate Credendi* XII, 26; PL 42, 84; and *De Civitate Dei* XI, 3; PL 41, 318 (PL= Patrologia Latina, Paris, J. P. Migne 1844-64).

23   See *The Protestant Era*, ch.VII, *Biblical Religion and the Search for Ultimate Reality*, 29-35, *ST1*, 194-7. In the following passages, Tillich sets out what he means by 'spirit': *ST1*, 276-9: *ST2*, 180-2: *ST3*, 20-5, ch.23 *passim*.

24   *Biblical Religion and the Search for Ultimate Reality*, 27.

25   Psalm 34.8.

26   E. Gilson *The Unity of Philosophical Experience*, 178-223; *Being and Some Philosophers*, 41-73.

27   See Bertrand Russell *The Philosophy of Leibniz*, and *An Introduction to Mathematical Philosophy*.

28   See *A History of Christian Thought*, 78-9, 110-11, 142-4, 184-5; *ST1*, 196-9; *Theology of Culture*, 16-19.

29   Immanuel Kant *The Critique of Pure Reason* B 29, A 19.

30   Tillich's 'Religionsphilosophie' and *Die religiöse Lage der Gegenwart* were published when Tillich was teaching with Heidegger at Marburg. In the previous year he published a critical review of Cassirer's *Die Begriffsform im mythischen Denken* in *Kant-Studien* XVII, no.6 (Mar. 22, 1924) entitled 'Probleme des Mythos'.

31   cf. Heidegger *Vorträge und Aufsätze*, 13 and 61 with Tillich *The Religious Situation* part 1, ch.1.

32   cf. Heidegger *Kant und das Problem der Metaphysik* and Tillich *The Religious Situation*, and *The Protestant Era*, 74-92.

33   cf. E. Cassirer *Die Begriffsform im mythischen Denken* and *The Philosophy of Symbolic Forms* vols. 1-3 with Tillich 'Probleme des Mythos' *Kant-Studien* XVII, no.6 (1924) and 'Das religiöse Symbol', *ST1*, 264-77 and *passim*, and *ST2*, 9-11 and *passim*.

34   E. Cassirer *The Philosophy of Symbolic Forms* vol.1, 288.

35   Tillich 'Religionsphilosophie'. See *What is Religion?*, 38. Compare Sigwart *Logik* (2nd rev. ed.), 1, 320ff. 'The advocates of [the theory of abstraction] also forget that abstraction presupposes some definition of the sphere of objects to be compared, and they tacitly posit a motive for selecting this particular grouping and for seeking its common characteristics. Ultimately this motive, if it is not absolutely arbitrary, can only be that these objects have been recognised as similar *a priori*.'

36   Sigwart *Logic*, 320ff.

37   E. Cassirer *Philosophy of Symbolic Forms* vol.1, 285.

38   ibid., 285.

39   cf. Michael J. Simpson 'Paul Tillich: Symbolism and Objectivity' *The Heythrop Journal* VIII, no.3, July 1967.

40   See 'Das Problem des Mythos' *Theologische Literaturzeitung* XLIX (1924) 115-17; *Religiöse Verwirklichung*, 99ff., and 'Symbol and Knowledge', *Journal of Liberal Religion* II (1941), 203-4. Cf. James Luther Adams *Paul Tillich's Philosophy of Culture, Science and Religion*, 244-7.

41   This is reminiscent of Aquinas's argument that every angel is a species, since angels are pure form and pure act,

without matter or potentiality.

42 Kierkegaard was more correct in maintaining that 'A logical system is possible, an existential system is impossible'. *Concluding Unscientific Postscript*, 99f.

43 Compare *The Protestant Era* ch.5, *The Religious Situation*, 85-101, *On the Boundary*, 27-30, and 'Art and Ultimate Reality' *Cross Currents* x, no.1, Winter 1960.

44 Kenneth Hamilton *The System and the Gospel*.

45 Wayne E. Mahan, *Tillich's System*.

46 'Mythus, begrifflich und religionspsychologisch' (op. cit. vol.IV, 363-70).

47 Klaus Rosenthal 'Myth and Symbol' *Scottish Journal of Theology* 18, 1965.

CHAPTER 7. The Metaphysics of Truth: Truth and Verification

1 See Flew and MacIntyre *New Essays in Philosophical Theology*, and Basil Mitchell (ed.) *Faith and Logic*.

2 Moritz Schlick 'Meaning and Verification' *Philosophical Review* 1936.

3 See K. Hamilton *The System and the Gospel*, 56-7; and L. F. Wheat *Paul Tillich's Dialectrical Humanism*, 118-19.

4 See above at pp.53 and 77-8.

5 St Thomas Aquinas *Disputate de Veritate* Article 1.

6 cf. his parallel distinctions between ontological reason and technical reason, and the distinctions, in his earlier writings, between the mystical approach and the methodical approach (*IH* 123ff.) and the dialectical, critical and meta-logical approaches (*WR* 41-51).

7 This, and what follows, is paraphrased from *Das System der Wissenschaften*, 125ff.

8 *Nichomachean Ethics* 1.3.

CHAPTER 8.
The Metaphysics of Logic

1 C. Sigwart *Logic* vol. 1, 1-21 (cf. ch.6, sect.2 above).

2 Osborne *New Being*, 59.

3 See Wm Wallace *The Logic of Hegel* ch.1, para.18. We have put 'Logic/Metaphysics' because Hegel goes on to say quite explicitly: '*Logic therefore coincides with Metaphysics, the science of things set and held in thoughts* – thoughts accredited able to express the essential reality of things', op. cit., ch.2, para.24.

4 ibid., ch.6, para.79. Compare with the Introduction to Hegel's *Science of Logic*, 53-75.

5 cf. Tillich *My Search for Absolutes*, 64-83 with *The Logic of Hegel*, ch.6, para.83 and chs 7-9.

6 cf. the discussion of 'the unhappy

consciousness' in Hegel's *Phenomenology of Mind* with Tillich's discussion of the alienation of consciousness in 'Participation and Knowledge – Towards an Ontology of Cognition' and parallel discussions in *STI*, 105f. and *Protestant Era*, 76f.

7 C. R. Morris *Idealist Logic*, 14.

8 See the section 'The Logic of the Concept' (Begriff) in Hegel's *Science of Logic*.

9 See *Werke*, Jubilee edition, H. G. Glockner vol.2, 22. Cf. *The Science of Logic* vol.1, 95f.

10 *The Science of Logic* vol.2, 460f. Cf. *Werke* vol.2, 14f.

11 *Werke* vol.2, 23-4.

12 See *The Phenomenology of Mind*, tr. J. Baillie (2nd ed.), especially the section 'The World of Spirit Estranged from Itself'.

13 C. R. Morris *Idealist Logic*, 11.

14 G. R. G. Mure *Introduction to Hegel*, 82.

15 ibid., 97.

16 ibid., 82.

17 See above, pp.177 and 178.

18 Kierkegaard *Concluding Unscientific Postscript*, 99.

19 This, and the previous quote, from C. R. Morris *Idealist Logic*, 7. Hegel anticipated by a generation the development of other logics, including multi-valued and modal logics, but was sidetracked into the apotheosis of his own dialectic.

20 ibid., 132.

21 cf. 'Über die Idee einer Theologie der Kultur' and 'Religionsphilosophie'. See *What is Religion?* parts 1 and 3.

22 cf. Werner Heisenberg *Physics and Philosophy*. 'In modern physics man confronts himself, contemplates himself'.

23 e.g. Descartes' demand for a calculus ratiocinator', Leibniz's demand for a 'mathesis universalis', and Spinoza's attempt to philosophise 'more geometrico'. Cf. *STI*, 22, 65-6.

24 Lotze *Logic*, 26, 110; C. Sigwart *Logic* vol.2, 25-65.

25 J. Heywood Thomas 'Some Aspects of Tillich's Systematic Theology'; *Paul Tillich; an Appraisal*, 28, 30 and 33f.; and 'The Correlation of Philosophy and Theology in Tillich's System', *London Quarterly Review* Jan. 1959.

26 J. Heywood Thomas 'Some Aspects of Tillich's Systematic Theology'. Cf. *Das System der Wissenschaften*, 127.

27 'Habitus quibus anima dicit verum'. See Robert W. Schmidt *The Domain of Logic according to St Thomas Aquinas*, 4.

28 See ch.3 above.

29 See W. L. Rowe *Religious Symbols and God*, 53-8.

30 See J. K. Feibleman *An Introduction to Peirce's Philosophy*, chs 4 and 5.

31 See ch.1 above

32 C. S. Peirce *Collected Papers* 2.231f. and 3.608.

33 This argument is repeated in *ST1*, 189, *ST2*, 36 and *ST3*, 61 and 65.

34 H. B. Veatch *Intentional Logic*, 112.

35 Jacques Maritain *Moral Philosophy*, 115.

36 ibid., 127.

37 cf. Robert W. Schmidt, s.j. *The Domain of Logic according to St Thomas Aquinas* chs 1-3; and H. B. Veatch *Intentional Logic* ch.2. On first and second intentions, see the important section in Schmidt, ch.5, which brings together the various texts of St Thomas on the subject. See also Parker & Veatch *Logic as a Human Instrument*, 16-29.

38 Veatch *Intentional Logic*, 13.

39 ibid., 15.

40 C. W. Morris 'Foundations of the Theory of Signs' in *International Encyclopaedia of Unified Science* vol.1, no.2.

41 cf. Maritain *An Introduction to Logic* Introductions to chs 1, 2 and 3; H. B. Veatch *Intentional Logic*, 17-20; Parker & Veatch *Logic as a Human Instrument*, 10.13.

42 As we have seen, the Ontological Argument plays a pivotal role in Tillich's thought. 'The so-called ontological argument points to the ontological structure of finitude. It shows that an awareness of the infinite is included in man's awareness of finitude.' *ST1*, 228.

Selected Bibliography

I. Books and articles by Paul Tillich

Gesammelte Werke (14 vols) ed. Renate Albrecht. Stuttgart. I
  Frühe Hauptwerke (1959); II *Christentum und soziale Gestalt-*
  ung (1962); III (1966); IV *Philosophie und Schicksal* (1961);
  V (1964); VI (1963); VII (1962); VIII (1970); IX (1975); X
  (1968); XI (1969); XII (1971); XIII (1972); XIV (1975).
Die religionsgeschichtliche Konstruktion in Schellings positiver
  Philosophie, ihre Voraussetzungen und Prinzipien. Breslau,
  H. Fleishmann 1910.
Mystik und Schuldbewusstsein in Schellings philosophischer Ent-
  wicklung. Gütersloh, C. Bertelsmann 1912.
Der Begriff des Übernatürlichen, sein dialektischer Charakter und
  das Princip der Identität, dargestellt an der supranaturalistischen
  Theologie vor Schleirmacher. Königsberg, H. Madrasch 1915.
Über die Idee einer Theologie der Kultur (1919). Tr. 'On the Idea
  of a Theology of Culture' in *What is Religion?* (1969) 155-83.
'Die Überwindung des Religionsbegriffs in der Religionsphilo-
  sophie' (1922). Tr. as 'The Conquest of the Concept of
  Religion in the Philosophy of Religion' in *What is Religion?*
  (1969) 122-55.
Das System der Wissenschaften nach Gegenständen und Methoden.
  Göttingen, Vandenhoeck & Ruprecht 1923. *GW* I.
'Ernst Troeltsch: Versuch einer geistesgeschichtlichen Würdig-
  ung' *Kant-Studien* XXIX, no. 3/4 (1924) 351-8.
'Rechtfertigung und Zweifel' *Vorträge der theologischen Konferenz*
  zu Giessen 39. Giessen, Alfred Töpelmann 1924, 19-32.
'Begriffsform im mythischen Denken' *Kant-Studien* XVII (1924)
  no. 6.
'Das Problem des Mythos' *Theologische Literaturzeitung* XLIX
  (1924).
'Religionsphilosophie' (1925). Tr. as 'The Philosophy of Religion'
  in *What is Religion?* (1969) 27-121.
Das Dämonische (1926). Tr. as 'The Demonic' in *The Interpreta-*
  tion of History, 77-122.
Kairos: Zur Geisteslage und Geisteswindung. Ed. Paul Tillich.
  Darmstadt, Otto Reichl 1926. 'Kairos: Ideen zur Geisteslage
  der Gegenwart' 1-21; and 'Kairos und Logos: Eine Untersuchung zur Metaphysik der Erkenntnis' 23-75, tr. as 'Kairos
  and Logos: a Study in the Metaphysics of Knowledge' in
  The Interpretation of History. GW IV.
'Gläubiger Realismus' (1927) *GW* IV, 77-87.
'Christentum und Idealismus' *Theologische Blätter* 6 (1927) 31ff.
'Das religiöse Symbol (1928). Tr. as 'The Religious Symbol' and
  rev. in *Journal of Liberal Religion* (Chicago) II, no. 1 (1940)
  13-33.
Mythus, begrifflich und religionspsychologisch. Tübingen, Mohr
  1930, vol. 4, 363-70. *GW* V, 187-95.
Hegel und Goethe. Tübingen, Mohr 1932.
The Religious Situation (1932). New York, Meridian Books 1956.
Die sozialistische Entscheidung. Potsdam, Protte 1933. *GW* II,
  219-365.

The Interpretation of History. Tr. N. A. Rasetzki (pt 1) and Elsa
L. Talmey (pts 2, 3 and 4). New York/London, Charles
Scribner's Sons 1936.
'The Conception of Man in Existential Philosophy' *Journal of
Religion* (Chicago) xix, no. 3 (July 1939) 201-15.
'Symbol and Knowledge' *Journal of Liberal Religion*, ii, no. 4
(Spring 1941) 202-6.
'Existential Thinking in American Theology' *Religion in Life* x
(Summer 1941) 452-56.
'Kierkegaard as Existential Thinker' *Union Review* (N.Y.) iv,
no. 1 (Dec. 1942) 5-7.
'Man and Society in Religious Socialism' *Christianity and Society*
viii, no. 4 (Fall 1943) 10-21.
'Existential Philosophy' *Journal of the History of Ideas* (N.Y.) v,
no. 1 (Jan. 1944) 44-70.
'Estrangement and Reconciliation in Modern Thought' *Review of
Religion* (N.Y.) ix, no. 1 (Nov. 1944) 5-19.
'Nietzsche and the Bourgeois Spirit' *Journal of the History of
Ideas* vi, no. 3 (June 1945) 307-9.
'The Relation of Religion and Health' *Review of Religion* x, no. 4
(May 1946) 348-84.
'The Problem of Theological Method' *Journal of Religion* xxvii,
no. 1 (Jan. 1947) 16-26.
The Protestant Era. Tr. J. L. Adams. Chicago, University of
Chicago Press 1948. Introd. R. H. Daubney. London, Nisbet
& Co. 1951.
The Shaking of the Foundations (1949). London, S.C.M. Press 1957.
'Beyond Religious Socialism' *Christianity and Society* (N.Y.) xv,
1 (1949).
'Existentialism and Religious Socialism' *Christianity and Society*
xv, no. 1 (Winter 1949-50) 8-11.
'Psychotherapy and a Christian Interpretation of Human Nature'
Review of Religion xiii, no. 3 (March 1949) 264-8.
'Anxiety-Reducing Agencies in our Culture' *Anxiety.* Eds Paul
H. Hoch and Joseph Zubin. New York, Grune and Stratton
1950, 17-26.
Systematic Theology Volume 1 (1951). London, Nisbet 1953.
Christianity and the Problem of Existence. Washington, D.C.,
Henderson Services 1951.
The Courage to Be. New Haven, Yale/London, Nisbet 19ς2.
Love, Power and Justice. New York/London, Oxford University
Press 1954.
'Psychoanalysis, Existentialism and Theology' *Faith and Freedom*
(Oxford) ix, pt 1, no. 25 (Autumn 1955) 1-11.
Biblical Religion and the Search for Ultimate Reality. Chicago,
University of Chicago Press 1955; London, Nisbet 1956.
The New Being. New York, Charles Scribner's Sons 1955; London,
S.C.M. Press 1956.
'Theology and Symbolism' *Religious Symbolism*, ed. F. Ernest
Johnson. New York, Harper Brothers 1955, 107-16.
'Participation and Knowledge: Problems of an Ontology of
Cognition' *Sociologica*, ed. W. Adorno and W. Dirks.
Frankfurt-am-Main, Europäische Verlagsanstalt 1955, 201-9.
GW iv.
'Erich Fromm's The Sane Society' *Pastoral Psychology* vi (Sept.
1955) 13-16.
A History of Christian Thought (1956). Ed. Carl E. Braaten.
London, S.C.M. Press 1968.

'Existential Analyses and Religious Symbols' *Contemporary Problems in Religion*, ed. Harold A. Basilius. Detroit, Wayne University Press 1956, 35-55.

'Relation of Metaphysics and Theology' *Review of Metaphysics* (New Haven) x, no. 1 (Sept. 1956) 57-63.

'The Nature and Significance of Existentialist Thought' *Journal of Philosophy* (N.Y.) LIII, no. 23 (Nov. 8, 1956) 739-48. *GW* IV.

'Existentialist Aspects of Modern Art' *Christianity and the Existentialists*, ed. Carl Michalson. New York, Charles Scribner's Sons 1956.

Systematic Theology Volume 2. London, Nisbet 1957.

Dynamics of Faith (World Perspectives Series, vol. x, ed. Ruth Nanda Anshen) New York, Harper Brothers/London, Allen & Unwin 1957.

'Protestantism and the Contemporary Style in the Visual Arts' *Christian Scholar* (N.Y.) XL, no. 4 (Dec. 1957) 307-11.

Theology of Culture: Essays by Paul Tillich. Ed. Robert C. Kimball. New York, Oxford University Press 1959.

'Existentialism and Psychotherapy' *Review of Existential Psychology and Psychiatry* (1961) 8-61.

'Existentialism, Psychotherapy, and the Nature of Man' *Pastoral Psychology* XI (June 1960) 10-18.

'Art and Ultimate Reality' *Cross Currents* (Winter 1960).

'The Impact of Pastoral Psychology on Theological Thought' *Pastoral Psychology* XI (Feb. 1960) 17-23.

'The Meaning and Justification of Religious Symbols' *Religious Experience and Truth*, ed. S. Hook. New York University Press 1961; Edinburgh, Oliver and Boyd 1968.

The Eternal Now: Sermons. London, S.C.M. Press 1963.

Christianity and the Encounter of World Religions. New York, Columbia University Press 1963.

Systematic Theology Volume 3 (1963) London, Nisbet 1964.

Morality and Beyond (1963). London & Kegan Paul Ltd. 1964.

Ultimate Concern. Ed. Mackenzie Brown. London, S.C.M. Press 1965.

The Future of Religions. Ed. Jerald C. Brauer. New York, Harper & Row 1966.

On the Boundary: an Autobiographical Sketch. London, Collins 1967.

Perspectives on Nineteenth and Twentieth Century Protestant Theology, ed. C. E. Braaten. New York, Harper & Row/London, S.C.M. Press 1967.

My Search for Absolutes. New York, Simon & Schuster 1967.

A History of Christian Thought. Ed. C. E. Braaten. London, S.C.M. Press 1968.

What is Religion? Ed. J. L. Adams. New York, Harper & Row 1969.

My Travel Diary: 1936 – Between Two Worlds. Ed. J. C. Brauer, tr. Maria Pelikan. London, S.C.M. Press 1970.

II. Books and articles on Tillich and General Works of Reference

ADAMS, James Luther *Paul Tillich's Philosophy of Culture, Science and Religion*. New York, Harper & Row 1965.

ALSTON, William P. 'Tillich's Conception of a Religious Symbol' in *Religious Experience and Truth: a Symposium*, ed. Sidney Hook. New York, New York University Press.

AQUINAS, St Thomas *Summa Theologiae*. London, Eyre &
Spottiswoode/N.Y. McGraw-Hill 1963.
—*Aquinas on Being and Essence*. Tr. Joseph Bobik. University
Notre Dame Press 1965/70.
—*The Disputed Questions on Truth*. Tr. R. W. Mulligan. Chicago,
Regnery Co. 1952.
ARISTOTLE *Metaphysics*. Ed. and Tr. J. Warrington. London,
J. M. Dent 1956.
—*Nicomachean Ethics*. Penguin Books.
—*The Rhetoric of Aristotle*. Tr. J. E. C. Weldon. London,
Macmillan 1886.
ARMBRUSTER, C. J. *Vision of Paul Tillich*. New York, Sheed &
Ward 1967.
AUGUSTINE, St *The City of God* (*De Civitate Dei*). Tr. J. Healey.
2 vols. London, Everyman's Library 1947.
—*De libero arbitrio voluntatis*, C. M. Sparrow, Charlottesville,
University of Virginia Studies, 1947.
—*The Confessions of St. Augustine*. Tr. Frank Sheed. London
1944.
—*Patrologia Latina*, Paris, J. P. Migne 1844-64. (Works of St
Augustine reprinted from the seventeenth-century Maurist
edition, in *Patrologia Latina* volumes 32-47.)
De Utilitate Credendi, 1844, in *P.L.* vol. 42.
AYER, A. J. et al. *The Revolution in Philosophy*. London,
Macmillan 1957.
BARTH, K. *Epistle to the Romans*. London 1933.
—'Von der Paradoxie des positiven Paradoxes, Antworten und
Fragen an Paul Tillich' *Theologische Blätter* 2, 287-96.
BECK, S. J. 'Implications for Ego in Tillich's Ontology of Anxiety'
Philosophy and Phenomenological Research XVIII (1958)
451-70.
BOAS, George 'Being and Existence' *Journal of Philosophy* LIII,
no. 23 (1956) 748-59.
BONHOEFFER, Dietrich *Letters and Papers from Prison*. London,
S.C.M. Press 1953.
CASSIRER, E. *Die Begriffsform im mythischen Denken*. Berlin
1922.
—*Philosophy of Symbolic Forms*. Tr. R. Manheim. 3 vols. New-
haven 1953-7.
CHESTERTON, G. K. *Introduction to the Book of Job*. Palmer &
Heywood 1916.
CLARK, B. L. 'God and the Symbolic in Tillich' *Anglican Theo-
logical Review* 18 (1961) 302-11.
COPLESTON, Frederick, S.J. *A History of Philosophy*. 7 vols.
New York, Doubleday 1965.
CROSS, W. O. 'Some notes on the Ontology of Paul Tillich'
Anglican Theological Review 39 (1957) 297-311.
CUSHMAN, R. E. *Therapeia: Plato's Conception of Philosophy*.
Chapel Hill, University of North Carolina Press 1958.
DEMOS, Raphael 'Tillich's Philosophical Theology' *Philosophy
and Phenomenological Research* XIX (1958-9) 74.
DIEM, H. *Kierkegaard's Dialect of Existence*. Edinburgh, Oliver
& Boyd 1959.
DILLENBERGER, J. 'Tillich's Use of the concept "Being"'
Christianity and Crisis XIII (1953) 30-1.
DILLISTONE, F. W. *Myth and Symbol* Theological Collections.
London, S.P.C.K. 1966.

DOOYEWEERD, H. *A New Critique of Theoretical Thought*, vol. 1. Amsterdam 1953.

DULLES, Avery R., S.J. 'Symbol, Myth and Biblical revelation' *Theological Studies* XXVII (1956) 1-26.

EMMET, Dorothy M. 'The Nature of Metaphysical Thinking' *Analogy*. London, Macmillan 1966.

—'The Ground of Being' *Journal of Theological Studies* 15 (1964) 280-92.

ERIKSON, Erik H. *Young Man Luther*. London, Faber & Faber 1958.

FEIBLEMAN, James K. *An Introduction to Peirce's Philosophy*. London, Allen & Unwin 1960.

FERRÉ, Nels F. S. 'Three Critical Issues in Tillich's Philosophical Theology' *Scottish Journal of Theology* X (1957) 225-38.

FICHTE, J. G. *Science of Knowledge*. Tr. A. D. Kroeger. Philadelphia 1868.

FLEW, A. and MACINTYRE, A. *New Essays in Philosophical Theology*. London, S.C.M. Press 1955.

FORD, L. 'The Three Strands of Tillich's Theory of Religious Symbols' *Journal of Religion* XLVI (1966).

—'Tillich and Thomas: the Analogy of Being' *Journal of Religion* XLVI (1966) 229-45.

GILL, Jerry H. 'Paul Tillich's Religious Epistemology' *Religious Studies* (1967-8).

GILSON, E. *The Christian Philosophy of St Thomas*. Tr. L. L. Shook. London, Gollanz 1961.

—*Being and Some Philosophers*. Toronto, Pontifical Institute of Mediaeval Studies 1952.

—*The Christian Philosophy of St Augustine*. Tr. L. E. M. Lynch. London, Gollanz 1961.

—*The Unity of Philosophical Experience*. London, Sheed & Ward 1938-55.

GRICE, H. P. 'Utterer's Meaning and Intentions' *Philosophical Review* 78 (1969) 147-77.

HAMILTON, Kenneth *The System and the Gospel: a Critique of Paul Tillich*. London, S.C.M. Press 1963.

—'Systematic Theology, volume III' *Journal of Religion* XLVI, no. 1, pt II (1963).

—'Paul Tillich and the Idealist Appraisal of Christianity' *Scottish Journal of Theology* XIII, 33-44.

HAMMOND, Guyton B. *Man in Estrangement: a Comparison of the Thought of Paul Tillich and Erich Fromm*. Nashville, Vanderbilt University Press 1965.

—'Tillich on the Personal God' *Journal of Religion* XLIV (1964) 289-93.

HAYNER, Paul Collins *Reason and Existence: Schelling's Philosophy of History*. Leiden, Brill 1967.

HEGEL, G. W. F. *Science of Logic*. Tr. W. H. Johnston and L. G. Struthers. 2 vols. London 1929.

—*Werke*. Jubilee edition, ed. H. G. Glockner. 26 vols. Stuttgart 1927-39.

—*The Phenomenology of Mind*. Tr. J. Baillie (2nd ed.). London 1931.

—*The Logic of Hegel*. Tr. W. Wallace (2nd rev. ed.). Oxford, Clarendon Press 1892.

—*The Philosophy of Religion*. Tr. E. B. Speirs and J. B. Sanderson. 3 vols. London 1895.

HEIDEGGER, M. *Vorträge und Aufsätze*. Pfullingen, Neske 1954.

—*Kant und das Problem der Metaphysik.* Frankfurt, Klostermann 1951.

—*Being and Time.* Tr. J. Macquarrie and E. Robinson. London, S.C.M. Press 1962.

HERBERGER, K. 'Historismus und Kairos: Die Überwindung des Historismus bei Ernst Troeltsch und Paul Tillich' *Theologische Blätter* 14 (1932) 896-900.

HEYWOOD THOMAS, J. *Paul Tillich: an Appraisal.* London, S.C.M. Press 1963.

—'The Correlation of Philosophy and Theology in Tillich's System' *London Quarterly and Holburn Review* 184 (Jan. 1959) 47-54.

—'Some Notes on the Theology of Paul Tillich' *Hibbert Journal* (April 1959) 253-8.

—'Some Aspects of Tillich's Systematic Theology' *Canadian Journal of Theology* IX (1963) 157-65.

—'Religious Language as Symbolism' *Journal of Religious Studies* (Oct. 1965).

HOOK, Sidney (ed.) *Religious Experience and Truth.* Edinburgh, Oliver & Boyd 1961 and 1968.

—'The Quest for Being' *Journal of Philosophy* no. 24 (1953) 709-31.

HOPPER, D. H. 'Towards Understanding of the Thought of Paul Tillich' *Princeton Seminary Bulletin* (1962) 36-43.

HUSSERL, Edmund *Logische Untersuchungen* (4th ed.). Halle, Niemeyer 1928.

—*Meditations cartésiennes.* Paris, Colin 1931.

JOHNSON, R. C. 'A Theologian of Synthesis' *Theology Today* 15 (1958) 36-42.

KANT, Immanuel *Critique of Pure Reason.* Tr. Norman Kemp-Smith. London, Macmillan 1929.

—*Critique of Practical Reason and Other Writings in Moral Philosophy.* Tr. L. W. Beck. Chicago, University of Chicago Press 1949.

KEEFE, Donald J., S.J. *Thomism and the Ontological Theology of Paul Tillich.* Leiden, Brill 1971.

KEGLEY, Charles and BRETALL, Robert W. (eds) *The Theology of Paul Tillich.* (Library of Living Theology vol. 1.) London, Macmillan 1956.

KELSEY, David H. *The Fabric of Paul Tillich's Theology.* New Haven, Yale University Press 1967.

KIERKEGAARD, Søren A. *Fear and Trembling.* Tr. W. Lowrie. Princeton University Press 1941.

—*Concluding Unscientific Postscript.* Tr. David F. Swenson and W. Lowrie. Princeton University Press 1941.

KILLEN, R. Allan *The Ontological Theology of Paul Tillich.* Kampen, J. H. Kok 1956.

KING, Magda *Heidegger's Philosophy.* Oxford, Basil Blackwell 1964.

KNEALE, W. and M. *The Development of Logic.* Oxford, Clarendon Press 1962.

KRAEMER, Hendrik *The Communication of the Christian Faith.* London, Lutterworth Press 1957.

KUCHEMANN, C. 'Professor Tillich: Justice and the Economic Order' *Journal of Religion* XLVI, no. 1 pt II (1966) 165-83.

LAM, E. P. 'Tillich's Reconstruction of the Concept of Ideology' *Christianity and Society* VI (1940) 11-15.

LANGER, S. *Philosophy in a New Key.* Cambridge, Mass. 1942.

LASWELL, H. D., CASEY, R. D. and SMITH, E. L. *Propaganda, Communication and Public Opinion* 1935. Princeton University Press 1946.
—*Propaganda and Promotional Activities.* University of Minnesota Press.
LEIBRECHT, Walter (ed.) *Religion and Culture. Essays in honour of Paul Tillich.* London, S.C.M. Press 1959.
LOOF, W. 'Paul Tillich's Theorie des religiösen Symbols' *Kant-Studien* 69 (1955) 52-73.
LOTZE, R. H. *Logic.* Tr. B. Bosanquet. Oxford 1884.
MCCULLOUGH, Thomas E. 'The Ontology of Tillich and Biblical Personalism' *Scottish Journal of Theology* 15, no. 3 (1962).
MCDONALD, H. D. 'The Symbolic Theology of Paul Tillich' *Scottish Journal of Theology* 17, no. 4 (1964).
MCKELWAY, Alexander J. *The Systematic Theology of Paul Tillich: a Review and Analysis.* Richmond, Va., John Knox Press/London, Lutterworth Press 1964.
MCLEAN, George F. *Man's Knowledge of God, according to Paul Tillich. A Thomistic Critique.* Washington D.C., Catholic University of America Press 1958.
MACLEOD, Alistair M. *Tillich: an Essay on the Role of Ontology in his Philosophical Theology.* London, Allen & Unwin 1973.
MAHAN, W. E. *Tillich's System.* San Antonio, Texas, Trinity University Press 1974.
MARITAIN, Jacques *Moral Philosophy.* London, Bles 1964.
—*Existence and the Existent.* Tr. L. Galantiene and G. Phelan. Pantheon Books 1948.
—*An Introduction to Logic.* London, Sheed & Ward 1946.
—*The Degrees of Knowledge.* Tr. B. Wall and Margot B. Adamson. London, Glasgow Pr. 1937.
MARTIN, Bernard *Paul Tillich's Doctrine of Man.* Welwyn, Nisbet 1966.
MARTIN, J. A. 'St Thomas and Tillich on the Names of God' *Journal of Religion* 37, no. 4 (1957).
MAY, Rollo *The Meaning of Anxiety.* New York, Ronald Press Co. 1950.
—*Paulus.* New York, Harper & Row 1973.
MEHTA, Ved *The New Theologian.* London, Weidenfeld & Nicholson 1966.
MITCHELL, B. (ed.) *Faith and Logic.* London, Allen & Unwin 1957.
MONDIN, Battista. *The Principle of Analogy in Protestant and Catholic Thought.* The Hague, Nijhoff 1968.
MORRIS, C. R. *Idealistic Logic.* London, Macmillan 1933.
MORRIS, C. W. 'Foundations of the Theory of Signs' Essay in *International Encyclopedia of Unified Science*, vol. 1, no. 2. Chicago University Press 1938.
MURE, G. R. G. *An Introduction to Hegel.* Oxford 1940.
NAUEN, F. G. *Revolution, Idealism and Human Freedom in Schelling, Hölderlin and Hegel.* The Hague, Nijhoff 1973.
NEWMAN, John Henry. *Grammar of Assent.* New York, Doubleday 1955.
NIETZSCHE, Friedrich *Beyond Good and Evil.* Chicago, Henry Regnery 1955.
O'HANLON, D. J. *The Influence of Schelling on the Thought of Paul Tillich.* Gregorian University of Rome thesis 1957.
O'MEARA, Thomas A., O.P. and WEISSER, Celestin D., O.P. *Paul Tillich in Catholic Thought.* London, Darton, Longman & Todd 1964.

OSBORNE, Kenan B. *New Being*. The Hague, Nijhoff 1969.
PARKER, Francis H. and VEATCH, Henry B. *Logic as a Human Instrument*. New York, Harper Brothers 1959.
PEIRCE, C. S. *Collected Papers*. Ed. C. Hartshorne and P. Weiss. Cambridge, Mass. 1933-4.
PETERS, E. 'Tillich's Doctrine of Essence, Existence and the Christ' *Journal of Religion* XLIII (1965).
PLATO. *Plato's Theory of Knowledge*. Tr. F. M. Cornford. London, Routledge & Kegan Paul 1935.
—*The Republic of Plato*. Tr. F. M. Cornford. London 1942.
RACINE, Louis, O.P. 'L'évangile selon Paul Tillich' *Théologie sans Frontières*. Paris 1970.
RATHBURN, J. W. and BURWICK, F. 'Paul Tillich and the Philosophy of Schelling' *International Philosophical Quarterly* IV, no. 3 (1964).
RICHARDS, I. A. *The Philosophy of Rhetoric*. Oxford, Oxford University Press 1936.
ROSENTHAL, K. 'Myth and Symbol' *Scottish Journal of Theology* XVIII (1965) 411-36.
ROWE, W. L. *Religious Symbols and God*. Chicago, University of Chicago Press 1968.
—'The Meaning of "God" in Tillich's Theology' *Journal of Religion* XLII (1962) 274-86.
RUSSELL, Bertrand 'On Denoting' *Logic and Knowledge*. London, Allen & Unwin 1956.
—*The Philosophy of Leibniz* (2nd ed.). London, Allen & Unwin 1937.
SCHARLEMANN, Robert P. *Reflection and Doubt in the Thought of Paul Tillich*. New Haven, Yale University Press 1969.
SCHELLING, F. W. *Werke*. Ed. M. Schröter. 6 vols. Munich 1927-8.
—*Of Human Freedom*. Tr. James Gutmann. Open Court Publ. Co. U S 1936.
—*The Ages of the World*. Tr. Frederick de Wolfe Bolman Jr. New York, A.M.S. Press Inc. 1967.
SCHICK, T. 'Reason and Knowledge in the Epistemology of Paul Tillich' *The Thomist* XXX, no. 1 (1966) 66-79.
SCHMIDT, W. S. J. *The Domain of Logic according to St Thomas Aquinas*. The Hague, Nijhoff 1966.
SIGWART, C. *Logic* vol. 1. Tr. Helen Dendy. London, Swan & Sonnenschein 1895.
SIMPSON, M., S.J. 'Paul Tillich: Symbolism and Objectivity' *The Heythrop Journal* VIII, no. 3 (1967).
SKINNER, J. E. 'Critique of Tillich's Ontology' *Anglican Theological Review* 39 (1957) 53-61.
SMART, R. N. 'Being and the Bible' *Review of Metaphysics* IX, no. 4 (1956) 589-607.
SOMMER, G. F. *The Significance of the Late Philosophy of Schelling for the Formation and Interpretation of the Thought of Paul Tillich*. Duke University thesis 1960.
SONNTAG, F. 'Ontological Possibility and the Nature of God: a Reply to Tillich' *Journal of Religion* XXXVI, no. 4 (1956) 234-40.
SPRAGUE, Elmer 'On Professor Tillich's Ontological Question' *International Philosophical Quarterly* II, no. 1 (1962).
TAUBES, J. 'On the Nature of the Theological Method: Some Reflections on the Methodological Principles of Tillich's Theology' *Journal of Religion* XXXIX, no. 1 (1954).

TAVARD, G. H. 'Christianity and the Philosophies of Existence' *Theological Studies* 18 (1957) 1-16.

—*Paul Tillich and the Christian Message*. London, Burns & Oates 1962.

THATCHER, A. *The Ontology of Paul Tillich*. Oxford, Oxford University Press 1978.

TIEBOUT, H. M., Jr. 'Tillich, Existentialism and Psychoanalysis' *Journal of Philosophy* LVI (1959) 605-12.

TILLICH, Hannah *From Time to Time*. New York, Stein & Day 1973.

TOULMIN, S. E. *The Uses of Argument*. Cambridge, Cambridge University Press 1958.

TROELTSCH, E. *Christian Thought: its History and Application*. London, University of London Press 1923.

VEATCH, H. B. *Intentional Logic*. New Haven, Yale University Press 1970.

—'Formalism and Intentionality in Logic' *Philosophical and Phenomenological Research* XI (1950).

—*Realism and Nominalism Re-visited*. Milwaukee, Marquette University Press 1954.

—'Tillich's Distinction Between Metaphysics and Theology' *Review of Metaphysics* X, no. 3 (1957) 529-33.

VEATCH, H. B. and PARKER, F. H. *Logic as a Human Instrument*. New York, Harper Brothers 1959.

VERSFELD, M. *Persons*. Cape Town, Buren 1972.

WATSON, M. 'The Social Thought of Paul Tillich' *Journal of Religious Thought* X (1952-3) 5-17.

WATTS, Alan *Beyond Theology of The Art of Godmanship*. London, Hodder & Stoughton 1964.

WEIGEL, Gustave, S.J. 'Recent Protestant Theology' *Theological Studies* (1953) 573-85.

—'Contemporaneous Protestantism and Paul Tillich' *Theological Studies* (1950) 177-202.

WHEAT, Leonard F. *Paul Tillich's Dialectical Humanism*. Baltimore, Johns Hopkins Press 1970.

WICK, W. A. *Metaphysics and the New Logic*. Chicago, University of Chicago Press 1942.

WITTGENSTEIN, L. *Philosophical Investigations*. Oxford, Basil Blackwell 1958.

Indexes

Subject Index